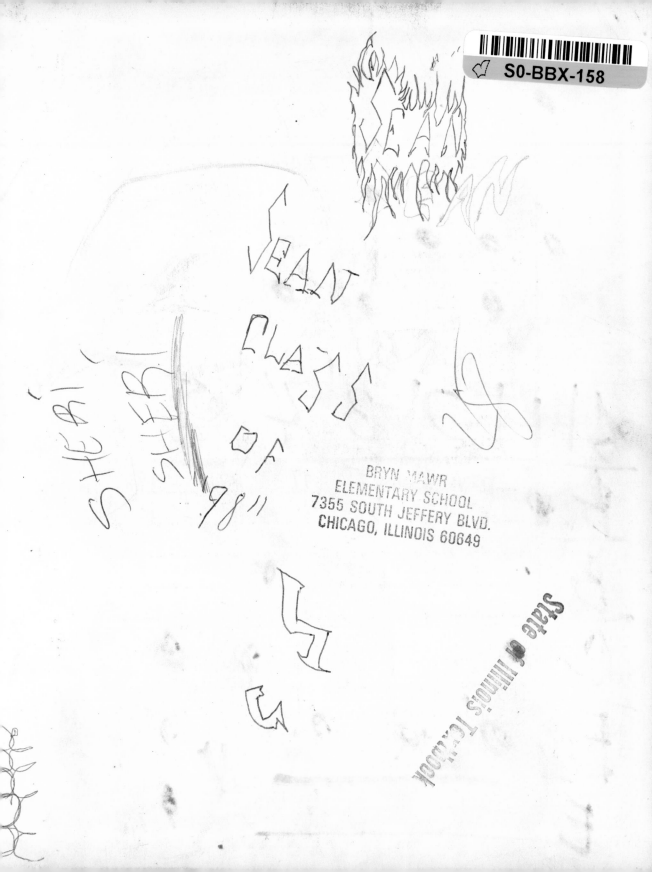

SEAN
SEAN
CLASS
OF
"98"
SHERI
SHERI

BRYN MAWR
ELEMENTARY SCHOOL
7355 SOUTH JEFFERY BLVD.
CHICAGO, ILLINOIS 60649

Reading
Literature

Purple Level
Yellow Level
Blue Level
Orange Level
GREEN LEVEL
Red Level

Reading Literature

The McDougal, Littell English Program

Jacqueline L. Chaparro
Curriculum Coordinator, English Language Arts
San Diego County Office of Education,
San Diego, California

Mary Ann Trost
Specialist in Educational Materials
for the Middle Grades, Cleveland Heights, Ohio

McDougal, Littell & Company

Evanston, Illinois
New York   Dallas   Sacramento

Consultants

James Dedes, Teacher, Holmes Junior High School, Mount Prospect, Illinois

Richard H. Gray, Chairman, English Department, Enfield High School, Enfield, Connecticut

Patricia West Jeffries, High school teacher and freelance writer on basic skills for the Memphis (Tennessee) City Schools.

Aramenta Kirkpatrick, Teacher, Warrensville Heights Junior High School, Cleveland, Ohio

Neeta Lewis, Teacher, Richardson Junior High School, Richardson, Texas

Sandra J. Nash, Teacher, Salt Rock Junior High School, Huntington, West Virginia

Jeane S. Travis, Teacher, Griffin Middle School, Smyrna, Georgia

Virginia Vargas, Teacher, Berta Cabaza Middle School, San Benito, Texas

H. Vance White, Department Chair, English, Walker Junior High School, La Palma, California

Frontispiece: The Unicorn Tapestries VII: *Unicorn in Captivity, about 1500.*
Metropolitan Museum of Art, Gift of John D. Rockefeller, Jr., the Cloisters Collection, 1937.

Acknowledgments

Ricardo E. Alegría: For "Lazy Peter and the Three-Cornered Hat" by Ricardo E. Alegría, from *The Three Wishes,* a Collection of Puerto Rican Folktales. Isaac Asimov: For "The Disappearing Man" by Isaac Asimov, as it appeared in *Boy's Life,* June 1978. Brandt & Brandt Literary Agents, Inc.: For "Western Wagons," "Abraham

(continued on page 605)

86 87 / 9 8 7 6 5 4 3

ISBN: 0-86609-229-3

Copyright © 1985 by McDougal, Littell & Company
Box 1667, Evanston, Illinois 60204

Contents

CHAPTER 5 *Poetry*   241

Poems About Animals

Reading Literature: More About Poetry

Poems About American History   321

CHAPTER 7 Drama 481

Handbook for Reading and Writing

Dear Educator,

Reading Literature brings to your students the greatest literature of all time. In this age of computers and VCR's, precious little of the world's great literary heritage filters through to our new generation. I don't believe you want your students to go through life without being acquainted with the tales of King Arthur. I don't believe you want your students to be unacquainted with the stories and poems of Geoffrey Chaucer, Pearl Buck, Emily Dickinson, and Henry Wadsworth Longfellow. This kind of reading can provide your students with a quickened sense of life's drama and a new sense of life's possibilities. The time is now. The opportunity is here.

Your students will be reading literature in its original form. Selections are not adapted. We have searched through the world's great literature to find selections that will stretch the students' minds, sharpen their senses, and enrich their lives.

Throughout, *Reading Literature* integrates reading and writing. Writing is presented as a process. A thorough foundation for writing is presented in a complete chapter, "How Writers Write" (see Chapter 3). The universal themes and ideas revealed by great literature make easy the task of teacher and text in guiding students to discover topics for their own writing.

I hope you will be as proud to offer *Reading Literature* to your students as we are to present it to you. I hope, too, that *Reading Literature* will assist you in helping the students to read happily, to think critically, and, above all, to meet the wondrous challenge that is life. Great writers of our time, and of earlier times, can help students in this process of growth. No other writers can do it as well.

Joseph L. Littell

Joseph F. Littell
Editor-in-Chief
McDougal, Littell & Company

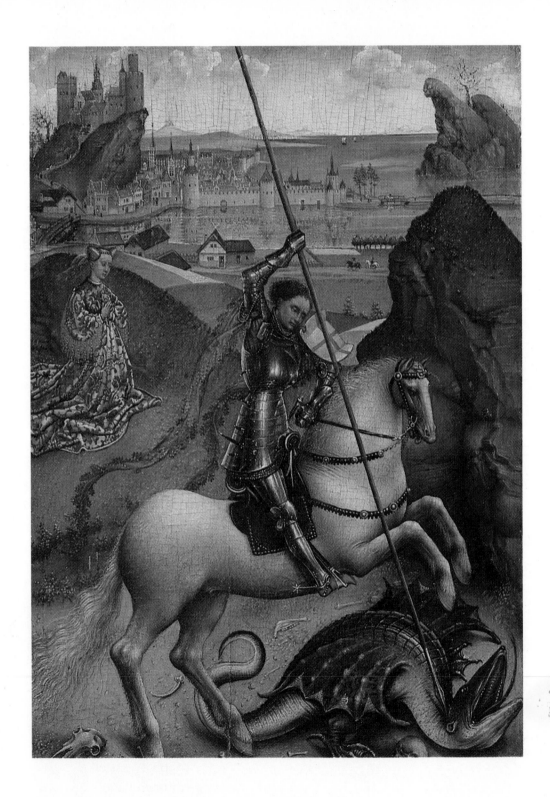

CHAPTER 1

Legends

St. George and the Dragon, about 1432, ROGIER VAN der WEYDEN.
National Gallery of Art, Washington, D.C., Ailsa Mellon Bruce Fund, 1966.

$\mathcal{R}$eading Literature: Legends

What Is a Legend?

A **legend** is a story about heroes and heroines and extraordinary events of the past. Some parts of legends are true and some parts are fictional. Legends are part of the **oral tradition.** That is, they have been passed on orally from parents and storytellers to children for many years.

The History of the Legend

People need heroes and heroines. When they find someone who is brave, strong, kind, and intelligent, they spread the good news. That is how legends begin.

Most legends are based on fact. However, when a true story is repeated many times, it changes. One teller may exaggerate a bit. The next teller adds a new event. Someone else remembers an old tale he or she once heard and includes that story, too. Soon, the true story is buried under exaggerations and additions. The new story that is created is a legend—a mix of fact and fiction.

Legends can be about characters as different as St. George, Robin Hood, and Pocahontas. Each group of people has its own favorite legends. Their heroes and heroines have qualities that the group admires, such as honesty or loyalty. There are some qualities that all of these characters have. They defend their beliefs bravely, they lead others, and they never give up.

For hundreds of years, people preserved legends by repeating them to each new generation. When printing was invented, people wrote the stories down. That is how we have them today.

From official records, we know that some of the characters in these legends, such as William Tell, were real people. However, we don't know if any of these adventures ever happened.

The Elements of a Legend

Legends are stories. The three major elements of any story are **characters, setting,** and **plot.**

Characters.   The characters are the people or animals who take part in the story. Usually, in a legend, one of the characters is a brave, good person. He or she may have powers greater than the normal person. This hero or heroine is often joined by followers. Opposing them, there is usually a powerful, evil character.

Setting.   The setting tells when and where the story takes place. It is often described early in the legend. However, details all through the story help you picture the setting.

Plot.   The plot is the series of events that take place in the story. The plot includes a struggle, or **conflict,** that the hero or heroine must face. In a legend, he or she must show courage or cleverness to win over evil forces.

Some events in legends are unbelievable. For example, one hero is carried down a mountain on an eagle's back. Uncommon happenings are common in legends.

Narrator.   The narrator is the person telling the story. Most legends are told by a narrator who does not take part in the plot. This narrator knows everything—even what characters think.

How To Read a Legend

When you read a legend, remember these guidelines:

1. Identify the setting. Does the legend take place in the time of knights and castles? Is it set in a forest or a jungle?
2. Accept impossible happenings. The imaginations of many storytellers are at work in legends. Enjoy their creativity.
3. Decide what the legend tells you about what makes a person heroic. Do the people who created the legend value courage, loyalty, patience, intelligence, or some other quality?

Comprehension Skills: Main Idea

Understanding Main Idea and Details

Every paragraph has a main idea. The **main idea** is the most important idea in the paragraph. Do not confuse the main idea with the topic of the paragraph. The topic is simply what the paragraph is about. The main idea is what the writer is telling you about the topic.

Read this sample paragraph.

Hamelin, a little German town, was overrun by rats. They were so fierce and numerous that they attacked the cats and drove the dogs away. All kinds of traps were laid, but the rats just flipped them about. They were everywhere.

The main idea of a paragraph is often stated in a topic sentence. In the paragraph above, the topic sentence is underlined. Read the paragraph again. See how the underlined sentence states the most important idea. Notice, also, that the other sentences give details about how Hamelin was overrun by rats. All the detail sentences tell more about the main idea.

Every sentence in a paragraph must be related to the main idea. To introduce a new idea, writers begin a new paragraph.

Important and Less Important Details

Some details are more important to the main idea than other details. Here is an example.

One evening in autumn, Blondel came to an unusually large castle in the middle of a wild forest. It had a grim look, dark and desolate. Two equally grim guards stood in front of the drawbridge.

You learn a lot of details in this short paragraph. The most important idea, or main idea, is that Blondel found an unusually large castle in a forest. One important detail is the grim look of the place. Another important detail is that it was guarded.

Some other details are not important to the story. For example, it does not matter much that Blondel came to the castle on one evening in autumn. It is not important to know that the forest was wild or where the guards were standing. These details make the story fun to read, but they are not absolutely necessary for an understanding of the story.

Exercises: Understanding Main Idea and Details

A. What is the main idea of this paragraph?

Their raid was not a success. The Pahani were watchful. The young warriors got nowhere near the Pahani horse herd. Not only did they capture no ponies, but they even lost their own mounts, because, while they were trying to creep up to their enemies' herd, the Pahani found their horses. The two young men had a hard time getting away on foot because their enemies were searching for them everywhere.

B. Read the following paragraph. Then match the items below.

Like autumn leaves in a storm, this promise was carried through the Hausa towns. It came to the ears of a certain young prince who was, himself, the son of a chief. Fadebi, he was called, and he was well known for his brave deeds.

1. This sentence states the main idea.

2. This sentence states an important detail.

3. This sentence tells a less important detail.

a. "The promise was carried like autumn leaves in a storm."

b. "The promise came to the ears of a certain young prince."

c. "Fadebi was well known for his brave deeds."

Vocabulary Skills: Context Clues

Using Context Clues

As you read, you often come upon new and unfamiliar words. Writers know that you may not understand every word. They leave clues in the context to help you. The **context** means the sentences and paragraphs in which a word appears. In this chapter, you will learn about different context clues, including definition or restatement clues, and synonyms.

Definition and Restatement Clues. Sometimes a writer gives you the meaning of a new word. The **definition clue** may appear in the same sentence as the new word or in the following sentence.

> The man held a pipe. A pipe is a tube of wood or metal used as a musical instrument.

Other times a writer repeats the new word in a slightly different way. This is a **restatement clue**.

> The children trooped, or marched, behind the piper.

Certain key words and key punctuation tell you to look for definition and restatement clues. Here are some of these keys:

is	*that is*	*in other words*	parentheses
or	*who is*	*which is*	commas	dashes

Find the definition or restatement clue that explains the underlined word in each sentence below. Identify any key words or punctuation.

1. A gale, which is a strong wind, blew the ships off course.
2. King John served sumptuous, that is, magnificent, meals.
3. He calls himself a patriot—a person who loves his country.

4. Blondel was a <u>minstrel</u>, a poet who was also a singer.
5. He looked into the <u>abyss</u> (a very deep hole in the earth).

Synonyms. A **synonym** is a word that means almost the same thing as another word. For example, a synonym for *azure* is *blue*. Writers often use a new word and then, as soon as they can, use a synonym for it. In this way, you understand the new word. This sentence uses a synonym to explain *lariat*. From the restatement clue in the sentence, you know that a lariat is a rope.

Black Crow took his rawhide *lariat,* made a loop in it, put the *rope* around Spotted Eagle's chest under his armpits, and lowered him down.

Exercises: **Using Context Clues**

A. For each underlined word, find the definition or restatement.

1. Gessler was a <u>tyrant</u>. A tyrant is a cruel ruler.
2. Tell took hold of the <u>rudder</u>, which is a movable piece of wood used for steering a boat.
3. All that you possess will be <u>forfeited</u>, that is, lost, to me.
4. The piper was <u>pied</u>. In other words, his clothes had patches of two different colors.

B. For each sentence, identify the word that has been restated, the key words or punctuation that helped you find the restatement clue, and the meaning of the restated word.

1. A deeper meaning was concealed—hidden—in the song.
2. The mayor summoned, or called together, his councilors.
3. Spotted Eagle lived on the ledge with the eagle fledglings (young birds).
4. Black Crow wore a sash, a type of scarf, around his waist.
5. The Abbot of Canterbury, the head of the English church, lived as well as the king.

Richard the Lion-Hearted:
Saved by a Song

Even heroes need saving sometimes. In this story, a hero is saved through something more powerful than weapons or treasure. As you read, look for that powerful quality.

TRADITIONAL TALE
Retold by Louis Untermeyer

Richard the First lived in the twelfth century. He is considered one of the greatest English kings although he spent comparatively little time in England. Wars in Europe as well as the Crusades in the Holy Land kept him abroad during most of his reign. He was in the forefront of every battle he fought. When he wielded his huge battle-axe, none could withstand him. So fearless was he that he was known not merely as King Richard the Mighty but as Richard the Lion-Hearted. Enemies fled when he charged upon them shouting his battle cry, "God be with us!"

Richard had gone on the Third Crusade against the Saracens, hoping to drive them out of Jerusalem so that Christians could visit the holy places in safety. He had been aided by two other European kings, but he quarreled with his allies and grew to respect his enemies more than

his friends. Saladin, king of Saracens, returned his respect and welcomed Richard as his guest. After mutual acts of courtesy and expressions of good will, a three-year truce was proposed.

"We of the East believe greatly in the number three," said Saladin. "It is a powerful number. Man is a threefold creature made of body, soul, and spirit, and the enemies of man are three: the world, the flesh, and the devil. Do you not believe so, you of the North?"

"It is so," replied Richard. "The Greeks taught us that man's life depends on the three fates—the three daughters of the night who spin the thread of life—that nature is divided into three kingdoms—animal, vegetable, and mineral—and that there are three prime colors: red, yellow, and blue."

"That being true," said Saladin, "let us make our truce really binding. Let it be

Stories of the Emperors: Soliman Against the Christians. Paris Biblioteque de l'Arsenale.
Courtesy of Art Resource, New York.

for three years, three months, three days, and three hours. And let us take an oath that nothing shall break such a truce."

The two leaders swore to keep the peace for that length of time and, if they were still friends, for the rest of their lives. Then Richard withdrew his troops from the Holy Land. He set sail for England by way of Cyprus, but a gale blew his ships off their course and drove them to Italy. Worse weather occurred when he resumed the journey. Storms overwhelmed the fleet with waves like battering-rams, and knife-sharp winds tore the sails. After a gruelling week, the boats lost contact with each other. King Richard's ship was thrown against a rocky coast and destroyed. His men were drowned, and he himself barely managed to survive.

After wandering for weeks, he found himself in the land of one of his worst enemies, Duke Leopold of Austria. He was recognized at once and captured. The Duke of Austria shut him up in a dungeon and then asked a huge ransom for his release. When Henry, Emperor of Germany, heard of this, he compelled Leopold to give up his prize. Instead of freeing Richard, Henry imprisoned him in one of his own castles and demanded a still more staggering ransom. So that no one would know where the King of

England was hidden and attempt to rescue him, he was moved at various times from one secret stronghold to another.

Meanwhile, things were going badly in England, where Richard's absence had caused much confusion. There were rumors that the demand for ransom was a deception to get money for the German emperor and that Richard was really dead. His brother John robbed the treasury and plotted to seize the throne; the country was in a state of turmoil and anxiety. No one thought of clarifying the situation by finding out whether Richard was alive or dead. No one except Blondel de Nesle.

Blondel was a minstrel, a poet who was also a singer. He had been a boon companion to Richard in his youth. Richard and Blondel had spent many hours together making up tunes, matching rhymes, and composing songs on any subject that came to mind. It was Blondel who asked for permission to look for the king.

"But how do you expect to conduct so wild a hunt?" inquired Richard's minister. He was the person who had been appointed by Richard to take care of his court duties while he was away. "Where will you start?"

"I cannot tell you how until I begin," answered Blondel. "But I can tell you where. The demands for the ransom have come from Germany, so Germany is the most likely place to start."

"How many men will you require?" asked the minister.

"None," said Blondel. "I will go alone."

"You will, I hope, be well armed. What weapons will you need?"

"One weapon only," said Blondel, "if you can call it that. I will take along my little hand harp. It will be all I need."

For three months Blondel wandered up and down Germany. He played his harp and sang his songs in taverns, inns, courtyards, and castles. He was always welcome, for people in every land delight to hear songs of war and wooing, of gallant deeds and lovely ladies, especially when they are sung as beautifully as Blondel sang them. He was offered large sums of money to remain in many a palace; he heard much gossip and was told many things in confidence. But never a word did he hear about King Richard.

One evening in autumn he came to an unusually large castle in the middle of a wild forest. It had a grim look, dark and desolate. Two equally grim guards stood in front of the drawbridge.

"Keep back," one of them said. "We make short work of spies."

"I am no spy," said Blondel. "I am a minstrel. I go from place to place to entertain lords and ladies. I am sure those inside would like to hear me."

"There is no one inside who cares for merrymaking," said the other guard. "Your eyes must be poor if you think this is a place for entertainment. It is not so much a castle as a prison."

"Indeed?" said Blondel. "I would not have suspected it."

"Yes," said the first guard, a note of pride coming into his voice. "It is one of the strongest prisons in Europe and one of the least known. And the curious part is this: it houses only one prisoner."

"And who might that be?" Blondel asked eagerly. "Who has an entire prison to himself?"

"That we can't tell you," replied the second guard. "In fact, we ourselves don't know. All we know is that he must be someone very important, someone who has to be watched very carefully."

"Well," said Blondel. "That is very interesting. But, after all, it has nothing to do with me. If I cannot get a welcome here I will try elsewhere. Before I go, perhaps you would like to hear a song."

"Go ahead," said the first guard. "A song never hurt anyone."

"Nor helped them, either," added the second. "But go ahead."

Blondel tuned his harp and began:

My lady sits within her bower;
She sings "alas" right dolefully:
She lingers hour after hour.
For her true lord. But where is he?

Blondel paused. It was a song that he and King Richard had made up and sung together years ago. It had a new meaning for them now.

Then another voice was added to his, completing the second stanza:

O tell my lady that the fates
Have kept her lord away from men;
But patiently her lover waits
The day he can come home again.

The guards were startled to hear the second voice. They did not guess the meaning concealed in the song. Nevertheless, they were angry with themselves for having let the minstrel linger.

"That's enough!" shouted the guards. "On your way!"

Blondel went, but he had found what he had been seeking. Also, the captured king knew that Blondel had discovered where he had been hidden. He did not have to wait long to be freed.

Three months later his release was accomplished and he was brought back to England. More powerful than ever, King Richard restored his country to peace.

A Twelfth-Century Signet Ring of Richard I (1189–99). The British Museum, London.

Developing Comprehension Skills

1. What led Richard and Saladin to make a truce? How long was the truce to last?

2. How did Richard come to be in Henry's prison?

3. How do you know that the relationship between Richard and his brother John was not good?

4. Why was Blondel the best person to find Richard?

5. Do you think any of the events in this story could really have happened? Which ones? Give reasons for your answer.

Reading Literature: Legends

1. **Recognizing Character Traits.** Heroes and heroines of legends are noted for their personal qualities, or **traits.** These traits are admired by the group that created the legends. Pick one of the three traits below and tell how Blondel showed that trait.

   a. self-confidence   b. loyalty   c. cheerfulness

2. **Understanding Setting.** The actions in a story may take place in several different settings. The storyteller or writer may describe one setting more clearly than other settings in the story.

   "Richard the Lion-Hearted" takes place in several settings: in the Holy Land, at sea, in Austria, in prisons in Germany, in England, in taverns and castles in Germany, and at one particular prison in Germany. Only one of these settings is described clearly. Which is it? Can you think of a reason why the writer described that one setting?

3. **Recognizing Irony.** Often a writer lets the reader know more than a character knows. The character thinks one thing is true, but the reader knows the opposite is true. When what appears to be true is not true at all, the writer is using **irony**.

   For example, on page 11, Blondel asks the guards if he may sing. Not knowing his real purpose, the guards agree:

   > "Go ahead," said the first guard. "A song never hurt anyone."
   >
   > "Nor helped them, either," added the second.

   Explain how both guards are wrong.

4. **Determining the Main Idea.** Reread paragraph 5 in column 2 on page 10. What is the main idea of the paragraph? State the main idea in your own words. Then list one of the details in the paragraph that explains the main idea.

Developing Vocabulary Skills

Using Context Clues in Sentences. The underlined words in the following sentences were drawn from the story. The meaning of each word can be figured out by a definition clue or a restatement clue. For each underlined word below, write the following on your paper:

  a. Whether each sentence contains a definition or a restatement clue
  b. The key words or key punctuation that helped you find the meaning of the word
  c. The meaning of the underlined word

1. The fighting between the two countries ended after <u>mutual</u> acts of courtesy. In other words, the leaders of the countries acted courteously toward each other.

2. Wars in Europe kept King Richard away during most of his <u>reign</u>—his time in power.

3. The Greeks believed that man's life depended on <u>fate</u>. Fate is what happens to a person beyond the person's control.

4. The Duke of Austria shut Richard up in a dungeon and then asked for a huge <u>ransom</u>, the price asked for his release.

5. When Henry heard of this he <u>compelled</u>, or forced, Leopold to give up his prize.

6. There were rumors that the demand for ransom was a <u>deception</u> (trick) to get money for the German Emperor.

7. The guards were angry with themselves for having let the minstrel <u>linger</u>, or stay around.

8. More powerful than ever, King Richard <u>restored</u>, that is, brought back, peace to his country.

Developing Writing Skills

1. **Relating the Parts of a Story.** After the first six paragraphs, the legend does not mention Saladin. Can you explain why Saladin was in

the story at all? What do we learn about Richard from his friendship with the Saracen leader? How does Richard's trip to the Holy Land set the stage for the rest of the legend? Write at least a paragraph that tells why the story mentions Saladin and Richard's activities in the Holy Land.

2. **Writing a Conversation.** The story says that Henry forced Leopold to hand over Richard. Create a short conversation that shows how Henry might have persuaded Leopold to give up Richard.

3. **Suggesting Another Ending.** If you had been a friend of King Richard, how would you have tried to find him? Write at least one paragraph explaining your solution to the problem. Use information from the story to make your plans. If you prefer, write a new version of the story, putting yourself in Blondel's place.

Developing Skills in Study and Research

Finding Information in the Library. This legend about Richard the Lion-Hearted may be based on fact. How could you find out what parts of the story are true? The way to begin is to learn what information your school or local library can give you.

All books in the library are separated into two large groups, fiction and nonfiction. The fiction books are shelved alphabetically, according to the author's last name. The nonfiction books can be separated into smaller groups, according to their topics.

One system for grouping books is the **Dewey Decimal system.** In this system, every nonfiction book is assigned to one of ten categories. Each category has a range of a hundred numbers between 0 and 999. When a book is assigned to a category, it is given a number within that range. For example, the category that includes history has the numbers from 900 to 999. Any history book will have a 900 number. Nonfiction books are shelved, then, in numerical order.

Another system, the **Library of Congress system,** assigns numbers in a different way.

Use information posted in your library to answer the questions below. If necessary, ask the librarian for help.

1. Which system does your library use to number nonfiction books?

2. What are the major categories used in the system?

King John and the Abbot:
The Three Questions

TRADITIONAL TALE
Retold by Louis Untermeyer

King John was noted for his greed, his jealousy, and his cruelty. However, this legend says that he had at least a few good qualities. As you read the legend, look for those good qualities.

Upon the death of Richard the Lion–Hearted, his younger brother, John, became king. King John lived not only richly and royally but, even for a king, extravagantly. He had many castles, and each of them outshone the other with lordly towers, marble floors, bronze doors, and tapestries that made the walls sing with color. He dressed his servants in cloth of gold; he presented his guests with garments of heavy silk, jewelled rings, and coats of precious furs. He served the most sumptuous meals on plates of pure silver. No one in the kingdom lived as well as its king—no one except the Abbot of Canterbury, the head of the English church.

For a while King John permitted the abbot to rival him in luxury. Finally, he could control his jealousy no longer. He summoned the abbot.

"Father Abbot," he began quietly, "I hear that you have a hundred knights to wait on you every day. I hear that you furnish them with velvet coats and gold chains. In short, I hear that you keep a far better household than I do. This, you know, is treason."

"Your Majesty," replied the abbot, "I would be the last man in your kingdom to have even the smallest thought of disloyalty. As to treason—I spend only what is my own. It is true that I entertain my guests in fair style; but that does credit to the abbey and, in a broad sense, to England."

"Yes, yes, I knew you would say something of the sort," said King John, beginning to lose his temper. "Surely you know that all property in England belongs to the crown. But I didn't bring you here to argue with you. I brought you here to tell you that you are guilty of treason, that you deserve to be executed, and that all your possessions should be given to me."

Royal Banquet Scene (detail) 19th Century, SPANISH FORGER. The Norton Simon Foundation.

"Your Majesty," cried the abbot. "I cannot believe—"

"Keep your belief for your sermons," angrily interrupted the king. "However," he resumed, calming himself, "as everyone knows, I am a merciful monarch. I will spare your life as well as your property if you can convince me of your wisdom by answering three questions."

"I shall try, your Majesty," said the abbot. "What are the three questions?"

"First," said King John, "as I sit here with this crown of gold on my head, you must tell me to the day how long I shall live. Second, you must tell me how long it will take me to ride around the entire world. Third, you must tell me what I am thinking."

"But—" began the abbot.

"No more buts," snapped the king. "I will give you seven days to decide on your answers. If you are not here with the right answers exactly one week from today, your life and lands and all the things you possess will be forfeit to me."

Sadly the abbot rode away. He went to Oxford, hoping a scholar at one of the great colleges there could supply the answers. When none could help, he rode to Cambridge; but the learned men there were no wiser. Shaking his head—a head that would, alas, soon be severed from his shoulders—he turned toward home. He had wasted four days; there were only three days left.

As he neared his abbey he met a shepherd. "Welcome back, master," said the shepherd. "What news do you bring from court and King John?"

"Bad news," replied the abbot. "Bad news indeed. I have only three days to live unless I answer three questions."

"Surely that should not be hard for you," said the shepherd. "What are the questions?"

When the doleful abbot told him what they were, the shepherd grinned. "Cheer up, master. Do not despair. Sometimes a fool may teach a wise man something. Let me, the fool, go to London. Lend me some of your servants, a few of your knights, your horse, and your gown. Begging your pardon, but it has often been said that my features resemble yours and, with a hood over my head, it would be hard to tell the difference between us. Let me do what I suggest—perhaps this fool can fool the king."

"But the questions?" said the abbot. "What will you do when you stand in front of King John?"

"I think I know a way to satisfy him—and save you, too," said the shepherd.

The next day the shepherd, accompanied by a splendid retinue, rode into London. Dressed like the abbot, he carried the gold staff and other symbols of the abbot's churchly office.

"Welcome, Sir Abbot," said King John. "You are prompt; you are even two days ahead of time. That is good. However, prompt as you are, I trust you haven't forgotten our bargain. You must answer my three questions in order to save your life and your property. Are you ready?"

"I am ready, your Majesty," said the disguised shepherd.

"First, as I sit here with this crown of gold on my head, tell me to the day how long I shall live."

"That's easy, your Majesty," replied the shepherd. "You will live until you die, not one day longer and not one hour less."

The king laughed. "A very clever answer. Your wit has saved you this time.

Now for the second question. How long will it take me to ride around the world?"

"That, your Majesty, is even easier. If at sunrise you get up and ride with the sun and continue to ride with it until it rises again the next morning, you will have ridden around the entire world in exactly twenty–four hours."

King John laughed still more heartily. "I didn't think it could be done so easily," he said. "You are as wise as you are witty. Now for the last and hardest question. Tell me what I am thinking."

This time it was the shepherd who laughed. "That's the easiest of all," he said. "You are thinking I am the Abbot of Canterbury, but I am only a poor foolish shepherd dressed in his robes. And I have come here to ask pardon for him."

For a moment the king frowned. Then he chuckled. Then he roared with laughter until he had to hold his sides.

"You rogue!" he cried. "I ought to have you hanged! Instead I will make you Lord Abbot of Canterbury, in place of the one who is hiding there."

"Thank you, your Majesty," said the shepherd, snatching off the abbot's cap and bowing deeply. "But that's impossible. I can neither read nor write."

"In that case," smiled the king, "I will see that you get a reward, four pieces of silver every week. The joke was worth it. And when you get home, you can tell the abbot that, thanks to your cleverness, he has a pardon from King John. Tell him I wish him to live long—but not quite so well."

Developing Comprehension Skills

1. Why was King John jealous of one of his subjects?

2. A **time line** is a way of showing the events of a story in a short form. To make a time line, begin by drawing a straight line. Then draw a dot on the line for each important event in the story.

| first event | third event | fifth event | last event |

| second event | fourth event | sixth event |

Next to each dot, write a few words describing the event.

Complete the time line for "The King and the Abbot."

(1) King John becomes jealous
of the abbot.

(2) King John sentences the abbot to die
unless he can answer three riddles.

3. What changes do you think the abbot will make in his lifestyle?

4. Create a new law you think King John might make for his country
after this experience.

5. Reread paragraph 4, column 2 on page 17. ("The next day the shepherd. . . .") State its main idea in one sentence. Then identify one
important detail. Last, identify one less important detail.

Reading Literature: Legends

1. **Examining a Character.** Who is the hero in this legend? What are
some of the qualities that make him a hero?

2. **Examining Setting.** Why is the setting of King John's castle important to this story?

3. **Identifying Conflict.** What is the conflict, or struggle, in this story?
How is it settled?

4. **Recognizing the Use of Three's.** In "Richard the Lion-Hearted,"
Richard and Saladin discussed the importance of the number three.
Many stories make use of this number. You have probably noticed
this in children's stories, such as "Cinderella," "The Three Bears,"
"The Three Billy Goats Gruff," and many others.

In "King John and the Abbot," events and other things come in
groups of three. Identify two groups of three in the tale.

Developing Vocabulary Skills

Using Synonyms as Context Clues. Sometimes a writer will give a clue
to the meaning of an unfamiliar word by repeating, or explaining, an idea
with a word or phrase that means the same thing. Words that have
almost the same meaning are called **synonyms**.

Each of the following sentences or groups of sentences uses words drawn from the story "King John and the Abbot." The meaning of the underlined word may be unfamiliar to you. Read over the sentence or group of sentences carefully. Find a synonym for each underlined word. On your paper, write the word and its synonym.

1. King John accused the abbot of <u>treason</u>, but the abbot declared he had no thought of disloyalty to his country.
2. The abbot hoped some <u>scholars</u> at Oxford could supply the answers, but none could help. He then rode to Cambridge, but the learned men there were no wiser.
3. "However," he resumed, "as everyone knows, I am a merciful <u>monarch</u>. As your king, I will spare your life as well as your property."
4. The next day the shepherd was accompanied by a splendid <u>retinue</u>. The attendants rode to London with him.
5. "Welcome, Sir Abbot," said King John. "you are <u>prompt</u>. However, on time as you are, I trust you haven't forgotten our bargain."

Developing Writing Skills

1. **Comparing Characters.** How is the hero of this story different from the hero of "Richard the Lion-Hearted"? How are the two characters alike?

2. **Writing a Defense.** Imagine that the abbot could not find the answers to the riddles, and no one volunteered to help him. Write a speech that the abbot could make to King John to save his life.

Developing Skills in Study and Research

Finding Information in the Library. In the library, nonfiction books are assigned numbers according to the Dewey Decimal system, the Library of Congress system, or some other system. After each book has been assigned a number, the number is stamped on the outside of the book. The books are shelved in numerical order.

At the same time, the librarians record the name and number of every book on cards that are placed in the **card catalog**. The author and the topic of the book are also recorded on the cards. Three cards are made for each book.

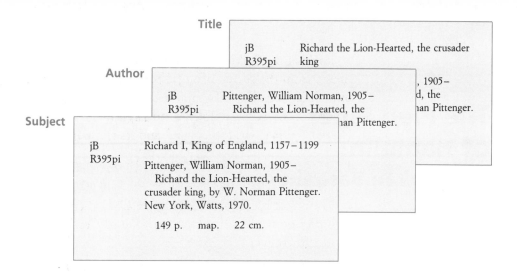

Title

jB
R395pi

Richard the Lion-Hearted, the crusader
king

Author

jB
R395pi

Pittenger, William Norman, 1905–
Richard the Lion-Hearted, the
...han Pittenger.

Subject

jB
R395pi

Richard I, King of England, 1157–1199

Pittenger, William Norman, 1905–
Richard the Lion-Hearted, the
crusader king, by W. Norman Pittenger.
New York, Watts, 1970.

149 p.   map.   22 cm.

title card—the title of the book appears on the first line
author card—the author's name appears on the first line
subject card—the subject of the book appears on the first line

If you want to find a book, you first look it up in the card catalog to find its number. You can look for the **title card**, the **author card**, or the **subject card**. Each one of these cards will tell the number of the book. Then you look on the shelves for the book with that number.

Investigate your school or local library. Find out if it has any books about King Richard the Lion-Hearted (Richard I) or King John (John I). Look up each ruler in the card catalog. Then find on the shelves at least one of the books listed in the catalog. On your paper, write the name, author, and number of the book you found. Tell whether you used a subject card, a title card, or an author card in your search.

Your local library may have this information on a computer.

Developing Skills in Speaking and Listening

Reading a Story Aloud. Legends were originally passed along by storytellers. Even though they have now been written down, they are still good entertainment when they are spoken rather than read silently.

Choose approximately one page of this legend. Prepare to read it to a group. If the part you choose includes the words of one or more characters, try to have your voice show that a character is speaking. The narrator's statements should sound different from each character, and each character should have a special sound.

When you are ready, present your selection to a group.

The Pied Piper of Hamelin:
The Broken Bargain

This story was made famous by Robert Browning in his poem of the same name. In the story, the mayor makes a fast decision that affects the lives of many other people. Did the mayor make the right decision?

TRADITIONAL TALE
Retold by Louis Untermeyer

Not many people know that this story was many hundred years old when the nineteenth century poet Robert Browning rewrote it. Here is the original.

Hamelin, a little German town in the duchy of Brunswick, was overrun by rats. They were so fierce and so numerous that they attacked the cats and drove the dogs out of the city. All kinds of traps were laid, but the rats just flipped them about. The creatures swarmed through the streets, broke into the houses, filled the attics, invaded the kitchens, sprang on the tables, and raced through the bedrooms. They were everywhere.

In poetry, Robert Browning describes them this way:

Rats!
They fought the dogs, and killed the cats,
    And bit the babies in the cradles,
And ate the cheeses out of the vats,
And licked the soup from the cook's
    own ladles,
Split open the kegs of salted sprats,
Made nests inside men's Sunday hats,
And even spoiled the women's chats,
    By drowning their speaking
    With shrieking and squeaking
In fifty different sharps and flats!

The townspeople complained bitterly. "What kind of a mayor have we got," they said, "who allows such a thing to happen! He sits in his elegant office, gazes out of the window, and does nothing about it!"

The mayor summoned his councilors, but they were no help. Day after day they met, but nothing they thought up had the slightest effect on the plague of rats. It grew worse every hour.

One summer morning—sometime around the year 1300—a tall, odd-looking stranger entered Hamelin and came straight to the town hall. Browning saw him this way.

His queer long coat from heel to head
Was half of yellow and half of red;
And he himself was tall and thin,
With sharp blue eyes, each like a pin,
And light loose hair, yet swarthy skin.
No tuft on cheek nor beard on chin,
But lips where smiles went out and in—
There was no guessing his kith and kin.
And nobody could enough admire
The tall man and his quaint attire.

The stranger entered the councilors' room, advanced to the council table, and spoke directly to the mayor.

"I hear," he said, "you are troubled with rats. I can help you, for I happen to be a rat-catcher. By means of a certain power—call it music or call it magic—I can rid your town of the pests that are such a plague to you. People call me the Pied Piper."

The mayor looked up at the man and noticed that at the end of the stranger's red and yellow scarf there hung a small pipe, and the stranger's fingers kept twitching as though they wanted to be playing on it.

"Yes," continued the strange figure, "I have freed many cities of rats, as well as gnats and bats. I will do the same for you—" he paused for a moment and coughed gently, "only you will have to pay me a thousand guilders."

"A thousand guilders?" echoed the mayor. "Make it fifty thousand! If you can really clear Hamelin of rats, it will be well worth it."

The piper stepped into the street and played a shrill tune on his pipe. As he played, rats came tumbling out of the houses. It was as if an army were on the run, murmuring and muttering. The muttering grew to a grumbling, the grumbling to a mighty rumbling, and still the rats kept coming. Great rats, small rats, lean rats, tall rats, young rats, old rats, big rats, bold rats, rats of every size and color. They followed the piper wherever he went. Still playing, he led them to the river Weser. Into the river went the rats, and every single rat was drowned.

The piper returned to the city hall, asked politely for his thousand guilders. The mayor looked blank.

"You must be joking," said the mayor. "Surely you wouldn't expect anyone to pay such a huge sum of money for getting rid of a few rats. Besides, the river did most of the work for you. A thousand guilders? Don't be silly, Come, take fifty."

The piper's face grew dark. "I don't drive bargains," he said. "I want the full payment agreed upon. If not, you will be sorry that you didn't keep your promise. See, I still have my pipe. And if you force me, I can play a different tune."

"What!" exclaimed the mayor angrily. "You dare to threaten me! The mayor of Hamelin is not to be insulted by a fool in crazy clothes! Do your worst! Blow on your pipe until you burst!"

The piper did not say another word. Instead he left the council room and stepped out into the street. Putting his lips to the pipe, he blew again. This time the sound was anything but shrill. It was sweet and low, a dreamy tune, full of delightful turns and twists, gentle and at the same time fun, promising all manner of marvelous things. As he played, there came a sound of little hands clapping and feet pattering, of small voices chattering, like chicks in a barnyard when corn and grain are scattering. Out of the houses came boys and girls, flocking to the piper, tripping and skipping, following after the magic music with shouting and laughter.

People looked on in amazement. The mayor cried "Stop!" But the children paid no attention to anything or anyone except the piper. Singing and dancing, they followed him out of town.

This time the piper did not guide them toward the river but toward the hills. When they came to the Köppelberg, a side of this mountain opened as though it were a door and all the children—one hundred and thirty of them—trooped inside. Then the hill closed up again. Not one of these boys and girls was ever seen again.

It would never have been known what the piper's music promised, what was inside the hill, had it not been for one lame boy. He never tired of saying how dull it was in Hamelin without his playmates nor of telling what he remembered.

Pied Piper, 1909, MAXFIELD PARRISH. Courtesy of the Palace Hotel, San Francisco.

"Because of my lame foot," he said, "I was a little behind the others. We were all happy as on a holiday. We were all looking forward to the place the piper—I mean the piper's music—told us about. It was a land where all things were beautiful and all people were good. A dozen rivers flowed there, each with a different sweet flavor. The flowers were larger and lovelier than anywhere else on earth. The sparrows were not dull brown, as they are here, but brighter than peacocks. Dogs ran faster than deer and never barked. Bees had lost their sting. Horses were born with eagles' wings. No one was ever sad or sick, and anyone who came to the place with anything wrong—like a lame foot—was instantly cured. Just as I was about to catch up with the other children, the door in the side of the mountain closed, the music stopped, and I was left on the Köppelberg, alone."

All of this happened (or was believed to have happened) centuries ago. But still, they say, no one is allowed to play the pipe in Hamelin. Besides, they say that in Transylvania (now a part of Romania) there lives a strange group of people who wear outlandish garments of red and yellow, and have names something like those of the families that once lived in Hamelin. Not one of them, they say, ever breaks a promise.

ED PIPER

Developing Comprehension Skills

1. How did the piper get the rats to leave?

2. Why do you think the mayor decided not to pay the piper?

3. Was the piper right to do what he did after the mayor's decision? Why or why not?

4. What good quality did the people of Hamelin learn to respect?

Reading Literature: Legends

1. **Recognizing Descriptions.** The setting of this story is described with many details. Both paragraph 2 on page 22 and the first section quoted from Browning's poem tell what the town was like when the rats were there. There are several other clear, detailed descriptions in this legend. Find three of them. Tell what is being described (the main idea). Then list several details that help the reader picture what is happening.

2. **Examining Characters.** In legends, the heroes and villains can be identified fairly easily. For example, the hero of this tale is the piper, while the villain is the mayor. However, heroes can have bad traits, and villains can have good ones. What bad trait do you find in the piper? Does the story suggest a good trait in the mayor? Explain.

3. **Identifying the Climax.** In every story, there is one point that is the turning point. Here the conflict, or struggle, reaches its peak. In "The Pied Piper," the conflict between the mayor and the piper reaches its peak quickly. What scene is the climax, the turning point of the story?

Developing Vocabulary Skills

Using Context Clues in Sentences. Read the following sentences about "The Pied Piper of Hamelin." Figure out the meaning of each underlined word from the context. Write **definition** or **restatement clue** or **synonym** to tell which clue you used to find the meaning of the word. Then write the meaning of the word.

1. Hamelin is a little German town in the duchy of Brunswick. A duchy is the land ruled by a prince or a duke.

2. The rats were so numerous that they attacked the cats. There were so many that they even drove the dogs out of the city.

3. The strange figure informed the mayor that he would have to give him a thousand <u>guilders</u>. He wanted the coins in exchange for freeing the town of rats.

4. When the piper asked politely for his thousand guilders, the mayor looked <u>blank</u>, without understanding.

5. The boy was behind the others because of his <u>lame</u> foot. In other words, he was unable to walk as well as the other children.

6. They say that in Transylvania there lives a strange group who wear <u>outlandish</u> garments of red and yellow. The same strange clothes were worn by the pied piper.

Developing Writing Skills

1. **Explaining Your Opinion.** In the first two legends that you read, the things that happened were all possible. We could call those stories **realistic**. That is, they could really have happened. In this legend, several things that happened were impossible. We would call this story **fantastic**. That is, there was fantasy in the story.

    Do you prefer one kind of story? If so, do you prefer realistic or fantastic stories? Or do you enjoy both kinds of stories? Write at least one paragraph telling your opinion and explaining your reasons.

2. **Putting Yourself into the Story.** Imagine that you are one of the townspeople of Hamelin. Describe what life is like with all the rats. If you wish, write your answer as a letter to a friend in another town.

Developing Skills in Critical Thinking

Separating Fact and Fiction. It is clear that most of this story was made up. However, some parts of it might have happened, and then a storyteller added the rest to make it interesting. Think about each event listed below. Tell which events might have happened. Tell which events could not have happened.

1. Rats overran a town.

2. The mayor and the council searched for a solution to the rat problem.

3. A stranger said he could help.

4. The stranger asked for a thousand guilders as pay.

5. The mayor promised to pay what the man asked.

6. The stranger charmed the rats with music on his pipe.

7. The mayor refused to pay.

8. The stranger threatened the mayor.

9. The stranger charmed the children of the town with pipe music.

10. The children went inside a mountain.

Developing Skills in Speaking and Listening

Expressing Mood. The **mood**, or the feeling you get from reading a story, changes several times in "The Pied Piper of Hamelin." For example, at the beginning of the story, when the rats are described, the mood is one of anxiety and disgust. Then there is a mood of excitement when the rats are being led into the river and, again, when the children are being led away. There is a mood of sadness and longing in the lame boy's explanation of what he saw and heard. Choose one of these passages. Prepare to read it to a group. Let your voice express the mood of the passage. Also, practice speaking clearly so that your listeners will understand every word. Then present your reading to a group.

William Tell:
The Archer and the Apple

TRADITIONAL TALE
Retold by Louis Untermeyer

William Tell, the hero of the Swiss people, was willing to die for a belief. What is this belief? What does this legend tell us about what is important to the people of Switzerland? As you read, look for the answers.

William Tell died in the fourteenth century, but he continues to live, not only in legend but in literature. The German poet Schiller wrote a stirring drama about this national hero of Switzerland, and the Italian composer Rossini glorified him in a popular opera.

William Tell was Switzerland's greatest champion in its war of independence against Austria. Albert of Austria had determined to deprive Switzerland of its long-held freedom and to bring it under his autocratic rule. To do this he had appointed Gessler, a real tyrant, to act as governor and subdue the people. A group of Swiss patriots met near the Lake of Lucerne to discuss what might be done. Their leaders were three mountain-men, Arnold von Melchtal, Walter Fürst, and Walter's son-in-law, William Tell.

"Gessler has sworn that he will break the country into pieces," said Arnold von Melchtal. "He has spies in every canton, and he will punish anyone who dares to utter the word 'liberty.'"

"I have heard that he is planning something worse," said Walter Fürst. "I hear that he's going to set his cap on top of a pole, and anyone who fails to salute it will be thrown into jail or banished from the country."

"Our people are too proud to bend the knee to a tyrant," said William Tell. "I, for one, would not bow to Gessler himself, let alone his cap."

A week later Tell was walking with his seven-year-old son through the town of Altdorf.[1] There, in the center of the village square, was a tall pole, and on top perched an Austrian cap. A dozen soldiers loafed in front of an inn facing the village square. Tell walked by without bending his head or even glancing at the

---

1. **Altdorf**, a Swiss town in the Alps at the foot of Lake Lucerne, is still in existence.

pole. The soldiers pounced upon him. Collaring the boy too, they dragged father and son to Gessler.

Gessler, dark and hateful, sat staring coldly at William Tell.

"They tell me you call yourself a patriot," he said. "They also tell me that you are quite an archer. Well, I give you a chance to prove your skill. I could have you imprisoned, but I am a kind man. I will give you a chance."

"I do not need your 'kindness,'" said Tell.

"We shall see about that," said Gessler. "You," he said, turning to one of his soldiers, "bring me an apple. Take that boy a hundred steps from here and place the apple on his head. Now you," he said turning back to Tell, "shoot that apple off your son's head. If you do it, both of you shall go free. If you fail, both of you shall die."

The crowd that had followed from the village square gasped with horror; even the soldiers shuddered. But Tell did not flinch. He looked at Gessler with contempt. He took two arrows from his quiver, hid one inside his shirt, and silently fitted the other to his crossbow. The shaft sped to its mark—the tense silence was broken as the apple split in half and fell to the ground. The Swiss shouted for joy, while the Austrian soldiers tried not to show their admiration.

"Very pretty," said Gessler sarcastically. "But I saw you take two arrows.

Evidently you weren't so sure of your first shot. You kept the second in case you should miss. Am I right?"

"You are wrong," said Tell. "The second arrow was for you had I as much as scratched my son."

"Enough!" cried Gessler. "You have spoken your own doom. Put him in chains," he told the soldiers. "Carry him across the lake to the castle at Küssnacht. Let him lie in the darkest dungeon, far from the light of the sun, and let him be a prey to the rats and reptiles that lodge there. I will go with you to see it done."

Tell was bound and thrown into a boat. Hardly had the vessel left the shore when the sky was covered with black clouds. A great storm sprang up bringing huge gusts of rain and driving the boat wildly in the darkness. The rowers were helpless.

"If you take off my chains," said Tell, "I will guide the boat for you. I know the lake, and I am used to this weather."

Gessler nodded, the chains were removed, and Tell took hold of the rudder. He steered straight toward the shore, heading for a slippery shelf of rock. Picking up his crossbow where it lay in the bottom of the boat, Tell leaped swiftly out. Then, as Gessler stood up in the tossing boat, he fitted the second arrow and shot the tyrant dead.

William Tell's example gave heart to other patriots. Crowds rose to challenge the rule of the Austrian oppressors. The land was cleared of tyranny, and the Swiss were—and have remained—a free people ever since. The rock where Tell leaped is now honored with a chapel, and a statue in the village square of Altdorf stands where the fearless archer shot the apple from his son's head.

William Tell 31

Developing Comprehension Skills

1. What did William Tell have to shoot from his son's head? Why did he have to do it?

2. Put these four events in the right order:
   a. Tell jumped out of the boat.
   b. Gessler was made governor.
   c. Gessler declared a new rule about his cap.
   d. Tell proved he was a good archer.

3. Why do you think Gessler hated William Tell?

4. Do you believe William Tell was right in shooting Gessler? Why or why not?

Reading Literature: Legends

1. **Examining a Character.** In this legend, it is easier than in most stories to pick out the hero and the villain. Reread the paragraphs that discuss Gessler. Look for information about what he does, what he says, and what others say or think about him. What qualities do you find in him? Do his own men like him? Refer to sentences or paragraphs in the story that support your answer.

2. **Recognizing the Value of a Legend.** Imagine that someone proved that William Tell never shot an apple off his son's head. However, the person also proved that everything else in the story was true. How would this affect the value of the legend? Would the legend no longer be worth telling? Or would the point of the story stay the same? Before you answer, be sure you understand the purpose of a legend. That is, be able to answer these questions: Why do people tell legends? Must they believe that every event in a legend is true? Must they believe that the qualities of the hero or heroine are worthwhile?

Developing Vocabulary Skills

Recognizing Antonyms as Context Clues. You can sometimes figure out the meaning of an unfamiliar word by looking for a word that is opposite in meaning. These words are called **antonyms.** An antonym may be found in the same sentence or in a nearby sentence. It is usually in the same position as the unfamiliar word. Read this example:

This lion cub is not *vicious*. He is *gentle*.

The opposite of vicious is gentle.

Read these sentences about legends you have read. Find the antonym of each underlined word. Write the word and its antonym.

1. Richard quarreled with his <u>allies</u>, but grew to respect his enemies.

2. The country was in a state of <u>turmoil</u>. During Richard's absence there was no peace.

3. The abbot was <u>doleful</u> as he rode away. He was not happy about his chances of answering the three questions.

4. When the shepherd heard the bad news, he grinned, "Do not <u>despair</u>, master. Be hopeful."

5. The shepherd knew the king would never recognize a poor, simple shepherd when he wore <u>elegant</u> clothes.

6. A dozen soldiers were <u>loafing</u> in front of the inn. Instead of working, they simply watched the people walk by.

7. The crowd was <u>tense</u> as the apple was placed on the boy's head, but Tell remained calm.

8. The land was cleared of <u>tyranny</u>, and the people have kept their freedom ever since.

Developing Writing Skills

1. **Understanding Legends.** All four legends that you have read had something to say about rulers. Only one ruler, Richard the Lion-Hearted, was pictured in a favorable way. Consider what these legends reveal about the people who told them. What do people expect of their rulers? What are some of the evils or failings that people criticize in their rulers? Write at least one paragraph to answer these questions.

2. **Rewriting a Legend.** Rewrite this story so that you can tell it to a first grader. Replace words that are too hard with easier words that mean almost the same thing. If you think that the story needs an explanation of what a tyrant is, add the explanation. If you feel the ending is too violent for a child, bring the story to an end after Tell successfully shoots the apple from his son's head.

Developing Skills in Study and Research

Becoming Familiar with Your Library. As the first paragraph of this story noted, William Tell has been made the hero of both a play and an opera. If you wanted to read the play or hear the opera, would your school or local library be of any help? In the Dewey Decimal system, plays are usually grouped with other literature, in the 800's. However, the play mentioned in the story was written in German. The play might be grouped with books in other languages, in the 400's. Records are shelved apart from books, and often they have a separate card catalog.

Investigate your library. Use the card catalog to find the following information:

1. Does the library have any writing by Johann Christoph Friedrich von Schiller?

2. Is that writing grouped under literature or languages?

3. Are records listed in the same card catalog as books? If not, where are they listed? How is the information organized?

4. Does the library have a record of the opera named *William Tell* by Gioacchino Rossini?

5. Does the library have any other recordings of works by Rossini? What are their titles?

Developing Skills in Critical Thinking

Recognizing Slanted Writing. Make two lists of words used in "William Tell." On one list, write all the words used to describe Gessler. On the other, write all the words used to describe Tell. Which list has almost all words with **positive,** or good, feelings? Which has almost all words with **negative,** or bad, feelings? What does this choice of words tell you about the writer's opinion of each of the characters?

Spotted Eagle and Black Crow

TRADITIONAL AMERICAN INDIAN LEGEND
Retold by Jenny Leading Cloud

The first four legends were from European peoples. This one is from American Indians. As you read, ask yourself: What qualities are admired by both groups? What other qualities of heroes are shown in this legend?

This is a story of two warriors, of jealousy, and of eagles. This legend is supposed to have been a favorite of the great *Mahpiya Luta*—Chief Red Cloud of the Oglalas.

Many lifetimes ago, there lived two brave warriors. One was named *Wanblee Gleska*—Spotted Eagle. The other's name was *Kangi Sapa*—Black Crow. They were friends but, as it happened, they both loved the same girl, *Zintkala Luta Win*—Red Bird. She was beautiful, a fine tanner and quill-worker, and she liked Spotted Eagle best, which made Black Crow very jealous.

Black Crow went to his friend and said, "Let us, you and I, go on a war party against the Pahani. Let us get ourselves some fine horses and earn eagle feathers." Spotted Eagle thought this a good idea. The two young men purified themselves in a sweat bath. They got out their war medicine and their war shields. They painted their faces. They did all that warriors should do before a raid. Then they went against the Pahani.

Their raid was not a success. The Pahani were watchful. The young warriors got nowhere near the Pahani horse herd. Not only did they capture no ponies, but they even lost their own mounts, because, while they were trying to creep up to their enemies' herd, the Pahani found their horses. The two young men had a hard time getting away on foot because their enemies were searching for them everywhere. At one time, they had to hide themselves in a lake, under the water, breathing through long, hollow reeds which were sticking up above the surface. They were so clever at hiding themselves that the Pahani finally gave up searching.

Brulé Sioux Shield with Feather Decoration.
Museum of the American Indian Heye Foundation.

The young men had to travel home on foot. It was a long way. Their moccasins were tattered, their feet bleeding. At last they came to a high cliff. "Let us go up there," said Black Crow, "and see whether our enemies are following us." They climbed up. They could see no one following them; but on a ledge far below them, halfway down the cliff, they spied a nest with two young eagles in it. "Let us at least get those eagles," Black Crow proposed. There was no way one could climb down the sheer rock wall, but Black Crow took his rawhide lariat, made a loop in it, put the rope around Spotted Eagle's chest under his armpits, and lowered him down. When his friend was on the ledge with the nest, Black Crow said to himself, "I will leave him there to die. I will come home alone, and then Red Bird will marry me." And he threw his end of the rawhide thong down and left without looking back and without listening to Spotted Eagle.

Spotted Eagle cried in vain. He got no answer, only silence. At last it dawned on him that his companion had betrayed him, that he had been left to die. The lariat was much too short for him to lower himself to the ground; there was an abyss of two hundred feet yawning beneath him. He was left with the two young eagles screeching at him, angered that this strange, two-legged creature had invaded their home.

Black Crow came back to his village. "Spotted Eagle died a warrior's death," he told the people. "The Pahani killed him." There was loud wailing throughout the village because everybody had liked Spotted Eagle. Red Bird grieved more than the others. She slashed her arms with a sharp knife and cut her hair to make plain her sorrow to all. But in the end she became Black Crow's wife, because life must go on.

But Spotted Eagle did not die on his lonely ledge. The eagles got used to him. The old eagles brought plenty of food— rabbits, prairie dogs, or sage hens—and Spotted Eagle shared this raw meat with the two chicks. Maybe it was the eagle medicine in his bundle, which he carried on his chest, that made the eagles accept him. Still, he had a very hard time on that ledge. It was so narrow that, when he wanted to rest, he had to tie himself with the rawhide thong to a little rock sticking out of the cliff, for fear of falling off the ledge in his sleep. In this way he spent a few very uncomfortable weeks; after all, he was a human being and not a bird to whom such a crack in the rock face is home.

At last the young eagles were big enough to practice flying. "What will become of me now?" thought the young warrior. "Once these fledglings have flown the nest for good, the old birds won't be bringing any more food up here." Then he had an inspiration. "Perhaps I will die. Very likely I will die. But I will try it. I will not just sit here and give

up." He took his little pipe out of the medicine bundle and lifted it to the sky and prayed, *"Wakan Tanka, onshimala ye.* Great Spirit, pity me. You have created man and his cousin, the eagle. You have given me the eagle's name. I have decided to try to let the eagles carry me to the ground. Let the eagles help me, let me succeed."

He smoked and felt a surge of confidence. He grabbed hold of the legs of the two young eagles. "Brothers," he told them, "you have accepted me as one of your own. Now we will live together or die together. *Hokahay."* And he jumped off the ledge. He expected to be shattered on the ground below, but with a mighty flapping of wings the two young eagles broke his fall and all landed safely. Spotted Eagle said a prayer of thanks to the Ones Above. He thanked the eagles, telling them that one day he would be back with gifts and have a giveaway in their honor.

Spotted Eagle returned to his village. The excitement was great. He had been dead and had come back to life. Everybody asked him how it happened that he was not dead, but he would not tell them. "I escaped," he said, "and that is all." He saw his love married to his treacherous friend, but he bore it in silence. He was not one to bring enmity to his people, to set one family against the other. Besides, what happened could not be changed. Thus he accepted his fate.

A year or so later, a great war party of Pahani attacked his village. The enemy outnumbered them tenfold, and there was no chance of victory for Spotted Eagle's band. All the warriors could do was to fight a slow rear-guard action, which would give the women, children, and old folks a chance to escape across the river. Guarding their people this way, the few warriors at hand fought bravely, charging the enemy again and again, making them halt and regroup. Each time, the warriors retreated a little, taking up a new position on a hill, or across a gully. In this way they could save their families.

Showing the greatest courage, exposing their bodies freely, were Spotted Eagle and Black Crow. In the end they alone faced the enemy. Then, suddenly, Black Crow's horse was hit by several arrows in succession and collapsed under him. "Brother, forgive me for what I have done," he cried to Spotted Eagle. "Let me jump up on your horse behind you."

Spotted Eagle answered, "You are a Fox. Pin yourself and fight. Then, if you survive, I will forgive you; and if you die, I will forgive you also."

What Spotted Eagle meant was this: Black Crow was a member of the Fox Warrior Society. The braves who belong to it sing this song:

> *I am a Fox.*
> *If there is anything daring,*
> *If there is anything dangerous to do,*

> *That is a task for me to perform.*
> *Let it be done by me.*

Foxes wear a long, trailing sash, decorated with quillwork, which reaches all the way to the ground even when the warrior is on horseback. In the midst of battle, a Fox will sometimes defy death by pinning his sash to the earth with a special wooden pin, or with a knife or arrow. This means: I will stay here, rooted to this spot, facing my foes, until someone comes to release the pin, or until the enemies flee, or until I die.

Black Crow pinned his sash to the ground. There was no one to release him, and the enemy did not flee. Black Crow sang his death song. He was hit by lances and arrows and died a warrior's death. Many Pahani died with him.

Spotted Eagle had been the only one to see this. He finally joined his people, safe across the river. The Pahani had lost all taste to follow them there. "Your husband died well," Spotted Eagle told Red Bird. After some time had passed, Spotted Eagle married Red Bird. And much, much later he told his parents, and no one else, how Black Crow had betrayed him. "I forgive him now," he said, "because once he was my friend, and because he died like a warrior should, fighting for his people, and also because Red Bird and I are happy now."

After a long winter, when spring came again, Spotted Eagle told his wife, "I must go away for a few days to fulfill a promise. I must go alone." He rode off by himself to that cliff. Again he stood at its foot, below the ledge where the eagles' nest had been. He pointed his sacred pipe to the four directions, down to Grandmother Earth and up to the Grandfather, letting the smoke ascend to the sky, calling out: "*Wanblee, misunkala.* Little eagle brothers, hear me."

High above him in the clouds appeared two black dots, circling. These were the eagles who had saved his life. They came at his call, their huge wings spread majestically, uttering a shrill cry of joy and recognition. Swooping down, they alighted at his feet. He stroked them with a feather fan, and thanked them many times, and fed them choice morsels of buffalo meat, and fastened small medicine bundles around their legs as a sign of friendship, and spread sacred tobacco offerings around the foot of the cliff. Thus he made a pact of friendship and brotherhood between *Wanblee Oyate*—the Eagle Nation—and his own people. After he had done all this, the stately birds soared up again into the sky, circling motionless, carried by the wind, disappearing into the clouds. Spotted Eagle turned his horse's head homeward, going happily back to Red Bird.

Sioux Shield, about 1870, LAKOTA
Courtesy of the Denver Art Museum.

Developing Comprehension Skills

1. Make a time line showing the major events in this story.

2. State two ways in which you can tell that Red Bird preferred Spotted Eagle.

3. Find a reason given in the story for each of these events.
   a. Black Crow abandoned Spotted Eagle on the eagles' ledge.
   b. Red Bird married Black Crow.
   c. Spotted Eagle told only his parents of Black Crow's actions.
   d. Black Crow pinned his sash to the ground and fought till he died.

4. Do you think that the events in this story could have really happened? Give reasons for your answer.

Reading Literature: Legends

1. **Examining Characters.** Unlike the narrator of "William Tell," the narrator of "Spotted Eagle and Black Crow" does not tell the reader that one character is a champion and the other is a villain. Instead, she tells what each young man does and lets the reader judge these actions. She even shows that Black Crow had some good qualities, despite his weaknesses.

   For each warrior, list those actions that suggest good qualities. Then list actions that suggest bad qualities or weaknesses.

2. **Identifying the Conflict.** What is the conflict, or struggle, in this story? Keep in mind that the conflict must be part of the story almost from beginning to end.

3. **Identifying the Climax.** What is the turning point in the conflict? In what scene does Black Crow face the result of his betrayal of his friend? How does he face this?

4. **Recognizing Elements of Legends.** Name some events in this story that are impossible.

Developing Vocabulary Skills

Choosing the Correct Meaning. A writer does not always give obvious clues to the meaning of an unfamiliar word. You may not find any key words or key punctuation to help you find a context clue. Then you must try to understand the important idea of the sentence or paragraph in which the word is found. From that, you may figure out the meaning of the word. In other words, you can **infer** the meaning of the word.

Read these sentences drawn from the story of "Spotted Eagle and Black Crow." For each underlined word, choose the meaning that best fits the sentence. Write the letter of your answer on your paper.

1. There was no way one could climb down the sheer rock wall.
   a. very steep   c. shiny
   b. beautiful   d. flat

2. Spotted Eagle cried in vain. He got no answer, only silence.
   a. too softly   c. unkindly
   b. too loudly   d. without success

3. At last it dawned on him that his companion had betrayed him, that he had been left to die.
   a. felt sorry for him   c. forgave him
   b. misled him   d. become angry with him

4. Red Bird grieved over the news of Spotted Eagle's death. She slashed her arms with a sharp knife and cut her hair to make plain her sorrow to all.
   a. was saddened   c. showed no feeling
   b. smiled shyly   d. lost interest

5. Over their shoulders, the Fox Indians wear a long, trailing sash, decorated with quillwork.
   a. soft-leathered shoes   c. headband
   b. a long strip of cloth   d. a piece of armor

Developing Writing Skills

1. **Understanding the Legend.** In this legend, both Spotted Eagle and Black Crow show courage. However, the legend suggests that courage is not enough to make a good warrior into a hero. What are some of the differences between Spotted Eagle and Black Crow? What qualities does Spotted Eagle show that make him a better person? Your answer should be at least one paragraph long.

2. **Changing the Point of View.** The term **point of view** refers to the narrator of a story. All of the legends have been told from the point of view of someone outside of the story. If this legend had been told by Spotted Eagle, we would say it was told from his point of view.

Rewrite the story from the point of view of one of the eagles who befriended Spotted Eagle. Imagine that you are one of the baby eagles. Tell what you see happening, the way an eagle might understand the events. In your version, tell about only the things that the eagles saw and heard.

Developing Skills in Speaking and Listening

Comparing Rhythms. Each legend you have read has a slightly different rhythm. **Rhythm** is the pattern of accented and unaccented syllables. The length of sentences is part of the rhythm. The way in which phrases go together is part of the rhythm. The length of individual words, the number of commas, and the amount of repetition are part of the rhythm. The rhythm can be fast or slow, regular or irregular, smooth or jerky, exciting or matter-of-fact or dull. Even when you read silently, you can tell differences in rhythm. When you read aloud, those differences should be much more noticeable.

Do this exercise in a small group. Each of you should take turns reading the passages listed below. Then discuss what you heard. What adjectives could you use to describe the rhythm of each passage?

1. "Richard the Lion-Hearted," page 9; three paragraphs beginning with "After wandering for weeks" through "to look for the king."
2. "The Pied Piper of Hamelin," page 22; two paragraphs beginning with "Hamelin, a little German town," through "and does nothing about it."
3. "Spotted Eagle and Black Crow," page 37; two paragraphs beginning with "Spotted Eagle returned to his village," through "they could save their families."

The Six Horsemen

TRADITIONAL WEST AFRICAN LEGEND
Retold by Frances Carpenter

This story has not one but six heroes. What quality enables them to succeed? What does the importance of that quality tell us about the people from whom we get this legend?

"The chief's daughter is gone!" they heard. "Nassa has been kidnaped by Ballo, the Robber."

The news spread through the Hausa towns of Northern Nigeria. People shook their heads with dismay. All knew this Ballo, the chief of a neighboring tribe. They called him "The Robber" because he often carried off a camel or a horse from right under their eyes.

Now he had taken Nassa, the fair daughter of the chief himself. Everyone loved this girl. She was known to be the kindest and the most beautiful of all the girls in that countryside. It is no wonder that this Ballo should wish her for his wife. The marvel was that he could have stolen her out of her bed without waking the guards. But that he had done.

The chief, father of Nassa, was beside himself with sadness. "I offer my daughter as bride to any good young man of our tribe who shall bring her home safe and sound. Half of my riches shall be their wedding gift."

Like autumn leaves in a storm, this promise was carried through the Hausa towns. It came to the ears of a certain young prince who was, himself, the son of a chief. Fadebi, he was called, and he was well known for his brave deeds.

"I will bring back the chief's daughter," Fadebi declared. He had seen Nassa. He admired her. Indeed, he was already in love with her. He saddled his fastest mare, and he galloped away toward the strong fortress where she was.

Fadebi had not ridden far before he met another traveler. After the custom on the highroad, the two reined in their steeds to give each other greeting.

"Allah give thee peace!" they said. When Fadebi was asked where he was going, he replied bravely: "I go to find Nassa, daughter of our chief. She is shut up in the fortress of Ballo, the Robber."

The other horseman shuddered. Everyone feared Ballo, the Robber in that part of Africa. His fortress of mud bricks was strong. His soldiers were just as cruel as he was himself.

"You should not go alone," he cried. "You should have a companion to help you. I'll give you my help." He, too, was young, and he, too, liked adventure.

"Two are always better than one," Fadebi agreed. "Come along if you wish." Then the two horsemen rode on together.

It was not long before they met a third traveler. When that one heard the story of their bold errand, he also wanted to join them.

"If two are better than one, then three are better than two, I suppose." Fadebi gave his consent. He did likewise to three other young horsemen whom they met on the highroad.

They were now a company of six. Their horses' hoofs made a clatter as they galloped over the land. With Fadebi in the lead, they swam their horses across the river that divided their country from that of Ballo, the Robber.

In the town on the other side of this river, they found shelter for the night in a small inn. The young woman who served their evening meal gave them news of fair Nassa.

"I know the girl well," she said. "Each morning I go into Ballo's fortress to dress the hair of his wives. Nassa is the prettiest of them all, but she also is the saddest. My heart aches when I see her tears. If I could, I would set her free."

Thus, Fadebi found out that even the people of Ballo's own tribe hated his fearful cruelty.

"My father is rich, girl," Fadebi said to the hairdresser. "You shall have a bolt of fine cloth, if you will do a service for me. Another bolt will come with it, if no one finds out that I come from Nassa's land." The girl nodded consent, and Fadebi continued.

"Tell Nassa I come from her father. I will bring her out of her prison, but she must help me find the way in."

Next morning, while the girl from the inn went to the fortress, Fadebi called his five companions around him. "You have offered your help," he said. "Pray tell me what each one of you can do best. If we succeed and I marry the chief's daughter, you shall have your rewards."

"I have great wisdom," said the first horseman. "There is no question on earth that I cannot answer."

"I can see into the future," the second horseman declared. "I know what is to happen before the time comes."

"I can dig a long tunnel in the wink of an eye." The third one was speaking now. The fourth then cried out, "I can build a large boat before anyone knows I have begun it."

"As for me," said the fifth horseman, "I have a strong JuJu. With my magic I can change myself into any form I wish."

You can know by these words that the six horsemen lived in the fairy-tale times of long ago.

At that very moment, in the fortress of Ballo, the Robber, the hairdresser was combing Nassa's long black hair. She was whispering Fadebi's message into the girl's listening ear.

"A handsome young man is this Fadebi who has come here from your father," she was saying. "He promises to get you out of this prison, if you will tell him how he may make his way into the fort."

Nassa was quiet until the hairdresser had finished combing her hair. Then, without speaking a word, she put into the girl's hands three little bundles.

The hairdresser hastened to hide them under her brushes.

"Will Fadebi know how to use them?" she asked. The chief's daughter nodded her head.

Fadebi, too, was puzzled when he opened the three bundles. In one there was a fig leaf. A strange leaf it was, like none the young man ever had seen. In the second bundle there was a bone, with bits of meat still upon it. And in the third, there was only a bunch of green grass.

"What am I to do with this fig leaf, this bone, and these blades of grass?" He turned to his companion who had said he could answer all questions.

"It is quite simple," the wise young fellow nodded his head. "The leaf is from the tree that reaches to Nassa's window.

Carved Ivory Equestrian Figure from the Oyo Area.
Private Collection. Courtesy of the Pace Gallery, New York City.

The bone is for the watchdog at the foot of the tree, so that he shall not bark. And when the Robber's horse, who is tied there, is about to whinny a warning to his master, this green grass will stop his cry."

This young man truly had wisdom. For that night, when the moon rose, Fadebi climbed over the garden wall. It was easy to find the tree with the strange leaf. Before the watchdog could bark, the bone was in his mouth. Then, before the Robber's horse could make even one whinny, it was munching the grass.

Without trouble, Fadebi went up the tree and in through the open window where Nassa was waiting. With sweet words he told her of her father's promise that she should marry that young man who would bring her home safe and sound. He spoke of how he would love her and how happy they would be. They talked and they talked as they waited for a dark cloud to cover the moon, so that they could get away without being seen.

Although they spoke softly, the watchful chief, Ballo, heard them as he walked in the garden. At once he called for the guards.

"A strange man is with Nassa! I have heard his voice. He must not escape. Beat the drums! Call all the people! I have work for them to do."

When all the town was wakened, Ballo, the Robber gave his commands. "A thief is in my fortress. You shall see it for yourselves. Lift off its roof. Take first one tile,

then another, so that he may not leap through. Then take down its walls, one mud brick at a time. The stranger cannot run away with so many of us in wait for him."

The people began the work. In the crowd, looking on, were the young hero's five companions.

"Our friend is in trouble," whispered the One-who-knew-what-was-going-to-happen-before-the-time. "Ballo means to kill him. I see it all clearly. We must find some way to get Fadebi and Nassa out of the fort."

Then the One-who-could-dig-a-long-tunnel-in-the-wink-of-an-eye began to work on the opposite side of the fortress. In the ground at the back, out of sight of the crowd, he dug and he dug. Before anyone knew it, Fadebi and Nassa had crept out through his tunnel. Their horses were waiting. With Nassa riding behind him on his swift mare, Fadebi led the way out of the Robber's town.

Meanwhile, the roof of the fortress had been taken off, tile after tile. Its walls were coming down, one brick at a time, but no stranger was there. Gone, too, was Ballo's pretty prisoner, Nassa. Ballo flew into a rage, "My horse! Bring me my horse!"

Ballo was soon in the saddle. With soldiers riding behind him, he was galloping across the land after Fadebi and Nassa.

The river slowed up the six fleeing young horsemen. They heard clearly the hoofbeats of their pursuers. They feared they would never be able to swim across the river in time.

Then it was the turn of the One-who-could-build-a-large-boat-in-a-jiffy. Before Ballo could come up with them, the six horsemen and the chief's daughter were safe in a huge vessel out in the stream. It was so big that their horses, too, were aboard.

Ballo leapt from his steed and threw himself into the river. With flashing arms and legs he swam like a big fish, trying to catch up with the boat. He might have succeeded if Fadebi's fifth companion had not remembered his JuJu. By its strong magic, he turned himself into a giant eagle. White as a cloud was this eagle. Larger than an elephant! So strong was the great bird that it could lift the boat high up into the air. Its passengers were well out of Ballo's reaching hands.

When they were set safely down on the other side of the river, the man's JuJu worked once more. It changed the giant eagle into a huge crocodile, with rows of teeth as big as an elephant's tusk. With one bite, that crocodile made an end of Ballo, the Robber. Never again would he trouble the chief's gentle daughter.

Her father rejoiced to have Nassa again at home, safe and sound. He gladly kept his promise to the young man who had saved her.

The wedding feast was splendid. The five horsemen who had helped Fadebi were the most honored guests. Each one of them went home with five handsome horses as his reward.

Developing Comprehension Skills

1. Which of these words names the chief's daughter? What or whom does each of the others name?

   a. Ballo   b. Hausa   c. Nassa   d. JuJu

2. How does each of the six horsemen contribute to the success of the adventure? Who else aids in Nassa's escape?

3. Reread paragraph 3 on page 46. Below are listed three ideas from that paragraph. Decide which is the main idea, which is an important detail, and which is a less important detail that was included just to make the paragraph more interesting.

   a. Fadebi used sweet words.
   b. Fadebi got into Nassa's room and explained his mission.
   c. Fadebi and Nassa waited for a dark cloud to cover the moon.

4. When the hairdresser tells Nassa that Fadebi needs her advice on how to get into the fortress, Nassa gives her three little bundles. What does Nassa's action tell about her? What does she expect from Fadebi?

5. Which events and characters in this legend are realistic, or believeable? Which ones are fantastic? Give reasons for your opinions.

Reading Literature: Legends

1. **Recognizing Elements of Legend: Magic.** The Pied Piper carried enchantment in his pipe. Spotted Eagle carried eagle medicine in his bundle. One of the six horsemen has a strong JuJu. How do these types of magic show similarities among the groups who made up these legends? What differences do the types of magic point out?

2. **Recognizing Elements of Legend: Riddles.** The three bundles that Nassa sends to Fadebi must be interpreted. They are like riddles he must answer to save her. What other legend involved riddles? What might be proved by an ability to answer riddles?

3. **Comparing Character Traits.** Like "Spotted Eagle and Black Crow," this legend says that courage is not enough to make a person a hero. What character trait shared by the six horsemen enabled them to defeat Ballo? Was this character trait important in any of the other legends you have read?

4. **Identifying Conflict and Climax.** What is the conflict in this story? Which scene is the climax, or turning point?

5. **Recognizing the Purpose.** Why do you think storytellers told this legend? Why did someone eventually write it down? Was the purpose mainly to teach about Hausa beliefs? Was it to tell a good story? Was it to show how good triumphs and evil is destroyed? Or was there a combination of reasons? Explain your opinion.

Developing Vocabulary Skills

Identifying Context Clues. You cannot always figure out the meaning of an unfamiliar word by looking for context clues, synonyms, or antonyms. You must refer to the dictionary or glossary to find the meaning of the word. Read this example of a sentence that contains no clue to the meaning of the underlined word.

Monica is a very loquacious person.

You cannot figure out from the context of the sentence that *loquacious* means "fond of talking."

Read each of these sentences using words drawn from the story. Try to figure out the meaning of the underlined word by using context clues. If there are clues, write the meaning of the word. If there are no clues, write *No clues—use dictionary.*

1. People shook their heads in dismay—sadness—at the news of Nassa's kidnapping.

2. Fadebi saddled his fastest mare and galloped toward the fortress.

3. Fadebi had ridden far on his steed and stopped to give the horse a drink of water and some rest.

4. The travelers reined, or guided, their horses in greeting each other.

5. Fadebi gave his consent—that is, he approved—and the third traveler joined them.

6. The hoofbeats of their pursuers could be heard easily.

Developing Writing Skills

1. **Understanding Setting.** What does this legend tell about life in the Hausa towns at the time of the story? Describe what you have learned about how people lived. For example, what were some of the jobs

they held? How were they ruled? What objects were valuable to them? What feelings did they respect?

2. **Rewriting a Legend More Realistically.** Most legends are based on actual events. However, as the legend is told and retold, other happenings are added to the actual events. These new happenings may be fantastic, that is, not possible in the real world. Suppose that "The Six Horsemen" started as an account of an actual rescue. Write a short version of the story the way you think it could have really happened. Replace the magical events with realistic adventures. Make your version about six to twelve paragraphs long.

Developing Skills in Study and Research

Using the Card Catalog To Find Reference Materials. In this story, the term *JuJu* may be unfamiliar to you. Because it is not used frequently in English, some dictionaries might not list it. If you wanted to know more about what it means, you might need to find it in an **unabridged dictionary** or a **specialized dictionary**.

Perhaps you want to know where each of the legends in this chapter came from. You would want to look at an **atlas**. An atlas would include an index of countries, listed in alphabetical order. The index would tell which of the maps in the atlas show each country.

To find the reference materials you want, you would begin with the card catalog. Start with the headings *Dictionaries* and *Atlases*. Under those classifications, there may be cards listing all the dictionaries and atlases in the library. There may be cards referring you to other headings, such as *Foreign Language Dictionaries*.

Make a list of the dictionaries and atlases your school or local library has. If you can find an entry for *JuJu* in any of the dictionaries, write down the name of the dictionary, its call number, and the information it gives about the term. In an atlas, find a map that shows western Africa. List five countries of western Africa.

Lazy Peter and His Three-Cornered Hat

The number three is used again and again in legends. Watch how important it is in this story.

TRADITIONAL PUERTO RICAN LEGEND

Retold by Ricardo E. Alegría and translated by Elizabeth Culbert

This is the story of Lazy Peter, a shameless rascal of a fellow, who went from village to village making mischief.

One day Lazy Peter learned that a fair was being held in a certain village. He knew that a large crowd of country people would be there selling horses, cows, and other farm animals and that a large amount of money would change hands. Peter, as usual, needed money, but it was not his custom to work for it. So he set out for the village, wearing a red three-cornered hat.

The first thing he did was to stop at a stand and leave a big bag of money with the owner, asking him to keep it safely until he returned for it. Peter told the man that when he returned for the bag of money, one corner of his hat would be turned down, and that was how the owner of the stand would know him. The man promised to do this, and Peter thanked him. Then he went to the drugstore in the village and gave the druggist another bag of money, asking him to keep it until he returned with one corner of his hat turned up. The druggist agreed, and Peter left. He went to the church and asked the priest to keep another bag of money and to return it to him only when he came back with one corner of his hat twisted to the side. The priest said fine, that he would do this.

Having disposed of three bags of money, Peter went to the edge of the village where the farmers were buying and selling horses and cattle. He stood and watched for a while until he decided that one of the farmers must be very rich indeed, for he had sold all of his horses and cows. Moreover, the man seemed to be a miser who was never satisfied but wanted, always, more and more money. This was Peter's man! He stopped beside him. It was raining, and, instead of keeping his hat on to protect his head, he took it off and wrapped it carefully in his cape, as though it were very valuable. It puzzled the farmer to see Peter stand there with the rain falling on his head and his hat wrapped in his cape.

After a while he asked, "Why do you take better care of your hat than of your head?"

Peter saw that the farmer had swallowed the bait. Smiling to himself, he said that the hat was the most valuable thing in all the world and that was why he took care to protect it from the rain. The farmer's curiosity increased at this reply, and he asked Peter what was so valuable about a red three-cornered hat. Peter told him that the hat worked for him. Thanks to it, he never had to work for a living because, whenever he put the hat on with one of the corners turned over,

people just handed him any money he asked for.

The farmer was amazed and very interested in what Peter said. As money–getting was his greatest ambition, he told Peter that he couldn't believe a word of it until he saw the hat work with his own eyes. Peter assured him that he could do this, for he, Peter, was hungry, and, since he had no money with which to buy food, the hat was about to start working.

With this, Peter took out his three–cornered hat, turned one corner down, put it on his head, and told the farmer to come along and watch the hat work. Peter took the farmer to the stand. The minute the owner looked up, he handed over the bag of money Peter had left with him. The farmer stood with his mouth open in astonishment. He didn't know what to make of it, but of one thing he was sure— he had to have that hat!

Peter smiled and asked if he was satisfied, and the farmer said yes, he was. Then he asked Peter if he would sell the hat. This was just what Lazy Peter wanted, but he said no, that he was not interested in selling the hat because, with it, he never had to work and he always had money. The farmer said he thought that was unsound reasoning because thieves could easily steal a hat. Wouldn't it be safer to invest in a farm with cattle? So they talked, and Peter pretended to be impressed with the farmer's arguments. Finally he said yes, that he saw the point.

If the farmer would make him a good offer, he would sell the hat. The farmer, who had made up his mind to have the hat at any price, offered a thousand pesos. Peter laughed aloud and said he could make as much as that by just putting his hat on two or three times.

As they continued haggling over the price, the farmer grew more and more determined to have that hat until, finally, he offered all he had realized from the sale of his horses and cows—ten thousand pesos in gold. Peter still pretended not to be interested, but he chuckled to himself, thinking of the trick he was about to play on the farmer. All right, he said, it was a deal. Then the farmer grew cautious and told Peter that, before he handed over the ten thousand pesos, he would like to see the hat work again. Peter said that was fair enough. He put on the hat with one of the corners turned up and went with the farmer to the drugstore. The moment the druggist saw the turned-up corner, he handed over the money Peter had left with him. At this the farmer was convinced and very eager to set the hat to work for himself. He took out a bag containing ten thousand pesos in gold and was about to hand it to Peter, when he had a change of heart and thought better of it. He asked Peter please to excuse him, but he had to see the hat work just once more before he could part with his gold. Peter said that that was fair enough, but now he would have to ask the farmer to

give him the fine horse he was riding as well as the ten thousand pesos in gold. The farmer's interest in the hat revived, and he said it was a bargain!

Lazy Peter put on his hat again and doubled over one of the corners. He told the farmer that, since he still seemed to have doubts, this time he could watch the hat work in the church. The farmer was delighted with this, his doubts were stilled, and he fairly beamed thinking of all the money he was going to make once that hat was his.

They entered the church. The priest was hearing confession, but when he saw Peter with his hat, he said, "Wait here, my son." He went to the sacristy and returned the bag of money Peter had left with him. Peter thanked the priest, then knelt and asked for a blessing before he left. The farmer had seen everything and was fully convinced of the hat's magic powers. As soon as they left the church, he gave Peter the ten thousand pesos in gold and told him to take the horse, also. Peter tied the bag of pesos to the saddle, gave the hat to the farmer, begging him to take good care of it, spurred his horse, and galloped out of town.

As soon as he was alone, the farmer burst out laughing at the thought of the trick he had played on Lazy Peter. A hat such as this was priceless! He couldn't wait to try it. He put it on with one corner turned up and entered the butcher shop. The butcher looked at the hat, which was very handsome indeed, but said nothing. The farmer turned around, then walked up and down until the butcher asked him what he wanted. The farmer said he was waiting for the bag of money. The butcher laughed aloud and asked if he were crazy. The farmer thought that there must be something wrong with the way he had folded the hat. He took it off and doubled another corner down. But this had no effect on the butcher. So he decided to try it out some other place. He went to the Mayor of the town.

The Mayor, to be sure, looked at the hat but did nothing. The farmer grew desperate and decided to go to the druggist who had given Peter a bag of money. He entered and stood with the hat on. The druggist looked at him but did nothing.

The farmer became very nervous. He began to suspect that there was something very wrong. He shouted at the druggist, "Stop looking at me and hand over the bag of money!"

The druggist said he owed him nothing, and what bag of money was he talking about anyway? As the farmer continued to shout about a bag of money and a magic hat, the druggist called the police. When they arrived, he told them that the farmer had gone out of his mind and kept demanding a bag of money. The police questioned the farmer, and he told them about the magic hat he had bought from Lazy Peter. When he heard the story, the druggist explained that Peter had left a bag of money, asking that it be returned when he appeared with a corner of his hat turned up. The owner of the stand and the priest told the same story.

I am telling you, the farmer was so angry that he tore the hat to shreds and walked home.

Developing Comprehension Skills

1. In this story, there are at least three sets of three. Tell, in order, three sets of events that come in threes.

2. Why did the farmer think the hat was worth a great deal of money?

3. Peter took advantage of one of the farmer's qualities. What was that quality? How did Peter use it against the farmer?

4. Would you call this story realistic? That is, do you think it could really happen? Why or why not?

Reading Literature: Legends

1. **Comparing Characters.** Lazy Peter, Blondel, and the shepherd in "King John and the Abbot" were all very clever. Did they use their cleverness in the same way? Which ones do you admire? Why?

2. **Identifying Theme.** The **theme** of a story is a general statement that it makes about life. For example, the theme of "William Tell" might be worded this way: "Liberty is more important than life itself." The theme of "The Six Horsemen" might be, "Cooperation will bring success." How would you state the theme of "Lazy Peter"?

3. **Identifying Conflict.** In "Lazy Peter," the conflict is not a physical one, as in "The Six Horsemen." What is the conflict in this story? How is it settled?

4. **Examining the Use of Three's.** What would happen to the story if Lazy Peter had left a fourth bag of gold with another person? Would that make the story even more interesting, or would it simply make the story longer? What would happen if the farmer had started shouting at the Mayor instead of going on to the druggist? Would that simply shorten the story, or would it lose a connection between the parts of the story? Explain your answer.

Developing Vocabulary Skills

Recognizing Context Clues, Synonyms, and Antonyms. Read each of the following sentences or groups of sentences. On your paper, write this information about each underlined word:

a. Whether you found a *definition or restatement clue*, a *synonym*, or an *antonym* to help you figure out the meaning of the word
b. Any key words or punctuation that helped you find the clue
c. The meaning of the word

1. Lazy Peter disposed of, or got rid of, three bags of money.

2. The farmer seems to be a miser who is never satisfied but always wants more and more money.

3. Seeing the bag of money was such a surprise, the farmer stood with his mouth open in astonishment.

4. Peter saw that the farmer had swallowed his bait. In other words, he had fallen for Peter's trick.

5. The farmer offered a thousand pesos, Spanish coins, for the hat.

6. The farmer said Peter used unsound thinking because thieves could easily steal a hat. Wouldn't it be more reasonable, he said, to invest in a farm with cattle?

7. When the druggist handed Peter the bag of money, the farmer was convinced of the hat's power. He was sure the hat would work for himself, too.

8. The priest had left the bag of money in the sacristy—the place where sacred items of the church were kept.

Developing Writing Skills

1. **Stating Your Opinion.** Is Lazy Peter a good model or a bad model? Give your opinion and explain your reasons. Use examples from the story to support your statements.

2. **Changing the Point of View.** Imagine that you are the farmer. Tell the story of "Lazy Peter and His Three-Cornered Hat" from the farmer's point of view.

Developing Skills in Critical Thinking

Classifying. There are many different ways in which to classify, or group, the legends in this chapter. For example, you could group those stories that are about kings and those that are about tricksters. The same story might be classified in more than one group. For example, "King John and the Abbot" was about both a king and a trickster.

Think of three different classifications in which to group these legends. Then decide which stories fit in each of your classifications.

Developing Skills in Speaking and Listening

Telling A Legend. Prepare to tell the story of "Lazy Peter and His Three-Cornered Hat" to a group of younger students. First, read the story several times until you know the order in which things happen. If you like, take notes that will help you remember the events. Then, practice telling the story to yourself. Use your own words. Make up speeches that Lazy Peter and the other characters might say to each other. Try to make their voices sound different from each other and different from the narrator. If you can find or make a three-cornered hat, practice showing how Peter used it throughout the tale.

Finally, tell the story to a group. Remember to look into your listeners' eyes. If your listeners start to laugh at the story, remember to pause until they can hear your next words. Make sure you sound interested in what you are saying.

Review

Using Your Skills in Reading Legends

The following paragraph is from a legend about Roland, a knight. Tell in your own words what you learn about him in this paragraph. What do you find out about him from the description of his armor?

Some of Roland's ancestors were the noblest heroes the world had ever seen. The blood of heroes flowed in the lad's veins. Of all the knights and warriors in Charlemagne's kingdom, Roland was the bravest and most skillful. When he reached manhood, he was given suitable armor for the knight of a king. His helmet was made of steel and inlaid with pearls, and engraved on it were battle scenes. His shield was made of copper and gold.

Using Your Comprehension Skills

The following is from a legend you will read in Chapter 2 of this book. Read the paragraph. Then state the main idea of the paragraph. Also, identify an important detail that makes the main idea clear.

Arthur immediately mounted his horse and led his men out of the castle. They fiercely attacked the enemy camp. Arthur was always at the front of the battle, doing marvelous deeds of arms. In the thick of fighting his horse was killed beneath him. King Lot came upon Arthur just then. To save himself, Arthur drew his magic sword. It was so bright that it blinded Lot and his men. They turned and ran, leaving Arthur the victor.

Using Your Vocabulary Skills

The following sentences are from "The Legend of King Arthur," which you will read in Chapter 2. Use context clues to determine the meaning of each underlined word. Tell the meaning in your own words. Then tell which kind of context clue you used: definition or restatement, synonym, antonym, or inference.

1. For many months, Lancelot <u>isolated</u> himself in the forests. He avoided all human contact.

2. When Arthur returned to his <u>lodgings</u>, he found the inn empty and locked.

3. Then Arthur's foster father <u>revealed</u> the secret of Arthur's birth. He told the boy that Merlin had arranged for Sir Ector to raise him, but his real father was King Uther Pendragon.

4. Arthur rode back quickly and, without stopping to read the <u>inscription</u>, yanked the sword from the stone.

5. When Joseph arrived in England, he brought with him the cup Jesus had used at the Last Supper. The cup was called the <u>Holy Grail</u>.

Using Your Writing Skills

Choose one of the writing assignments below.

1. Choose one of the legends you have read in this chapter. Identify which of the following can be found in the legend: (a) a powerful hero or heroine; (b) a powerful evil character; (c) some unbelievable event or events.

2. Create your own hero or heroine. Decide on one admirable quality for which your character will be known. Write a one-paragraph description of this character. Be sure to describe both the character's physical appearance and his or her admirable quality.

Using Your Study and Research Skills

The following questions can be answered through the information available in a library. Read each question; then look at the card-catalog headings listed below. For each question, identify the headings that would be useful in locating answers.

1. Who are the other members of the family of Richard the Lion-Hearted and King John I?

2. Did the German town of Hamelin ever really exist?

3. How do the Swiss honor their national hero, William Tell?
   a. William   b. Richard I (the Lion-Hearted)   c. Hamelin
   d. towns   e. Tell, William   f. Germany

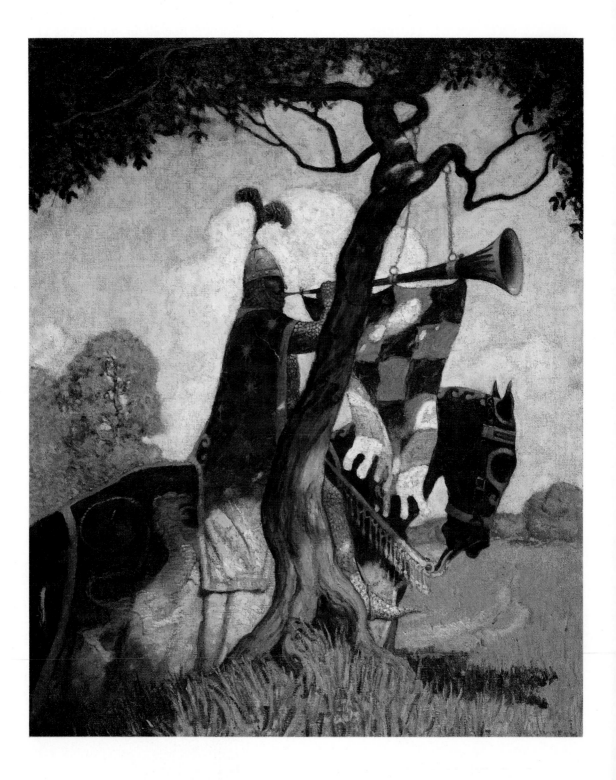

CHAPTER 2

The Legend of King Arthur

He Blew Three Deadly Notes, 1917, N.C. WYETH.
Brandywine River Museum, Chadds Ford, Pennsylvania.

Reading Literature: The Legend of King Arthur

What Is the Legend of King Arthur?

The legend of King Arthur is one of the best loved legends of Britain, France, and the United States. It is also called the Arthurian legend. This legend tells about the noble Arthur, King of Britain, his court of knights, and their bold adventures.

The History of the Legend of King Arthur

Like most legends, the legend of King Arthur is probably based on fact. It is believed that the real Arthur was a leader of a group called the Celts. He lived in Britain in the sixth century. When the Saxons from Germany began to invade Britain, Arthur and his followers defended their land. Arthur was defeated and was killed in battle, but his courage was not forgotten.

Some of his followers fled south to Wales and some to Brittany in France. There they told everyone about Arthur. They began to create a legend that was more exciting than the facts.

Arthur's bravery was first mentioned in print in a Welsh poem as early as 600 A.D. By the twelfth century, Arthur was a national hero in Britain. Some people even believed that King Arthur, as he was soon called, would someday return.

The legend of Arthur also had become popular in France. The French wrote stories and poems about King Arthur, adding details to his legend. For example, during the age of knighthood, some writers decided that Arthur must have been a knight. A French writer invented the Round Table, King Arthur's table where all seats were of equal importance. His knights, the story-tellers said, were known for their bravery, honesty, and courtesy.

In 1470, Sir Thomas Malory of England combined many French and British poems and stories about Arthur in a work called *Le Morte d'Arthur.* In the nineteenth century, Alfred, Lord Tennyson of England wrote a stirring poem, "Idylls of the King," based on this legend. In our own century, T. H. White wrote a book about Arthur, *The Once and Future King,* and an American musical play, *Camelot,* retold the legend for modern audiences.

The Elements of the Legend of King Arthur

Characters. In the legend of King Arthur, you will meet many people. Besides the noble Arthur and his wife Guinevere, there are his knights Lancelot, Galahad, and many others. These characters are not always presented realistically. They are often symbols of qualities such as loyalty, purity, or greed.

Setting. This legend is set in Britain about 500 A.D. It pictures Arthur and his friends as knights. In reality, the age of knighthood would come hundreds of years later. To enjoy the story, ignore that fact and imagine the action taking place in castles among knights in armor and ladies in flowing gowns.

Plot. Many stories were combined over hundreds of years to make this legend. The version you will read, based on Malory's *Le Morte d'Arthur,* is a combination of shorter stories. Each story has its own plot, or series of events. When you read the whole legend, you read all these plots one after the other.

How to Read the Legend of King Arthur

1. Notice all the ways in which King Arthur shows his goodness and courage. By studying Arthur, you can understand why this legend has survived for so long.
2. Read each name carefully the first time it appears. The names may be hard to remember. Especially important and possibly confusing are Merlin, Morgan Le Fay, and Mordred.
3. Appreciate the way this legend takes you out of this ordinary world and into a land of magic and beauty.

Comprehension Skills: Inferences and Conclusions

Getting All the Meaning from the Words

Reading is an activity. It does not just happen. You make it happen. Good readers throw themselves into their reading. They are always thinking and looking for relationships. As they read, they make inferences and draw conclusions.

Making Inferences

An **inference** is information that the reader draws from the evidence by reasoning. That is, he or she uses what the writer states as clues. By thinking about these clues, the reader can discover ideas or facts that the writer did not state.

When people write, they count on readers to catch the hints they drop. They try not to make their writing so detailed that it becomes boring. Writers expect you to recognize and use the clues in their writing. Only when you make logical guesses based on evidence in the story can you understand what happens and why.

What evidence should you look for? Keeping these questions in mind as you read will help you make sensible inferences.

1. **Characters:** How is the character described? Does the character grow and develop during the story? What is the mood of the character? How does he or she treat other people? What do other characters say about this character? Does the writer give any clues about what has happened to the character in the past? Are there clues that suggest the character's hopes for the future? Do these clues explain the character's actions?

2. **Setting:** What is the setting? How does the setting affect what happens in the story? Why does the author mention details about the setting at particular points in the story?

3. **Mood:** Can you find words or phrases that give you a certain feeling? Which events or situations are described strongly enough to make you feel certain emotions?

Drawing Conclusions

Think of how detectives work. They collect all the evidence, put all the clues together, and come up with a conclusion. A **conclusion** is the final decision in a chain of thinking or reasoning. When you read, you are often asked to draw conclusions. Here is a model for you to follow.

You know these facts:

1. Only the true king can pull the magic sword from the stone.
2. Many people try to pull the sword out, but they fail.
3. Arthur pulls the sword from the stone easily.

You draw this conclusion: Arthur is the true king.

Exercise: Getting All the Meaning from the Words

Read the following paragraphs from "The Legend of King Arthur." They tell what happens when Sir Kay sends Arthur to get a sword for him. Then decide which inferences are sensible.

Arthur yanked the magic sword from the stone. Then he hurried back to Sir Kay with the borrowed sword.

As soon as he saw the sword, Sir Kay knew where it had come from. He grabbed it, ran to his father, and said, "Sir! Look! I have the sword from the stone, so I must be the rightful King of England!"

1. Sir Kay is the rightful King of England.
2. Sir Kay is not very honest.
3. Sir Kay is not very old.
4. Arthur tries to please Sir Kay.
5. Arthur is handsome.
6. Arthur has no time to lose.

Vocabulary Skills: Word Parts

Using Word Parts

Words in our language are formed in many ways. Some words are formed by adding a beginning or an ending to a **base word**. A word part added to the beginning of a base word is called a **prefix**. A word part added to the end of a word is called a **suffix**.

Prefix	+	Base Word	=	New Word
re	+	use	=	reuse

Base Word	+	Suffix	=	New Word
care	+	ful	=	careful

Adding a prefix or a suffix to a base word makes a new word with a different meaning. Read the following lists of prefixes and suffixes. What is the meaning of each new word?

Prefixes	New Words
re– means "again."	retake
mis– means "wrong" or "wrongly."	miscount
in–, im–, ir–, il–, and **un–** mean "not."	inactive, immortal, irresistible, illegal
dis– means "the opposite of."	displease

Suffixes	New Words
–ness means "the quality of" or "state of being."	goodness
–less means "without."	hopeless
–ful, –ous mean "full of" or "having."	wonderful, dangerous

Word Parts from Greek and Latin

Many English words are based on Greek and Latin words. Greek and Latin words are shortened and used as prefixes and suffixes. Here are some Greek and Latin word parts that you may find in your reading. Knowing their meanings will help you understand the meaning of the English words that they are part of.

Meaning	Greek	Latin	Examples
one	mono–	uni–	monotone, unicycle
two	di–	bi–, duo–	dioxide, bicycle, duet
three	tri–	tri–	triangle
ten	deca–	deci–	decade, decimal
many	poly–	multi–	polygon, multitude
half	hemi–	semi–, hemi–	semiannual, hemisphere
all	pan–	omni–	panorama, omnipresent
science of	–ology		biology

Exercises: Using Word Parts

A. In each sentence, find a word with a prefix or suffix from page 66. Identify each word part and tell what the word means.

1. One seat at the Round Table was called the "Seat Perilous."

2. Merlin could vanish and reappear by magic.

3. The punishment for being disloyal was death.

4. The knights tried to avoid needless fighting.

B. Use the chart of Greek and Roman forms. Answer these questions.

1. How many colors are there in a *tricolored* flag?

2. If *lateral* means "sided," what does *multilateral* mean?

3. If *cornu* is the Roman word for "horn," how many horns does a unicorn have?

4. If *bios* is Greek for "life," what does *biology* mean?

The Legend of King Arthur: Part One

A retelling of Le Morte d'Arthur
by Sir Thomas Malory

In this part of the legend, you will learn how the young Arthur gained the throne and began his court. Which men did Arthur trust? Why? Why did other men trust Arthur? As you read, look for clues to these answers.

Centuries ago, when Uther Pendragon reigned as King of England, he and his wife Igraine had a son named Arthur. Uther's close aide, the magician Merlin, foresaw that Arthur would need special training. Therefore, he talked the King into keeping the birth of his son secret. At Merlin's urging, Uther sent his baby son away. Safe from the dangers and distractions of court life, Arthur could learn the ways of knighthood.

Merlin took Arthur to Sir Ector and his wife to raise, along with their own son Kay. Together the boys trained to become knights.

While Arthur was still a young boy, King Uther Pendragon became seriously ill. Merlin asked him, "Do you wish Arthur to become king after your death?"

The King replied, "Yes, the throne is his by right of birth."

Shortly after that, Uther died. His enemies began to take over his lands and there was much unrest. When Merlin saw this, he went to the Archbishop of Canterbury. He suggested that a call be issued to all the lords of the kingdom. He asked that the lords gather on Christmas Eve in a church in London. There they could search for a sign that would show who should be the next King of England.

When they assembled, everyone was amazed. In the churchyard they found a large block of marble. In the marble was a steel anvil with a sword driven into it. Gold letters on the sword read: "Whoever pulls this sword out of the stone and anvil is the King of England by right of birth."

Immediately, several knights tried to pull the sword out of the stone. No matter how hard they tried, no man could even budge it. The sword in the stone was left in the churchyard, a challenge to all.

On New Year's Day, there was to be a tournament of jousts and matches in the fields outside London. Each man would test his strength and skill against each of the others. Sir Ector brought Sir Kay, recently knighted, and Arthur to witness this great event. On New Year's Eve, the three arrived in London and found an inn at which to stay. The next day they rode out to the site of the tournament.

When they arrived at the field, Sir Kay realized he had forgotten his sword. He asked Arthur to ride back to their lodgings in town and get it for him.

Arthur found the inn empty and locked. Upset, he remembered the sword and anvil he had seen as he had ridden past the church. He rode back quickly and, without stopping to read the inscription, yanked the sword from the stone. Then he hurried back to Sir Kay with the borrowed sword.

As soon as he saw the sword, Sir Kay knew where it had come from. He grabbed it, ran to his father, and said, "Sir! Look! I have the sword from the stone, so I must be the rightful King of England!"

Sir Ector took his son and Arthur to the church. There he demanded that Sir Kay tell the truth. Unwilling to lie in a holy place, Sir Kay admitted that Arthur had brought the sword to him. Sir Ector questioned Arthur, and then pondered things over in his mind. At last he told Arthur, "Now I know you must be the rightful King of England."

Arthur asked, "But, sir, how can this possibly be?"

First, Sir Ector explained the magic of the sword in the stone. Only the man fit to be the next King of England would have the power to draw that sword out of the stone. Then Arthur's foster father revealed the secret of Arthur's birth. He told the boy that Merlin had arranged for Sir Ector to raise him, but his real father was King Uther Pendragon.

Arthur declared, "You, Sir, and your wife have raised me from my birth. I owe you love and honor for all you have done for me."

Sir Ector replied, "Arthur, I ask only one thing of you when you become King of England. Make Sir Kay the keeper of all your lands."

Arthur was mightily surprised at this news of his birthright and at the thought that he should be king. Yet something inside him told him what to do and say. Without hesitation he answered, "Sir, your wish is granted. Sir Kay shall retain his office as long as he and I shall live."

Sir Ector took Arthur to the Archbishop. He pointed out the magic sword in Arthur's hands and explained how Arthur had drawn it from the stone. As the word spread, onlookers hurried from the tournament fields to the church. The crowds watched Arthur put the sword back into the stone. Several knights and barons tried to pull the sword out again. Over and over they tried, but no one could do so. Finally, Arthur stepped up to the stone once more. Effortlessly, he slid the sword out and raised it before all the people.

Many knights were angry that a mere boy could accomplish this feat. They convinced the Archbishop that many more knights deserved a chance to draw the sword. Several times over the next few months, nobles and knights gathered so that all might have an opportunity to pull the sword from the stone. Still, none could do so except Arthur.

Finally, the people cried, "We will wait no longer. We want Arthur for our king. We will fight anyone who opposes him."

Then the knights accepted Arthur despite his youth. He was immediately declared a knight. Shortly after that, Sir Arthur was officially crowned King of England.

As soon as he took office, the young king promised to right the wrongs that had been committed since his father's death. The people's hearts were filled with joy. Once again peace and justice would rule the land.

Excalibur

After he was made king, Arthur decided to give a great feast. He sent messengers out with gifts for all the kings of the neighboring counties. He dressed in his finest clothes and waited for their arrival.

However, when his messengers returned they brought back his gifts. They told him that the neighboring kings had refused the presents. They had called Arthur a boy of low birth. They did not recognize his right to rule as king. In fact, they were on their way to take Arthur's lands away from him.

Alarmed, Arthur gathered an army of men to help him. He and his five hundred followers gathered supplies and went into a strong castle.

When the rivals came, Arthur and his men withstood a siege that lasted for fifteen days. Then Merlin made his way into the camp of Arthur's enemies. The leaders recognized Merlin and asked him, "Why has a young boy like Arthur been made king?"

Merlin told them how Sir Ector had raised Arthur, but that Arthur's father actually was King Uther Pendragon and the throne was his by right of birth. He convinced some of the leaders of Arthur's claim to the throne. Others, however, laughed at Merlin.

"Even if your story is true," they said, "the boy Arthur hasn't proved himself. He must show by victories that he deserves to be our king."

Merlin warned them, "It would be good for you to accept him and end this resistance. Even if there were ten times as many of you as there are now, you would never defeat Arthur."

"Should we be afraid of this dream-reader?" King Lot, one of the leaders, mocked Merlin.

At that, Merlin vanished. He reappeared before King Arthur, inside his fortress.

"Begin the attack," Merlin told Arthur. "They won't listen to reason. But be careful. The fighting will be fierce. Do not use the sword you have acquired by magic until you have no choice. Then do your best with it."

Arthur immediately mounted his horse and led his men out of the castle. They fiercely attacked the enemy camp. Arthur was always at the front of the battle, doing marvelous deeds of arms. In the thick of the fighting, his horse was killed beneath him. King Lot came upon Arthur just then. To save himself, Arthur drew his magic sword. It was so bright that it blinded Lot and his men. They turned and ran, leaving Arthur the victor.

Now that he had established himself as a leader, Arthur relaxed by going out hunting. In the forest, he came across a knight who insisted on fighting him. They were both strong and skillful swordsmen. For a long time the fight was even, each man giving and taking wounds. Then the two swords smashed together, and King Arthur's magic sword broke in two. The strange knight was about to kill Arthur. Suddenly Merlin arrived. He quickly put an enchantment on the knight, who fell to the ground in a deep sleep.

"What have you done, Merlin?" Arthur cried. "Have you killed this good knight by your crafts? He was the bravest and strongest knight I have ever come across! I would have wanted him to fight under me."

"Don't worry," Merlin assured him. "He's in better health now than you are. He will wake soon. In the future he will do you much good service."

For three days King Arthur rested from the fight. Then he became worried because he had no sword.

"Come with me," Merlin said. "I will take you to one."

Merlin led Arthur to a wide lake. At the center of the lake was an arm reaching up out of the water. Its hand held up a sword encased in a sheath.

"Look," said Merlin. "That is the sword I spoke of. And here comes the Lady of the Lake. Speak courteously to her, and she will give you a sword."

"Fair Lady," Arthur asked the Lady of the Lake, "what sword is this which an arm holds above the water? I wish to have that sword because I no longer have my own."

"The sword is mine," said the Lady. "You may have it, if you will give me a gift when I ask for it."

Arthur agreed. The Lady pointed out a barge that Arthur could use. He rowed across the lake. When he reached the arm, he grasped the sword by the handle. The arm slowly went back under the water.

When Arthur returned to the shore, Merlin told him, "Your sword is called

Excalibur. Keep it close to you as long as you live."

As they rode back to court, Merlin asked Arthur, "Which do you like better, the sword or the sheath?"

Arthur answered, "The sword, of course."

"The sheath is far more valuable than the sword," said Merlin. "While you wear it, you will lose no blood, even if you are badly wounded. Always keep it nearby."

From that day on, Arthur felt more capable of fighting against his enemies. He began to have a large following who recognized him as a good and strong leader.

Arthur and Guinevere

Once Arthur began to get his kingdom in order, he decided it was time to marry. He consulted with Merlin.

"Have you seen anyone fit to be the Queen?" Merlin asked.

"Yes," said Arthur. "The most beautiful woman I have ever seen is Guinevere, the daughter of King Leodegrance. She is the woman I wish to marry."

Merlin wasn't happy about Arthur's choice. With his gift of foresight, he knew that Guinevere would love another as well as Arthur. Merlin advised Arthur, "She is not the woman I would have chosen for you. I could find you a woman who would make you even happier."

Arthur answered, "No. I want only Guinevere for my wife. Go and settle matters for me with her father."

King Leodegrance had been an ally of Arthur's father. For his wedding present, Uther Pendragon had sent Leodegrance an enormous round table. The table was so large that one hundred and fifty knights could sit around it.

King Leodegrance was very happy that Arthur wanted to marry his daughter. He told Merlin, "Arthur does not need any more lands. I will give him the finest gift I can offer him. I will give him the Round Table that his father gave to me long ago."

With the Round Table went one hundred knights who would help Arthur to make decisions and protect his lands. Still, there were fifty empty seats to be filled.

Merlin, Guinevere, and the Knights of the Round Table set off for Arthur's castle at Camelot. When Arthur saw Guinevere, she looked even more beautiful than he had remembered her. He was delighted with the gift of the Round Table and the hundred knights. These were men of maturity and experience whom he could count on.

Arthur set a high standard for his knights. He declared that the knights of the Round Table could not fight each other and could not start battles just to gain power or riches. Instead, they were to protect people in need, including the poor. They were to guard the kingdom against dangers from lawbreakers within the country and enemies outside the borders. They must always show courage and courtesy.

In order that the empty seats of the Round Table would be filled, a custom was established. The feast of Pentecost came in early summer, the seventh Sunday after Easter. Every year at this time more knights would be added to the Round Table, as they proved themselves worthy of this great honor. When a new knight sat in one of the seats, the seat was magically labeled with his name in letters of gold. One seat, called "Seat Perilous," was left empty. If anyone unworthy sat there, he would be destroyed.

When Guinevere became Arthur's queen, she was overwhelmed by the splendor of Arthur's kingdom. She quickly established herself in his court, and his knights became devoted to her. Her love for Arthur, and Arthur's love for her, grew steadily.

In the meantime, Merlin also fell in love. The lake in which Arthur had found his sword, Excalibur, also held a great rock. Underneath the great rock was a palace. The Lady of the Lake lived there. One day she cast her spell and persuaded Merlin to come and live with her. That was the last time anyone ever saw Merlin the magician.

Developing Comprehension Skills

1. Arrange the following events from the legend in the correct order.

    a. Arthur visited the Lady of the Lake and got a sword.

    b. Merlin suggested that Arthur be raised by Sir Ector.

    c. Arthur married Guinevere and received the gift of the Round Table.

    d. Merlin disappeared and was not heard from again.

    e. Arthur pulled the sword from the stone.

2. At first, Arthur was not accepted easily as king. Name two objections against him. Then tell at least two ways Arthur proved his right to be king.

3. After Arthur drew the sword from the stone, Sir Ector told him his real father was Uther Pendragon and that Arthur was the rightful King of England. Arthur immediately declared, "I owe you love and honor for all you have done for me," and he promised to make his foster brother the keeper of his lands. What can you infer about Arthur's character from these statements? That is, what do these statements tell you about the kind of person Arthur was?

4. Did Arthur put too much trust in Merlin? In your answer, identify several important instances in which Arthur did exactly as Merlin advised. Also, identify other instances in which Arthur acted without Merlin's help or approval. Do you think Merlin's disappearance will be good or bad for Arthur? Explain your answer.

Reading Literature: The Legend of King Arthur

1. **Understanding Setting.** The term **setting** refers to the place and the time in which a story is set. When a story is set in a time different from our own, the characters often think differently from modern people. Use clues in this story to decide what the characters might think about these modern statements. Explain your answers.

    a. Magic is just tricks.

    b. In a good government, people elect their leaders.

    c. A woman should decide for herself whether to marry.

2. **Studying Plot.** In the introduction to Chapter 2, you learned that the legend of King Arthur was a combination of many shorter tales. In this part of the legend there are at least five separate **episodes,** or

series of events. Identify as many of the five short tales as possible. How are these short tales related to each other?

3. **Examining Character.** The hero or heroine of a legend must be better than the average person in some ways. Name some of the ways in which Arthur is special. Are there other ways in which he is like other men? Describe them.

4. **Appreciating the Legend.** Magic is an important element in "The Legend of King Arthur." It sets off Arthur's world from ours and makes everything that happens unusual. Point out several places where magic affects the story.

Developing Vocabulary Skills

Using Word Parts from Greek and Latin. Examine the chart below. Note the meaning of each Greek and Latin word and word part listed. Then read the sentences below the chart. The underlined word in each sentence is based on one or more of the words or word parts on the chart. Use the information on the chart and the context clues in each sentence to figure out the meaning of each underlined word.

mono–, uni–	one	hemi–	half	scientia	knowledge
di–	two	omni–	all	archein	to rule
multi–	many				

1. Arthur wanted to unite all of England under his rule.

2. His enemies led a multitude against Arthur's men.

3. Since the author knows everything that happened, we can tell the story uses an omniscient point of view.

4. The government of England has been a monarchy for about 1200 years.

5. Arthur was faced with a dilemma. Should he listen to Merlin or should he listen to his heart?

Developing Writing Skills

1. **Examining a Character.** Does Merlin act like a real person? What is special about his abilities? What kinds of unusual feats can he accomplish? Write at least one paragraph describing Merlin.

2. **Describing Actions.** Imagine that you were one of the people at the tournament on the day that young Arthur drew the sword from the stone. Write an eyewitness account of what happened for your hometown paper. Remember to use only the information that a traveler to the tournament would know.

Developing Skills in Study and Research

Using the Encyclopedia. A general encyclopedia is a collection of articles on a wide variety of topics. The articles are arranged alphabetically by title and often fill several separate books, or **volumes.** The encyclopedia **index** lists all the titles of the articles and tells the volume and page where you will find each article. Sometimes one article may discuss several related topics. The title of the article may name only one of the topics. The other related topics are also listed in the index as separate entries. There you will find the title of the article or articles that discuss the topic.

You can often get an idea of how important a topic is by seeing how much space an encyclopedia gives to that topic. In your school or local library, choose one set of encyclopedias. Look up each of the following names and terms in that encyclopedia. Find out which names and terms are given separate articles, and how long each article is. Find out which names and terms are discussed only in articles under other titles. Use the index to save yourself from looking up entries that do not exist.

Arthur or King Arthur	Guinevere
Round Table	Merlin
Arthurian Legend	Uther Pendragon
Lady of the Lake	Sir Ector
Knighthood	Camelot

The Legend of King Arthur: Part Two

A retelling of Le Morte d'Arthur by Sir Thomas Malory

Lancelot, Tristram, and Galahad are three of the bravest and noblest of King Arthur's knights. Each is faced with a different challenge. As you read, look for the qualities that enable each man to meet his challenge.

These are the stories of three of the most respected of King Arthur's knights.

Sir Lancelot

One of the finest and bravest knights of King Arthur's court was a young man named Lancelot. He became Arthur's closest friend. Earlier in his life, he had met Guinevere at her father's castle and had fallen in love with her. Now that she was King Arthur's wife, he kept his love for her in his heart and tried to avoid her in the court.

Lancelot fought valiantly in battles. No one could win over him. One night he was attacked by four knights. He killed two and the other two fled in terror.

Later, he discovered Sir Kay in the midst of a battle. He fought off the three attackers easily. Then he exchanged horses and armor with Sir Kay, so that Sir Kay could ride home in safety.

Lancelot was often pursued by the ladies of the court. Since none of them seemed to him as beautiful as Guinevere, he had no time for them. Once, Arthur's sister, Morgan Le Fay, found Lancelot asleep in a forest. She cast a spell on him and had him transported to her castle. When he woke up, four women were standing over him. They told him they knew his heart belonged to Guinevere, but he must choose one of them for his wife or face death in prison.

After thinking it over, Lancelot declared, "I choose to die rather than to have one of you as my wife. As for Guinevere, she is faithful to her husband."

Very discouraged and knowing they were defeated, the four women let Lancelot go on his way. When his friends at the court heard this story, they respected him even more.

By this time, Guinevere had learned of Lancelot's love for her. She had no desire to leave King Arthur or to offend him. Still, she enjoyed the fact that the finest knight in all the court would love no woman but her. She became jealous if she heard any rumor that Lancelot had paid attention to anyone else.

Once she believed that Lancelot had fallen in love with the lady Elaine, daughter of King Pelleas. Furious with Lancelot, Guinevere insulted him, calling him a traitor. "Leave the court immediately!" she demanded. "And never again come into my sight!"

Filled with sorrow, Lancelot went mad and fled to the countryside. Guinevere soon regretted her angry words. She sent messengers to find him, but he could not be found anywhere.

For many months, Lancelot isolated himself in the forests and lived like an animal. He survived by eating fruits and berries. He avoided all human contact. When he at last went into a town, he could not remember who he was. The people of the town, feeling sorry for the crazy man, gave him enough food to survive.

Finally, Elaine happened to see this crazy person, and she recognized Lancelot. As he slept, her knights carried him to a tower.

In the tower was hidden the most precious object in all England. Hundreds of years before, Joseph of Arimathea had come to England. This was the man who had given his tomb to the Apostles for the burial of Jesus. When Joseph arrived in England to spread the Gospel, he brought with him the cup Jesus had used at the Last Supper. This cup was called the Holy Grail. Joseph left the Grail in the keeping of a good family.

After a time the people of England fell into evil habits. They were no longer worthy to see the Holy Grail. From then on, the Grail was hidden in the tower of the good family with whom it had been left. It was that tower to which Elaine had Lancelot taken.

As Lancelot lay near the Grail, he was cured of his madness. When he awoke, he remembered who he was. He recognized Elaine and her father Pelleas. He became ashamed of his madness and what he had done while he was out of his mind.

Elaine wanted him to marry her, but Lancelot would not listen. As soon as he heard that Guinevere wanted him back in court, he returned to Camelot.

Sir Tristram

Another of King Arthur's knights was named Tristram. His name meant "sorrowful birth." He got his name from his mother shortly before she died. Tristram's mother had heard that her husband, King Melodius, had unjustly been thrown into prison. She set off to help him and died from exposure to the cold on a winter's night. The next day, King Melodius was freed. He returned home to find that his son had been born and his wife had died.

Seven years later, King Melodius married again. His new wife became jealous of Tristram and decided to poison him. By mistake, one of her own sons drank the potion and died.

When Melodius heard about this, he condemned his wife to be burned at the stake as a traitor. Tristram begged for her life to be spared. He could not accept the severity of this punishment. The King agreed, but sent his son off for his own safety to learn the ways of knighthood.

Tristram left for France. There he learned to play beautiful music on the harp. He also learned to fight bravely, and he became a knight.

When Tristram returned home to Cornwall, he threw himself into battle. When he was fighting with the Irish Sir Marhaus, Tristram thrust his sword into his opponent's skull. Tristram's sword was chipped, and the chip stayed in Marhaus's skull. Sir Marhaus went home to Ireland to die.

Tristram had been wounded seriously in this fight. He boarded a ship, intending to go in search of a doctor who could heal him. Strong winds drove the ship to Ireland. There he was given hospitality by King Anguish. Tristram fell in love with Anguish's daughter, Isoud.

One day a servant noticed Tristram's broken sword. It matched the piece that had killed Isoud's uncle, Sir Marhaus. Tristram was asked to leave King Anguish's house immediately. Before he left,

he pledged his love for Isoud. She promised to keep her love for him, too.

On his return home, Tristram talked constantly of his fair maiden Isoud. His uncle, King Mark, jealous of Tristram, decided to marry Isoud himself.

To overcome his grief at the marriage of Mark and Isoud, Tristram plunged into his duties as a knight. Once he saved a knight from being killed by two enemies and discovered that it was King Arthur he had rescued.

In gratitude, Arthur awarded Tristram a seat at his Round Table. There the knight became well known and loved. The knights and ladies of Camelot appreciated his gift for music.

Tristram's uncle, hearing of his latest honor, traveled to Camelot with two knights. He planned to surprise and kill Tristram. However, when he told his plan to the knights, they rejected it in horror. Instead, they went to King Arthur and told him of Mark's treachery. Arthur quickly had Mark arrested.

Brought before King Arthur, Mark confessed his crime. Arthur forgave him this time. However, he warned Mark that if he tried again to harm Tristram, he would be severely punished. Mark agreed to leave Tristram alone. Then he returned to Cornwall.

Trying to forget Isoud, Tristram went to Brittany in search of adventure. There he fought bravely for King Hoel. In gratitude, the king offered to Tristram marriage with his daughter, another Isoud. She was known as Isoud of the White Hands.

By now, Tristram realized that he was never to win his first love. He liked Isoud of the White Hands well enough, and he decided to marry her. They lived happily for a while, until Tristram was badly wounded in another battle. Despite the loving care of his wife, Tristram grew weaker and weaker.

Tristram remembered how badly wounded he had been when he had landed in Ireland. He remembered how Isoud, his first love, had nursed him to health. He asked his wife to send for her.

Perhaps, he reasoned, she might bring him back to health again.

At first, Isoud of the White Hands agreed. She sent messengers to Cornwall to ask Isoud to come and help. If Isoud agreed to come, the ship was to return bearing white sails. If Isoud refused, the ship was supposed to use black sails.

After the ship with the messengers left, Tristram's wife began to worry. What was to stop her husband from falling in love once more with the first Isoud?

When she saw the ship return with white sails, Isoud of the White Hands made up her mind. She went to her husband where he lay ill. She told him that the ship had returned with black sails. Tristram turned away sorrowfully.

"Alas, my beloved," Tristram sighed, "we shall never see each other again." Then he died.

When the ship landed, Isoud heard the terrible news. She was led to Tristram's bedroom. There she, too, died of grief.

The bodies of Tristram and Isoud were returned to Cornwall. King Mark sadly buried them in his own chapel.

Sir Galahad

Throughout the years, the seat at the Round Table called "Seat Perilous" had remained empty. Finally, a man came to court who was worthy to sit there.

A young man named Galahad, the son of Elaine, King Pelleas's daughter, had been raised by the nuns in a quiet cloister. He had been taught wisdom, understanding, and purity of heart. Now that Galahad had become a young adult, he had been sent out to learn the ways of knighthood.

It was the feast of Pentecost, and the knights were waiting for one of the seats at the Round Table to be filled.

A squire came into the court and told the knights that he had seen a great red stone with a sword stuck in it floating on the river. Immediately, they all rushed out to the river see if they could capture the sword. When they got there, not one man could do so. Disappointed, they returned to the court.

Later, when they were again seated at the Round Table, an old man led a young man into the room. In the young man's hand was the sword from the red rock in the river. Amazed, they watched the old man lead this young man to the Table. He led the youth to the "Seat Perilous," but now the words read, "This is the seat of Sir Galahad, the high prince." King Arthur remembered how he, too, had pulled a sword from a stone. From that moment on, Sir Galahad was treated with the greatest honor and respect.

At this same season, a vision appeared to the knights as they sat at the Round Table. There was a bright light and a clap of thunder. Then the Holy Grail, covered so that no one could see it, appeared at one end of the hall. It passed before all the knights and disappeared. After a moment Sir Gawaine stood up.

"I make a holy vow," he declared. "I am starting now on a search for the Holy Grail. I will not return until I have succeeded in finding it."

All the knights knew that only a man of pure heart could see this holy vessel. In spite of this, each one of them wanted to be the first person to see it.

Every Knight of the Round Table took up the challenge to search for the Holy Grail. King Arthur's heart was filled with sadness. He knew his Round Table would never be the same. Many knights would never return from this quest.

Galahad rode off unarmed. He had no

shield to protect himself. While he was riding, he saw a white abbey. When he stopped there, a white knight told him, "Here is a shield which only you, sir, are fit to wear. Take it and ride in safety."

As Galahad rode on, he discovered the Castle of Maidens. He wounded and chased away seven knights who were barring his entrance to it. Once inside, Galahad set free hundreds of people who had been imprisoned there by the seven wicked knights he had just fought.

As he traveled on, Galahad stopped at a hermitage to share a meal with an old man who lived there. A woman came to the door and asked for him by name. "Galahad, come with me. I will show you the greatest vision you have ever seen."

She led Galahad to a ship. He with two of his friends, Sir Bors and Sir Percival, sailed to a castle in the city of Sarras.

When they arrived, Galahad was met by the vision of Joseph of Arimathea.

Joseph told Galahad that he would take him to see the Holy Grail. Galahad entered the holy place in fear and trembling. He knew that he would not survive once he had seen the vision. He also knew it would be the greatest vision he had ever seen. When he saw the Holy Grail, he fell on his knees in a state of rapture and happiness. Galahad felt his life had now been fulfilled.

He came out, briefly, to say farewell to his friends. Before their eyes, they saw Galahad's soul carried up into the heavens. With him went the Holy Grail.

After this remarkable experience, Sir Bors entered a holy hermitage. Sir Percival returned to King Arthur's court to recount the amazing story.

Now that the search for the Holy Grail had ended, the remaining knights returned to the Round Table. King Arthur was overjoyed at their return.

Developing Comprehension Skills

1. Explain what the Holy Grail was and how it came to be in England.

2. Tristram's uncle, Sir Mark, wanted to marry Isoud after he found out that Tristram loved her. What inferences can you draw from this?
   a. Sir Mark was brave and gallant.
   b. Sir Mark was jealous of Tristram.
   c. Sir Mark loved Isoud and didn't want to hurt Tristram.
   d. Sir Mark cared only about himself.

3. Why did King Anguish order Tristram to leave his house? What evidence upset him? What conclusion did he draw?

4. Sir Galahad was the only man who saw the vision of the Holy Grail. What can you guess about his character that made this possible?

5. Lancelot's character was shown in two extremes, as very gallant and brave in defending Sir Kay and as outraged and crazy after his fight with Guinevere. Do you think an ordinary person would act as he did in those two incidents? Give reasons for your answer.

Reading Literature: The Legend of King Arthur

1. **Examining Characters.** Lancelot, Tristram, and Galahad were three of the greatest Knights of the Round Table. Each one **represents,** or stands for, a particular quality that was admired by people who heard this legend. What quality does each of the three knights stand for? Give a reason for your answer.

2. **Making a Time Line.** As you learned in Chapter 1, a time line is a list, in order, of the main events in a story. Each event is represented by a dot printed on a straight line. (See page 18, question 2.) Choose one of the three episodes in Part 2. Make a time line for that episode.

3. **Recognizing Mood.** Each story gives its readers a certain **mood,** or feeling. For example, in the story of Sir Galahad there is a feeling of suspense and anticipation. Each event—from Galahad's appearance at court with the magic sword to his disappearance in the sky with the Grail—carries the story steadily forward. What do you think is the mood of the story of "Tristram and Isoud"? What feeling or feelings do you get reading it?

Developing Vocabulary Skills

Using Prefixes and Suffixes To Determine Word Meaning. Each of the following sentences from "The Legend of King Arthur" includes a word built from a base word and one of the prefixes and suffixes discussed on page 66. Identify the word, separate it into its base word and prefix or suffix, and tell what it means.

1. The Holy Grail passed before all the knights and then disappeared.

2. Furious with Lancelot, Guinevere insulted him, calling him a traitor.

3. Tristram saved a knight from being killed by two enemies and discovered that it was King Arthur he had rescued.

4. Arthur slid the sword from the stone with an effortless pull.

5. Arthur was always at the front of the battle, doing marvelous deeds of arms.

6. The sorrowful Tristram died when he thought Isoud would not come to him.

7. Lancelot told the women that Guinevere was faithful to her husband.

8. The knights dismounted and fought with swords.

Developing Writing Skills

1. **Comparing Characters.** Compare Sir Galahad with King Arthur. Think about what each one does. Also think about what sort of person each one is. How are they alike? How are they different? Write at least one paragraph comparing the two characters.

2. **Creating Other Solutions.** When Lancelot faced the trickery of Morgan Le Fay and the other women, he made a daring statement and they spared his life. How else could he have outwitted them? Write an original solution to his problem. Keep Lancelot's character true to the legend: He would never harm the women or forget his love for Guinevere.

3. **Writing a New Ending.** Is there any way that the story of Tristram and Isoud could have a happy ending? Write a new ending for the story. Keep the characters the same but change enough of the happenings to make a different ending.

Developing Skills in Study and Research

Comparing Encyclopedias. Most school and local libraries have at least two different sets of encyclopedias. One reason for this is that each encyclopedia includes slightly different amounts of information. One encyclopedia may provide more information on one topic, while a second encyclopedia may tell more about a different topic.

Look up each of these topics in at least two different encyclopedias. Compare the amount and the kinds of information given by the different encyclopedias. Which encyclopedia has more lines of writing about the topics? Which one has more pictures, charts, or maps? Which one looks easier to read and understand? If you were going to buy one of the sets, which one would you choose?

Arthur *or* King Arthur
Knights *or* Knighthood
Legends
Britain, Great Britain, *or* United Kingdom

Developing Skills in Speaking and Listening

Interpreting a Character's Speech. In "The Legend of King Arthur," the characters use a language that is a bit more formal than our everyday language. This helps to make the characters sound like the knights and ladies they were. Choose one of the characters whose exact words are given in one of the passages. Prepare to read that character's words to the class. Make sure you speak clearly, so that everyone can hear each word. However, try to make the words sound natural, as if the character would normally speak that way.

The Legend of King Arthur: Part Three

*A retelling of Le Morte d'Arthur
by Sir Thomas Malory*

King Arthur loves his queen, Guinevere. He also values highly the trust and friendship of his knights. What happens when he must choose between wife and friends? Is there any easy solution?

Spring was at hand, so Queen Guinevere decided to go "a-Maying." She and ten of her knights went out, unarmed, to pick the lovely flowers from the fields.

Sir Meliagrance, who had fallen in love with the Queen, seized this opportunity to strike. He rode out into the field to capture the Queen. When he declared his love and asked her to come with him, she responded angrily. She told him she would rather cut her throat than go with him. However, when his men began attacking her unarmed knights, she agreed to go with him if her knights could go, too.

When they arrived at Meliagrance's castle, Queen Guinevere waited for her chance. Then she sent a secret message to Sir Lancelot telling him of her plight. Lancelot set out immediately. While he was still at a distance, Meliagrance's men shot his horse from under him. Lancelot walked a long way, hampered by his heavy armor. Then he borrowed a woodsman's cart to ride the rest of the way.

When he finally arrived at the castle, Lancelot shouted to Meliagrance that the "knight of the cart" had come to fight. Meliagrance, knowing he couldn't win against Lancelot, begged and obtained mercy from the Queen. Lancelot, greatly disappointed that he couldn't fight with Meliagrance, rode away with Guinevere and delivered her safely home.

The Breakup of the Round Table

Two of King Arthur's nephews, Sir Mordred and Sir Agravaine, hated Queen Guinevere. They knew their words would be much more powerful than their swords. Therefore, they began to plant vicious rumors about the love Queen Guinevere felt for Sir Lancelot.

Together, they set a trap for Lancelot. They arranged for King Arthur to stay out hunting one night. Then they hid outside Guinevere's chamber. As they had hoped,

Lancelot came to talk with the queen. As soon as he entered her room, they pounded on the door.

"Come out, traitor," they cried.

Lancelot had no choice. He had to open the door to try to escape. When he did so, the fight began.

Lancelot wounded Mordred. He killed Agravaine and the other knights. Finally, he escaped. Mordred rushed to tell King Arthur about Lancelot's disloyalty and his killing of the knights.

King Arthur's heart was broken. He could no longer trust his queen or his good friend Lancelot. They must both be punished.

One of Arthur's nephews, Sir Gawaine, was a good friend of Lancelot. He argued in Lancelot's defense. "Lancelot has defended the queen several times," Gawaine pointed out. "Perhaps she called him to her chamber to reward him. And perhaps she feared the rumors that would start if he were seen visiting her. That may be why she called him at night, when she thought no one was about.

"Lancelot is your best friend, your finest knight. You must believe that he and your queen wish you no harm."

Still, Mordred argued strongly against Gawaine. "They have loved each other for a long time. Everyone knows it!"

At last, Mordred convinced Arthur that Guinevere was guilty. Sorrowfully, the king sentenced Guinevere to be burned at the stake for treason.

Just as the wood piled about Guinevere was to be set afire, Lancelot rushed in with his forces and saved the queen. He rode off with her to his castle, Joyous Gard. In the chaos of the fight and the escape, Lancelot unknowingly killed two brothers of his friend Sir Gawaine.

When Gawaine heard that news, his friendship turned to vengeful hatred.

Hearing all that had taken place, King Arthur arrived with his men to lay siege on Lancelot's castle. For fifteen weeks Lancelot kept his men inside, refusing to fight Arthur.

At last Arthur stood before Lancelot's castle and called to him, "Come forth, if you dare, and fight me!"

"I cannot fight my king, the man who made me a knight," Lancelot replied.

"I am no longer your king! I am your enemy! You have killed my men and stolen my queen."

"I never wanted to hurt your men. They forced me to, in order to save myself. And how could I let your innocent queen die because of me! I had fought to defend her often enough before. I am heartily willing to return her to you. She is here only for her safety. She is true to you. Take her back, I beg you, and end this needless war."

Arthur weakened. He wanted to believe his old friend. Yet, Sir Gawaine remembered his dead brothers.

"Liar! Traitor! Killer!" Gawaine yelled. "I will forever make war against you!"

"I repent of your brothers' deaths," Lancelot said. "I will do whatever penance you ask."

Gawaine would not listen. Angrily he reminded Arthur of all the evidence against Lancelot and Guinevere. He pointed out the damage they had caused to the Round Table. Arthur once again resolved to fight Lancelot, and he broke off discussions with him. Sadly, Lancelot told his men that they could leave the castle to fight. He ordered them, however, not to harm his friends Arthur and Gawaine.

For the next several days, the fighting was hard and bloody. Several times Lancelot came upon Arthur and Gawaine. Each time he held back from killing either man. When he saw his own men attacking his old friends, he stepped in to save Arthur and Gawaine.

Hundreds of knights were killed on both sides. The number of deaths became so great that the Pope decided to intervene. He issued a decree that Arthur must take back Queen Guinevere and that peace must once again exist between King Arthur and Sir Lancelot.

Lancelot sent word to King Arthur that he would personally deliver the queen back to the court. The queen's ladies and knights arrived riding in a procession, all dressed in the finest green velvet. Behind them rode Lancelot and Guinevere, dressed in robes of white. They dismounted and knelt before the king. All who stood by wept.

Lancelot addressed the king in his finest words. He repeated what he had said before the battle. He blamed all the trouble on lies and swore unending loyalty to Arthur. Once more he asked that their friendship begin anew.

Gawaine, at Arthur's side, answered first. "The king may do as he pleases," Gawaine said bitterly, "but I will never forgive you."

"I am taking back Guinevere as my queen only because the Pope has commanded me to do so," Arthur stated wearily. "As for you, I will not fight you. But you must leave Camelot at once, forever."

Lancelot, hearing these words, turned and rode away. He bent his head in the deepest sorrow he had ever known.

Feeling he had lost everything, Lancelot called his knights together. He told them about his banishment from King Arthur's court. They cried, "We will remain with you forever. Wherever you go, we go."

Lancelot felt comforted. Together, he and his knights sailed for France. When they arrived, they were well accepted. Their reputation for helping the poor and downtrodden had preceded them.

Sir Mordred

Even though Lancelot had declared his sorrow at killing Gawaine's brothers, Gawaine was not satisfied with Lancelot's banishment. He continued to stir up King Arthur to take revenge. Despite the Pope's order, Arthur decided to take up the fight with Lancelot once again.

Before leaving for France, King Arthur gave his nephew Mordred complete charge of his kingdom and power to rule over his affairs.

Lancelot, hearing of Arthur's and Gawaine's arrival in France, sent a message to them, begging for peace. They would not hear of it, and the siege began again.

Both sides were equally matched. Hundreds were again killed in battle. Lancelot seriously wounded Gawaine. The battle raged on for months.

In the midst of the fighting, King Arthur received word that Sir Mordred had taken over all his lands in England. Mordred had ordered his men to write from abroad proclaiming that King Arthur had been killed. He had persuaded the Archbishop to crown him king. Now he was planning to make Guinevere his queen.

Guinevere had reluctantly agreed to Mordred's demands, but she first made a special request. She asked to travel to London to buy a new wardrobe. Mordred agreed. Once in the city, Guinevere locked herself up in the Tower of London to protect herself from Mordred.

King Arthur and his men left the siege in France and quickly returned to England. Mordred and his men attacked them as they left their ships. Sir Gawaine, not fully recovered from the wound Lancelot had given him in France, was again wounded seriously. Arthur found him lying half-dead. The king mourned, "Are you going to leave me too? You and Lancelot were my best knights. Will I lose you both? In you two I most had my joy. Losing you, I will lose all joy in life."

Sir Gawaine, realizing death was near, at last regretted his actions.

"I see now," he said, "that my willfulness has caused this disaster. If I had forgiven Lancelot, you and he would have come to terms. Then he would have been at your side, and this war with Mordred would never have begun. And now you will miss Lancelot."

Then Gawaine asked for ink and paper. He wrote a letter to Lancelot, asking his forgiveness for the pain he had caused. He begged Lancelot to come to Arthur's aid. Then he took his last breath.

The End of the Round Table

On the next morning, Arthur's army took the field against Mordred's. Many were slain, but at the end Mordred fled. Arthur took several days to have the dead buried and to let the wounded recover. Then he set a date to meet Mordred again.

The night before the battle, Arthur had a strange dream. In the dream Gawaine appeared to him.

"I advise you," Gawaine said, "in no way should you go to battle tomorrow. If you fight tomorrow, you will cause your own death and the death of many others. Postpone the battle for a month. By then Lancelot will arrive and slay Mordred."

Then Gawaine vanished.

Arthur told his councilors about his dream. He asked them to make a treaty with Mordred. In order to postpone the battle, he would agree to any conditions.

The councilors arranged the treaty. All that was left was for Arthur and Mordred to meet to complete the arrangements. Each was to bring fourteen men.

Before going to the meeting, Arthur warned his men, "I don't trust my nephew. This may be a trap. If any sword is drawn, strike immediately." Mordred gave his men the same message.

While they were negotiating, a snake crawled onto a knight's foot and bit him. Without thinking, the knight pulled his sword and struck at the snake. With that movement, fighting broke out at once.

The battle raged all day. Hundreds of men were killed. At the end, King Arthur had only two knights left, Sir Lucan and Sir Belvidere. Sir Mordred stood alone.

"Look, Sir Lucan," Arthur cried, "there is the man who has caused all this woe. Give me my spear."

"Sir," Lucan argued, "remember your dream. Leave him alone. We can finish this tomorrow."

Arthur ignored the warning. He shouted to Mordred, "Even if this is the end of me, I will not leave this life without killing such a traitor as you are, Mordred."

With that, Arthur grabbed his spear and ran at Mordred. The spear passed into Mordred and through his body. Mordred knew he was dying. Despite the spear, he pushed himself closer to Arthur and brought his sword down on Arthur's helmet. The blow was so strong that it cut through the helmet and into Arthur's head. Then Mordred fell dead.

Sir Lucan and Sir Belvidere carried Arthur to a chapel near the lake to recover. Arthur said to Belvidere, "Take my sword, Excalibur, and throw it into the water. Then tell me what you see."

Twice Sir Belvidere pretended to do so, each time returning and saying nothing had happened. Arthur said to him, "Would you betray me at the very end? Do as I say!"

Belvidere finally threw the sword into the water. As soon as he did so, an arm and a hand reached out of the water, grabbed the sword, shook it three times, and vanished with the sword underneath the water.

Arthur was greatly relieved when he heard the report. "Now," he said, "take me to the waterside."

When Sir Belvidere carried him there, they found a small barge on the lake. In the boat were Arthur's sister, Morgan Le Fay, and two other women. The women took Arthur into the boat and rowed him across the lake.

Sir Belvidere cried, "My lord Arthur, what will become of me? You are leaving me alone among my enemies!"

"Comfort yourself," Arthur replied. "Do as well as you can by yourself, for in me there is nothing left to trust. I am going to the valley of Avalon. If you never hear of me again, pray for my soul."

The next morning, Sir Belvidere discovered a chapel with a freshly-dug grave outside it. The hermit who lived at the chapel said that during the night several women had brought to him the body of a warrior to be buried.

Belvidere knew that the warrior must have been King Arthur. He decided to stay in this chapel and spend the rest of his life in prayer and fasting.

Lancelot and Guinevere

The news finally reached Lancelot that Sir Mordred had been crowned King of England and would not allow Arthur to return. He also heard that Guinevere had locked herself up in the Tower of London for safety.

Quickly, Lancelot gathered his men and returned to England. In the meantime, Guinevere, learning that Arthur had been killed, fled to the peace and quiet of a convent in Almesbury.

Arriving in England, Lancelot learned about King Arthur's death. He set out to search for Guinevere. He finally found her in the cloister where she was living.

When Guinevere saw Lancelot, she cried, "Lancelot, because of us, a good king and thousands of knights have been killed. We must never see each other again. I will stay here and live a life of prayer. You must leave at once."

Lancelot left, greatly saddened, knowing that he, too, must find peace. As he rode along, he heard a bell ringing from a chapel. There he found Sir Belvidere and vowed to spend the rest of his life at the chapel with his friend and the hermit who had buried Arthur.

Six years went by. One day Lancelot received a sad message. Guinevere had died, leaving a note for Lancelot. She asked that he bury her beside her husband, King Arthur. Lancelot obeyed her request and brought her body back to the chapel.

There, he and the others buried Guinevere in a grave next to that of Arthur. Losing all interest in life, Lancelot grieved for the death of his king and his queen. He sorrowed for his part in the destruction of their kingdom.

And there, in six weeks, Lancelot died. His body was carried to his castle, Joyous Gard, as he had requested. At last he would rest in peace.

Developing Comprehension Skills

1. Make a time line showing the end of King Arthur's reign. Begin with Mordred's setting the trap for Lancelot and Guinevere. Show all the important events. Be sure to include each point at which Arthur makes a major decision.

2. Find a reason stated in the story for each of these actions:
   a. Gawaine's friendship for Lancelot turned to hate.
   b. King Arthur stopped fighting Lancelot in France and returned to England.
   c. Guinevere locked herself up in the Tower of London.
   d. Bedivere threw Excalibur into the lake.

3. Reread paragraph 2 on page 90. The main idea of the paragraph is that Lancelot brought Guinevere back to Camelot. Identify two or three important details in this paragraph. Then identify two less important details.

4. When Sir Gawaine lay dying, he realized that Arthur needed Lancelot's friendship and help. He also saw that Arthur and Lancelot would have made up their quarrel long before if only he, Gawaine, had not stood between them. How did Sir Gawaine try to correct this situation before he died? Do you feel he was doing the right thing? Tell why or why not.

5. After Arthur's death, both Lancelot and Guinevere chose to live the rest of their lives in prayer and fasting. Which of the following inferences can be reasonably drawn from that fact?

   a. Lancelot and Guinevere were searching for peace.
   b. They were tired of the glory of King Arthur's court.
   c. They wanted to repent for their part in causing Arthur's death.
   d. They were hiding from enemies.

Reading Literature: The Legend of King Arthur

1. **Recognizing Contrasts.** Part 3 begins with the story sometimes called "The Knight of the Cart" and ends with the death of Guinevere and Lancelot. What are some of the contrasts that you see between the two episodes? Are the characters the same, or have they changed? How has the setting changed? Is the mood of the story (the feeling it gives you) the same in the two episodes? What other differences do you find?

2. **Recognizing the Author's Purpose.** Review your answer for the question above. Then suggest an answer for this question: Why did the author begin this section with the story of the knight of the cart?

3. **Understanding Reasons for Actions.** The story states that Mordred and Agravaine hated Queen Guinevere and plotted against her and Lancelot. It does not state reasons for their hate. Consider what happened both before and after they hatched their plot. Can you infer any reasons for Mordred's eagerness to make Lancelot look bad? Can you think of any possible reasons for Agravaine's attitude?

4. **Examining Characters.** In Part 2, the characters of Lancelot, Tristram, and Galahad were not drawn very fully. Each character could stand for a single human quality. In Part 3, however, the characters are drawn more fully. Arthur, Lancelot, Gawaine, and Mordred all have good qualities and bad qualities. Choose one of these four characters. Describe both the good and bad qualities of this character. Tell whether you think the character is believable—that is, whether you learn enough about him to believe he could be a real person you might know.

5. **Recognizing Themes.** A **theme** is a general statement that the writer makes about life. For example, in Part 1 the writer pictured Sir Ector

as wise, honest, and concerned about both his son and his foster son. In this way, the writer made the statement that a good knight could also be a good and loving father.

In Part 3, the writer is very concerned about the idea of friendship and the demands that friendships make on a person. Review what Arthur does in his struggle to keep both of his friends, Lancelot and Gawaine. Reread Arthur's statements to his friends, particularly to the dying Gawaine. What are some of the statements about friendship that you find in this legend?

Developing Vocabulary Skills

Forming Words with Prefixes and Suffixes. In each sentence below, a word is missing. The base word is given in parentheses, but one of the prefixes or suffixes from page 66 must be added to the base word. Read the rest of the sentence. Choose the correct **affix** (prefix or suffix) that will change the base word into a word that makes sense in the sentence. On your paper, write the complete sentence, filling in the new word.

1. Guinevere caused problems when she acted in a ___(thought)___ manner.

2. The damage to the Round Table could never be repaired; in other words, it was ___(reparable)___ .

3. When Arthur became king, the identity of his father was ___(known)___ .

4. For several weeks, Lancelot raved in delirium. Elaine found him while he was ___(wit)___ .

5. It was ___(legal)___ for a knight to visit the Queen alone.

6. Despite his ___(sorrow)___ life, Tristram brought music and many pleasant moments to the people of the court.

7. Galahad was noted for his ___(truthful)___ and other virtues.

8. Merlin accomplished by magic many tasks that were otherwise ___(possible)___ .

Developing Writing Skills

1. **Presenting Your Opinion.** Who was responsible for the ruin of King Arthur's court? Was it one person? Was it a combination of people? Was there any one point at which a different decision by Lancelot or

Gawaine or Arthur could have saved the kingdom? State your opinion and give reasons.

2. **Writing a New Legend.** In the story of the knight of the cart, Guinevere saves her unarmed knights but must wait for Lancelot to free all of them from Sir Meliagrance. Write a new ending to this episode. Have Guinevere outwit Meliagrance and free herself and her knights. However, do not use any modern inventions in your new legend. All of the characters and the setting should remain the same as they are described in the original legend.

Developing Skills in Study and Research

Finding Other Reference Sources. A general encyclopedia has articles on topics in many fields—history, science, literature, art, and so on. There are also encyclopedias in special fields, such as history, science, literature, and art. A school library or public library will have numerous specialized encyclopedias and other reference books as well as general encyclopedias.

Examine the reference section of your school or local library. Make a list of any reference books in which you can find information about either the book entitled *Le Morte d'Arthur* or its author, Sir Thomas Malory. Write down both the title and the author(s) or editor(s) of each reference book on your list.

Developing Skills in Speaking and Listening

Interpreting Mood. Do this activity with a partner. One member of the team should prepare to tell the story of the knight of the cart, while the other should prepare "The End of the Round Table."

First, review your answers to the first question in Reading Literature: The Legend of King Arthur. Decide what the mood is in the knight of the cart and in "The End of the Round Table." Decide for each story whether you want your listeners to laugh or to cry. Then prepare your story. You may read the text. If you prefer, you may tell the story in your own words, adding details to make the effect you want.

Then tell your stories, one after another, to a group. Ask the group to let you know if the mood of each story was clear and different from the other.

Using Your Skills in Reading the Legend of King Arthur

Read the following paragraph from another adventure about King Arthur's knights. Explain what is magical and unreal in the events.

Once, a rich gentleman asked Arthur's knights for help.

"Not long ago," the gentleman said, "I was in a joust. During the contest I was twice defeated by a certain knight. He attacked my son and wounded him. Now my son cannot be healed until I have defeated the knight in combat. Yet how can I find him? I don't even know his name. I only know that, when he wants to, he can become invisible."

Using Your Comprehension Skills

The following paragraph is from a short story you will read in Chapter 4. Read it carefully. From the information given by the speaker, what do you think his attitude is toward his family? Is he ashamed or proud of his background? How can you tell?

We were poor. We had no money. Our whole tribe was poverty-striken. Every branch of the Garoghlanian family was living in the most amazing and comical poverty in the world. Nobody could understand where we ever got money enough to keep food in our bellies, not even the old men of the family. Most important of all, though, we were famous for our honesty. We had been famous for our honesty for something like eleven centuries, even when we had been the wealthiest family in what we liked to think was the world.

Using Your Vocabulary Skills

In the following paragraph, there are five words that use Greek or Latin word parts listed on page 67. Read the paragraph and locate those five words. Review the information on the chart on page 67. Then use that information and the context clues in the paragraph to figure out a possible meaning for each word.

> It was common knowledge around King Arthur's court that Merlin, the multi-talented magician, was a very special person. He was thought to have a monopoly on magic. He alone knew how to cast spells. His powers were so great that he seemed almost omnipotent. King Arthur knew that, even if he searched for a decade, he would never find another person like Merlin. Merlin was unique.

Using Your Writing Skills

Choose one of the writing assignments below.

1. Choose an instance when magic is used in "The Legend of King Arthur." Explain why the magical event appears believable. To support your explanation, list the details used to make the scene seem possible. Think about the ways the character or characters involved react to the event. List any way you believe their reactions make the magic seem realistic.

2. Write another adventure for some of the characters in this legend. Use the adventure to show off certain personality traits that you have seen in the characters. For example, you might "test" the goodness of a knight by having him tempted by a rich or beautiful enemy of the king. In your adventure, make the characters agree with what they were like in the legend. Continue the same relationships among the characters.

Using Your Skills in Study and Research

In addition to providing written information, an encyclopedia provides maps, photographs, charts, and other illustrations. Imagine that you have been asked to examine an encyclopedia. Your assignment is to locate drawings of King Arthur and the knights and ladies of this legend. Describe the steps you would follow. Under what headings or guide words would you look? How would you determine which pictures would best illustrate the characters in this story?

How Writers Write

Mimosa, 1945–51, HENRI MATISSE.
Ikeda Museum of 20th Century Art, Japan.

Using the Process of Writing

Writers do not possess a magical power that enables them to write masterpieces on the first attempt. Writers work hard and long to produce good writing. Usually they follow a set of steps called the **process of writing.** The three main stages are:

> **pre-writing**—a planning stage
> **writing**
> **revising**—a rewriting or reworking stage

Morning Light, 1916, OSCAR BLUEMNER. Hirshhorn Museum and Sculpture Garden, Smithsonian Institution, Washington, D.C.

Understanding the Process of Writing

Have you ever seen professional musicians play a piano or a guitar or a saxophone? They make it look easy. In fact, it looks so simple that you may think you could do as well with a little practice.

If you really do learn to play an instrument, you will find out how difficult it is. You will begin to appreciate how well the musician plays.

If you study an instrument such as the piano for awhile, you will become a better listener. Instead of simply listening to the entire sound of a piano piece, you will listen for certain techniques. You can decide whether the pianist performs well or poorly. You would probably be happier listening to a good performance than would someone who had never studied piano.

Reading someone else's writing is similar to hearing someone play an instrument. When you know what to listen for at a concert, you can better appreciate the quality of the performance. When you know what to look for as you read, you can enjoy the writing more fully.

In this chapter, you will learn how writers produce their writing. You will learn about techniques they use to make their writing clear and vivid. You will get a chance to try some of these techniques yourself. As a writer, you will become a more appreciative reader.

Pre-Writing

The first stage of the writing process is called **pre-writing.** During the pre-writing stage, writers prepare to write. They think and plan before they put one word down on paper. These are the pre-writing steps writers follow:

1. Choose and limit a topic. Think of possible topics. Do you know a great deal about one topic? Would you like to learn more about another? List all the topics that interest you. Then go over this list of ideas again. Choose the one that you most want to write about.

Professional writers search for ideas for topics too. Jean Craighead George describes where she gets her ideas.

> Ideas for my stories come from memories of my childhood, from events that happen to the people I love, live, and work with—and from reading. I mean all reading—ads, books, magazines, newspapers, scientific journals, trashy stuff, classics, my children's homework, postcards, even legal papers. Ideas do not come out of thin air.

Now think about the topic you have chosen. Make another list. This time include anything you can say about the topic. Decide which of these ideas belong in your story, poem, or other writing. Then limit your topic. Which of these ideas can be covered adequately in the space available?

As you choose and limit your topic, keep in mind two related considerations: your purpose and your audience.

2. Decide on your purpose.   What do you want to accomplish with your writing? Do you want to entertain your readers? Do you want to teach them facts they didn't know before? Do you want to persuade them to think a certain way? Do you want to share a feeling? The way you treat your topic depends on your purpose.

3. Decide on your audience.   In any library, you can probably find a variety of books about a popular topic such as race car driving. You may find a story about a trip to the race track in the pre-school room. In the children's room there may be a book describing important races that have been run. The adult room may have a biography of a famous driver. Each book on this topic is aimed at a different audience.

For each audience, you write differently. If you are writing for pre-schoolers, you use simple words and tell about events five-year-olds can understand. For school-age children, you might write about fast-paced action. You might use slang words. Writing for adults, you would probably use a more formal style.

Once she has chosen her topic, author Mary Lewis thinks about her audience carefully.

> When a story idea seems to be a good one, I next must think of exactly what age group I am going to write it for. The age group must be more definite than just for children. I write the story for children of one special age and then try to make the story interesting also to children who are a few years younger or older.

4. Gather supporting information. The next pre-writing step is to gather information about your chosen topic. Make a list of things you already know about the topic. Then list questions you need to answer before you can write. Use every possible resource to help you find the answers.

Author Frank Bonham gives this advice to writers beginning their research: "Take notes—notes on anything you might possibly need later. Never trust your memory." He varies his research.

> For a book I wrote about dolphins, I read all I could find about these delightful animals in books and scientific journals. I visited them at Marineland. Then I talked to marine biologists. I talked, finally, to tuna fishermen who find the tuna by spotting schools of dolphins feeding on the fish.

Carol Ryrie Brink wrote *Caddie Woodlawn,* a book based on her grandmother's childhood adventures. Looking at her information, she began to see how each piece was related to the other.

> My grandmother had told me many stories of her childhood. I had to sort them out in my mind and decide which things were most important, where natural climaxes should come, and how one story could be woven into another so that they made a unified whole.

5. Organize your ideas. Read over the list of details you have gathered. Some will be useful for your writing. Others will not fit in. Cross out any details that are not related to what you want to say. Your research may have uncovered interesting new information on a different topic. You may decide to change your topic.

Once you have settled on a topic, it is time to organize your information. In what order will you present your ideas or appropriate facts? Choose an order. Stories are usually arranged in time order. Details of descriptions often are arranged according to the order in which they are noticed. Writing meant to convince or persuade lists reasons in the order of importance.

As you begin to picture the direction your writing will take, you may discover areas where your information is incomplete. If so, go back and continue your research.

Most writers organize their material in some type of outline. Matt Christopher, writer of sports books, tells how he goes about writing his outline.

> Working with sheets of paper containing the scenes of my proposed book, I begin my outline, writing chapter after chapter, usually about half a page in length.

Mary Lewis finds that her outline depends on the type of writing she is doing.

> For a short picture book I do not find I need a detailed outline, just a list of notations of what is going to happen. But for a longer and more complicated story, I need a long and detailed outline.

Other writers organize their writing in special ways that make sense to them. Marguerite Henry, writer of exciting books about horses, has her own method of organizing:

> Conventional outlines are not for me. I construct a kind of skeleton skyscraper which foretells the story as visibly as steel girders and beams give promise of the building to come. This framework tells me more, in one glance, than all the I, II, III's and a, b, c's of a normal outline.

You, the writer, can choose any type of organizing or outlining that makes sense to you.

Writing the First Draft

You have done your research. You have organized your ideas. Now begin to write. Write quickly. Concentrate on getting your ideas down. Try to follow your outline as much as possible. As you write, skip lines to leave room for later corrections and changes.

Writers know that facing a blank sheet of paper can be frightening. Nevertheless, anyone who writes has to overcome that fear and plunge in, as these writers advise:

> Get your ideas into words and put the words down on paper. Don't worry about how you scribble them down or about anything else. —Louis Slobodkin

> Get it down. Take chances. It may be bad, but it's the only way you can do anything really good.
> —William Faulkner

Pura Belpré, storyteller and author, describes the way she begins to write:

> I write my first draft by hand and always in pencil. I do it just as soon as I finish doing the research, and I am careful that I have covered everything that is needed for the story. Drafting quickly is important so that the freshness of the material is not lost.

Writers write the first draft quickly, knowing that they will come back to it later when they begin to revise.

Revising

> Just because you wrote it doesn't mean it's good.
> —Frank Bonham

When you revise, you have another chance to get your ideas and words written just right. To begin revising, read over what you have written with these questions in mind:

1. Will readers think my writing is interesting? Will my writing hold their attention?
2. Did I stick to my topic? Did I include any unnecessary words or sentences? Do I need to add any important details?
3. Is my organization logical? Will the readers be able to follow my ideas as I've connected them?
4. Did I use complete sentences? Did I choose the best words to express my meaning?

On your first draft, mark any changes or corrections. Draw lines through words you have decided to omit. Note the words and sentences you want to add. Don't be surprised if your paper becomes so marked up that you have trouble reading it. If that happens, copy the page.

Beginning writers are not the only ones who have to revise. All writers think of revising as the natural and logical next step in the writing process.

Each writer has favorite techniques for revising.

> Sometimes words seem stubborn and don't say what we have in mind. So we try again and sometimes again and again. Having someone else read what we have written often helps. So does leaving it alone for a while and then coming back to give it another try. Both of these help us find a "fresh" look. Reading it aloud, or sometimes just telling it as though you were talking to someone, helps in rewriting.   —Glenn O. Blough

> In rewriting, I add details here and there, rearrange sentences for more directness, and where a sentence is long, shorten it or turn it into two sentences.   —Holling C. Holling

By the end of that winter it was clear ~~to~~

~~everyone~~ that Barry was the best rescue dog ~~the~~

~~monks had ever had.~~ _when it was snowing_ ~~In a snow storm~~ Barry was the first

to find people buried under the snow. He was the

fastest ~~at~~ _to_ dig~~ging~~ them free. He worked _the_ hardest ~~at~~ _to_

warm~~ing~~ them up. Sometimes, ~~after~~ the other dogs

gave up, _But_ Barry went on licking a frozen face until

~~finally~~ there was _some_ movement, a moan, ~~an opening eye.~~

Then the great dog grew wild with joy.

Years passed. Werner grew tall and thin. ~~He~~ _Now_

~~put aside his school books and~~ gave all of his time

to the dogs. He worked with Bro~~ver~~ _ther_ Luigi every day,

He fed ~~feeding~~ the dogs, playing with them, _and helped_ train~~ing~~ the

pups. He was completely happy.

~~In 1806~~ _When_ Barry was six years old, ~~and~~ Werner

was eighteen. _That_ ~~It~~ was the most terrible winter ~~ever~~ _the monks_

had known ~~to strike the mountains.~~ Rescue trips were made

every day. Half of the _monastery_ dogs ~~in the monastery~~ died

that winter, trying to save the travelers' lives.

Almost half of the monks died in icy traps as they

went about their rescues.

One night in March, Werner and Barry were walking

slowly up the trail toward home. Werner's face was

stiff with cold, and even Barry seemed tired. It

had been a terrible winter for both of them.

Author Lynn Hall shows how she corrected a page of her manuscript while writing the story Barry, the Bravest St. Bernard.

I read and write my drafts with a critical ear. I test every sentence for meaning and for sound. I keep testing the book as I type. I'm a noisy writer. I mumble as I work because I have to find out how a sentence sounds when read aloud.

—Ann Petry

One thing is certain: you have to be able to look at your own writing objectively and critically, as a stranger would.

—H. A. and Margaret Rey

"Revise!" urges writer Frank Bonham. "Only the sculptor has the disadvantage of being stuck forever with what he has chipped out."

Proofreading.   You have revised your writing so it says what you want it to say. Now make sure that careless mistakes don't prevent readers from understanding you. Reread your marked-up draft. This time look for errors in grammar, spelling, punctuation, and capitalization. Mark any corrections.

Preparing the Final Copy.   Your final copy should be neat and easy to read. When you write it or type it for the last time, remember to make all necessary changes and corrections.

Finally, proofread your writing again to check yourself.

Practicing the Process of Writing

Use the ideas in this chapter when you write. Also, refer to the Process of Writing section in the Handbook for Reading and Writing. It contains guidelines for the process of writing, for revising, and for proofreading.

As you read, think as a writer would think. Do as Carol Ryrie Brink suggests:

If you have enjoyed a passage in a book, ask yourself why. Was it because the words were well chosen or because it expressed a feeling that you had often had yourself? Could you write such a passage? You could try.

Using the Sounds of Language

Every word has both a sound and a meaning. Writers use sound and meaning to appeal to readers' senses as well as their reason. In this chapter, you will see how writers use the sounds of language in five ways:

alliteration	rhyme	onomatopoeia
assonance	rhythm	

The Blue Guitar, 1982, DAVID HOCKNEY. Courtesy of the Pantechnicon, London.

Alliteration

> **Alliteration** is the repetition of consonant sounds.
>
> Example: <u>r</u>ough and <u>r</u>eady
>
> Usually, the repeated consonant sound appears at the beginning of the words.

Alliteration in Prose. You probably already use alliteration without knowing it. It is fun to use. We find alliteration in phrases such as "tried and true" and "making a mountain out of a mole-hill." We use it in comparisons such as "hungry as a horse" and "green as grass." And our tongue twisters are usually built with alliteration: "She sells seashells by the seashore."

When writers want to be sure the readers will pay attention to certain words, they often use alliteration. Here are some examples. Notice how sometimes the writers repeat the consonant sound in places other than the beginning of words.

> The silver rocket lay in the light of the moon. And beyond the rocket stood the yellow lights of his home, a block away, burning warmly. —Ray Bradbury, "The Rocket"

> Again the stream slowed into long, lazy stretches sparkling in the sun. —Edwin Way Teale, *Journey into Summer*

Alliteration in Poetry. Sometimes poets use alliteration for a humorous effect, as in the following example.

GAZELLE

O gaze on the graceful gazelle as it grazes
It grazes on green growing leaves and on grasses
On grasses it grazes, go gaze as it passes
It passes so gracefully, gently, O gaze!
—Mary Ann Hoberman

Alliteration is a favorite way of using sound in poetry. Read this example from Longfellow. Look for the many repeated consonant sounds.

> The tide rises, the tide falls,
> The twilight darkens, the curlew calls;
> Along the sea-sands damp and brown
> The traveler hastens toward the town,
>   And the tide rises, the tide falls.
>   —Henry W. Longfellow, "The Tide
>   Rises, the Tide Falls"

Exercises: Using Alliteration

A. Each of these selections uses alliteration. Identify the consonant sounds that are repeated at the beginnings of words.

1. The fair breeze blew, the white foam flew,
   The furrow followed free;
   We were the first that ever burst
   Into that silent sea.
              —Samuel Taylor Coleridge, "The Rime
                  of the Ancient Mariner"

2. There once was a witch of Willowby wood,
   and a weird wild witch was she.
              —Rowena Bennett, "The Witch of
                  Willowby Wood"

3. He sprang through the sleeping camp and in swift silence dashed through the woods.
              —Jack London, *The Call of the Wild*

4. They climbed higher on the hill, cutting the briers and brushes and tree branches and stacking them neatly into piles.
              —Jesse Stuart, "The Clearing"

5. All that day Hugh sat at the clearing's edge, still as a stone.
              —Jane Yolen, "The Hundredth Dove"

B. Write three sentences using alliteration. Try to repeat the consonant sound at least three times at the beginning of words.

Assonance

Assonance is the repetition of vowel sounds within words.

Example: R<u>ai</u>n, r<u>ai</u>n, go aw<u>ay</u>!

Assonance in Prose.   The repetition of vowel sounds helps writers produce a musical quality in their writing. Your ears simply enjoy hearing certain sounds over and over. In addition, assonance creates different moods, depending on which sounds are repeated.

In the following selections, assonance emphasizes the meanings the writer wants his or her words to express. The *oo* sound in the first sample emphasizes the sadness that the character felt. On the other hand, the sharp, rough, short *a* sound in the second sample suggests a more active mood.

> All day Buck br<u>oo</u>ded by the p<u>oo</u>l or roamed restlessly above the camp.

> It was no t<u>a</u>sk for him to learn to fight with cut and sl<u>a</u>sh and the quick wolf sn<u>a</u>p.
> —Jack London, *The Call of the Wild*

Assonance in Poetry.   Poets use assonance in poetry for the same reasons that other writers use it in prose. It creates moods and it emphasizes the music-like qualities of our language.

In this sample, notice how the poet has combined assonance with alliteration.

> Our echoes roll from soul to soul,
>   And grow for ever and for ever.
> Blow, bugles, blow, set the wild echoes flying,
> And answer, echoes, answer, dying, dying, dying.
>   —Alfred, Lord Tennyson, "The Splendor Falls"

This poem repeats both sounds and words to create its mood.

> Alone, alone, all, all alone,
> Alone on a wide wide sea!
> —Samuel Taylor Coleridge, "The Rime of the
> Ancient Mariner"

Exercises: Using Assonance

A. Find the assonance in each selection. Identify the vowel sounds that are repeated.

1. Break, break, break
   On thy cold grey stones, O Sea!
   —Alfred, Lord Tennyson, "Break, Break, Break"

2. I saw . . . the soft and nearly imperceptible waving of the sable draperies . . . —Edgar Allan Poe, "The Pit and the Pendulum"

3. who knows if the moon's
   a balloon, coming out of a keen city
   in the sky—filled with pretty people?
   —e.e. cummings, "who knows if the moon's"

4. O beautiful for spacious skies,
   For amber waves of grain.
   —Katharine Lee Bates, "America, the Beautiful"

5. The first second of flight was only a flurry of awkward wings. Then Itchi-ban surged away, the air thick about it, its body beating against the dark, the feel of life on a leash, spinning, cartwheeling to dive, crashing into the river.
   —Eve Bunting, "Magic and the Night River"

B. Write three sentences using assonance. Each sentence should use the same vowel sound at least twice. Assonance can sound comical or beautiful, depending on how you use it. Make sure that the effect of the assonance fits with the meaning of the sentence.

Rhyme

> **Rhyme** is the repetition of sounds at the ends of words.
>
> Example: Jack and Jill
>   Went up the hill.
>
> In poems, rhymes are usually found at the ends of lines.

Rhyme in Prose.   Prose does not usually use rhyme. Sometimes, though, it is used for special effect. For example, the near-rhyme of *poem* and *home* in this final speech of a play stresses the fact that the play is ending.

> That's why, when I look at her now through this window, I remember that time and that poem, and she really seems to say, Whoever you are, wherever you come from, Welcome All. Welcome Home.   —Arthur Miller, *Grandpa and the Statue*

Rhyme in Poetry.   Poems rhyme in different patterns. Sometimes the lines that rhyme come one after another.

> Dreaming of honeycombs to share
> With her small cubs, a mother bear
> Sleeps in a snug and snowy lair.
>   —Harry Behn, "Waiting"

Sometimes every other line rhymes, as in the following poem.

> All day the snow fell on that Eastern town
> With its soft, pelting, little, endless sigh
> Of infinite flakes that brought the tall sky down
> Till I could put my hands in the white sky.
>   —Stephen Vincent Benét, *John Brown's Body*

This poem has a third pattern of rhyme. Can you find it?

Whose woods these are I think I know.
His house is in the village though;
He will not see me stopping here
To watch his woods fill up with snow.
> —Robert Frost, "Stopping by Woods on a
> Snowy Evening"

The pattern of rhyme in a poem is called a **rhyme scheme**. We use a special code to represent the rhyme scheme. The ending sound in each line of a poem is assigned a different letter of the alphabet. If one ending sound is repeated at the end of another line, the same letter is used to label both lines. Here is an example:

I never saw a moor,	a
I never saw the sea;	b
Yet I know how heather looks,	c
And what a wave must be.	b

> —Emily Dickinson, "I Never Saw a Moor"

Notice that the second and fourth lines rhyme. Therefore, they are both labeled with the same letter.

Here are the rhyme schemes for the other examples:

WAITING	JOHN BROWN'S BODY	STOPPING BY WOODS
a	a	a
a	b	a
a	a	b
	b	a

Exercises: **Using Rhyme**

A. Turn to pages 114 and 115. Show the rhyme scheme for each of the poems you find there.

B. Make a list of rhyming words for each of the words below. Then, using any rhyme scheme, write a two- or a four-line poem. Use your list of rhyming words.

moon	tree	skate	ball	race	money

Rhythm

Rhythm is the pattern of accented and unaccented syllables in a sentence or a line of poetry. The pattern is shown by marking each syllable with these symbols:

/ for accented, or stressed syllables

⌣ for unaccented, or light syllables

Example: Jáck bĕ nímblĕ, Jáck bĕ quíck.
Jáck júmp ŏvĕr thĕ cándlĕstíck.

Rhythm in Prose. Language has a natural rhythm. Occasionally, the rhythm of some prose is so strong that we can easily hear the rhythm pattern, as in the following example. The accent marks above each word tell you which syllables to stress.

The wínd wăs hówlĭng úp frŏm thĕ séa, béatĭng thĕ wáves ăgáinst thĕ whárves.

—Esther Forbes, *Johnny Tremain*

Writers use the rhythm of language to express mood. In the following example, the writer uses the rhythm of his words to stress their meaning. The result is growing excitement.

They had drums among the Indians, the Chinese, the Egyptians, thousands of years ago. And the words of their poetry move along like drum-beats, keeping time, now fast, now slow, drumming easy and slow at the opening of a war dance, drumming faster and faster, wild and furious, till it is so swift only the best-trained warriors can stand the speed of the dance that is drummed.

—Carl Sandburg, *Early Moon*

The rhythm of the writing speeds up with the drum beats.

Rhythm in Poetry. Rhythm in poetry catches and holds your attention. In addition, it works with the meaning of the words to express the poet's thought. The first stanza of this poem has a gentle, easy rhythm. Can you find where the rhythm changes slightly to emphasize the words?

> I'm going out to clean the pasture spring;
> I'll only stop to rake the leaves away
> (And wait to watch the water clear, I may):
> I shan't be gone long.—You come too.
> —Robert Frost, "The Pasture"

Exercises: Using Rhythm

A. Read these two prose selections from the same story. Compare their rhythms. Describe the mood that the words and the rhythm express.

Somehow the people who made tennis shoes knew what boys needed and wanted. They put marshmallows and coiled springs in the soles and they wove the rest out of grasses bleached and fired in the wilderness. Somewhere deep in the soft loam of the shoes the thin hard sinews of the buck deer were hidden. The people who made the shoes must have watched a lot of winds blow the trees and a lot of rivers going down to the lakes. Whatever it was, it was in the shoes, and it was summer.

"Bang! I deliver your packages, pick up packages, bring you coffee, burn your trash, run to the post office, telegraph office, library! You'll see twelve of me in and out, in and out every minute."
> —Ray Bradbury, "The Sound of Summer
> Running"

B. Copy these lines. Mark the stressed and unstressed syllables.

> Honey, pepper, leaf-green limes,
> Pagan fruit whose names are rhymes,
> Mangoes, bread-fruit, ginger-roots,
> Grenadillas, bamboo-shoots.
> —Agnes Maxwell-Hall, "Jamaica Market"

Onomatopoeia

> **Onomatopoeia** is the use of words that imitate sounds.
>
> Examples: bang, thump, whizz

Onomatopoeia in Prose. When writers need a word to tell about a sound, they often invent a new word, for example:

> The pounding of the cannon increased; there was the rat-tat-tatting of machine guns, and from somewhere came the menacing pocketa-pocketa-pocketa of the new flame throwers.
> —James Thurber, "The Secret Life of Walter Mitty"

Onomatopoeia in Poetry. In the example below, the poet imitates sounds you might hear at a July Fourth fireworks display.

> A white sky bomb fizzed on a black line.
> A rocket hissed its red signature into the west.
> —Carl Sandburg, "Fourth of July Night"

Exercises: Using Onomatopoeia

A. Find the onomatopoeia in the following sentences.

1. The bells in the steeples cling-clanged, telling people it was time to be up and about.
   —Esther Forbes, *Johnny Tremain*

2. The tuba oomphs, the flutes tweet-tweet;
   —William Cole, "Here Comes the Band"

B. Write three sentences using words that sound like their meanings. Your words might imitate the sounds of animals, weather, tools, musical instruments, or anything else that makes a sound.

Using Figures of Speech

Figures of speech are a special way of using language. Writers and speakers use figurative language and figures of speech often because they make language colorful and lively. In this part of the chapter, you will read and study these figures of speech:

simile	personification
metaphor	hyperbole

The Starry Night, 1889, VINCENT VAN GOGH. Oil on canvas, 29 × 36¼". Collection, The Museum of Modern Art, New York; Acquired through the Lillie P. Bliss Bequest.

Simile

> A **simile** is a comparison that uses *like* or *as*. It points out how two unlike things are alike in some way.
>
> Examples: The star is like a diamond in the sky.
> The dancer was as graceful as a cat.

Similes in Prose.   By using similes, writers help you see your familiar world in a new way. A good simile should make you say, "That's exactly what it's like! I never thought of it that way before."

Writers, therefore, try to invent similes that are fresh and original. Overused similes can become **clichés**. You have heard them so often that you do not really listen to them anymore.

The following samples use similes. Look for the two things that are compared in each one.

> A pale smile, like a gleam of cold sun on a winter's evening, passed over the old man's face.
> —J.R.R. Tolkien, *The Return of the King*

> The mothers stayed back in the kitchen, washing and drying, putting things away, recrossing their traceless footsteps like the lifetime journeys of bees.
> —James Agee, *A Death in the Family*

Similes in Poetry.   This poem compares trees to pencil strokes. At the same time, it puts a clear image into our minds.

> Scene
> Little trees like pencil strokes
> black and still
> etched forever in my mind
> on that snowy hill.
> —Charlotte Zolotow

The next poem takes objects we can see—candles—and compares them to things we cannot see.

The days of our future stand before us
Like a row of little lighted candles—
Golden, warm, and lively little candles.
>   —C.P. Cavafy, "Candles", translated by Rae
>   Dalven

Exercises: Using Simile

A. For each example, tell what two things are being compared. Also tell what they have in common.

1. I wandered lonely as a cloud
   That floats on high o'er vales and hills.
   >   —William Wordsworth, "I Wandered Lonely
   >   as a Cloud"

2. The fence had lost many of its pickets and stood propped against the tangle like a large comb with teeth missing.
   >   —Elizabeth Enright, "Nancy"

3. The fuel was in the rocket and the men ran away from it on the ground like ants running lickety from a metal god—
   >   —Ray Bradbury, "R Is for Rocket"

4. Black snake! Black snake!
   Curling on the ground,
   Rolled like a rubber tire,
   Ribbed and round.
   >   —Patricia Hubbell, "The Black Snake"

B. Write three original similes. If you are having trouble getting started, you may want to use these beginnings.

1. The engine sounded as quiet as _____.
2. The wind was like _____.
3. The cake we made in cooking class tasted like _____.
4. The water in the pool looked like _____.

Metaphor

> A **metaphor** is a comparison that states that one thing is another, unlike thing. It shows how the two things have something in common.
>
> Examples: Your mind is a complex computer.
> The spider's web was strung with diamonds.
>
> In the first example, your mind is compared to a computer. In the second example, drops of water on a spider's web are compared to diamonds.

Metaphors in Prose.   Read the sample below. Try to picture the street scene in this comparison.

> The air was filled with snowstorms of torn paper; strangers hugged each other in the streets. The war was over.
> —Alice Dalgliesh, *The Silver Pencil*

Metaphors are stated in a variety of ways. They don't always say clearly that one thing *is* another. It is up to the reader to figure out what two things are being compared and how they are alike. What two things are compared in each example below?

> Now and then Tom and Huck came upon snug nooks carpeted with grass and jeweled with flowers.
>
> . . . long lances of sunlight pierced down through the dense foliage far and near. . . .
> —Mark Twain, *The Adventures of Tom Sawyer*

Grass is compared to a carpet. Flowers are compared to jewels. Shafts of sunlight are compared to lances.

Metaphors in Poetry.   Read the following part of a poem called "Steam Shovel." To what is the steam shovel compared?

The dinosaurs are not all dead.
I saw one raise its iron head
To watch me walking down the road
Beyond our house today.
Its jaws were dripping with a load
Of earth and grass that it had cropped.
It must have heard me where I stopped,
Snorted white steam my way,
And stretched its long neck out to see,
And chewed, and grinned quite amiably.
     —Charles Malam, "Steam Shovel"

In this poem, the steam shovel is like a huge dinosaur.

Exercises: **Using Metaphor**

A. Find the metaphors in the following selections. What two things are compared? How are they alike?

1. The bones of the sea
 are on the shore,
 shells
 curled into the sand.
     —Lilian Moore, "Shells"

2. The tundra was an ocean of grass.
     —Jean Craighead George, "Amaroq, the Wolf"

3. All the world's a stage,
 And all the men and women merely players.
     —William Shakespeare, *As You Like It*

4. Fingers of fear squeezed his stomach.
     —Carl Henry Rathjen, "The Runaway Rig"

B. Write three sentences containing original metaphors. These questions may start you thinking. Use these ideas or your own.

1. To what can you compare your school when the bell rings?

2. To what can you compare snow?

3. To what can you compare a rocket?

Personification

Personification is the giving of human qualities to an object, an animal, or an idea.

Examples: The train whistle screamed.
The hail tap-danced on the roof.

Personification in Prose. Personification, like other figures of speech, puts a picture in the reader's mind.

In this sample, a whole city takes on the qualities of one person. The reader can picture the way that person wakes up.

> Boston slowly opened its eyes, stretched, and woke.
> —Esther Forbes, *Johnny Tremain*

Personification also helps the writer express a mood.

> In the distance a beautiful island covered with palm trees and flowers beckoned invitingly from the sparkling water.
> —Norton Juster, *The Phantom Tollbooth*

> The ice talked, grinding its teeth, sending out every now and then a singing crack.
> —Norah Burke, "Polar Night"

Personification in Poetry. In this poem, another city is personified. Read how Carl Sandburg describes Chicago. See how he uses the meaning and rhythm of his words as well as personification to communicate an image and a mood.

> Hog Butcher for the World,
> Toolmaker, Stacker of Wheat,
> Player with Railroads and the Nation's Freight Handler;
> Stormy, husky, brawling,
> City of the Big Shoulders.
> —Carl Sandburg, "Chicago"

Each of these examples of poetry gives human qualities to different things. How is each shown to be like people?

Snowy Benches
Do parks get lonely
in winter, perhaps,
when benches have only
snow on their laps?
—Aileen Fisher

The telephone poles
have been holding their
arms out a long time now.
—Donald Justice, "Crossing Kansas by Train"

Exercises: **Using Personification**

A. In each example, tell what is being compared to humans. Tell why it is like humans.

1. On all sides, green-clad mountains gazed down upon us.
   —Edwin Way Teale, *Journey into Summer*

2. Ten thousand daffodils saw I at a glance,
   Tossing their heads in sprightly dance.
   —William Wordsworth, "Daffodils"

3. The wind stood up, and gave a shout;
   He whistled on his fingers, and
   Kicked the withered leaves about,
   And thumped the branches with his hands.
   —James Stephens, "The Wind"

B. Use personification to describe each thing listed below. Consider how the object looks and what it does. Then think about similar ways people look and act. If possible, let your personification express a mood.

1. a mailbox

2. an apple tree bearing fruit

3. a radio

Hyperbole

Hyperbole is exaggeration that puts an image into the reader's mind. A hyperbole is often funny.

Example: It was so hot, you could fry an egg on the sidewalk.

Hyperbole in Prose.   In hyperbole, the exaggerated pictures fit in well with the fun-loving mood of tall tales and folk humor. The following examples of hyperbole are from American tall tales.

> There is a family in this town that is so lazy it takes two of them to sneeze. One throws his head back. And another goes AH-CHOO!

> There is a man nearby whose feet are so large that, when it rains, he lies down and uses them as umbrellas.

Writers also use hyperbole to describe exciting moments, as in the following example.

> The swing accelerated ever more wildly: soon it would take off entirely, depart from its hinges, fly through the air, burn a hole through the sky!
> —Elizabeth Enright, "Nancy"

Hyperbole in Poetry.   Hyperbole gives this poem a carefree and humorous mood.

> What a strange wind it was today,
> Cool and clear from a sky so grey
> And my hat stayed on but my head blew away—
> What a strange wind it was today.
> —Shel Silverstein, "Strange Wind"

The writer of this poem chose hyperbole to express her strong emotions.

> I will be the gladdest thing
>   Under the sun!
> I will touch a hundred flowers
>   And not pick one.
> > —Edna St. Vincent Millay, "Afternoon on
> > a Hill"

Exercises: Using Hyperbole

A. Identify which of the following selections use hyperbole.

1. And I will love thee still, my dear,
   Till all the seas go dry.
   > —Robert Burns, "A Red, Red Rose"

2. It was hot. Only the black ants didn't feel it, and they would be happy in a furnace.
   > —"Arap Sang and the Cranes," retold by
   > Humphrey Harman

3. Mr. Johansen was a gentle, white-haired, elderly man; he walked slowly with a slight stoop and had a kindly, sad face with large, dark eyes. —Joan Aiken, "The Serial Garden"

4. I heard all things in the heaven and in the earth. I heard many things in hell. —Edgar Allan Poe, "The Tell-Tale Heart"

5. There is a man who is so forgetful that one night he put his cat to bed and put himself outside. He did not discover his mistake until a dog chased him and he found he could not climb a tree.

B. Write an original hyperbole. If you wish, you may begin with one of these phrases.

1. My bedroom is so messy that _____.

2. Our car is so small that _____.

3. The speaker talked so long that _____.

Understanding the Process of Writing

Read the following statements by writers. Each one tells about one stage of the writing process—pre-writing, writing or revising. About which stage is each one speaking?

1. I read the manuscript aloud to myself and discover awkward words or phrases that had escaped me when I read them silently. In the final draft I have been known to spend several hours working over one page, or sometimes one paragraph, in order to get it as close to what I am trying to create as possible.
   —Robert M. McClung

2. Many writers find it useful to keep a notebook. In my own, I keep ideas for plots, characters observed from real life, scenes, scraps of speeches, even single phrases that flash into the mind.
   —Geoffrey Trease

3. I do not worry about length or the order in which the material is written down. Neither do I worry about incomplete sentences, spelling, or grammar. . . . This first draft is like an artist's quick sketch of a landscape or a figure.
   —Ann Petry

Understanding the Sounds of Language

Read each of the following samples. Look for examples of these sounds of language. Identify each example you find. If you can, tell how the use of sound helps the reader to understand the example.

alliteration   rhythm
assonance   onomatopoeia
rhyme

CYNTHIA IN THE SNOW

It SUSHES.
It hushes
The loudness of the road.
It flitter-twitters,
And laughs away from me.
It laughs a lovely whiteness,
And whitely whirs away
To be
Some otherwhere,
Still white as milk or shirts.
So beautiful it hurts.
                    —Gwendolyn Brooks

It was a beautiful afternoon. The street was very high with elms. The light that came through their roof of leaves was green and trembling like light through water. Fiona became a little crab crawling among the roots of seaweed. The parked cars were fishes which would eat her up, danger was everywhere. . . .

The houses sat back from their green laps of lawn, silent and substantial, regarding her like people wearing glasses.
                    —Elizabeth Enright, "Nancy"

Understanding Figures of Speech

Reread each sample above. Look for the following figures of speech:

simile	personification
metaphor	hyperbole

Identify each figure of speech you find. If you find a comparison, identify the two things being compared and tell how they are alike.

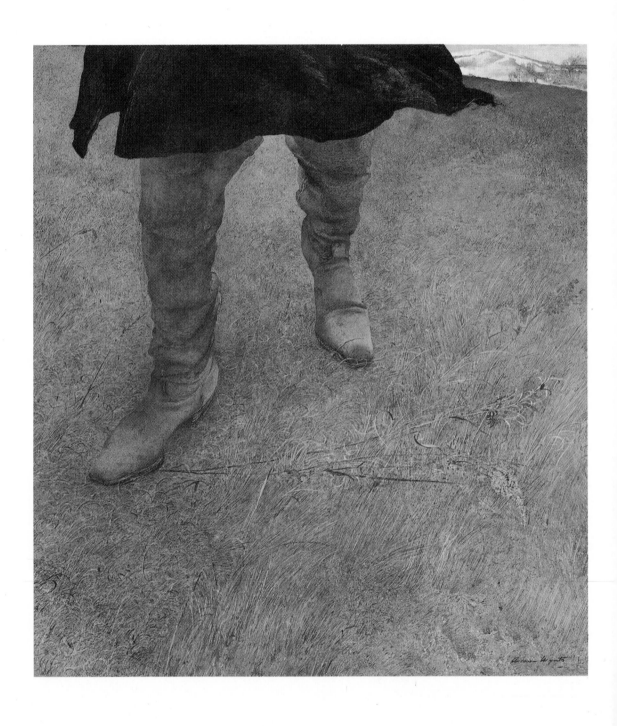

CHAPTER 4

Short Stories

The Trodden Weed, 1951, ANDREW WYETH.
Private Collection.

Reading Literature: Short Stories

What Is a Short Story?

A **short story** is a story short enough to be read from beginning to end at one time. A short story is fiction. It comes from the imagination of a single writer. A short story usually focuses on a single important event in the life of one character.

The History of the Short Story

The short story is a very old form of literature. Stories were told by storytellers long before they were written. Short, fictional stories were written down in Egypt as early as 3000 B.C. The Bible contains many short stories called **parables**.

Two outstanding collections of short stories were written around the year 1350. (This was about one hundred years before Malory wrote *Le Morte d'Arthur*.) An Italian writer, Giovanni Boccaccio, wrote a collection of tales called *The Decameron*.

A few years later, an English writer, Geoffrey Chaucer, wrote *The Canterbury Tales*. In this book, each member of a group of travelers tells a story.

In the 1800's, great writers all over the world became interested in the short story. They each developed slightly different ways of writing short stories.

American poet and writer Edgar Allan Poe studied the short story thoroughly. In his writings, he explained how he thought a short story should be written. He said that the goal of a short story should be to communicate a single idea. Every sentence and every word should be chosen carefully. If it was written correctly, Poe thought, the short story could communicate the writer's entire message before the reader became tired of reading. Poe's ideas strongly influenced later writers.

The Elements of the Short Story

The three main elements in a short story are the same as in a legend. They are characters, setting, and plot.

Plot. Many short stories follow the same general plan. It is a logical way of telling a story. Here is that plan.

Introduction: This comes at the beginning of the story. You meet the characters, learn about the setting, and see the beginning of a conflict, or struggle.

Rising Action: The struggle grows more intense.

Climax: This is the most exciting part in the story. It is the turning point.

Falling Action: After the climax, events follow their logical course to the end.

Resolution: All loose ends are tied up. The story ends.

Point of View. If the story is told by a character in the story, it is written from the **first-person point of view.** Then the writer uses words such as *I* and *we.* If a narrator who is not a character in the story is telling what happened, the story is written from the **third-person point of view.** Sometimes this narrator tells only what one person could know. That is the **limited** third-person point of view. Sometimes this narrator knows everything that happens. That is the **omniscient** third-person point of view.

How To Read a Short Story

1. Read carefully. Since these stories are so short, each word is important. You may miss something if you skip words.
2. Decide who is telling the story. Is it a narrator outside the story? Is it one of the characters in the story?
3. Keep track of the order of events.
4. Try to understand why one event leads to the next.

Comprehension Skills: Relationships

Finding Relationships Among Events

As you read, it is important to see how one event is connected to another. If you do not see the connections, the story will not make sense. Sometimes the writer tells how one event is related to others. Sometimes he or she gives clues, and you must figure out what the relationship is. Two important relationships to watch for are **time order** and **cause and effect**.

Time Order. Writers know that the order of events in their stories should be clear. Often, they leave clues to help you. Certain words are signals that tell you that time order is being explained. A few of these signal words are *after, before, finally, then, now, soon, next,* and *at last.*

Read the following paragraph. What event comes first? What comes last? The underlined words give you clues about time order.

There was a meeting, about eleven in the morning, at the Town Hall. <u>After</u> that, everyone had a picnic on the green. <u>Then</u> the procession formed to escort the old soldiers out to the Burying Ground, where they put flags on the graves.

Cause and Effect. Sometimes the events in a story just occur in a certain order. Other times an early event is the reason for a later event. Then the early event is a **cause**, a reason why something happens. The later event is an **effect**, what happens as a result of the cause. Here is an example.

I can't run <u>because</u> my running shoes are worn out.

Cause   **Effect**
My running shoes are worn out. Therefore, I can't run.

shorty G

Notice the underlined word in the sample sentence. *Because* is a key word to look for when you want to identify the reasons for something happening in a story. Some other key words are *so*, *for this reason*, *since*, *therefore*, and *that is why*.

A writer will not always provide signal words. However, you may still find a cause-and-effect relationship. For example, the sample sentence could have been stated in any one of these ways:

I can't run. My running shoes are worn out.
I need new running shoes. My old shoes are worn out.
My running shoes are worn out and I can't run.

As you can see, you cannot only look for key words. You must think about each event and how it goes with other events.

Exercises: Understanding Time Order and Cause and Effect

A. Read this sentence from one of the stories in this chapter. Does it show a time order relationship or cause and effect?

The old man hadn't heard this because he was so deaf.

B. Read this selection. Then answer the questions below.

Esmeralda stared at the coin she held in her hand. It was a shilling. She had never had any money before and was quite puzzled to know what she should buy with it. Almost without realizing what she was doing, she began to wander along the stalls, looking at different things offered for sale. Then she came to the toy counter.

1. What did Esmeralda do first? second? third?
2. The writer used two key words to show time order. Name one.
3. Why was Esmeralda puzzled?
   a. She stared at the coin in her hand.
   b. She had never had any money before.
   c. She began to wander along the stalls.
4. How was Esmeralda going to decide what to buy?

Vocabulary Skills: Multiple Meanings

Using Words with Multiple Meanings.

Can potatoes see with their eyes? If you're bright, do I need sunglasses to look at you? The underlined words in these sentences have more than one meaning. Many words in our language have multiple meanings. Often this fact makes it difficult for us to understand what a speaker or writer is saying.

For example, here are seven dictionary definitions for *bit*.

1. *n.*, a metal mouthpiece on a bridle
2. *n.*, the part of the key that turns the lock
3. *n.*, the cutting part of a tool
4. *n.*, a tiny piece
5. *n.*, a short time
6. *adj.*, very small: as, *he has a bit part*
7. *n.*, in computers, the smallest unit of information

The dictionary can tell you all the meanings of a word. However, in order to know exactly which definition is meant, you need to read the word in **context**—in a sentence or a paragraph.

Which definition of *bit* is meant in each sentence below?

1. The wild horse hated the feel of the bit in its mouth.
2. I'll be happy if I get even a bit part in the play.
3. In computer class, we learned that a bit is zero or one.

Levels of Language

Often the meaning of a word depends on the level of language in which it is used. The two major levels of our language are standard and nonstandard English. **Standard English** is accepted anywhere. **Formal standard English** is used in most writing. **Informal standard English** is used in everyday conversations.

Nonstandard English, unlike standard English, is not accepted everywhere. Baby talk, for example, is a kind of nonstandard English. Another kind of nonstandard English is **slang**. Slang includes new words or words with new meanings that are not used by everyone. For example, in standard English, you might say that an accident left your bike a total wreck. In slang, you might say that you totalled your bike. Some dictionaries label nonstandard words or meanings as slang.

Exercises: Using Multiple Meanings

A. Choose the correct definition for each underlined word.

1. Let us decide by <u>lot</u> which of us shall go into town.
   That movie was filmed on the back <u>lot</u>.

   a. lot—an object used to decide a matter by chance; the person who draws it from a container of like objects wins
   b. lot—in movies, a studio and its surrounding area

2. Be sure to lock the door with the <u>bolt</u>.
   How many <u>bolts</u> of cloth will it take to make the drapes?

   a. bolt—a roll of cloth or paper
   b. bolt—a sliding bar used to lock a door or gate

3. She had never met her cousins who lived in a <u>distant</u> city.
   The young woman's glance fell upon the prisoner with a <u>distant</u>, swift disinterest.

   a. distant—cool in manner, reserved
   b. distant—widely separated, far away

B. Choose one of the numbered definitions to answer each question.

tip (1) in baseball, to hit the ball a glancing blow
     (2) **tip off** to give secret information to
     (3) **tip one's hand** [slang] to reveal a secret

1. Which definition gives a meaning that is special for one sport?
2. Which definition gives a slang meaning?
3. Which definition gives a meaning used mostly in conversation?

Great Classic Stories

The first meaning of *classic* listed in the dictionary is "being a model of its kind." These stories by famous writers of the past are truly models for today's writers. They suggest how a short story can make a certain setting or character or event real for the reader. Even though they range in age from about eighty years to over five hundred years old, they still touch our feelings and lead us to think.

Eskimo Finger Masks, 1880, Private Collection. Photograph by Peter Furst.

How the Three Young Men Found Death

This story is set in the Middle Ages, when the disease called the Black Death killed one out of every four people throughout Europe. Read to find out what happened when three young men tried to stop Death.

GEOFFREY CHAUCER

In Flanders there was once a company of young men who devoted themselves to folly of all kinds: rioting, gambling, and drinking. They danced and played dice both day and night and drank more than they should.

One day, as three of these young men sat in a tavern, they heard the clanging bell of a funeral procession. One of them called out to a waiter, "Go and ask what corpse is passing by here."

"Why, sir," said the boy, "there is no need to ask. Only a short time ago someone told me. The dead man was a friend of yours. Last night as he sat drinking on his bench, suddenly the thief that men call Death came by and, with his spear, cut his heart in two and then went away without another word. He has taken thousands with his plague, and I would suggest that you be careful to avoid his presence."

The innkeeper then said, "The boy is telling the truth; for Death has taken many—men, women, and children—in the village this year. It seems as if he has made his home here."

"Is there such danger in meeting him?" one young man asked. "Why, then I shall look for him in every street. Let the three of us make a pact. Let us hold up our hands and swear to be brothers and to find and kill this traitor who has killed so many others!"

So together these three made their pact: to live and die for each other as brothers. And they started off to find Death, shouting that Death was as good as dead, if only they could find him.

When they had gone less than half a mile, they came upon an old man, who gave them a friendly greeting.

The proudest of the three young men spoke for all three. He said to the man, "You scoundrel, why are you all covered except for your face? How have you lived to be so old?"

The Hunt of the Unicorn II: The Unicorn Dips His Horn into the Stream To Rid It of Poison (detail)
The Metropolitan Museum of Art, Gift of John D. Rockefeller, Jr., the Cloisters Collection, 1937.

The old man answered, "Even if I were to walk as far as India, I would not be able to find, in any town or village, a man who would be willing to exchange his youth for my age. And, therefore, I shall keep my age for as long as I live. So I walk around the earth in my shroud like a restless slave and hope for death. But you show no manners in speaking unkindly to an old man. You should treat an old man who has done you no harm as kindly as you would want to be treated in your old age—if you live so long. Now I must go."

"Oh, no, old dog," said the youth. "You shall not leave so easily. You just spoke now of the traitor Death, who has been killing all our friends in this area. I think that you are his spy, and I demand that you tell me where he is. Surely you are one of his helpers."

"Now, sirs," the old man said, "if you are so eager to find Death, turn up this crooked path. I left him under a tree in that grove, and there he will stay. Death will not hide from your boasting. Do you see that oak? <u>You will find him there.</u>"

So together the three young men ran until they came to the tree. But there was no one there; instead they found eight bushels of coins—round and shiny gold pieces. The sight of such wealth drove all thoughts of Death from their minds, and they sat down by their treasure.

"Brothers," said one, "listen closely to what I say. Fortune has given us this treasure, and we shall spend it as easily as we found it. Once this gold is carried away from this place, to my house or to yours (for we know that all this gold is ours), then all will be well.

"But, after all, we cannot do it by daylight. Then people would say that we were thieves and hang us for our treasure. It must be carried away by night as carefully and secretly as we can. Therefore, let us draw lots to see which of us shall go into town to bring back food and drink. And two of us shall keep guard over the treasure. Then, when it is night, we shall carry it to wherever we agree is the best place."

The lot fell on the youngest of the three, and he went off toward the town.

As soon as he was gone, one said to the other, "You know that you are my sworn brother, and now I will tell you your reward. Our friend has gone into town, but here is the gold (and plenty of it!) to be divided among the three of us. But if I can help it, it shall only be divided between us two. Isn't this a great favor to do a friend?"

The other answered, "I don't know how that can be. What will we do? What will we say to him?"

"Will you keep it a secret?" asked the first man. "If so, I will tell you in a few words how we will bring it about."

"I promise, by my honor," said the other, "that I will not betray you."

"Now," said the first, "there are two of us, and two are stronger than one. When he comes back, watch when he sits down and right away stand up as though you want to wrestle with him; and while you struggle with him, as in sport, I will run him through the side. Then, with your dagger, you do the same. And then, my dear friend, all this gold will be divided only between you and me; and we can both have everything we want and gamble as much as we like." And so these two agreed to kill the third.

On his way into town, the youngest thought of nothing but the bright and shiny gold coins. He thought, "If only I could have all that gold for myself; then there would be no man in all the world so happy as I."

At last he thought that he would buy poison with which to kill his two partners. When he got into town, he went straight to the apothecary and asked for poison to kill some rats.

The apothecary answered, "I will give you something that no being can withstand. Once you have given it, the creature will be dead before you have walked a mile—it is so strong and violent."

The young man took the box of poison; and on the next street he met a man from whom he bought three large bottles. He poured the poison into two and kept the third clean for his own drink. When he had filled the three bottles with wine, he returned to the grove where his friends waited for him.

Just as they had planned, the other two killed him as soon as he returned. And when they had done this, one said, "Let us sit down and drink and celebrate. We will bury him later." So he took one of the bottles with the poisoned wine and drank it down. Then he gave the other to his friend.

And soon, like their friend, the two found Death.

Vanitas, 1603, JACQUES de GHEYN the ELDER.
The Metropolitan Museum of Art; Curtis Marquand, Victor Wilbour Memorial, Charles B. and Alfred N. Punnett Endowment Funds 1974.

Developing Comprehension Skills

1. Why do the three young men go to look for Death?

2. How do you think the old man knew exactly where Death was? Why do you think so?

3. These three young men put their desire for gold above their loyalty to each other. Can you think of any situation in which you would be justified in turning against a friend?

4. Rearrange the events listed below in terms of time order. Identify which happen first, second, and so on.

   a. The youngest is killed by the other two young men.
   b. The three young men find the coins.
   c. All three young men find Death.
   d. A corpse is carried past the tavern.
   e. The three young men meet the old man.
   f. The two young men drink the poisoned wine.
   g. The youngest man goes to town for food and drink.
   h. The three young men swear to be brothers.

5. In looking at this story as a whole, what do you think the author is telling you about life? In other words, what is the theme of this story? Can you identify another theme? What might it be?

Reading Literature: Short Stories

1. **Identifying Character Traits.** Reread the conversation of the three young men with the old man. Only one young man spoke, but the others did not object, so they must have agreed with their friend. What does this conversation tell you about the qualities, or traits, of the three young men? Find two other parts of the story that make you sure that your opinion of them was right.

2. **Making Inferences.** Often a writer will drop a hint about, or fore-shadow, an event that happens later in the story. What is there in the old man's speech that contains a clue to the outcome of the story?

3. **Making a Plot Diagram.** Review the events listed in Developing Comprehension Skills, 4, above. Find the place for each event in the plot diagram below. More than one event may belong in each category. The correct position of two events has already been marked on the

diagram. The letters *b* and *d* refer to the letters identifying the items in the Comprehension exercise on page 145.

Climax

Rising Action (b)   Falling Action

Introduction (d)   Resolution

4. **Examining the Effect of Personification.** Death is a person in this story. How does this add to the interest of the story? How does it provide humor? Find at least three sentences in which there is a double meaning caused by thinking of Death as a person. Do you think these lines are humorous?

Developing Vocabulary Skills

Recognizing Multiple Meanings of a Word. Read the following pairs of sentences. In each pair, both sentences use a word drawn from the story. However, each sentence uses a different meaning of the word. Choose the correct meaning of the underlined word in each sentence from the definitions given.

1. Death came by and took away thousands with his <u>plague</u>.
2. Mosquitoes were annoying all day, but at dusk they became a <u>plague</u>.

   a. a very dangerous disease that spreads rapidly and often causes death
   b. a thing or person that torments or troubles

3. The sailors tied a secure <u>shroud</u> to the mast of the ship.
4. The old man had walked around the earth in his <u>shroud</u> like a restless slave.

   a. a rope stretched from a ship's side to the top mast.
   b. a wrap or garment used for burial

5. Not a <u>spear</u> of grass was found in the garden.
6. Death took his <u>spear</u> and cut the man's heart in two.

   a. a weapon used for thrusting or throwing
   b. a sprout or shoot of a plant

7. The young man thought of nothing but the <u>bright</u> gold coins.
8. Alexis is very <u>bright</u> in math but not in science.

   a. clever
   b. radiating or reflecting light

9. Jon's favorite <u>area</u> of science is astronomy.
10. Many people in the <u>area</u> of the village had died suddenly.

    a. a field of study
    b. a particular geographical region

Developing Writing Skills

1. **Appreciating Point of View.** "How the Three Young Men Found Death" was written from the point of view of the all-knowing, or omniscient, author. Imagine that, instead, one of the young men had told the story to a passerby who found him dying of poison. Then the story would have been written from the first-person point of view. What parts of this story would the young man not know? What would he have left out? Would he have added anything? Write one or more paragraphs explaining how the story would have been different if it had been told from the first-person point of view.

2. **Using Personification.** Write a story of no more than twelve paragraphs about three young people of today who go searching for one of these: Peace, Happiness, Excitement, or Wisdom. Personify the quality you choose. If you like, your heroes or heroines can meet and talk with the personified quality.

Developing Skills in Critical Thinking

Making Generalizations from Specific Details. List details given in this selection that show the character of the three young men. From this list, write three generalizations about the men. A **generalization** is a statement about a group that supposedly is true of all the members of the group. Your generalizations should be as accurate as possible.

Then make one generalization that is inaccurate and unfair to the men. Rewrite your generalizations in any order. Then exchange papers with a partner. The partners must identify the unfair generalizations.

The Bishop's Candlesticks

VICTOR HUGO

In this short story, which is part of a novel, the two major characters act in ways that may surprise you. Try to find and understand the reasons each man had for acting as he did.

Les Miserables tells the story of Jean Valjean, a French peasant who stole a loaf of bread for his sister's starving children. He was sentenced to the galleys for five years. Because he repeatedly tried to escape, Jean's time in prison was increased until he had served nineteen years.

At last he was set free; and four days later something happened that changed his whole life.

The scene is the small house the bishop chose to live in rather than in the bishop's palace, which he had turned over for use as a hospital. The time is 1815.

As the bishop entered the dining-room, Mme. Magloire, the old servant, had just finished setting the table for supper. She was talking with some warmth to Mdlle. Baptistine, the bishop's sister, about the need for a lock for the front door. It seems that while she had been out making provision for supper, she had heard talk about a suspicious vagabond who was lurking somewhere in the town. It was said that some unpleasant adventures might befall those who came home late that night, and that everyone ought to bolt his door most carefully.

"We are not safe at all," said Mme. Magloire, "for nothing could be more horrible than a door that opens by a latch on the outside. And monseigneur has the habit of always saying, 'Come in,' even at midnight."

At this moment there was a violent knock on the door.

"Come in," said the bishop.

The door opened.

A man entered. He was a man of middle height, strong and hardy; he might have been forty-six or forty-seven years old. A slouched leather cap half hid his face, tanned by the sun and wind. He wore a coarse yellow shirt, open at the neck; shabby blue trousers, white on one knee and with holes in the other; an old ragged gray blouse patched on one side with a piece of green cloth sewed with twine. Upon his back was a well-filled knapsack, strongly buckled and quite new. In his hand he carried an enormous knotted stick; his stockingless feet were in hobnailed shoes; his hair was shorn but bristly, for it seemingly had not been cut for some time.

He came in, took one step, and paused, leaving the door open behind him. There was a rough, hard, tired, and fierce look in his eyes, as seen by the firelight. He was hideous.

Mme. Magloire had not even the strength to scream. She stood trembling, with her mouth open.

Mdlle. Baptistine turned, saw the man enter, and started out half alarmed; then slowly turned back again toward the fire. She looked at her brother, and her face resumed its usual calmness and serenity.

The bishop looked upon the man with a tranquil eye.

As he was opening his mouth to speak, doubtless to ask the stranger what he wanted, the man, leaning with both hands upon his club, glanced from one to another in turn, and, without waiting for the bishop to speak, said in a loud voice:

"See here! My name is Jean Valjean. I am a convict; I have been nineteen years in the galleys. Four days ago I was set free; today I have walked twelve miles. When I reached this place this evening, I went to an inn, and they sent me away. I went to another inn; they said: 'Get out!' I went to the prison and the turnkey would not let me in. In the square I laid down upon a stone; a good woman showed me your house and said: 'Knock there!' I have knocked. What is this place? Is it an inn? I have money; my savings, 109 francs and 15 sous, which I have earned in the galleys by my work for nineteen years. I will pay. I am very tired—and I am so hungry. Can I stay?"

"Mme. Magloire," said the bishop, "put on another plate."

The man stepped foward. "Stop," he exclaimed, as if he had not been understood. "I am a galley slave—a convict—I am just from the galleys." He drew from his pocket a large sheet of yellow paper, which he unfolded. "This is my passport, yellow, as you see. That is enough to have me thrown out wherever I go. It says, 'This man is very dangerous.' There you have it. Everybody has thrust me out. Will you receive me? Can you give me something to eat? Have you a stable where I can sleep?"

"Mme. Magloire," said the bishop, "put some sheets on the bed in the alcove." Then he turned to the man. "Monsieur, sit down and warm yourself. We are going to take supper presently, and your bed will be made ready."

At last the man understood; his face, the expression of which till then had been gloomy and hard, now expressed stupefaction, doubt and joy, and became absolutely wonderful. He began to stutter like a madman.

"What? You will keep me? You won't drive me away—a convict? You call me 'monsieur' and don't say, 'Get out, dog!' as everybody else does. I shall have a supper! a bed like other people, with mattress and sheets—a bed! It is nineteen years since I have slept on a bed. I will pay well. I beg your pardon, Mr. Innkeeper, what is your name? You are an innkeeper, aren't you?"

"I am a priest who lives here."

"A priest," said the man. "How stupid I am. I didn't notice your cap."

While speaking, he deposited his knapsack and stick in the corner, replaced his passport in his pocket, and sat down.

Mme. brought in a plate and set it on the table.

"Mme. Magloire," said the bishop, "put this plate as near the fire as you can." Then turning toward his guest, he added: "The night wind is raw in the Alps; you must be cold, monsieur."

Every time he said the word "monsieur" with his gently solemn and heartily hospitable voice, the man's face lighted up. "Monsieur" to a convict is a glass of water to a man dying of thirst at sea.

"The lamp," said the bishop, "gives a very poor light."

Mme. Magloire understood him and, going to his bedchamber, took from the mantel the two silver candlesticks, lighted the candles and placed them on the supper table.

"Monsieur, you are good; you don't despise me. You take me into your house, you light your candles for me, and I haven't hid from you where I come from."

The bishop touched his hand gently and said, "You need not tell me who you are. This is not my house; it is the house of Christ. It does not ask any comer whether he has a name, but whether he has an affliction. You are suffering; you are hungry and thirsty. Be welcome. Whatever is here is yours. What need have I to know your name? Besides, before you told me, I knew it."

The man opened his eyes in astonishment. "You knew my name?"

"Yes," answered the bishop, "Your name is my brother."

Meantime Mme. Magloire had served up supper. It consisted of soup, a little pork, a scrap of mutton, a few figs, a green cheese, and a large loaf of rye bread. She had added, without asking, a bottle of fine old wine.

"To supper!" said the bishop briskly. When they were seated, he asked the blessing and then served the soup. Suddenly he said: "It seems to me something is lacking on the table."

Mme. Magloire understood the remark; without a word she went out and, a moment afterward, returned with the three extra silver plates that they always had on the table when there were guests.

The man ate with the voracity of a starving man, paying no attention to anyone. Meanwhile, the bishop chatted pleasantly of Pontarlier, to which place Jean Valjean said he must be on his way by daybreak. He told of the many papermills, tanneries, and iron foundries there, saying that, during the revolution when his family was ruined, he himself had worked there. Without giving the stranger any advice, he let him know where there was a place that he could stay and where he was sure to find work. Never once did he bring into the conversation any sermonizing.

Immediately after the dessert, the bishop said, "You must be in great need of sleep." Bidding goodnight to his sister, he took one of the silver candlesticks from the table, handed the other to his guest, and said to him:

"Monsieur, I will show you to your room."

To reach the alcove where Jean Valjean was to sleep, they had to pass through the bishop's sleeping-chamber. As they went through this room, Mme. Magloire was just putting up the silver in the cupboard at the head of the bed. The bishop left his guest in the alcove before a clean, white bed. The man set down the candlestick upon a small table.

"A good night's rest to you," said the bishop. "Tomorrow morning before you go, you shall have a cup of warm milk from our cows."

"Thank you, monsieur," said the man. A moment afterward, so completely exhausted was he that, after blowing out the candle, he fell on the bed, dressed as he was, into a sound sleep.

As the cathedral clock struck two, Jean Valjean awoke.

He had slept only four hours, but he could not get to sleep again. Many thoughts came to him, but there was one that continually presented itself and that drove away all others. He had noticed the six silver plates and the large ladle that Mme. Magloire placed in the cupboard at the head of the bishop's bed. They were solid and old silver. With that big ladle, they would bring at least 200 francs; dou-

ble what he had got for nineteen years' labor.

His mind wavered a whole hour, in fluctuation and in struggle. The clock struck three. He opened his eyes, got up hastily in bed, and put his feet on the floor. All at once, he stooped down and took off his shoes. Then he rose to his feet, hesitated for a moment longer, and listened. He placed his belongings near the window and, with stealthy steps, moved toward the door of the bishop's room. On reaching it he found that it was unlatched. He pushed it a little, then more boldly. This time a rusty hinge sent out into the darkness a harsh creak. For a moment he thought he was lost. But minutes passed, and he ventured to look into the room. The bishop had not stirred.

A deep calm filled the chamber. As Jean Valjean paused before the bed, suddenly the dark clouds parted, and a ray of moonlight, crossing the window, lighted up the bishop's face. The effect was startling. The expression of content, hope, and happiness on his countenance became radiant, and he appeared as if in a halo.

Jean Valjean, standing in the shadow, erect, motionless, was terrified. He had never seen anything comparable to it. He did not remove his eyes from the old man. One would have said he was hesitating between two realms—that of the doomed and that of the saved.

In a few moments, he raised his left hand slowly to his forehead and took off his cap. He stood for some time looking at the sleeping bishop. Then, suddenly he put on his cap, passed quickly to the cupboard, turned the key, opened it, took the basket of silver, passed quickly to the window in the alcove, stepped out, ran across the garden, leaped over the wall like a tiger, and fled.

The next day at sunrise, as the bishop was walking in the garden, Mme. Magloire came running, quite beside herself, to tell him that the silver was stolen, the man was gone! The bishop was silent for a moment, then, raising his serious eyes, he said mildly:

"Mme. Magloire, I have for a long time wrongfully withheld this silver. It belonged to the poor. Who was this man? A poor man evidently."

A short time later, the bishop and his sister were having breakfast when there was a knock at the door.

"Come in," said the bishop.

The door opened. A strange, fierce group appeared on the threshold. Three men were holding a fourth by the collar. The three were gendarmes; the fourth, Jean Valjean. One of them stepped forward and addressed the bishop.

"Monsiegneur," said he.

The bishop rose and approached as quickly as his great age permitted. "Ah, there you are," he said, looking toward Jean Valjean. "I am glad to see you. But I gave you the candlesticks also, which are silver like the rest and would bring 200 francs. Why did you not take them along with your plates?"

Jean Valjean opened his eyes and looked at the bishop with an expression that no human tongue could describe.

"Monseigneur," said the gendarme, "then what this man said was true? We met him. He was going like a man who was running away, and we arrested him in order to see. He had this silver."

"And he told you," interrupted the bishop, with a smile, "that it had been given him by a good old priest with whom he had passed the night. I see it all. And you brought him back here? It is all a mistake."

"If that is so," said the gendarme, "we can let him go."

"Certainly," replied the bishop.

The gendarmes released Jean Valjean, who shrank back.

"You can go. Do you not understand?" said one of them.

"My friend," said the bishop, "before you go away, here are your candlesticks. Take them." He went to the mantelpiece, took the two candlesticks, and brought them to Jean Valjean, who was trembling in every limb. He received the two candlesticks mechanically.

"Now," said the bishop, "go in peace." To the gendarmes he said, "Messieurs, you can retire." The gendarmes withdrew.

Jean Valjean felt like a man who is about to faint.

The bishop approached him and said in a low voice, "Forget not, never forget that you have promised me to use this silver to become an honest man."

Jean Valjean, who had no recollection of this promise, stood confused. The bishop had laid much stress upon these words as he uttered them. He continued solemnly:

"Jean Valjean, my brother, you belong no longer to evil, but to good. It is your soul that I am buying for you. I withdraw it from dark thoughts and from the spirit of perdition, and I give it to God."

Developing Comprehension Skills

1. Why was Jean Valjean directed to knock on the bishop's door?

2. Describe Jean Valjean's life for the past nineteen years. What things had happened to him that would make it possible for him to consider taking the silver?

3. What does the bishop say his reasons are for giving the silver to Jean Valjean? Do you think these are his real reasons? Explain your answer.

4. Do you think Jean Valjean will use the silver to become an honest man, able to support himself? Why or why not? Quote any passages you can find from the story to support your answer.

Reading Literature: Short Stories

1. **Identifying the Plot Line.** On your paper, fill in the missing parts of this plot diagram for "The Bishop's Candlesticks."

   a. Introduction: Jean Valjean comes to the Bishop's house and is fed and housed.

   b. Rising Action: Jean Valjean wakes in the night and runs off with the bishop's silver, but is brought back by three gendarmes.

   c. Climax:

   d. Falling Action: the gendarmes leave him with the bishop.

   e. Resolution:

2. **Identifying Internal Conflict.** When he woke at 2:00 A.M., Jean Valjean's "mind wavered a whole hour, in fluctuation and in struggle." Describe the two opposing courses of action that Valjean was considering. For each course, list both advantages and disadvantages for him. Then tell why you think he chose the one he did.

3. **Identifying Tone.** The tone of a story is the author's attitude toward the theme, plot, and characters. The approach may be a serious one, a somber one, or a light and happy one. For example, the tone of "How the Three Young Men Found Death" was somewhat amused. The narrator seemed to think the young men were foolish and not worth feeling sorry for. How would you describe the tone of "The Bishop's Candlesticks"? Is the author making fun of the characters, or is he concerned about them? What parts of the story make you think as you do?

4. **Understanding Character.** In the third paragraph from the end of the selection, the bishop tells Jean Valjean, "Forget not, never forget that you have promised me to use this silver to become an honest man." Valjean cannot remember the promise. Did he make it? Is the bishop imagining things? Consider the bishop's other actions and statements, particularly his reaction to Mme. Magloire's news that the silver was stolen and his final statement. Then tell what reasons you think he might have had for telling Valjean about his "promise."

Developing Vocabulary Skills

Identifying Multiple Meanings in a Dictionary Entry. Several words in "The Bishop's Candlesticks" have more than one dictionary meaning. Each of the following pairs of sentences uses one of those words with two of its meanings. Below the pair of sentences is part of the dictionary entry for the underlined word. For each, choose the definition that best fits the context of the sentence. On your paper, write the letter of your choice.

1. There was a <u>rough</u>, tired, and fierce look in the man's eyes.
2. Miss David asked for a <u>rough</u> outline of the project.

    a. having a coarse or uneven surface: *rough road*
    b. shaggy and tangled: *a dog with a rough coat*
    c. harsh; rude; ungentle: *a rough manner*
    d. not completed; hastily done as a first try: *a rough idea*
    e. in golf, any part of the course bordering the fairway

3. The convict was looking for a <u>stable</u> in which he could sleep.
4. The concrete poles supporting the tent were quite <u>stable</u>.

    a. a building for lodging and feeding of horses
    b. not likely to fall or give way
    c. able or likely to continue or last: *a stable government*
    d. in chemistry, resisting molecular or chemical change: *a stable compound*

5. In the town <u>square</u>, Jean Valjean lay down upon a stone.
6. "Find the <u>square</u> of four," asked Mr. Jenkins.

    a. a rectangle having all four sides of equal length
    b. an open area bounded by streets in a city or town, used as a park
    c. in math, the product of a number multiplied by itself.

7. While speaking, the man had <u>deposited</u> his knapsack and stick in the corner.
8. The miners found rich <u>deposits</u> of iron.

    a. to put, place, or set down
    b. to insert (a coin) in a coin-operated device
    c. to place money for safekeeping in a bank account
    d. a natural accumulation of oil or ore
    e. money placed in a bank account

9. Mrs. Barnes hurried to the sale to <u>bid</u> for the old chair.
10. The bishop <u>bid</u> goodnight to his sister and took one of the silver candlesticks from the table.

    a. to say as a greeting, or wish: *to bid the visitors farewell*
    b. in cards, to enter a bid of a given suit: *to bid hearts*
    c. to make an offer to purchase at a price
    d. an invitation

Developing Writing Skills

1. **Understanding a Minor Character.** Look at the beginning of the selection and list the details that are given about Mme. Magloire. What is her role in the Bishop's household? What does she talk about? What are her fears?

    Why did Victor Hugo write about Mme. Magloire in the beginning of this selection? What was the author's purpose? How does the description of Madame Magloire achieve this purpose? Write at least one paragraph discussing her role in setting the mood of the story.

2. **Creating a Mood.** In this story, Victor Hugo and the translator chose words deliberately. They carefully created the mood of fear and suspense that hovers about the character of Jean Valjean. List at least ten of the words and phrases used to describe Valjean that establish this mood. Then use several of those words and phrases in a single paragraph describing Valjean.

Developing Skills in Study and Research

Comparing Reference Sources. Read the short biography of Victor Hugo in the Handbook for Reading and Writing in this book. What does it tell you about this author? Also, look up Victor Hugo in at least two other reference books:

a dictionary   an almanac
an encyclopedia   your choice of any other reference books

Find the answers to these questions: Do both of the books you looked into list Victor Hugo? Which tells the most about him? Which tells the least? Which entry is the most interesting to you?

Hearts and Hands

O. HENRY

Have you ever walked down a street in a strange town and met someone you once knew? How do you explain what has happened to yourself in the meantime? Read the story to see how these two handled this.

At Denver there was an influx of passengers into the coaches on the eastbound express. In one coach there sat a very pretty young woman dressed in elegant taste and surrounded by all the luxurious comforts of an experienced traveler. Among the newcomers were two young men, one of handsome presence with a bold, frank countenance and manner; the other a ruffled, glum-faced person, heavily built and roughly dressed. The two were handcuffed together.

As they passed down the aisle of the coach, the only vacant seat offered was a reversed one facing the attractive young woman. Here, the linked couple seated themselves. The young woman's glance fell upon them with a distant, swift disinterest; then with a lovely smile brightening her face and a tender pink tingeing her rounded cheeks, she held out a little gray-gloved hand. When she spoke, her voice, full, sweet, and deliberate, proclaimed that its owner was accustomed to speak and be heard.

"Well, Mr. Easton, if you will make me speak first, I suppose I must. Don't you ever recognize old friends when you meet them in the West?"

The younger man roused himself sharply at the sound of her voice. He seemed to struggle with a slight embarrassment which he threw off instantly, and then clasped her fingers with his left hand.

"It's Miss Fairchild," he said, with a smile. "I'll ask you to excuse the other hand; it's otherwise engaged just at present."

He slightly raised his right hand, bound at the wrist by the shining "bracelet" to the left one of his companion. The glad look in the girl's eyes slowly changed to a bewildered horror. The glow faded from her cheeks. Her lips parted in a vague, relaxing distress. Easton, with a little laugh as if amused, was about to speak again when the other forestalled him. The glum-faced man had been watching the girl's expression with veiled glances from his keen, shrewd eyes.

"You'll excuse me for speaking, miss, but I see you're acquainted with the marshal here. If you'll ask him to speak a word for me when we get to the pen, he'll do it, and it'll make things easier for me there. He's taking me to Leavenworth prison. It's seven years they give for counterfeiting."

"Oh!" said the girl, with a deep breath and returning color. "So that is what you are doing out here? A marshal!"

"My dear Miss Fairchild," said Easton, calmly, "I had to do something. Money has a way of taking wings unto itself, and you know it takes money to keep step with our crowd in Washington. I saw this opening in the West, and—well, a marshalship isn't quite as high a position as that of ambassador, but—"

"The ambassador," said the girl, warmly, "doesn't call any more. He needn't ever have done so. You ought to know that. And so now you are one of these dashing Western heroes, and you ride and shoot and go into all kinds of dangers. That's different from the Washington life. You have been missed."

The girl's eyes, fascinated, went back, widening a little, to rest upon the glittering handcuffs.

"Don't you worry about them, miss," said the other man. "All marshals handcuff themselves to their prisoners to keep them from getting away. Mr. Easton knows his business."

"Will we see you again soon in Washington?" asked the girl.

"Not soon, I think," said Easton. "My butterfly days are over, I fear."

"I love the West," said the girl, irrelevantly. Her eyes were shining softly. She looked away out the car window. She began to speak truly and simply, without the gloss of style and manner: "Mamma and I spent the summer in Denver. She went home a week ago because Father was slightly ill. I could live and be happy in the West. I think the air here agrees with me. Money isn't everything. But people always misunderstand things and remain stupid—"

"Say, Mr. Marshal," growled the glum-faced man. "This isn't quite fair. I'm needin' a drink, and haven't had a smoke all day. Haven't you talked long enough? Take me in the smoker now, won't you? I'm half dead for a pipe."

The bound travelers rose to their feet, Easton with the same slow smile on his face.

"I can't deny a petition for tobacco," he said, lightly. "It's the one friend of the unfortunate. Good-bye, Miss Fairchild. Duty calls, you know." He held out his hand for a farewell.

"It's too bad you are not going East," she said, reclothing herself with manner and style. "But you must go on to Leavenworth, I suppose?"

"Yes," said Easton, "I must go on to Leavenworth."

The two men sidled down the aisle into the smoker.

The two passengers in a seat nearby had heard most of the conversation. Said one of them: "That marshal's a good sort of chap. Some of these Western fellows are all right."

"Pretty young to hold an office like that, isn't he?" asked the other.

"Young!" exclaimed the first speaker, "why—Oh! didn't you catch on? Say—did you ever know an officer to handcuff a prisoner to his right hand?"

Developing Comprehension Skills

1. Which man was the prisoner and which the marshal? How do you know? When, in reading the story, did you know?

2. Where, when, and how well had Miss Fairchild and Mr. Easton known each other before this meeting? Give statements from the story to support your answer.

3. Why does Miss Fairchild say, "I could live and be happy in the West"? What is she trying to tell Easton?

4. What does the author mean when he says Miss Fairchild "reclothed herself with manner and style"? When had she removed manner and style and for what reason?

5. Do you think the marshal showed good manners and sensitivity by doing what he did? Which person did he help more, Miss Fairchild or Easton? Do you think he showed the proper regard for his office?

Reading Literature: Short Stories

1. **Identifying Time Order.** List these events in the proper time order. Number them from one to five.

   Miss Fairchild and Mr. Easton meet and speak on the train.
   Mr. Easton is arrested and convicted for counterfeiting.
   Miss Fairchild and Mr. Easton part forever.
   Mr. Easton goes West to seek his fortune.
   The marshal pretends to be the prisoner.

   At which of these events does this story begin?

2. **Understanding the Introduction.** In a short story, the reader should be made to feel at home in the story as soon as possible. In the first paragraph of this story, what do you learn about these topics:

   a. who the characters are
   b. what kind of person each character is
   c. where the action will take place

3. **Understanding Cause and Effect.** The marshal acts quickly when he decides to pretend he is the prisoner. What occurrence on the train caused him to make this decision? What are some of the effects of the decision?

4. **Recognizing Irony.** This story uses a special form of irony. Dramatic irony occurs when the truth is known to everyone in the story except the principal character. The facts of this story are known to everyone except Miss Fairchild. She must talk and act on the wrong assumption until the end. She takes at face value everything that is said by Easton or the sheriff. What is the second meaning that can be understood in the following quotations from their conversations?

   a. Easton: "I found this opening in the West."

   b. Easton: "It takes money to keep step with our crowd in Washington."

   c. Marshal: "Mr. Easton knows his business."

   d. Easton: "My butterfly days are over, I fear."

   e. Miss Fairchild: "But people always misunderstand things and remain stupid—"

   f. Marshal: "This isn't quite fair."

   g. Easton: "I must go on to Leavenworth."

Developing Vocabulary Skills

1. **Using Parts of Speech To Determine Meanings.** Many words in the English language can be used as more than one part of speech. For example, the word *design* is used as a noun in the first sentence below and as a verb in the second.

> That wallpaper has a bold design.
> Ms. Forbes will design a new building.

Several words in "Hearts and Hands" may be used as more than one part of speech. Find the words *express, coach, taste,* and *comforts* in the first paragraph of the story. Decide from the context of the sentence how each word is used. Then read the dictionary entry below for each word. On your paper, write the part of speech of the word in that sentence. Then write the dictionary definition that best fits the context of the sentence.

   a. **express** *v*. **1.** put into words. **2.** show by look, voice, or action. **3.** to press or squeeze out. *-adj.* **4.** clear and definite. **5.** especially direct or fast. *-n.* **6.** a train or bus that carries passengers, packages, money. **7.** a quick means of sending, *by express.*

b. **coach** *n.* **1.** a large old-fashioned, horse-drawn carriage. **2.** a passenger car of a railroad train. **3.** a class of airline travel. **4.** a person who trains or teaches athletes. **5.** a private tutor. -*v.* **6.** to give instruction or advice. **7.** to study with or be instructed by a coach.

c. **taste** *v.* **1.** to try or test the flavor of something. **2.** to eat or drink a little bit of. **3.** to experience; have: *to taste freedom.* **4.** to have a particular flavor; *this tastes of garlic.* -*n.* **5.** sensation, flavor, or quality of something: *the taste of lemons.* **6.** a liking for something: *taste for art.* **7.** the sense of what is fitting or beautiful.

d. **comfort** *v.* to soothe or console; cheer; *comfort him in his loss.* **2.** to make physically comfortable. -*n.* **3.** a person or thing that gives consolation: *The child was a great comfort to her.* **4.** a cause of satisfaction: *It was a comfort to see him.* **5.** freedom from hardships: *He enjoys his comforts.*

2. **Recognizing the Meaning of Slang Words.** Many slang words are used about and by criminals. Identify the meaning of each word listed below. Tell whether you used context clues, the dictionary, or both to find the meaning.

   a. bracelet   (page 158, column 2, paragraph 5)
   b. pen   (page 159, column 1, paragraph 2)

3. **Recognizing the Meaning of Colloquialisms.** A phrase used mostly in everyday conversation is called a **colloquialism**. Find these colloquialisms in the story. Use context clues to determine their meanings. On your paper, tell what each phrase means.

   a. to keep step   (page 159, column 2, paragraph 2)
   b. I'm half dead   (page 160, column 2, paragraph 1)
   c. speak a word for me   (page 159, column 1, paragraph 2)

Developing Writing Skills

1. **Comparing Characters.** In both "The Bishop's Candlesticks" and "Hearts and Hands," one of the major characters is a lawbreaker. Jean Valjean and Mr. Easton are very different characters, however. Write a paragraph or more comparing Valjean and Easton. How do you feel toward each of them?

2. **Changing the Outcome of a Story.** Imagine that the marshal in "Hearts and Hands" had not pretended to be the prisoner. Then write a short story of what might have happened in this encounter on the train. Before you write, consider these questions:

a. What elements in the O. Henry story will be missing in yours?

b. How will the characters change in different circumstances? For instance, does Miss Fairchild get angry, or does Mr. Easton show remorse?

Developing Skills in Critical Thinking

Making Inferences. Now that you know the story of "Hearts and Hands," reread it for clues that might have told you the truth, that Mr. Easton was the prisoner and the burly man was the marshal. Identify at least two clues.

The Bet

ANTON CHEKHOV

Think of how you have changed in the last five years. Then imagine spending three times as long, alone. What might those years do to you? In this story, does the lawyer expect what happens to him?

It was a dark autumn night. The old banker was pacing from corner to corner in his room, recalling to his mind the party he had given in the autumn fifteen years before.

There had been many clever people at that party. There was much good talk. They talked, among other things, of capital punishment. The guests for the most part disapproved of it. They found it old-fashioned and evil as a form of punishment. They thought it had no place in a country that called itself civilized. Some of them thought that capital punishment should be replaced right away with life in prison.

"I don't agree with you," said the host. "In my opinion, capital punishment is really kinder than life in prison. Execution kills instantly; prison kills by degrees. Now, which is better? To kill you in a few seconds, or to draw the life out of you for years and years?"

"One's as bad as the other," said one of the guests. "Their purpose is the same, to take away life. The government is not God. It has no right to take a human life. It should not take away what it cannot give back."

Among the company was a young lawyer, a man about twenty-five. "Both are evil," he stated, "but if offered the chance between them, I would definitely take prison. It's better to live somehow than not to live at all."

"Nonsense!"

"It is so!"

"No!"

"Yes!"

The banker, who was then younger and more nervous, suddenly lost his temper. He banged his fist on the table. Turning to the young lawyer, he cried out:

"It's a lie! I bet you two million you couldn't stay in a prison cell, even for five years."

"Do you mean that?" asked the young lawyer.

The banker nodded eagerly, his face an angry red.

"Then I accept your bet," the lawyer said simply. "But I'll stay not five years but fifteen."

"Fifteen! Fifteen!" cried the banker. He was now wild, as though he had already won the bet. "Done, then. The people here are our witnesses. I stake two million rubles. You stake fifteen years of your freedom."

So this foolish, senseless bet came to pass. At the time, the banker had too many millions to count. He was beside himself with joy. All through dinner he kept talking about the bet. He said to the lawyer jokingly, "Come to your senses, young man. It's not too late yet. Two million is nothing to me, but you stand to lose three or four of the best years of your life. I say three or four, not fifteen. You'll never stick it out longer than that, I can tell you. And they'll just be wasted years. Not the smallest coin do I give you if you leave earlier than fifteen years. Why, just think of it! My jail will have no bars, no locks. You'll be able to walk out of it any time you want to. That thought will be like poison to you. So you will walk out, I know that. Sooner or later, you will!"

Now the banker, pacing from corner to corner, recalled all this and asked himself, "Why did I make this bet? What's the good? The lawyer loses fifteen years of his life, and I throw away two million. That bet was a mistake. On my part, it was the foolishness of a well fed man. On the lawyer's part, it was pure greed for gold."

He remembered, further, what happened after the evening party. It was decided that the lawyer's "prison" would be in the garden wing of the banker's house. For fifteen years the lawyer was not to go through its door. He was not to see living people or to hear a human voice. He was not to receive letters or newspapers. Musical instruments, however, were to be permitted. He could also read books and write letters. Some other things, he could order. He had only to pass his order note through a special window. A guard would bring anything allowed.

Thus, the smallest details of the bet were discussed and settled. At twelve noon on November 14, 1870, the prison term began. It was to last until twelve noon on November 14, 1885. The lawyer must make no attempt to break the rules agreed upon. Any attempt to escape, even for two minutes, would free the banker from having to pay the two million.

The lawyer's first year, as far as it was possible to judge from his short notes, was one of suffering. He grew lonely and bored. From his wing, day and night, came the sound of the piano. Short, easy novels were his only reading—love stories, crime, and comedy.

In the second year, the piano was heard no more. The lawyer asked only for classics. By the fifth year, music was heard again. Guards who peeked into his room said that he yawned often and talked angrily to himself. Books he did not read

Later on, after the tenth year, the lawyer sat before his table and read only the New Testament. Then he went on to the history of religions.

During the last two years, the prisoner read a huge amount, quite haphazardly. He would ask for books on science. Then it would be Shakespeare. Notes used to come from him, asking at the same time for books on chemistry, religion, and medicine, as well as for a novel. He read as though he were swimming in a sea among broken pieces of wreckage. In his desire to save his life, he was eagerly grasping at one thing after another.

The banker recalled all this and thought, "Tomorrow at noon he receives his freedom. Under the agreement, I shall have to pay him two million. But if I pay, it's all over with me. I shall be ruined forever."

Fifteen years before, he had had too much money to count. Now, he did not know which he had more of, money or debts. He had gambled on the stock market—and lost. He had made business deals that turned sour. The fearless, proud man of business had become an ordinary person, trembling with worry about money.

"That cursed bet!" murmured the old man. "Why didn't the lawyer die? He's only forty years old. He will take all my money. He will marry and enjoy life. To him, I will look like an envious beggar, and he will say, 'Look, let me help you.

now. Sometimes at night, he would sit down to write. He would write for a long time and then tear it all up in the morning. More than once, he was heard to weep.

In the second half of the sixth year, the prisoner began zealously to study languages, philosophy, and history. He fell on these subjects with hunger. The banker hardly had time to get books enough for him. In four years' time, about 600 volumes were brought at his request.

After all, I owe my happiness to your money.' Oh, such shame!

"Ruin and shame," the banker went on. "No—it's too much. Too much for anyone. I must escape ruin and shame, even if he has to die—even if he has to die!"

The clock struck three. The banker stood, listening. In the house everyone was asleep, and he could hear only the frozen trees whining outside the windows. He put on his overcoat and went out of the house. The garden was dark and cold. It was raining. A damp wind argued with the noisy trees. Nearing the garden wing, he called the guard twice. There was no answer. "Good," the banker thought. Evidently the guard had taken shelter from the bad weather. The man was probably sleeping in the kitchen or greenhouse.

"If I have the courage to kill this man," thought the old banker, "the guard will get the blame."

In the darkness he groped for the door. It opened without a sound. In the prisoner's room, a candle was burning dimly. The prisoner sat by the table. Only his back, the hair on his head, and his hands were visible. Open books lay everywhere—on the table, on the two chairs, on the carpet.

Five minutes passed, and the prisoner never once stirred. "Probably asleep," thought the old banker. He stepped forward. Before him, at the table, sat a man

unlike an ordinary human being. It was a skeleton, with tight skin, long curly hair like a woman's, and a shaggy beard. The face was yellow. The cheeks were sunken. The hands were so long and skinny that they were painful to look upon. His hair was already silvering with gray, and no one who looked at the thin, aging face would have believed that he was only forty years old. On the table before his bent head, lay a sheet of paper covered with tiny handwriting.

"Poor devil," thought the banker. "He's asleep and probably seeing millions in his dreams. I only have to throw this half-dead thing on the bed. Then I'll smother him in a moment with the pillow. But first, let's read what he has written."

His eyes dropped to the paper:

Tomorrow, at noon, I am to have my freedom. I shall have the right to mix with people. But before I leave this room, I want to say a few words to you. My conscience is clear, and I stand before God, who sees me. I declare to you that I despise all that your books call the blessings of the world.

For fifteen years I have studied earthly life. In your books I hunted deer and sang songs. In your books I climbed Mt. Blanc. I saw from there how the sun rose in the morning. In your books I worked miracles, burned cities to the ground, preached new religions, conquered whole countries—

Your books gave me wisdom. I know that I am cleverer than you all. You are mad and gone the wrong way. You worship things, not ideas. You take falsehood for truth and ugliness for beauty. So do I marvel at you, you have traded heaven for earth. I do not want to understand you.

To show that I despise all that you live by, I give up the two million I once so desired. Can your money buy wisdom? No. I shall come out of here five minutes before noon tomorrow. I shall thus break our agreement.

When he had read this, the banker kissed the head of the strange man. He began to weep. He went out of the wing. Never, not even after his terrible losses in the stock market, had he felt such hatred for himself. Back in his own room, he lay down on the bed. Tears of guilt kept him a long time from sleeping.

The banker slept late the next morning. About noon the poor guard came running to him. The prisoner had escaped! He had walked out into the garden! He had gone to the gate and disappeared!

The banker instantly went with his servants to the wing. Yes, the prisoner was gone. To avoid rumors, he picked up the note on the table. He made two neat folds. And on his return, he locked it in his safe.

Developing Comprehension Skills

1. What is being discussed at the party? What are the young lawyer's thoughts on this topic? What are the banker's thoughts on the topic?

2. Rearrange the events listed below in terms of time order. Identify which happened first, second, and so on.
   a. The banker reads the letter written by the lawyer.
   b. The banker and lawyer make the bet at the party.
   c. The banker decides to kill the lawyer.
   d. The banker is pacing from corner to corner in his room, worried about the consequences of his bet.
   e. The guard finds the prisoner has escaped.
   f. The prisoner reads books on many different subjects.
   g. The banker places the letter in the safe.
   h. The banker loses his temper and challenges anyone to a bet.

3. According to the letter found on the lawyer's desk, why was he going to break the bet? What does this suggest about the reason he took the bet in the first place?

4. Because the lawyer left the room before the noon deadline, the banker won the bet. Remembering that the original argument was about capital punishment as opposed to life imprisonment, who do you think won the argument?

5. Did the lawyer walk out before the deadline for the reason the banker said he would?

Reading Literature: Short Stories

1. **Understanding Cause and Effect.** As you know, a **cause** is a reason why something happens. An **effect** is what happens as a result of the cause. Read each passage below and identify at least one cause and one effect discussed in each.

   a. "Why did I make this bet? What's the good? The lawyer loses fifteen years of his life, and I throw away two million. That bet was a mistake. On my part, it was the foolishness of a well fed man. On the lawyer's part, it was pure greed for gold."

b. "Tomorrow at noon he receives his freedom. Under the agreement, I shall have to pay him two million. But if I pay, it's all over with me. I shall be ruined forever."

2. **Recognizing Character Development.** The banker changes from a confident, arrogant man, to an insecure, troubled person. Scattered through the story are passages that show him as he was at the time of the party and as he was fifteen years later. These passages show how he has changed. Here is an example:

Young Banker	Old Banker
At the time, the banker had too many millions to count. (page 167, column 2, pp. 5)	"He will take all my money. He will marry and enjoy life. To him I will look like an envious beggar." (page 167, column 2, pp. 4)

Can you find at least two more descriptions of the young banker and two more of the old banker? Then find at least three descriptions of the lawyer at the beginning of the bet and three of him at the end of the bet.

3. **Understanding Conflict.** Both external and internal conflicts are presented in this story. The external conflict involves the disagreement between the lawyer and the banker. What is the internal conflict the lawyer has to cope with during the fifteen years? What is the internal conflict the banker has to cope with on the night before the fifteen years ends?

4. **Making a Plot Diagram.** Review the events listed in Developing Comprehension Skills, 2, above. Choose the most important of these events, and add others as needed to fill in the plot diagram below.

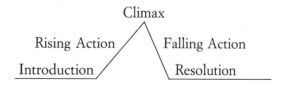

Climax

Rising Action   Falling Action

Introduction   Resolution

5. **Identifying Mood.** How would you describe the mood of this story—the feelings you get as you read it? Reread the first paragraph. Can you point out words that set that mood?

Building Vocabulary Skills

Completing Analogies. In an analogy there are two pairs of related words. Each pair is related in the same way. Here are two examples:

a. <u>Lion</u> is to <u>cat</u> as <u>wolf</u> is to <u>dog</u>.

b. <u>Tall</u> is to <u>short</u> as <u>pretty</u> is to <u>ugly</u>.

In the first example, the relationship between *lion* and *cat* is that the lion is a wild animal and the cat is a tame animal in the same family. In the same way, the *wolf* and *dog* are wild and tame members of the same family.

In the second example, the words in each pair are opposites.

In an analogy question, you are given the first pair of words and must complete the second pair. To work the question, you must first figure out the relationship between the first two words. Then you must find the missing word that will form the same relationship with the third word given. Here is an example:

<u>Really</u> is to <u>actually</u> as <u>seemingly</u> is to _____.

usually   apparently   carefully   terribly

The first two words are synonyms. Therefore, the missing word must be a synonym for *seemingly*. If you remember the meaning of *seemingly,* you will choose the answer *apparently.*

The following analogies use words you have read in the stories in Chapters 1, 2, and the first part of Chapter 4. Choose the word that will complete each analogy. If necessary, refer to the glossary of this book or to a dictionary for help.

1. <u>Principal</u> is to <u>teachers</u> as <u>abbot</u> is to _____.
   knights   robbers   monks   councilors

2. <u>Joy</u> is to <u>sadness</u> as <u>order</u> is to _____.
   chaos   cloister   contempt

3. <u>Teach</u> is to <u>school</u> as <u>preach</u> is to _____.
   house   court   market   cathedral

4. <u>Car</u> is to <u>road</u> as _____ is to <u>water</u>.
   train   barge   horse   eagle

5. <u>Raise</u> is to <u>lower</u> as <u>welcome</u> is to _____.
   rouse   pace   shudder   banish

6. Room is to chamber as castle is to _____.
   cliff   fortress   passport   disposition

7. Pillow is to pillowcase as person is to _____.
   hassle   garments   jousts   grove

8. Up is to down as peak is to _____.
   abyss   apothecary   blubber   feat

Developing Writing Skills

1. **Examining Literary Techniques.** This story uses the technique of a **flashback**, a passage that tells what happened at a time before the story began. Without the flashback, the story would have begun at the party and moved forward, year by year, to the night before the bet was to end.

   Write one, two, or three paragraphs discussing the use of the flashback in "The Bet." How does it affect the introduction? How does it keep the story short? How does it focus attention on the conflict between the two men?

2. **Writing a Diary.** "The Bet" gives a short description of the activities of the lawyer during his fifteen-year confinement. There is a slow change in his behavior and reading habits. Find the part in the story that describes this and reread it carefully.

   Write a diary that tells about the changes in the lawyer. Write the diary from the first-person point of view. Imagine that you are the lawyer, speaking to no one but yourself for fifteen years. Use the following time divisions to indicate the changes in your thinking and personality. For each time division, write one or two paragraphs.

   a. first year   c. fifth year   e. last two years
   b. second year   d. tenth year

Developing Skills in Critical Thinking

Understanding Analogies. Refer to Building Vocabulary Skills, above. Explain the reason for each of your choices.

The Story of Keesh

JACK LONDON

In the Arctic only strong people or those with strong friends and family can survive. Usually, a thirteen-year-old is not considered to be a strong person. Find out how young Keesh proves his strength.

The winter darkness, when the north gales make their long sweep across the ice pack and the air is filled with flying white and no man may venture forth, is the chosen time for the telling of how Keesh, from the poorest igloo in the village, rose to power.

Keesh lived long ago on the rim of the polar sea. He was a bright boy, healthy and strong, who had seen thirteen years. His father had been a very brave man who had met his death in a time of famine, when he sought to save the lives of his people by taking that of a great polar bear. In his eagerness, he had come to close grapples with the bear, and his bones had been crushed. But the bear had had much meat on him, so the people were saved.

Keesh was his only son and lived alone with his mother. But people are forgetful, and the deed of his father was forgotten. Keesh being but a boy, and his mother only a woman, they, too, were swiftly for-gotten. Soon they were reduced to living in the meanest of all the igloos.

At a council one night in the big igloo of Klosh-Kwan, who was chief, Keesh showed the blood that ran in his veins and the manhood that stiffened his back. With the dignity of an elder, he rose to his feet and waited for silence amid the babble of voices.

"It is true that meat is apportioned me and mine," he said. "But it is ofttimes old and tough, this meat, and, moreover, it has an unusual quantity of bones."

The hunters, both the grizzled and gray and the lusty and young, were aghast—a child that talked like a grown man and said harsh things to their very faces!

Steadily and with seriousness, Keesh went on. "Because I know my father, Bok, was a great hunter, I speak these words. It is said that Bok brought home more meat than any of the best hunters, that with his own hands he attended to the division of it, that with his own eyes he saw to it that the least old woman and the last old man received fair share."

"Na! Na!" the men cried. "Put the child out!" "Send him off to bed!"

He waited calmly till the uproar died down.

"My mother has no one save me; wherefore I speak. As I say, though Bok be dead because he hunted overkeenly, it is just that I, who am his son, and that Ikeega, who is my mother and was his wife, should have meat in plenty so long as there is meat in plenty in the tribe. I, Keesh, the son of Bok, have spoken."

He sat down.

"That a boy should speak in council!" old Ugh-Gluk was mumbling.

"Shall the babes in arms tell us men the things we shall do?" Massuk demanded in a loud voice. "Am I a man that I should be made a mock by every child that cries for meat?"

Their anger boiled to white heat. They ordered him to bed, threatened that he should have no meat at all, and promised him sore beatings. Keesh's eyes began to flash and his blood to pound darkly under his skin. In the midst of the abuse, he sprang to his feet.

"Hear me, ye men!" he cried. "Take this now for my last word. Bok, my father, was a great hunter. I, too, his son, shall go and hunt the meat that I eat. And be it known now, that the division of that which I kill shall be fair. And no widow nor weak one shall cry in the night be-cause there is no meat, when the strong men are groaning in great pain because they have eaten overmuch. And in the days to come there shall be shame upon the strong men who have eaten over-much. I, Keesh, have said it!"

Jeers and scornful laughter followed him out of the igloo, but his jaw was set and he went his way, looking neither to right nor to left.

The next day he went forth along the shore line where the ice and the land met together. Those who saw him go noted that he carried his bow, with a goodly supply of bone-barbed arrows, and that across his shoulders was his father's big hunting spear. And there was laughter, and much talk, at the event. It was an unprecedented occurrence. Never did boys of his tender age go forth to hunt, much less to hunt alone. Also, there were shaking of heads and prophetic mutter-ings. The other women looked pityingly at Ikeega, and her face was grave and sad.

"He will be back ere long," they said cheeringly.

"Let him go; it will teach him a lesson," the hunters said. "He will come back shortly, and he will be meek and soft of speech in the days to follow."

But a day passed, and a second, and on the third a wild gale blew, and there was no Keesh. Ikeega tore her hair and put soot of the seal oil on her face in token of her grief; and the women assailed the men with bitter words in that they had mis-

Polar Bear and Cub in Ice, 1959, NIVIAKSIAK.
Reproduced by permission of the West Baffin Eskimo Cooperative, Cape Dorset, N.W.T. Canada.

treated the boy and sent him to his death; and the men made no answer, preparing to go in search of the body when the storm abated.

Early the next morning, however, Keesh strode into the village. He came not shamefacedly. Across his shoulders he bore a burden of fresh-killed meat. There was importance in his step and arrogance in his speech.

"Go, ye men, with the dogs and sledges, and take my trail for the better part of a day's travel," he said. "There is much meat on the ice—a she-bear and two half-grown cubs."

Ikeega was overcome with joy, but he received her demonstrations in manlike fashion, saying, "Come, Ikeega, let us eat. And after that I shall sleep, for I am weary."

He passed into their igloo and ate profoundly, and, after that, he slept for twenty running hours.

There was much doubt at first, much doubt and discussion. The killing of a polar bear is very dangerous, but thrice dangerous is it, and three times thrice, to kill a mother bear with her cubs. The men could not bring themselves to believe that the boy Keesh, single-handed, had accomplished so great a marvel.

But the women spoke of the fresh-killed meat he had brought on his back, and this was an overwhelming argument against the men's unbelief. Finally, the men departed, grumbling greatly that in all probability, if the thing were so, he had neglected to cut up the carcasses.

Now, in the north it is very necessary that this should be done as soon as the kill is made. If not, the meat freezes so solidly as to turn the edge of the sharpest knife, and a three-hundred-pound bear, frozen stiff, is no easy thing to put upon a sled and haul over the rough ice. However, arriving at the spot, they found not only the kill, which they had doubted, but that Keesh had quartered the beasts in true hunter fashion and removed the entrails.

Thus began the mystery of Keesh, a mystery that deepened and deepened with the passing of the days. His very next trip he killed a young bear, nearly full grown, and, on the trip following, a large male bear and his mate. He was ordinarily gone from three to four days, though it was nothing unusual for him to stay away a week at a time on the ice field. Always he declined company on these expeditions, and the people marveled.

"How does he do it?" they demanded of one another. "Never does he take a dog with him, and dogs are of such great help."

"Why dost thou hunt only bear?" Klosh-Kwan once ventured to ask him.

Keesh made fitting answer. "It is well known that there is more meat on the bear," he said.

However, there was also talk of witchcraft in the village. "He hunts with evil spirits," some of the people contended, "wherefore his hunting is rewarded. How else can it be, save that he hunts with evil spirits?"

"Mayhap they be not evil, but good, these spirits," others said. "It is known that his father was a mighty hunter. May not his father hunt with him so that he may attain excellence and patience and understanding? Who knows?"

Nonetheless, his success continued, and the less skillful hunters were often kept busy hauling in his meat. In the division of it, Keesh was just. As his father had done before him, he saw to it that the least old woman and the last old man received a fair portion, keeping no more for himself than his needs required. Because of this and of his merit as a hunter, he was looked upon with respect and even awe; and there was even talk of making him chief after old Klosh-Kwan. Because of the things he had done, they looked for him to appear in the council, but he never came, and they were ashamed to ask.

"I am minded to build me an igloo," he said one day to Klosh-Kwan and a number of the hunters. "It shall be a large igloo, wherein Ikeega and I can dwell in comfort."

"Aye," they nodded gravely.

"But I have no time. My business is hunting, and it takes all my time. So it is but just that the men and women of the village, who eat my meat, should build me my igloo."

The igloo was built accordingly, on a generous scale that exceeded even the dwelling of Klosh-Kwan. Keesh and his mother moved into it, and it was the first prosperity she had enjoyed since the death of Bok. Nor was material prosperity alone hers, for, because of her wonderful son and the position he had given her, she came to be looked upon as the first woman in all the village; and the women were given to visiting her, to asking her advice, and to quoting her wisdom when arguments arose among themselves or with the men.

But it was the mystery of Keesh's marvelous hunting that took chief place in all their minds. And one day Ugh-Gluk taxed him with witchcraft to his face.

"It is charged," Ugh-Gluk said ominously, "that thou dealest with evil spirits, wherefore thy hunting is rewarded."

"Is not the meat good?" Keesh made answer. "Has one in the village yet to fall sick from the eating of it? How dost thou know that witchcraft be concerned? Or dost thou guess, in the dark, merely because of the envy that consumes thee?"

Ugh-Gluk withdrew, discomfited, the women laughing at him as he walked away. However, in the council one night after long deliberation, it was determined to put spies on Keesh's track when he went forth to hunt, so that his methods might be learned. So on his next trip Bim and Bawn, two young men, the craftiest of hunters, followed after him, taking care

not to be seen. After five days they came back, their eyes bulging and their tongues a-tremble, to tell what they had seen. The council was hastily called in Klosh-Kwan's dwelling, and Bim took up the tale.

"Brothers! As was commanded, we journeyed on the trail of Keesh, and cunningly we journeyed, so that he might not know. And midway of the first day, he picked up with a great he-bear. It was a very great bear."

"None greater," Bawn corroborated and went on himself. "Yet was the bear not inclined to fight, for he turned away and made off slowly over the ice. This we saw from the rocks of the shore, and the bear came toward us, and after him came Keesh, very much unafraid. And he shouted harsh words after the bear, and waved his arms about, and made much noise. Then did the bear grow angry, and rise up on his hind legs, and growl. But Keesh walked right up to the bear."

"Aye," Bim continued the story. "Right up to the bear Keesh walked. And the bear took after him, and Keesh ran away. But as he ran he dropped a little round ball on the ice, and the bear stopped and smelled of it, and then swallowed it up. And Keesh continued to run away and drop little round balls, and the bear continued to swallow them up."

Exclamations and cries of doubt were being made, and Ugh-Gluk expressed open unbelief.

"With our own eyes we saw it," Bim affirmed.

Bawn repeated, "Aye, with our own eyes. And this continued until the bear stood suddenly upright, and cried aloud in pain, and thrashed his forepaws madly about. And Keesh continued to make off over the ice to a safe distance. But the bear gave him no notice, being occupied with the misfortune the little round balls had wrought within him."

"Aye, within him," Bim interrupted. "For he did claw at himself, and leap about over the ice like a playful puppy— save from the way he growled and squealed it was plain it was not play but pain. Never did I see such a sight!"

"Nay, never was such a sight seen," Bawn took up the strain. "Furthermore, it was such a large bear."

"Witchcraft," Ugh-Gluk suggested.

"I know not," Bawn replied. "I tell only of what my eyes beheld. And after a while the bear grew weak and tired, for he was very heavy and he had jumped about with exceeding violence, and he went off along the shore ice, shaking his head slowly from side to side and sitting down ever and again to squeal and cry. And Keesh followed after the bear, and we followed after Keesh, and for that day and three days more we followed. The bear grew weak and never ceased crying from his pain."

"It was a charm!" Ugh-Gluk exclaimed. "Surely it was a charm!"

"It may well be."

Bim relieved Bawn. "The bear wandered, now this way and now that, doubling back and forth and crossing his trail in circles, so that at the end he was near where Keesh had first come upon him. By this time the bear was quite sick and could crawl no farther, so Keesh came up close and speared him to death."

"And what then?" Kosh-Kwan demanded.

"Then we left Keesh skinning the bear and came running that the news of the killing might be told."

In the afternoon of that day, the women hauled in the meat of the bear while the men sat in council assembled. When Keesh arrived, a messenger was sent to him, bidding him come to the council.

Keesh sent reply, saying that he was hungry and tired; also that his igloo was large and comfortable and could hold many men.

Curiosity was so strong on the men that the whole council, Klosh-Kwan to the fore, rose up and went to the igloo of Keesh. He was eating, but he received them with respect and seated them according to their rank. Ikeega was proud and embarrassed by turns, but Keesh was quite composed.

Klosh-Kwan recited the information brought by Bim and Bawn, and at its close he said in a stern voice: "So explanation is wanted, O Keesh, of thy manner of hunting. Is there witchcraft in it?"

Keesh looked up and smiled. "Nay, O Klosh-Kwan. It is not for a boy to know aught of witches, and of witches I know nothing. I have but devised a means whereby I may kill the ice bear with ease, that is all. It be headcraft, not witchcraft."

"And may any man?"

"Any man."

There was a long silence. The men looked in one another's faces, and Keesh went on eating.

"And—and—and wilt thou tell us, O Keesh?" Klosh-Kwan finally asked in a tremulous voice.

"Yea, I will tell thee." Keesh finished sucking a marrowbone and rose to his feet. "It is quite simple. Behold!"

He picked up a thin strip of whalebone and showed it to them. The ends were sharp as needle points. The strip he coiled carefully, till it disappeared in his hand. Then, as he suddenly released it, it sprang straight again. He picked up a piece of blubber.

"So," he said, "one takes a small chunk of blubber, thus, and thus makes it hollow. Then into the hollow goes the whale bone, so, tightly coiled, and another piece of blubber is fitted over the whalebone. After that it is put outside where it freezes into a little round ball. The bear swallows the little round ball, the blubber melts, the whalebone with its sharp ends stands out straight, the bear gets sick, and, when the bear is very sick, why, you kill him with a spear. It is quite simple."

Ugh-Gluk said, "Oh!" and Klosh-Kwan said, "Ah!" and each said something after his own manner, and all understood.

This is the story of Keesh, who lived long ago on the rim of the polar sea. Because he exercised headcraft and not witchcraft, he rose from the meanest igloo to be head man of his village, and, through all the years that he lived, it is related, his tribe was prosperous. Neither widow nor weak one cried aloud in the night because there was no meat.

Eskimo Ivory Bag Fastener. Department of Anthropology, Smithsonian Institution, Washington, D.C.

Developing Comprehension Skills

1. Why did Keesh complain to the council?

2. Why did Keesh's talk to the council make its members so angry?

3. When Keesh hunted, he followed a definite method. Tell, in order, the steps he used to kill a bear.

4. What did Keesh mean when he said that he exercised headcraft, not witchcraft?

5. Keesh is a very mature thirteen-year-old boy. Do you think that he is a realistic character? Considering what you know of teenagers, do you believe a thirteen-year-old could do what he did? Explain your answer.

Reading Literature: Short Stories

1. **Appreciating the Setting.** This story could be set only above the Arctic Circle in the lands of the Eskimos. It tells about the people in one Alaskan village and shows some of the customs of these people. What are some of the customs or activities that are different from your own? Would you have as much difficulty persuading your town council that a particular need of yours should be met?

2. **Recognizing Point of View.** Who is the narrator of this story? Is it one of the characters in the story or someone outside the story who knew and told everything that happened? Or is it someone outside the story who knew and told something, but not everything, about what was going on? We call these points of view the first-person, the third-person omniscient, and the third-person limited. Which did you choose? Select several passages from the story to support your answer.

3. **Outlining the Plot.** In the order of their happening, list the events in this story. List only the most important events, because a great many things happen in this story. Then tell which event is the climax of the story. You can identify the climax because everything that happens after it explains how the characters in the story react to their new knowledge.

4. **Recognizing Special Uses of Language.** In "The Story of Keesh," the author was writing about a culture quite different from ours. He

wanted the reader to keep that in mind throughout the story. One way to show the difference was by having the characters speak in an unusual way. Therefore, the writer had the characters use old forms of common words, as in "He will be back ere long" instead of "he will be back before long." In addition, the characters—and even the narrator—use very formal sentence patterns and unusual word choices. For example, Keesh says, "My mother has no one save me; wherefore I speak" instead of "Since my mother has no one else to help her, I have to say something to you."

Choose five other sentences from the story that use old-fashioned forms or unusual sentence patterns and words. Restate each sentence as you would say it naturally.

Developing Vocabulary Skills

Choosing the Correct Meaning from a Dictionary Entry. Sometimes it is not easy to choose the correct definition of a word in the dictionary. The meanings of the word may be only slightly different. There may be many to choose from. Often there is a sample sentence after the definition. This sentence will help you choose the correct meaning.

Read these sentences drawn from the story. Find each underlined word in the dictionary. Choose the best meaning. Examine how the word is used in each sentence. On your paper, write the word, its part of speech, and the dictionary definition you chose.

1. With the dignity of an elder, he rose to his feet and waited in silence.

2. The men prepared to go in search of the body when the storm abated.

3. The igloo was built on a generous scale that exceeded even the dwelling of Klosh-Kwan.

4. One day Ugh-Gluk taxed him with witchcraft to his face.

5. He received the men of the council with respect and seated them according to their rank.

6. Ikeega was proud and embarrassed by turns, but Keesh was quite composed.

Developing Writing Skills

1. **Comparing Literature to Your Life.** After Keesh proved himself a worthy hunter and a fair provider of meat, he received rewards from the villagers. Can you think of ways a thirteen-year-old could achieve similar honor in our culture? Write at least a paragraph describing how a thirteen-year-old boy or girl could win recognition and respect from the community.

2. **Comparing Plots to Reality.** While reading a well written story, a reader believes that the events could really happen, even though he or she knows they did not. Afterwards, the reader often sees ways that the story does not match reality. Think about the last three stories: "Hearts and Hands," "The Bet," and "Keesh." Choose one and write a paragraph that points out hard-to-believe events in that story.

3. **Preparing for an Interview.** In an interview, one person questions another to obtain information. The questions are usually prepared in advance and should be worded so that the person interviewed gives in-depth answers.

   Imagine that you will interview Keesh after the village finds out his unique way of killing bears. Write six questions that you could ask him. The questions may be on his personal background, his hunting method, how he worked out his method, or his plans for the future.

4. **Changing Point of View.** Rewrite the story of Keesh as he might have told it to his son, many years later. Remember that the point of view will change. You will write the story as though you had lived it yourself. What character traits of Keesh would show as he tells this story to his son? Your story should be from six to twelve paragraphs long.

Developing Skills in Study and Research

Conducting a Poll. A poll is a collection of opinions on a subject. The poll can be of a selected group or a random group. A selected group would be one certain type, for example, all eighth-grade students in your school or all people over thirty years of age. A random group would be without a definite pattern, for example, people at the supermarket or people on the street.

Conduct a random poll of five people outside this class. The poll will be about voting age. Ask each person: "Are you in favor of lowering the voting age to sixteen?" The answer must be one of the following:

a. Yes, I am.
b. No, I am not.
c. Only under certain conditions.
d. I don't know.

After everyone in the class has obtained five responses, pool the results. Add all the responses in each of the four categories. Then work together to show the combined results using all of the following reporting methods:

a. raw numbers
b. percentages
c. a bar graph
d. a circle graph

Examples:
a. 100 total: 40 in favor, 40 opposed, 15 conditional, 5 undecided
b. 40% in favor, 40% opposed, 15% conditional, 5% undecided

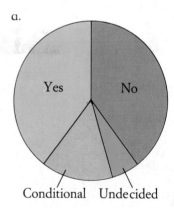

Developing Skills in Speaking and Listening

Presenting an Interview. With a partner, act out a news interview. Use the questions you wrote for the third activity in Developing Writing Skills, page 183. When one partner asks his or her prepared questions, the other partner takes the part of Keesh.

Great Modern Stories

These stories were all written in the middle of the twentieth century. In most of them, the plot covers a longer time span than it does in the classic stories you read. Also, there are more minor characters. However, like the older stories, each of these focuses attention on one particular problem faced by the characters. Each one helps us see a certain part of life more clearly.

The Great Wave Off Kanagawa, 1823–31. KATSUSHIKA HOKUSAI.
The Metropolitan Museum of Art; Bequest of Mrs. H.O. Havemeyer, 1929. The H.O. Havemeyer Collection.

More About the Elements of a Short Story

You know that the most important elements of a short story are its characters, setting, and plot. On these pages you will learn more about characters and about the element of the plot called **conflict**. You will also learn about the theme and the mood of a short story.

Characters. Characters can be either major or minor. A **major character** is a main character. The story is really about the major characters. In a short story, there is often only one major character. A **minor character** is less important to the story. His or her actions matter only if they are connected in some way to the main character. In "Hearts and Hands," for example, the young woman, the sheriff, and the prisoner are the major characters. The other two passengers are included in the story only to bring out the truth about the major characters.

Characters are either static or dynamic. **Static characters** stay the same throughout the whole story. **Dynamic characters**, on the other hand, change and grow during the story. This difference can be seen in a comparison of "Hearts and Hands" with "The Bet." In "Hearts and Hands," the reader finds out the truth about the characters; they do not change. In "The Bet," the characters also find out some truths; they do change.

Conflict. The plot of a short story describes the struggle between opposing forces, called the **conflict**. Every story needs conflict. There are two kinds.

External conflict is a struggle between a character and another character or the forces of nature. External conflict can even include the character's battle with supernatural forces. Examples of external conflict include the struggles of the three young men with each other and with Death, in the tale "How the Three Young Men Found Death."

Internal conflict refers to the clash of different feelings and thoughts inside a character. The struggle within Jean Valjean in "The Bishop's Candlesticks" is an example.

Learning About Theme and Mood

Theme. In each piece of writing, a writer focuses on one thing he or she has learned about life. That main idea that the writer shares with the reader is called the **theme**.

To determine the theme, review the story. Decide what the writer is telling you about the characters. Then, decide how the things you learned from them can be applied to your own life. Last, state this idea so that it can be applied to everyone.

It is possible that different readers will find somewhat different themes in the same story. This is because each of us brings different experiences to the story. For example, in "The Story of Keesh," a reader might find any of these themes:

Age doesn't necessarily make a person wise.
In order to survive, a person must use his or her wits.
Determination and bravery will bring success.

Mood. The **mood** of a piece of writing is the feeling you get as you read it. You may feel worried, joyful, or fearful. Writers know the kind of mood they want you to feel. To create that mood, they choose their words carefully. They choose words both for their meanings and for the feelings the words give you.

Note how the beginning of this story reminds you of a fairy tale. The mood is funny in one way and scary at the same time.

There was once a little girl called Esmeralda who lived with her wicked stepmother. Her father was dead. The stepmother, who was called Mrs. Mitching, was very rich and lived in a large but hideous house in a suburb.

The Old Soldier

DOROTHY CANFIELD

The title of this story gives attention to one character. Is he the most important character? As you read, decide whether the story is mainly about the old soldier or about someone else.

No matter how I set this story down, you will take it, I fear, as a fable. But it is not. It is as literally true as a local news item in your this-morning's newspaper. It happened up the state aways from our town, "over the mountain," as we call that middle upland valley of Vermont.

For a long time, after the Revolution, the citizens of the little town of Sunmore had made a great day out of the Fourth of July. They seemed to hear, more clearly than some other towns, the very sound of the old Liberty Bell in Philadelphia as it rang out in joy over the signing of the Declaration of Independence. They had not at all forgotten what the Fourth meant. As the years went by, a set form grew up for the day's celebration. At dawn, the big boys fired off again and again the old cannon that stood on the village common. There was a meeting, about eleven in the morning, at the Town Hall, where people made speeches and sang patriotic songs. After that, a picnic lunch was eaten out on the green. If it rained, the lunch was eaten inside the Town Hall. Then, rain or shine, the procession formed to escort the old soldiers out to the Burying Ground, a mile from town, where they put flags on the graves of their comrades among the Sunmore men who, like them, had been soldiers in the Revolution.

The boys looked forward to this celebrating from one year to the next chiefly, of course, because to share in the firing of the cannon marked a long step forward in growing up. The cannon was generally said to have been in the Battle of Bennington in 1777. Ordinary people said yes, of course it was. But more careful folks said this was not sure. As the years went by after that battle, twenty, forty, fifty; and finally by the time of this story, in 1848, seventy years, fewer and fewer people could remember it. Also, of course, there were fewer and fewer old Sunmore men who had been Revolutionary soldiers.

Until they were past eighty, they had walked in the procession like everybody else. After that, Dr. White, who of course took care of them all when they were sick, said their joints were too stiff. He took them out in his own chaise, behind his slow, ancient roan horse. Dick was rather stiff in his joints too, and was glad to walk with ceremonial slowness.

Dr. White knew more about medicine than anyone else in town. This was to be expected because nobody else knew anything at all about it. But on the subject— local history—of which many people knew a great deal, he was also the local specialist. On the shelves of his library, mixed up with his medical books, stood more histories of Vermont than the rest of Sunmore people had, all put together. When anyone wanted to find out something about what had happened in the past, Dr. White was asked. He always knew the answer.

When May and June came in, people began to plan for the Fourth of July celebration. But there were no old soldiers left. For four or five years there had been only two. Both of them were very old, of course, for the year 1848 was seventy-one years after the Battle of Bennington. One had been ninety, and the other eighty-six. Now both were gone. The older one had died in the winter, and the family of the other one had moved away out west into York State and taken the old man with them.

It was too bad. Everybody was saying that the celebration wouldn't be much without an old soldier in it, to connect the town with the Revolution. Without one, how would people remember what the Fourth of July was really about? The ancients had always sat on the platform of the Town Hall, while the singing and speech-making went on, their long fire-arms across their knees, their soldier's leather belts strapped on over their Sunday coats. Of course what uniforms they had had, had gone all to pieces, if they'd ever had any, which was unlikely, buck-skin being the wear in those early days. They had ridden in Dr. White's chaise, just behind the fife and drum corps and the little girls in white dresses carrying the bouquets, ahead of the marching men and women, four abreast in the road. When the procession reached the cemetery, the little girls handed the flowers to the big boys, and they passed them out to the hobbling old soldiers, who laid them on the graves of their comrades in the Revolution. The smaller boys had the honor of planting fresh American flags on the graves, waving above the flowers.

One of the boys in town, one of the Bostwick family, heard his folks lamenting that the celebration would not seem right with no old soldiers at all. He was the third child; Andrew was his name. He was about ten years old when this happened. He went to the nearby district school and read in the fourth reader, but long before he knew his alphabet, he knew about the Battle of Bennington and the Revolutionary War.

He was just getting to be old enough to help fire off the cannon, and to hand the flowers to the old soldiers in the cemetery. And now they were all gone.

One day in June, when he was sent out to look for a cow which, the night before, hadn't come back to the barn from the mountain pasture, he met a schoolmate up there, Will Hunter. Will's mother had sent him out to pick wild strawberries on that sloping clearing. After the two boys met, the cow and the strawberries were forgotten. They sat down on a ledge to have a talk. Before long, Andrew said something about the Fourth of July celebration with no old soldier left, not a single one.

The other boy said, "There's an old fellow lives with the Hawleys, 'way up Haw-

A Beautiful World, 1948, GRANDMA MOSES. Copyright © 1982, Grandma Moses Properties Co., New York.

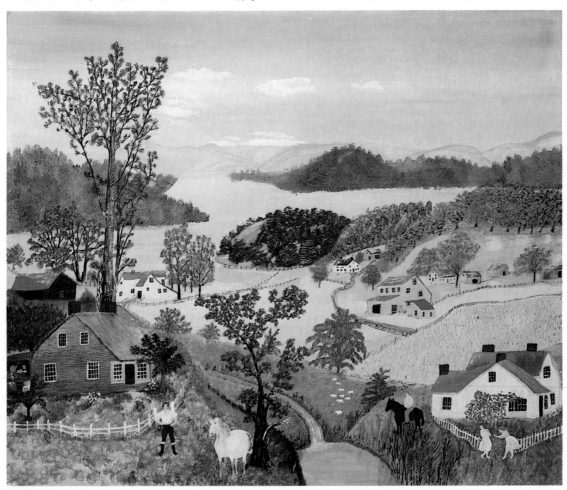

ley Hollow from our house. He's their great-grandfather, I think. Maybe he was a soldier in the Revolution. He's old enough. They say he's ninety. More."

Andrew's ten-year-old mind was already firmly lodged behind the tight narrow wall of the idea of the Town. "They don't live in Sunmore," he said. "We have to have a Sunmore old soldier for our Fourth."

"Yes, they do too, live in Sunmore," said the other boy. "They don't trade at the Summore stores, because from that end of the Hollow where their house is, it's easier to go out the far end to Canbury. But they vote in our Town Meeting.[1]"

The two boys looked at each other. Thinking no more of the missing cow and the wild strawberries, they set out for the Hollow.

So there was to be a Revolutionary soldier after all for the Fourth of July celebration! Everybody was talking about the old man, eighty-nine years, or maybe ninety, maybe more, back up on the far side of Westward Mountain, who had been remembered just in time.

When the two boys told their fathers about him, two of the Selectmen of the town had gone over the mountain to see him. They said his back was bent with rheumatism, he was almost stone deaf,

and he hobbled along with two canes to steady him. But he still had his old rifle, and even his cracked leather soldier's belt, just as the others had. And they reported that when, shouting loudly in his ear, they had asked him if he had fought in the Revolutionary War, he had nodded his head. Then they asked had it been in the Battle of Bennington? When he finally heard what they were asking, he nodded his head and told them, "Yes, yes, sir, it certainly was."

They said the Hawleys up there, for all he was so old, thought a great deal of him. It was his great-grandson's family he was with—young people they were, had been married only five or six years. When the last of his grandchildren had died, these young people had left their little cottage in Canbury and gone up to take care of him. An arrangement often made, in our country—he was to leave them his house and farm and they were to provide for his old age. They had never heard, naturally, what he had been doing seventy years ago—neither of them was over twenty-five—but they had always seen the old long gun, laid on the pegs over the fireplace, and the old belt hung with it.

On the morning of the Fourth, Andrew's father got up early, took the boys, and drove his farm wagon all the way around the mountain and up into the Hollow to bring the old man back. It was ten o'clock when they came back into Sunmore Street. A crowd was waiting in

---

1. **Town Meeting.** In New England, an annual meeting of citizens 18 years and older. They vote on issues affecting the town. The town is an area larger than a village, much like the Midwest township.

front of the Town Hall. They began to clap their hands and cheer when Mr. Boswick helped lift the bent old man out of the wagon and led him into the Hall. Andrew and Will, the Young Guard of Honor, carried his ancient gun in and put it across his knees. He had his rusty belt strapped on over his coat.

When they took his gun to carry, he gave them such a pleasant smile of thanks that they understood why his great-grandchildren thought so much of him. He was a very nice-looking old man, everybody thought, clean and neat, with quiet, gentle eyes; and although he hadn't a tooth left, his mouth still looked as though he liked jokes.

The people came into the Town Hall, took their seats, and began fanning themselves. It was a hot day, as the Fourth often is. The speaker was there, a lawyer from Canbury. The chorus of local singers stood below the platform, facing the audience. Their leader rapped his stick. They stood at attention. But they did not begin to sing. For at this point Dr. White, who always sat on the platform with the Selectmen and the speaker, called out to Andrew, "Here! Let me look at that gun! Pass it over to me."

Andrew was surprised. He put his hand on the gun and, leaning down to the old man's ear, said as loudly as he could, "Dr. White wants to see your gun."

He shouted with all his might but he could not make himself heard. The old soldier was almost stone deaf. But he was willing to do anything that was wanted. His cheerful old face was bright. He felt the friendliness that was all around him. He smiled, nodded, and passed his gun to Andrew.

The doctor took one sharp look at it and motioned to the singers in the chorus. "Wait a minute!" he told them.

Then he put on his glasses and looked very carefully at a certain place near the trigger. Everybody kept still, wondering what was in his mind.

When he looked up, his face was all astonishment. He spoke so loudly that everybody in the whole Town Hall could hear him. "This is a Hessian[2] gun! The old man must have been one of the Hessians who fought against the Americans."

There was such a silence in the Town Hall you could hear a wasp buzzing at one of the windows.

He was a Hessian! He had fought on the other side. People's mouths dropped open, they were so taken back.

The old man hadn't heard any of this because he was so deaf. He sat quietly there, between the two little boys, his gentle old eyes looking around at the people in the hall.

For a minute nobody said a word. Nobody could think of what to say. Or what to do.

2. **Hessians.** Well-trained soldiers from Hesse-Kassel, Germany, hired by the British to fight the colonists during the Revolutionary War

Then Andrew ran out to the front of the platform and began to talk very fast. "Listen," he said. "That was a hundred years ago. Well, more than seventy years, anyhow. No matter how mad you are at somebody, you don't keep it up forever. He's lived close to us all that time, and farmed it like anybody, and had his family, and paid his taxes. He's old, so old—it would be mean of us to—"

Andrew had never even spoken a piece in school. He had forgotten where he was. When he realized what he was doing, he stopped talking and hung down his head. He went back and put one hand on the old man's shoulder. The wrinkled face lifted to smile at him. Andrew smiled back. But his lips were trembling.

People began to rustle and move their feet. But when Dr. White stood up as if to say something, they became still again, to listen.

He said, "I remember now, when I first came to Sunmore to practice medicine and first began to be interested in Vermont history, I did hear some very old people talk about a young Hessian soldier who had been wounded in the Battle of Bennington, and was picked up unconscious, in the woods, the day after. One of the old history books in my Vermont collection says that he was carried to a farmhouse and taken care of there. By the time he was well enough to get around, many months afterwards, there were no more soldiers or armies around. He was only

nineteen by that time, and he had come to love the way of life he saw around him. He wanted to be an American and live here.

"That history book didn't say anything more about him. But I heard something else from old Mr. Hale." The doctor looked down into the audience at a middle-aged man in the second row. "He was your grandfather, Jim Hale. He was sort of connected, in-laws somehow, with the Bennington family that took in the Hessian boy. He told me they always liked him, the young soldier, I mean. When he learned enough English, he told them his story. He had always had it hard in the Old Country, he said. He was an orphan, very poor, seventeen years old, when a recruiting gang picked him up off the street and carried him off to the barracks in Brunswick. He never liked soldiering, he said. He never understood what the fighting was about. He never knew any English till he learned it from the Vermont family who cared for him."

The doctor still held the old rifle in his hands. He turned around now and laid it back on the old man's knees. Then he said to the audience, "I rather think Andrew Bostwick was right. Seventy years is too long to go on being mad. I think our celebration would better go on. Maybe the Reverend Hardwick might have something to say to us about this."

The minister stood up, stooped in his black clergyman's clothes. He stood silent a long time. Then he said, "May war pass and peace be with us. Amen."

He sat down. The Moderator of the Town stood up. He was a burly, powerful, middle-aged man, with a serious, responsible face. He said, soberly, "I think this is something we ought to take a vote on. Don't you think so, Mr. Hardwick?"

The minister nodded. "Yes. It is something for each one of us to decide. But before we vote, I think we ought to sit quiet for a moment. And think."

The Moderator reached for the clergyman's cane, and with it struck a gavel-like blow on the table. In his Moderator's voice, he said, "The question before this House, is whether we can live in peace when war has long gone by."

They all sat still.

The deaf ears of the old soldier had, of course, not heard any of this. It looked all right to him. He was very much bent with rheumatism. His hands lay thin and knotted on the arms of his chair. His clean old

Colonel Glover's Fishermen Leaving Marblehead for Cambridge, 1775, about 1920, J.O.J. FROST.
New York Historical Association, Cooperstown.

face was calm. In the silence, he looked from one person to another in the audience. He smiled a little. After a moment, he turned his white head to look back at his little-boy guard of honor. There they were, one on each side of his chair. He nodded and leaned back as if to say, "It's all right, if you are there."

The water came into Andrew's eyes.

The people in the rows of chairs on the floor were all looking up at the old soldier and the little boys.

A man stood up and said, "Mr. Moderator, I move that our celebration proceed."

Several voices said, "I second the motion."

Then the vote was taken. Everybody voted "aye."

That afternoon, after the usual speaking and singing had been done, and the picnic lunch eaten out on the Common, the procession formed as usual, to march out to the cemetery.

The old soldier looked very tired by this time, but still cheerful. He came out of the Town Hall on Dr. White's arm, and was helped up into the chaise. The Young Guard of Honor held their flags high, so that they stirred in the breeze. The little girls in white dresses were pushed by their mothers into line, two by two. They carried the flowers——lilies, roses, carnation pinks.

The men and women formed, four by four. The doctor slapped the reins over the old horse's back. The leader of the band lifted his hand and said, commandingly, "A–a–ll ready!"

The marchers held their flags straight, ready to go.

"Forward, march!" cried the bandmaster.

The fifes sang out, "Whee-dee-deedle-dee" in thin high voices.

In a deep roar, the drums said, "Boom! boom! boom!"

And away they all went.

Developing Comprehension Skills

1. Why did the townspeople of Sunmore need an old soldier for the Fourth of July celebration? How would the ceremonies have been different without an old soldier?

2. Of what importance was the celebration to the boys of Sunmore? Why was Andrew so interested in this year's celebration?

3. Would you have voted to continue or not to continue with the ceremony? Explain your answer.

4. Why was the idea of the soldier being Hessian such a surprise to the townsfolk? Why had they never thought of this possibility?

Reading Literature: Short Stories

1. **Appreciating the Setting.** Why is the small-town setting important for an understanding of this story? How is the date important?

2. **Understanding Metaphor.** Examine this passage from the story.

   > Andrew's ten-year-old mind was already firmly lodged behind the tight narrow wall of the idea of the Town. "They don't live in Sunmore," he said. "We have to have a Sunmore old soldier for our Fourth."

   How is "the idea of the Town" like a wall? What is it holding in? What is it keeping out?

3. **Identifying Unstated Cause and Effect.** Reread the passage in question 2, above. It states that Andrew thought of the town as a wall. Then it reports that Andrew insisted on the old soldier being from Sunmore. What is the relationship between these two facts?

4. **Understanding Character Descriptions.** Sometimes the author wants the reader to feel a certain way about a character. What feeling does the author want the reader to develop about the old soldier? Find several passages from the story that support your answer.

5. **Identifying Theme.** In the first paragraph, the author assures the reader that the story is not a fable. She insists that the story is as true as a newspaper notice. However, one way the story is like a fable is that its theme is stated as the moral of a fable often is. Find the theme as stated in Andrew's words.

6. **Identifying Conflict.** What is the external political conflict that almost started because of the Hessian soldier? How is it avoided?

Developing Vocabulary Skills

Identifying Homographs. In the dictionary you may find two or three entry words that look the same. For example, there are three words that are spelled *r-o-w*. Read these dictionary entries:

row[1] (rō), a line or rank
row[2] (rō), to move by oars
row[3] (rou), a noisy quarrel

Words like *row* are called **homographs.** They are spelled the same, but their meanings are completely different. These words often have the same pronunciation, but sometimes, as in *row,* they do not. The dictionary enters and defines each homograph separately.

The following sentences are drawn from stories you have read. Each underlined word is a homograph. Find each homograph in a dictionary. On your paper, write the definition that fits the context of the sentence.

1. The young woman had a lovely smile, and her rounded cheeks were a tender pink.
2. "The other hand is engaged at present," he told Miss Fairchild.
3. He would write for a long time and then tear it all up.
4. They were reduced to living in a mean igloo.
5. Several voices said, "I second the motion."

Developing Writing Skills

1. **Identifying the Narrator.** "The Old Soldier" is told by a specific character. The author asks you to imagine the character from the first sentence, where the narrator refers to himself or herself twice:

    No matter how I set this story down, you will take it, I fear, as a fable.

    Throughout the story, the narrator uses conversational phrases and offers personal opinions.

    What image did you develop of the narrator as you read the story? What sort of person do you think he or she is? Write a paragraph explaining what you think the narrator is like. Include references to lines of the story that led you to your conclusions.

2. **Developing a Character.** Begin to assemble the parts of a short story. Think of a character. You can base your character on someone you know but change the name and at least one character trait, or quality. Describe this character in as much detail as you can. Tell about things such as these:

how the person dresses
the color of the person's hair
his or her size
his or her personality traits

Give examples of how this person does things.

Developing Skills in Study and Research

Using the Encyclopedia. Sometimes a great deal of information is presented about a subject or topic in the encyclopedia. So much information is presented that it is necessary to divide or outline the subject. Boldface headings or titles are used to introduce the different sections within a single article.

In your school or local library, select an encyclopedia. Find the volume that has the article on the "American Revolution" or the "Revolutionary War." On your paper, list the boldface headings or titles that are used to organize the information in the article. Then describe the type of organization used. Was it chronological? Were certain periods discussed separately? Were the periods broken down further by topics or themes? Were the same topics or themes discussed for each time period?

The Big Wave

PEARL S. BUCK

In this story of a Japanese fishing village, the destructive forces of nature win a major victory. Read the story to see how the good in people helps them deal with the situation.

Kino lived on a farm that lay on the side of a mountain in Japan. The mountain rose so steeply out of the ocean that there was only a strip of sandy shore at its foot. Upon this strip was a small fishing village where Kino's father sold his vegetables and rice and bought fish.

Kino often looked down upon the thatched roofs of the village. The village houses faced one another, and those which stood beside the sea did not have windows toward it. Since Kino enjoyed looking at the waves, he often wondered why the village people did not, but he never knew until he came to know Jiya, whose father was a fisherman. Jiya's house did not have a window toward the sea either.

"Why not?" Kino asked him. "The sea is beautiful."

"The sea is our enemy," Jiya replied.

"How can you say that?" Kino asked. "Your father catches fish from the sea and sells them, and that is how you live."

Jiya shook his head. "The sea is our enemy," he repeated.

It was hard to believe this. On hot sunny days Kino and Jiya threw off their clothes and swam far out toward a small island that they considered their own. Actually, it belonged to an old gentleman whom they had never seen except at a distance.

Kino longed to sleep on the island some night, but Jiya was never willing. Even when they spent only the afternoon there, he looked often out over the sea.

"What are you looking for?" Kino asked one day.

"Only to see that the ocean is not angry," Jiya replied.

But certainly the ocean was not angry now. The sun sparkled deep into the clear water, and the boys swam over the silvery surface of rippling waves. Beneath them, the water was miles deep. When Kino dived, he went down, down, down, until he struck icy-still water.

The Coast of Tago, 1823–31, KATSUSHIKA HOKUSAI. The Metropolitan Museum of Art, Rogers Fund, 1922.

Today when he felt the coldness grasp his body, he understood why Jiya was afraid, and he darted upward again to the sun. On the beach he threw himself down and was happy again. But Jiya looked often at the sun. When he saw it sinking toward the west, he called to Kino: "Come quickly. We must swim home."

After supper that evening, Kino turned to his father. "Why is Jiya afraid of the ocean?" he asked.

"The ocean is very big," Kino's father replied. "We do not understand the ocean."

"I am glad we live on the mountain," Kino went on. "There is nothing to be afraid of on our farm."

"But one can be afraid of the land too," his father replied. "Do you remember the volcano we visited last autumn?"

Kino did remember. They had gone to visit a great volcano twenty miles away. Kino had looked down into the yawning mouth of the volcano, and he had not liked it. Great curls of yellow smoke were rolling about it, and a white stream of melted rock was crawling slowly from one corner.

"Must we always be afraid of something?" Kino asked.

His father looked back at him. "No," he replied. "I did not mean that. It is true that on any day, an ocean may rise into storm and a volcano may burst into flame. We must accept this fact, but without fear. We must say, 'Some day I shall die, and does it matter whether it is by ocean or volcano, or whether I grow old and weak?' "

"I don't want to think about such things," Kino said.

"It is right for you not to think about them," his father said. "Enjoy life and do not fear death. That is the way of a good Japanese."

There was much in life to enjoy. In the winter Kino went to a school in the fishing village, and he and Jiya shared a seat. In the summer Kino worked on the farm, helping his father. Even his little sister, Setsu, and the mother helped when the rice seedlings had to be planted and when the grain was ripe and had to be threshed.

Sometimes if it were not seedtime or harvest, Kino went fishing with Jiya and Jiya's father. "I wish my father were a fisherman," he would say. "It is stupid to plow and plant and cut the sheaves, when I could just come out like this and reap fish from the sea."

Jiya shook his head. "But when the storms come, you would wish yourself back upon the earth," he said.

On days when the sky was bright and the winds mild, the ocean lay so calm and blue that it was hard to believe that it could be cruel and angry. But when the deep water moved and stirred, ah, then Kino began to be glad that his father was a farmer and not a fisherman!

Yet it was the earth that brought the big wave. Deep under the deepest part of the ocean, fires raged in the heart of the earth. At last the fires grew so strong that they forced their way through the mouth of the volcano. That day Kino saw the sky overcast halfway to the zenith. "Look, Father!" he cried. "The volcano is burning again!"

His father gazed anxiously at the sky. "It looks very angry," he said. "I shall not sleep tonight."

All night Kino's father kept watch. When it was dark, the sky was lit with red and the earth trembled under the farmhouse. Down at the fishing village, lights in the little houses showed that other fathers watched too.

When morning came, the sky was red and, even here upon the farm, cinders fell from the volcano.

In the house the mother took down everything from the walls that could fall or be broken. Her few good dishes she packed into straw in a basket and set them outside.

"Shall we have an earthquake, Father?" Kino asked as they ate breakfast. "After the volcano burns?"

"I cannot tell, my son," his father replied. "Earth and sea are struggling together against the fires inside the earth."

No fishing boats set sail that hot summer morning. The sea lay dead and calm, but when Kino looked at it he felt afraid.

No one stirred from home that day. Kino's father sat at the door, watching the sky and the oily sea, and Kino stayed near him. He did not know what Jiya was doing, but he imagined that Jiya, too, stayed by his father.

Early in the afternoon, the sky began to grow black. The air was as hot as though a forest fire were burning. The glow of the volcano glared over the mountaintop, blood-red against the black. All at once a deep-toned bell tolled over the hills.

"What is that bell?" Kino asked.

"It is a bell in the temple inside the walls of Old Gentleman's Castle," his father replied. "Old Gentleman is calling people to come up out of the village and find shelter within his walls."

"Will they come?" Kino asked.

"Not all of them," his father replied. "Parents will try to make the children go, but the children will not want to leave their parents. Mothers will not want to leave fathers, and the fathers will stay by their boats. But some will want to be sure of life."

"I wish Jiya would come up to our farm," Kino said. "Do you think he will see me if I stand on the edge of the terrace and wave my sash?"

"Try it," his father said.

Kino took off the strip of white cloth which he wore instead of a belt, and he waved it high above his head. Jiya, far down the hill, saw the two figures and the waving strip of white. For Jiya was already on his way up the mountain toward Old Gentleman's Castle. He was crying as he climbed and trying not to cry. He had not wanted to leave, but his father said, "If the ocean yields to the fires, you must live after us."

"I don't want to live alone," Jiya said.

"It is your duty to obey me, as a good Japanese son," his father told him.

So Jiya had run out of the house, crying. Now when he saw Kino, he decided that he would go there instead of to the castle, and he began to hurry up the hill to the farm.

Kino's father put out his hand to help Jiya climb over the stone wall of the terrace, and Kino was just about to shout out his welcome, when suddenly a hurricane wind broke out of the ocean. Kino and Jiya clung together and wrapped their arms about the father's waist.

"Look, what is that?" Kino screamed.

The purple rim of the ocean seemed to lift and rise against the clouds. Under the deep waters of the ocean, the earth had yielded at last to the fire. It groaned and split open, and the cold water fell into the middle of the boiling rocks. Steam burst out and lifted the ocean high into the sky in a big wave.

The Red Fuji, 1823–31, KATSUSHIKA HOKUSAI. The Metropolitan Museum of Art, Rogers Fund, 1914.

The wave rushed toward the shore, green and solid, frothing into white at its edges.

"I must tell my father!" Jiya screamed. But before Jiya could scream again, the wave reached the village and covered it fathoms deep in swirling wild water. Upon the beach where the village had stood, not a house remained.

Jiya gave a wild cry, and Kino felt him slip to the ground. Jiya was unconscious. What he had seen was too much for him. His family and his home were gone.

Kino's father gathered Jiya into his arms and carried him into the house. "It is better that he is unconscious," he said gently. "Let him remain so until his own will wakes him. I will sit by him."

"What shall we say to Jiya when he wakes?" Kino asked his father.

"We will not talk," his father replied. "We will give him warm food and let him rest. We will help him to feel he has a home still."

"Here?" Kino asked.

"Yes," his father replied.

"I don't think Jiya can ever be happy again," Kino said sorrowfully.

"Yes, he will be happy some day," his father said. "Life is always stronger than death. Soon now he will open his eyes, and we must be there, you to be his brother and I to be his father. Call your mother, too, and little Setsu."

So they went back into the house. Jiya's eyes were still closed, but he was sobbing in his sleep. Kino ran to fetch his mother and Setsu, and they all gathered about the bed, kneeling on the floor.

In a few minutes, Jiya's eyelids fluttered and then he opened his eyes. He did not know where he was. He looked from one face to the other as though they were strangers.

None of them said anything for a long time. They continued to kneel about him, waiting. But Setsu could not keep quiet. She clapped her hands and cried, "Jiya has come back!"

The sound of her voice made him fully awake. "My father—my mother," he whispered.

Kino's mother took his hand. "I will be your mother now, dear Jiya," she said.

"I will be your father," Kino's father said.

"I am your brother now, Jiya," Kino faltered.

"Jiya will live with us!" Setsu said joyfully.

Then Jiya understood. He got up from the bed and walked to the door. He looked down the hillside to the beach where the fishing village had stood.

Kino's heart ached for his friend–brother. Kino's mother was wiping her eyes, and even little Setsu looked sad. She stood beside Jiya and took his hand and stroked it. "Jiya, I will give you my pet duck," she said.

But Jiya could not speak. He kept on looking at the ocean.

"We ought all to eat something," Kino's mother said. "I have a fine chicken for dinner."

"I'm hungry," Setsu cried.

"Come, my son," Kino's father said to Jiya. Jiya was not hungry, but, when Kino begged him, he took up his chopsticks and ate some of the meat and rice. His mind was still unable to think, but his body was young and strong and glad of the food.

When they had all finished, Kino said, "Shall we go up the hillside, Jiya?"

But Jiya shook his head. "I want to go to sleep again," he said.

Each day Jiya was still tired. He did not want to think or to remember. He only wanted to sleep. One day when the work was over and Jiya still had not waked, Kino and his father sat together on the threshold. "Father, are we not very unfortunate people to live here?" he asked.

"Why do you think so?" his father asked in reply.

"Because the volcano is behind our house and the ocean is in front and, when they make the earthquake and the big wave, we are helpless. Often many of us are lost."

"To live in the midst of danger is to know how good life is," his father replied.

"But if we are lost in the danger?" Kino asked anxiously.

"To live in the presence of death makes us brave and strong," Kino's father replied.

"What is death?" Kino asked.

"Death is the great gateway," Kino's father said. His face was not at all sad.

"The gateway—where?" Kino asked again.

Kino's father smiled. "Can you remember when you were born?"

Kino shook his head. "I was too small."

Kino's father laughed. "I remember very well when you were born," he said. "And oh, how hard you thought it was to be born! You cried, and you screamed."

"Didn't I want to be born?" Kino asked.

"No," his father told him, smiling. "You wanted to stay where you were, in the warm dark house of the unborn. But the time came to be born, and the gate of life opened."

"Did I know it was the gate of life?" Kino asked.

"You did not know anything about it, and so you were afraid," his father replied. "But see how foolish you were!

Here we were waiting for you, your parents, already loving you and eager to welcome you. And you have been very happy, haven't you?"

"Until the big wave came," Kino replied. "Now I am afraid again because of the death that the big wave brought."

"You are only afraid because you don't know anything about death," his father replied. "Some day you will wonder why you were afraid, as today you wonder why you feared to be born."

While they were talking, the dusk had deepened, and now, coming up the mountainside, they saw a flickering light. "I wonder who comes?" Kino exclaimed.

In a few minutes they saw that their visitor was Old Gentleman coming from the castle. "Is this the house of Uchiyama, the farmer?" Old Gentleman asked.

At this, Kino's father stood up, and so did Kino. "Please, Honored Sir," Kino's father said. "What can I do for you?"

Old Gentleman came forward. "Do you have a lad here by the name of Jiya?"

"He lies sleeping inside my house," Kino's father said.

"It is my habit when the big wave comes to care for those who are orphaned," said Old Gentleman. "Three times the wave has come, and three times I have searched out the orphans and widows, and I have fed them and sheltered them. I have heard of this boy Jiya and I wish to do even more for him. I will make him my own son."

"But Jiya is ours!" Kino cried.

"Hush," his father replied. "We must think of Jiya's good. We are only poor people." Then he said to Old Gentleman, "Sir, it is very kind of you to propose this for Jiya. I had planned to take him for my own son, now that he has lost his parents, but I am only a poor farmer and I cannot pretend that my house is as good as yours. Tomorrow when he wakes, I will tell him of your kind offer. He shall decide."

"Very well," Old Gentleman said. "But let him come and tell me himself, so that I will know how he feels."

As soon as Kino woke the next morning, he remembered Jiya and the choice he had to make. After breakfast Kino went to the field to weed the cabbages, but his father stayed home to talk to Jiya.

For a long time Kino stayed in the field, working alone. Then, when the sun was nearing zenith, he heard his father calling. He got up at once and walked between the terraces until he reached the doorway. There his father stood with Jiya.

"I have told Jiya that he must not decide until he has seen all that Old Gentleman can give him for a home," Kino's father said. "Jiya, you know how our house is—these four rooms and the kitchen, this little farm upon which we have to work so hard for our food. We have only what our hands can earn."

Then he returned to Kino again. "You are to go with Jiya, and when you see the castle you must persuade him to stay there, for his own sake."

So the two boys went down the mountainside to the castle. The gate was open, and the garden was most beautiful. A gardener was sweeping the green moss, but he left his work to lead them to the house. There they took off their shoes and followed the gardener through a great door. Inside this, they met a manservant who dismissed the gardener and said to the boys, "Follow me."

So they followed him through a wide passageway. On both sides of the passageway, panels slid back to show beautiful rooms, and in each room were a vase of flowers, an exquisite scroll, a few pieces of dark polished furniture. Neither Jiya nor Kino had ever seen such a house.

Then far in the distance, they saw Old Gentleman sitting beside a small table. The table was set in front of the open sliding panels that looked into the garden, and Old Gentleman was writing.

When the two boys came near, he looked at Jiya. "Well," he said. "Will you be my son?"

Jiya turned very red. He had not expected to have the question put to him so directly.

Old Gentleman saw he found it hard to speak. "Say yes or no," he told Jiya.

"No," Jiya said. "I thank you, but I have a home—on the farm," he added.

For a moment Kino was filled with pure joy. Then he remembered the small farmhouse, the four little rooms and the old kitchen. "Jiya," he said solemnly, "remember how poor we are."

Old Gentleman was smiling a half-sad little smile. "They are certainly very poor," he said to Jiya. "And here, you know, you would have everything."

Jiya looked about him. Then he shook his head again.

Old Gentleman took up his brush[1] again. "Very well," he said. "I will do without a son."

The manservant motioned to them and they followed, and soon they were out in the garden.

"How foolish you are," the manservant said to Jiya. "You would have everything here."

"Not everything," Jiya replied.

They went out of the gate and across the hillside and back to the farmhouse. Setsu came running to meet them, the sleeves of her bright kimono flying and her feet clattering in wooden sandals.

"Jiya has come back home!" she cried.

And Jiya, seeing her happy little face, opened his arms and gave her a great hug. For the first time, he felt comfort creep into his heart.

Their noonday meal was ready, and Kino's father came in from the field. When he had washed, they all sat down to eat. "How happy you have made us," he told Jiya.

"Happy indeed," Kino's mother said.

"Now I have my brother," Kino said.

Jiya smiled. Happiness began to live in him again. The good food warmed him, and his body welcomed it. Around him, the love of the people who received him glowed like a warm and welcoming fire upon the hearth.

The Suido Bridge and Suruga Plain from "One Hundred Famous Views of Edo," 1857, ANDO HIROSHIGE.
Cooper Hewitt Museum, Smithsonian Institution, Washington, D.C.

---

1. **Brush.** The written Japanese language consists of pictographs, or characters that have evolved from pictures. The writer uses a brush to draw them.

Developing Comprehension Skills

1. At first Kino and Jiya have different ideas about the sea. How does Jiya feel about the sea? How does Kino feel about the sea?

2. List the following events from the story in the order in which they happened. Some are related only by time. Others are connected by cause-and-effect relationships. Identify at least two events that are related by cause and effect, and explain which is the cause and which is the effect.

   a. Jiya's father and mother died.
   b. Kino and Jiya went swimming.
   c. The Old Gentleman talked with Kino's father.
   d. A tremendous wave washed over the fishing village.
   e. The Old Gentleman talked with Jiya.

3. Kino's father uses a comparison, a metaphor, to explain his idea of death. What is the comparison? What is the father saying about death?

4. What did the Old Gentleman have to offer Jiya? What did Kino's family have to offer Jiya? Why did Jiya choose Kino's family as opposed to the Old Gentleman's castle?

5. Do you agree with Jiya's choice? Why or why not?

Reading Literature: Short Stories

1. **Identifying the Conflict.** The external conflict in this story is the characters' struggle against a force in nature. This force in nature is the sea. Who wins the conflict?

   Kino and Jiya both must face internal conflict. Explain the internal conflict for Jiya after his parents die. How does he resolve it?

2. **Appreciating Description.** In the following paragraphs from the story, the author paints a clear word picture of the sea and the volcano. She wants the readers' senses to come alive. She uses concrete, vivid words to create these descriptive word pictures.

   Read the two descriptions. Then write the words and phrases that help you see the ocean and the volcano.

   Certainly the ocean was not angry now. The sun sparkled deep into the clear water, and the boys swam over the silvery surface of rippling waves. Beneath them, the water was miles deep. When Kino dived, he went down, down, until he struck icy-still water.

Kino did remember. They had gone to visit a great volcano twenty miles away. Kino had looked down into the yawning mouth of the volcano, and he had not liked it. Great curls of yellow smoke were rolling about it, and a white stream of melted rock was crawling slowly from one corner.

Find at least three other examples of descriptive phrases. These do not necessarily have to describe the sea or the volcano.

3. **Recognizing Mood.** How would you describe the mood of this story, the feeling you get when reading it? Is it fearful and pessimistic or carefree and optimistic or some combination of these and other feelings? Do the examples you chose for 2 make the mood clear?

4. **Recognizing Exposition.** The introduction, or **exposition**, in a short story introduces the characters and the setting. This must be done in the opening paragraphs of the story. The exposition also gives clues or signals that tell the reader what to look for in the coming pages. These clues or signals may be what the characters say, what the narrator says, and even the title of the story.

List the facts that are told in the first five paragraphs of "The Big Wave," the exposition portion of this story. How does this introduction prepare the reader for what happens in the story?

Developing Vocabulary Skills

Recognizing Different Pronunciations of a Word. Sometimes a word can be pronounced two different ways, but it is not a homograph. There is only one dictionary entry for the word. The accent may change from one syllable to another, depending on its part of speech. Read these sentences.

Owen's *present* was a ten-speed bike. (pres′ent)
The drama class will *present* a play tonight. (pre sent′)

In the first sentence, *present* is accented on the first syllable and is used as a noun. In the second, *present* is accented on the second syllable and is used as a verb. The dictionary gives both pronunciations for the word. It also indicates which definitions use each of the pronunciations.

Read each of these sentences concerning stories you have read. Find each underlined word in your dictionary. On your paper, write the following:

   a. The underlined word, from each sentence below, separated into syllables, with the correct accent marked.
   b. The part of speech of the word as it is used in the sentence.
   c. The meaning of the word as it is used in the sentence.

1. The man said in a loud voice, "See here! I am a <u>convict</u>; I have been nineteen years in the galleys."

2. When she spoke her voice was full, sweet, and <u>deliberate</u>.

3. He said with a smile, "Will you please <u>excuse</u> the other hand?"

4. Then, rain or shine, the procession would <u>escort</u> the old soldiers out to the Burying Ground.

5. During the lawyer's fifteen years in prison, they did <u>permit</u> him to have musical instruments.

Developing Writing Skills

1. **Recognizing Irony.** The term **irony** is used to describe a situation in which what is expected does not happen. Write a paragraph explaining what is ironic about Jiya's decision to live with Kino's family rather than with the Old Gentleman.

2. **Developing a Setting.** Continue preparing for the short story you started in connection with "The Old Soldier." Then, you wrote about a character. Now, describe the setting in which you imagined this character. Tell about the time and place in which he or she lives. Use specific words and phrases.

Developing Skills in Speaking and Listening

Reading a Dialog. There are several places in "The Big Wave" where two or more people are speaking. Find each of the passages described below. Decide what the mood of each dialog is. Then work with one or two partners. Prepare to read one of these dialogs. Try to express the mood of the story in your voices.

Kino and Jiya talk about the sea.
The father explains about death to Kino.
The Old Gentleman, Jiya, and Kino discuss Jiya's future.

The Summer of the Beautiful White Horse

WILLIAM SAROYAN

William Saroyan wrote about growing up in the San Joaquin Valley area of California. Note his use of the first-person point of view. How does this help to make the account of this magical summer enjoyable?

One day back there in the good old days when I was nine and the world was full of every imaginable kind of magnificence and life was still a delightful and mysterious dream, my cousin Mourad, who was considered crazy by everybody who knew him except me, came to my house at four in the morning and woke me up by tapping on the window of my room.

"Aram," he said.

I jumped out of bed and looked out the window.

I couldn't believe what I saw.

It wasn't morning yet but it was summer, and with daybreak not many minutes around the corner of the world it was light enough for me to know I wasn't dreaming.

My cousin Mourad was sitting on a beautiful white horse.

I stuck my head out of the window and rubbed my eyes.

"Yes," he said in Armenian. "It's a horse. You're not dreaming. Make it quick if you want to ride."

I knew my cousin Mourad (Mōō′räd) enjoyed being alive more than anybody else who had ever fallen into the world by mistake, but this was more than even I could believe.

In the first place, my earliest memories had been memories of horses and my first longings had been longings to ride.

This was the wonderful part.

In the second place, we were poor.

This was the part that wouldn't permit me to believe what I saw.

We were poor. We had no money. Our whole tribe was poverty-stricken. Every branch of the Garoghlanian (Gar′ə glän′yən) family was living in the most amazing and comical poverty in the world. Nobody could understand where we ever got money enough to keep us with food in our bellies, not even the old

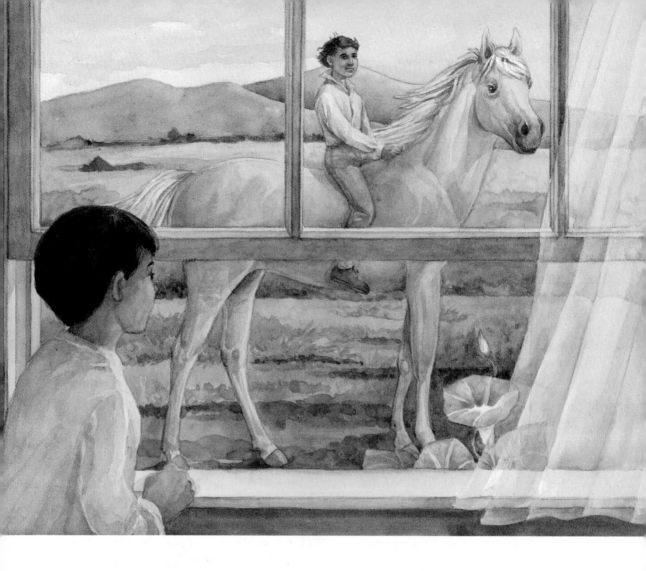

men of the family. Most important of all, though, we were famous for our honesty. We had been famous for our honesty for something like eleven centuries, even when we had been the wealthiest family in what we liked to think was the world. We were proud first, honest next, and after that we believed in right and wrong. None of us would take advantage of anybody in the world, let alone steal.

Consequently, even though I could see the horse, so magnificent; even though I could smell it, so lovely; even though I could hear it breathing, so exciting; I couldn't believe the horse had anything to do with my cousin Mourad or with me or with any of the other members of our family, asleep or awake, because I knew my cousin Mourad couldn't have bought the horse, and, if he couldn't have bought it he must have stolen it, and I refused to believe he had stolen it.

No member of the Garoghlanian family could be a thief.

I stared first at my cousin and then at the horse. There was a pious stillness and humor in each of them, which on the one hand delighted me and on the other frightened me.

"Mourad," I said, "where did you steal this horse?"

"Leap out of the window," he said, "if you want to ride."

It was true, then. He had stolen the horse. There was no question about it. He had come to invite me to ride or not, as I chose.

Well, it seemed to me stealing a horse for a ride was not the same thing as stealing something else, such as money. For all I knew, maybe it wasn't stealing at all. If you were crazy about horses the way my cousin Mourad and I were, it wasn't stealing. It wouldn't become stealing until we offered to sell the horse, which of course I knew we would never do.

"Let me put on some clothes," I said.

"All right," he said, "but hurry."

I leaped into my clothes.

I jumped down to the yard from the window and leaped up onto the horse behind my cousin Mourad.

That year we lived at the edge of town, on Walnut Avenue. Behind our house was the country: vineyards, orchards, irrigation ditches, and country roads. In less than three minutes we were on Olive Avenue, and then the horse began to trot. The air was new and lovely to breathe. The feel of the horse running was wonderful. My cousin Mourad, who was considered one of the craziest members of our family, began to sing. I mean, he began to roar.

Every family has a crazy streak in it somewhere, and my cousin Mourad was considered the natural descendant of the crazy streak in our tribe. Before him was our uncle Khosrove (Käsh'rôv), an enormous man with a powerful head of black hair and the largest mustache in the San Joaquin Valley, a man so furious in temper, so irritable, so impatient that he stopped anyone from talking by roaring, "It is no harm; pay no attention to it."

That was all, no matter what anybody happened to be talking about. Once it was his own son Arak running eight blocks to the barber shop, where his father was having his mustache trimmed, to tell him their house was on fire. This man Khosrove sat up in the chair and roared, "It is no harm; pay no attention to it." The barber said, "But the boy says your house is on fire." So Khosrove roared, "Enough, it is no harm, I say."

My cousin Mourad was considered the natural descendant of this man, although Mourad's father was Zorab (Zōō'räb), who was practical and nothing else. That's how it was in our tribe. A man could be the father of his son's flesh, but that did not mean that he was also the father of his spirit. The distribution of the various kinds of spirit of our tribe had been from the beginning capricious and vagrant.

We rode and my cousin Mourad sang. For all anybody knew we were still in the old country where, at least according to some of our neighbors, we belonged. We let the horse run as long as it felt like running.

At last my cousin Mourad said, "Get down. I want to ride alone."

"Will you let me ride alone?" I said.

"That is up to the horse," my cousin said. "Get down."

"The horse will let me ride," I said.

"We shall see," he said. "Don't forget that I have a way with a horse."

"Well," I said, "any way you have with a horse, I have also."

"For the sake of your safety," he said, "let us hope so. Get down."

"All right," I said, "but remember you've got to let me try to ride alone."

I got down and my cousin Mourad kicked his heels into the horse and shouted, *Vazire,* run. The horse stood on its hind legs, snorted, and burst into a fury of speed that was the loveliest thing I had ever seen. My cousin Mourad raced the horse across a field of dry grass to an irrigation ditch, crossed the ditch on the horse, and five minutes later returned, dripping wet.

The sun was coming up.

"Now it's my turn to ride," I said.

My cousin Mourad got off the horse. "Ride," he said.

I leaped to the back of the horse and for a moment knew the worst fear imaginable. The horse did not move.

"Kick into his muscles," my cousin Mourad said. "What are you waiting for? We've got to take him back before everybody in the world is up and about."

I kicked into the muscles of the horse. Once again it reared and snorted. Then it began to run. I didn't know what to do. Instead of running across the field to the irrigation ditch, the horse ran down the road to the vineyard of Dikran Halabian (Dik′rən Hä läb′yän) where it began to leap over vines. The horse leaped over seven vines before I fell. Then it continued running.

My cousin Mourad came running down the road.

"I'm not worried about you," he shouted. "We've got to get that horse. You go this way and I'll go this way. If you come upon him, be kindly. I'll be near."

I continued down the road and my cousin Mourad went across the field toward the irrigation ditch.

It took him half an hour to find the horse and bring him back.

"All right," he said, "jump on. The whole world is awake now."

"What will we do?" I said.

"Well," he said, "we'll either take him back or hide him until tomorrow."

He didn't sound worried and I knew he'd hide him and not take him back. Not for a while, at any rate.

"Where will we hide him?" I said.

"I know a place," he said.

"How long ago did you steal this horse?" I said.

It suddenly dawned on me that he had been taking these early morning rides for some time and had come for me this morning only because he knew how much I longed to ride.

"Who said anything about stealing a horse?" he said.

"Anyhow," I said, "how long ago did you begin riding every morning?"

"Not until this morning," he said.

"Are you telling the truth?" I said.

"Of course not," he said, "but if we are found out, that's what you're to say. I don't want both of us to be liars. All you know is that we started riding only this morning."

"All right," I said.

He walked the horse quietly to the barn of a deserted vineyard, which at one time had been the pride of a farmer named Fetvajian (Fet va'jən). There were some oats and dry alfalfa in the barn.

We began walking home.

"It wasn't easy," he said, "to get the horse to behave so nicely. At first it wanted to run wild, but, as I've told you, I have a way with a horse. I can get it to want to do anything I want it to do. Horses understand me."

"How do you do it?" I said.

"I have an understanding with a horse," he said.

"Yes, but what sort of an understanding?" I said.

"A simple and honest one," he said.

"Well," I said, "I wish I knew how to reach an understanding like that with a horse."

"You're still a small boy," he said. "When you get to be thirteen you'll know how to do it."

I went home and ate a hearty breakfast.

That afternoon my uncle Khosrove came to our house for coffee. He sat in the parlor, sipping and remembering the old country. Then another visitor arrived, a farmer named John Byro, an Assyrian who, out of loneliness, had learned to speak Armenian. My mother brought the lonely visitor coffee, and he sipped and then at last, sighing sadly, he said, "My white horse which was stolen last month is still gone. I cannot understand it."

My uncle Khosrove became very irritated and shouted, "It's no harm. What is the loss of a horse? Haven't we all lost the homeland? What is this crying over a horse?"

"That may be all right for you, a city dweller, to say," John Byro said, "but what of my surrey? What good is a surrey without a horse?"

"Pay no attention to it," my uncle Khosrove roared.

"I walked ten miles to get here," John Byro said.

"You have legs," my uncle Khosrove shouted.

"My left leg pains me," the farmer said.

"Pay no attention to it," my uncle Khosrove roared.

"That horse cost me sixty dollars," the farmer said.

"I spit on money," my uncle said.

He got up and stalked out of the house, slamming the screen door.

My mother explained.

"He has a gentle heart," she said. "It is simply that he is homesick and such a large man."

The farmer went away, and I ran over to my cousin Mourad's house.

He was sitting under a peach tree, trying to repair the hurt wing of a young robin which could not fly. He was talking to the bird.

"What is it?" he said.

"The farmer, John Byro," I said. "He visited our house. He wants his horse. You've had it a month. I want you to promise not to take it back until I learn to ride."

"It will take you a year to learn to ride," my cousin Mourad said.

"We could keep the horse a year," I said.

My cousin Mourad leaped to his feet.

"What?" he roared. "Are you inviting a member of the Garoghlanian family to steal? The horse must go back to its true owner."

"When?" I said.

"In six months at the latest," he said.

He threw the bird into the air. The bird tried hard, almost fell twice, but at last flew away, high and straight.

Early every morning for two weeks my cousin Mourad and I took the horse out of the barn of the deserted vineyard where we were hiding it and rode it, and every morning the horse, when it was my turn to ride alone, leaped over grape vines and small trees and threw me and ran away. Nevertheless, I hoped in time to learn to ride the way my cousin Mourad rode.

One morning on the way to Fetvajian's deserted vineyard, we ran into the farmer John Byro who was on his way to town.

"Let me do the talking," my cousin Mourad said. "I have a way with farmers."

"Good morning, John Byro," my cousin Mourad said to the farmer.

The farmer studied the horse eagerly.

"Good morning, sons of my friends," he said. "What is the name of your horse?"

"*My Heart,*" my cousin Mourad said in Armenian.

"A lovely name," John Byro said, "for a lovely horse. I could swear it is the horse that was stolen from me many weeks ago. May I look into its mouth?"

"Of course," Mourad said.

The farmer looked into the mouth of the horse.

"Tooth for tooth," he said. "I would swear it is my horse if I didn't know your parents. The fame of your family for honesty is well known to me. Yet the horse is the twin of my horse. A suspicious man would believe his eyes instead of his heart. Good day, my young friends."

"Good day, John Byro," my cousin Mourad said.

Early the following morning we took the horse to John Byro's vineyard and put it in the barn. The dogs followed us around without making a sound.

"The dogs," I whispered to my cousin Mourad. "I thought they would bark."

"They would at somebody else," he said. "I have a way with dogs."

My cousin Mourad put his arms around the horse, pressed his nose into the horse's nose, patted it, and then we went away.

That afternoon John Byro came to our house in his surrey and showed my mother the horse that had been stolen and returned.

"I do not know what to think," he said. "The horse is stronger than ever. Better-tempered, too. I thank God."

My uncle Khosrove, who was in the parlor, became irritated and shouted, "Quiet man, quiet. Your horse has been returned. Pay no attention to it."

Developing Comprehension Skills

1. Why was Aram so surprised to see his cousin with a horse?

2. Why do you think the speaker presented so much information on his Armenian "tribe"? List some of the characteristics of his "tribe."

3. When he met Mourad and Aram on the road in the early morning, John Byro inspected the white horse. Why did he not take the horse from Mourad and Aram? Do you think he knew that it was his horse? Explain your answer.

4. Byro mentions two positive things that happened to the horse during its absence. What are these positive things? Why do you think the horse had made these changes in attitude?

5. Comment on this statement from the story: "Well, it seemed to me stealing a horse for a ride was not the same thing as stealing something else, such as money." Do you agree or disagree with this statement? Explain your answer.

Reading Literature: Short Stories

1. **Recognizing Tone.** The attitude that an author shows toward his or her work is called **tone**. The author must choose words very carefully to let the reader recognize the tone. In "The Summer of the Beautiful White Horse," the boys keep a horse without permission, knowing they should not. Is the author's tone critical of the boys? Is it preachy? Would you describe the tone as forgiving or amused, or would you describe it with some other term? How does Saroyan's use of the first-person point of view affect the tone?

   Pick out two or three passages that support your comments on the tone of the story.

2. **Appreciating Setting.** Is the setting important in "The Summer of the Beautiful White Horse"? Could the setting have been in present-day New York City or some other large urban area? Explain your answer.

3. **Understanding Characters.** What type of person was Uncle Khosrove? What do you think Uncle Khosrove meant when he said, "It's no harm, pay no attention to it"? Do you believe there are real people like Uncle Khosrove? Explain your answer.

4. **Recognizing Sounds of Language.** Throughout this story, the author uses various kinds of repetition. This repetition helps Saroyan to express his ideas clearly and to create interesting patterns of sound.

There is repetition of ideas.

> We were poor. We had no money. Our whole tribe was poverty-stricken.

There is repetition of phrases.

> I have a way with a horse.
> I have a way with farmers.
> I have a way with dogs.

There is repetition of sentence patterns.

> Consequently, even though I could see the horse, so magnificent; even though I could smell it, so lovely; even though I could hear it breathing, so exciting; I couldn't believe the horse had anything to do with my cousin Mourad or with me.

Saroyan avoids monotony by letting some patterns grow more complex gradually. For example, "We were poor" grows into "Our whole tribe was poverty-stricken." Another way he avoids monotony is by making a sudden change in sentence length. An example of this occurs at the end of the sentence above, beginning with "Consequently." Only part of the sentence is shown above; the complete sentence is eighty-eight words long. The sentence following it is only ten words long. In other places, several very short sentences are followed by a very long one.

Find at least one other example of each of these techniques:

a. Repetition of ideas   c. Repetition of sentence patterns
b. Repetition of phrases   d. Sudden change in sentence length

Developing Vocabulary Skills

Choosing the Best Meaning. Each of the following sentences was drawn from "The Bet" or "The Summer of the Beautiful White Horse." Most of the underlined words have more than one meaning. Find the entry in the dictionary for each underlined word. Test each listed meaning in the context of the sentence. Find the meaning that best fits the sentence. Write that meaning on your paper.

1. The old banker was <u>pacing</u> from corner to corner in his room.
2. Execution kills instantly; prison kills by <u>degrees</u>.
3. In the second year the piano was heard no more. The lawyer asked only for <u>classics</u>.
4. I must escape <u>ruin</u> and shame.
5. In the darkness he <u>groped</u> for the door.
6. The <u>feel</u> of the horse running was wonderful.
7. A man could be the father of his son's flesh, but that did not mean that he was also the father of his <u>spirit</u>.
8. Don't forget that I have a <u>way</u> with horses.

Developing Writing Skills

1. **Evaluating a Character.** In this story, Aram mentions several times that his cousin Mourad was considered crazy by everyone. Was he crazy? Make a list of the things you learned about Mourad. You can begin with the following:

   He woke Aram up before daybreak.
   He was riding a white horse.

   Add ten or more items to this list. When you have listed about a dozen specific things that Mourad did, make a judgment on what kind of person Mourad is. Write a paragraph explaining your opinion of whether Mourad was crazy or not.

2. **Describing a Conflict.** You have written about a character and you have imagined a setting for that character. Now describe a conflict for that character in that setting. For example, the character may have to move away from the setting or possibly the setting changes. Write a few paragraphs describing this conflict and giving details about how the character feels about it.

Developing Skills in Critical Thinking

Recognizing the Need to Define Terms. Frequently, we use terms whose definitions we think we know. However, not everyone may agree on those definitions. In the story of "The Summer of the Beautiful White Horse," for example, Aram thinks he understands what honesty and stealing are. Then Mourad brings a horse to his window, and suddenly Aram is no longer sure what *stealing* means. The term *crazy,* too, is used to describe Mourad. Aram's meaning for *crazy,* however, is probably different from another person's meaning.

For one day, carefully listen to conversations, commercials, and other announcements. Listen particularly for words that seem familiar, but whose meanings you cannot easily explain. List at least three such words, and keep a record of how you heard each word used. Then, in class or in a small group, discuss the words you and the other group members listed. Without using a dictionary, try to agree on meanings that fit the situations in which you heard the words.

Spring Tryout, 1944, THOMAS HART BENTON. Charles H. MacNider Museum, Mason City, Iowa.

The Rocking Donkey

JOAN AIKEN

In this story you will find a wicked stepmother, an innocent child, and magic. Does it sound like a fairy tale? As you read it, try to decide whether "The Rocking Donkey" is a fairy tale or not.

There was once a little girl called Esmeralda who lived with her wicked stepmother. Her father was dead. The stepmother, who was called Mrs. Mitching, was very rich, and lived in a large but hideous house in a suburb with a dusty, laurelly garden, and a lot of ornamental iron fencing.

Mrs. Mitching was fond of opening things, and getting things up. The things she opened were mostly hospitals, or public libraries, or new bypasses, or civic centers. The things she got up were sales of work,[1] and bazaars, and flag days. She was, in fact, a public figure and was very little at home. When she was, she spent her time receiving callers in her fringy, ornamented drawing room.

"How is your little girl?" they would sometimes ask. "Is she still at home, or has she gone to boarding school?"

"Oh, she's at home," Mrs. Mitching would reply, "but she has her own playroom, you know, so that we needn't disturb one another. I don't believe in grownups bothering children all the time, do you?"

Mrs. Mitching could not afford school for Esmeralda, as she needed all her wealth for opening and getting up. She always took Esmeralda along to the openings in a white muslin dress, painfully starched at the neck and wrists, because people liked to see a child on the platform. But for the rest of the time, Esmeralda had to manage in her old brown dress, much too short now, and a torn pair of gym shoes. She had her meals in the kitchen, and they were horrible—bread and margarine, boiled fish, and prunes.

However, the most melancholy part of Esmeralda's life was that she had nothing to do. The playroom which Mrs. Mitching spoke of was a large, dark basement

---

1. **Sale of work.** Sale of handmade goods, such as needlework and crafts

room, shadowed by the laurels which overhung the area. There was nothing in it at all, not even a chair. No one ever came into it; and it would have been thick with dust had not Esmeralda, who was a tidy creature, once a week borrowed a broom from the housemaid's cupboard and swept it. She had no toys. Once Mr. Snye, the man who came to cut the laurels, had given her a length of garden twine. She used this as a skipping rope, to keep herself warm. She became a very good skipper, and could polka, double-through, swing the rope, and other fancy variations. If she felt inclined to do plain skipping, she could go on almost all day without a fault.

There were no books to read in the house. She was not encouraged to go into Mrs. Mitching's rooms or outside because of her shabby clothes, though she sometimes took a stroll at dusk.

One day Mrs. Mitching was to open a jumble sale.[2] She was being driven to it by the mayor in his Rolls-Royce; so she told Hooper, the housemaid, to bring Esmeralda by bus, dressed in her white muslin, and meet her at the hall. Then she went off to keep an appointment.

"Drat," said Hooper. "Now what am I do to? Your muslin's still at the laundry from last week."

---

2. **Jumble sale.** British name for rummage sale, a sale of assorted new or used items, usually to raise money for charitable causes

"I'll have to go as I am," said Esmeralda, who quite liked openings. At least, they made a change from wandering about in the basement.

"I don't know what Madam'll say," said Hooper doubtfully, "but I should catch it if I didn't take you, sure enough." So they went as they were, Esmeralda in her old brown dress and shoes.

When Mrs. Mitching saw them, she gave a cry of dismay.

"I can't let you be seen like that! You must go home at once," and she hurriedly left them before anyone should connect her with the shabby child.

Hooper had set her heart on a violet satin pincushion she had noticed on one of the stalls, so she pushed Esmeralda into a corner and said, "You wait there. I shan't be a moment. It won't matter; no one will know who you are."

Esmeralda stood looking quietly about her. An elderly gentleman, Lord Mauling, making his way to the platform, noticed what seemed to him a forlorn-looking little creature. Stopping by her, he took a coin from his pocket and said, "Here, my dear. Buy yourself a pretty toy."

Esmeralda gave him a startled look as he went on his way. Then she stared at the coin she held in her hand. It was a shilling. She had never had any money before and was quite puzzled to know what she should buy with it. Almost without realizing what she was doing, she began to wander along the stalls, looking at the different things offered for sale. There were books, clothes, bottles of scent, flowers—all the things she saw seemed beautiful, but she could not imagine buying any of them. Then she came to the toy counter. Toys! She had never had one. The only time she ever touched a toy was sometimes when Mrs. Mitching opened a children's ward at a hospital, and Esmeralda would present a ceremonial teddy bear to a little patient. She gazed at dolls, puzzles, engines, without noticing that most of them were shabby and secondhand. Then at the end of the counter, she saw what she wanted. There was no hesitation in her mind; she knew at once.

It was a rocking donkey—gray, battered, weather-beaten, with draggling ears and tangled tail. On the side of his rockers his name was painted—"Prince." It hardly seemed the name for someone so ancient and worn. The price ticket pinned to his tail said one shilling.

"I'd like the donkey, please," said Esmeralda timidly to the lady at the stall, holding out her coin. The lady glanced from the coin to the ticket and said, "Good gracious. Can this really be going for only a shilling? Surely they mean ten? Mr. Prothero," she called to a gentleman farther down the room, but he was busy and did not hear.

"Oh, well," she said to Esmeralda. "You take it. You won't often get a bargain like that, I can tell you." She took the coin and put the donkey on the floor.

"How will you get him home?" she asked.

"I don't know," said Esmeralda. She was lucky though. As she stood hesitating with her hand on Prince's bridle, someone familiar stopped beside her. It was Mr. Snye, the man who cut the hedges.

"You bought that donkey?" he said. "Well, I'm blest. That'll be a bit of fun for you, I reckon. Like me to take it home for you in the van? I've got it outside—been bringing some flowers along for the platform."

"Oh thank you," Esmeralda said. So he shouldered Prince, nodded to her, and said, "I'll be home before you are, like as not. I'll just leave him in the shrubbery for you."

Esmeralda went to find Hooper, who had bought her pincushion, and they caught their bus home.

As soon as dusk fell and no one was about, she slipped up the back steps and half dragged, half carried Prince from his hiding place down through the basement passage to her playroom. She put him in the middle of the floor and sat down beside him.

It was a strange moment. For as long as she could remember, she had had no company at all, nothing to play with. Now here, all of a sudden, was a friend. She felt sure of that. She put an arm over his cold, smooth neck. He rocked down and gently touched the top of her head with his nose.

"Prince," she said quietly and almost wondered if he would reply, but he was silent. She combed out his tangled mane and tail. Then she sat with him until the room was quite dark, and it was time to put herself to bed.

As she went to her tiny room upstairs, it occurred to her that he might be cold, alone in that dark basement. She took one of the two blankets off her bed, slipped down again in her nightdress, and tucked it over him. Back in bed, she tried to settle but could not. It was a chilly night, and one blanket was not enough to keep her warm. Also, she could not help wondering if Prince felt lonely and perhaps homesick for wherever he had come from? So presently she was tiptoeing back to the playroom with the other blanket. She made a sort of nest for the two of them and slept all night on the floor, curled up between his front rockers. If she wanted company, all she had to do was reach up, and pull on a rein to bring down his cold, friendly nose against her cheek.

She was never lonely again. She never rode on Prince—she felt that would be almost an impertinence with someone who was so much a friend and who, moreover, looked so weary and battered. But she would set him off rocking while she skipped, so that they seemed to be keeping each other company; and she talked to him all the time, while he nodded intelligently in reply. Every night she crept

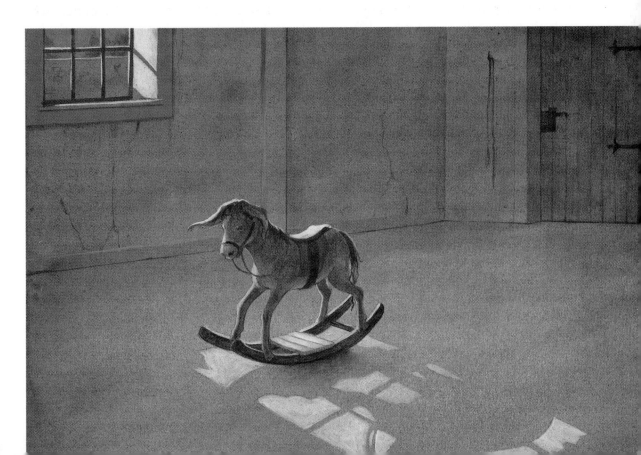

down with her two blankets and slept curled up between his feet.

One day, Mrs. Mitching decided to give a whist drive[3] in her house for the wives of chimney sweeps. It occurred to her that the basement playroom would be just the right size for the purpose. She went along to inspect and found Esmeralda having her weekly cleanout with brush and dustpan.

"That's right, that's right," she said absently, glancing about. "But what is this? A rocking horse?" Esmeralda stood mute.

"Do you not think you are a little old for such toys? Yes, yes, I think it had better be given away to some poor child. It is the duty of children who live in rich houses, such as you, Esmeralda, to give away your old toys to the little slum children who have nothing. It can be taken away when the van for the Bombed Families[4] calls here tomorrow morning. But you must certainly clean it up a little first. You should be quite ashamed to pass on such a shabby old toy without doing your best to improve its appearance. After all, you know, it may gladden some poor little life in Stepney or Bethnal Green. So give it a good scrub this evening. Now what

was I doing? Ah, yes, seventeen feet by sixteen, ten tables—let me see—"

Esmeralda passed the rest of the day in a sort of numbness. After tea, she took some sugar soap and a scrubbing brush from the housemaid's cupboard and started to scrub Prince.

"Well," she thought, "perhaps I didn't deserve to be so happy. I never thought of scrubbing him. Perhaps someone else will take better care of him. But oh, what shall I do, what shall I do?"

She scrubbed and scrubbed and, as the shabby gray peeled away, a silvery gleam began to show along Prince's back and sides. His mane and tail shone like floss. By the time she had finished, it was quite dark. A long ray of moonlight striking across the floor caught his head and, for a moment, dazzled her eyes.

For the last time she went up, fetched her blankets, and settled herself beside him. Just before she fell asleep, it seemed to her that his nose came down and lightly touched her wet cheek.

Next day Esmeralda hid herself. She did not want to see Prince taken away. Mrs. Mitching superintended this.

"Good gracious," she said, when she saw him shining in the sun. "That is far too valuable to be taken to Stepney. I shall give it to the museum." So the Bombed Families van dropped Prince off at the museum before going on to Stepney.

All day Esmeralda avoided the basement playroom. She felt that she could

---

3. **Whist Drive.** A fund-raising activity involving the card game of whist, a game that is similar to bridge

4. **Bombed Families.** Families left homeless as a result of the bombing raids over England during World War II

not bear to look at the empty patch in the middle of the floor.

In the evening, Hooper felt sorry for her, she seemed so restless and moping, and took her out for a stroll. They went to the museum, where Hooper liked to look at the models of fashions through the ages. While she was studying crinolines and bustles, Esmeralda wandered off. Soon, around a corner, she came on Prince, railed off from the public with a red cord, and with a notice beside him that read, "Donated by the Honorable Mrs. Mitching, November 19—"

Esmeralda stretched out her hand, but she could not quite touch him over the cord.

"Now, miss," said an attendant. "No touching the exhibits, please." So she looked and looked at him until Hooper said it was time to go home.

Every day after that she went to the museum to look at Prince. Hooper said to Cook, "That child doesn't look well." Mrs. Mitching was away from home a good deal, organizing the grand opening of a new welfare center and clinic, so she did not notice Esmeralda's paleness or her constant visits to the museum.

One night something woke Esmeralda. A long finger of moonlight lay lightly across her closed eyes. She got up quietly and put on her old brown dress and thin shoes. It was easy to steal out of that large house without anyone hearing. Once outside, she slipped along the empty streets

like a shadow. When she reached the museum, she went at once, as if someone had called her, to a little door at one side. Somebody had left it unlocked, and she opened it softly and went into the thick dark.

The museum was a familiar place by now. She went confidently forward along a passage and presently came out into the main hall. It did not take her long to find Prince, for there he was, shining like silver in the moonlight. She walked forward, stepped over the rope, and put her hand on his neck.

"Esmeralda," he said. His voice was like a faint, silvery wind.

"You never spoke to me before."

"How could I? I was choked with gray paint."

"Oh," she cried, "I'm so terribly lonely without you. What shall I do?"

"You never rode on me," he said.

"I didn't like to. You were so old and tired, it would have seemed like taking a liberty."

"Ride on me now."

Timidly she put her foot into the stirrup and swung herself onto his back.

"Settle yourself in the saddle and hold tight. Are you all right?"

"Yes," she said.

Like a feather in the wind, they went rocking up the ray of moonlight and passed through the high window as if it had been a mist. Neither of them was ever seen again.

Developing Comprehension Skills

1. How did Mrs. Mitching treat Esmeralda? To Esmeralda, what was the worst part of her treatment?

2. Describe a typical day and night for Esmeralda and Prince. How was this different from Esmeralda's life before Prince came?

3. Mrs. Mitching said that the rocking donkey should be cleaned up before being given away to the slum children. What was Esmeralda's reaction? Was this typical of Esmeralda?

4. Do you think Mrs. Mitching knew how badly she treated Esmeralda? Have you ever met someone like Mrs. Mitching? Can you believe in this type of character? Why or why not?

5. Do you think the ending was happy? Why or why not?

Reading Literature: Short Stories

1. **Finding Character Traits.** As we have seen, the reader can determine the personality of a character by considering the following:
   a. what the character says
   b. what others say about the character
   c. what the narrator says about the character
   d. what the character does

   Describe the personality of Mrs. Mitching. List ways the author tells about her personality. For each method, select an example.

2. **Comparing Types of Stories.** Certain features or elements appear over and over in fairy stories. The tales usually begin with "Once upon a time . . ." or "Long, long ago . . ." Both good and bad characters usually appear in the same story. Good characters are totally good and bad characters are totally bad. One incident often occurs three times in a fairy tale. Fairies have magical powers. They can take the shape of humans or animals. Most fairy tales end happily, with ". . . and they lived happily ever after."

   Identify at least three ways in which "The Rocking Donkey" is like a fairy tale. Also, identify any ways you can think of in which it is different. Then tell your opinion of whether or not it is a fairy tale.

3. **Identifying Elements of a Plot.** Make a plot diagram for this story.

4. **Recognizing Theme.** A writer can say something about real life even in a story that is not realistic. Can you identify the theme of "The Rocking Donkey," what the author wanted to say about life?

Developing Vocabulary Skills

Reviewing Context Clues. Read each of the following groups of sentences from the stories you have read. Use context clues to figure out the meaning of each underlined word. Look for definitions, restatements, synonyms, and antonyms. You may have to infer the meaning from the other words in the sentence. Write the meaning of each word from the clues given.

1. Mdlle. Baptistine looked at her brother, and her face resumed its usual calmness and serenity.

2. One would have said he was hesitating between two realms—that of the doomed and that of the saved.

3. We were poor. We had no money. We were poverty-stricken.

4. Uncle Khosgrove was a man so furious in temper, so irritable, so impatient, that he stopped anyone from talking by roaring.

5. Esmeralda had horrible meals in the kitchen. However, the most melancholy part of Esmeralda's life was that she had nothing to do.

6. Esmeralda, who was a tidy creature, would borrow a broom from the housemaid's cupboard and sweep the room.

7. It was a shilling. She had never had any money before and was quite puzzled to know what she should buy with it.

8. It was a gray rocking horse—battered, weather-beaten, with draggling ears and tangled tail.

Developing Writing Skills

1. **Writing a New Ending.** The ending of this story may have seemed too sudden to you. You may have felt that the rest of the story seemed possible, but the ending brought in impossible events. Perhaps you felt that the ending was too sad or left too many loose ends. Can you think of an ending more satisfying to you? Decide at what point you would begin to change the story. Then write your own ending, beginning at that point.

2. **Planning Your Own Story.** In writing activities for the first three stories of this section, you have had an opportunity to create a character and a setting, and to describe a conflict facing the character. To do this activity, you may use that character, setting, and conflict, or you may invent new ones.

Develop a plot outline for a story about your character. The outline should be between five and ten sentences long. Write at least one sentence for each of the parts in the plot diagram below.

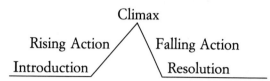

Climax

Rising Action / Falling Action

Introduction / Resolution

3. **Discussing Point of View.** Try to imagine "The Rocking Donkey" being told in the first-person point of view. How would the story have changed if Esmeralda had told it? How would it have changed if Mrs. Mitching had given her view? Could the yardman have told the story in the way it is written? Write at least a paragraph about the point of view in this story. Point out some of the effects of the third-person, omniscient point of view on the story and on the reader.

Developing Skills in Study and Research

Doing Background Reading. The story of "The Rocking Donkey" is by an English author. She used many terms common in England, but not necessarily in America. For example, the phrases "sales of work," "jumble sale," and "whist drive" probably were unfamiliar to you. To understand the story a bit better, you might want to know something about customs in England. An encyclopedia article is very limited; it might not tell you much about how the average person lives. To learn more about life in England, you might want to do some background reading, that is, reading of fiction and nonfiction books on the topic.

Use the card catalog of your school or local library. Find the titles of at least three books that might give you information about the lives of typical people in England or another country of your choice. Begin by looking up the name of the country and go on to the other categories listed there. To select the three books, read the short descriptions that are given on the cards. You could include biographies, novels, or books about events in the country of your choice since World War II.

The Disappearing Man

ISAAC ASIMOV

In detective stories the reader should be aware of evidence or small clues that help in solving the crime. Can you find the clues in this story? Can you predict the outcome?

I'm not often on the spot when Dad's on one of his cases, but I couldn't help it this time.

I was coming home from the library that afternoon, when a man dashed by me and ran full speed into an alley between two buildings. It was rather late, and I figured the best thing to do was to keep on moving toward home. Dad says a nosy fourteen-year-old isn't likely to make it to fifteen.

But in less than a minute, two police officers came running. I didn't wait for them to ask. "He went in there," I said.

One of them rushed in, came out, and shouted, "There's a door open. He went inside. Go 'round to the front."

They must have given the alarm, because in a few minutes three police cars drove up, there were plainclothes officers on the scene, and the building was surrounded.

I knew I shouldn't be hanging around. Innocent bystanders get in the way of the police. Just the same, I was there when it started and, from what I heard the police saying, I knew they were after this man, Stockton. He was a loner who'd pulled off some pretty spectacular jewel robberies over the last few months. I knew about it because Dad is a detective on the force, and he was on the case.

"Slippery fellow," he said, "but when you work alone, there's no one to double-cross you."

I said, "Doesn't he have to work with someone, Dad? He's got to have a fence—someone to peddle the jewels."

"If he has," said Dad, "we haven't located him. And why don't you get on with your homework?" (He always says that when he thinks I'm getting too interested in his cases.)

Well, they had him now. Some jeweler must have pushed the alarm button.

The alley he ran into was closed on all sides but the street, and he hadn't come out. There was a door there that was open, and he must have gone in. The police had the possible exits guarded. They even had a couple of officers on the roof.

I was just beginning to wonder if Dad would be involved, when another car came up, and he got out. First thing, he saw me and stopped dead. "Larry! What are you doing here?"

"I was on the spot, Dad. Stockton ran past me into the alley."

"Well, get out of here. There's liable to be shooting."

I backed away, but I didn't back off all the way. Once my father went into the building, I got into his car. The driver knew me, and he said, "You better go home, Larry. I'm going to have to help with the search, so I can't stay here to keep an eye on you."

"Sure, you go on," I said. "I'll be leaving in a minute." But I didn't. I wanted to do some thinking first.

Nobody leaves doors open in New York City. If that door into the alley was open, Stockton must have opened it. That meant he had to have a key; there wasn't time to pick the lock. That must mean he worked out of that building.

I looked at the building. It was an old one, four stories high. It had small businesses in it, and you could still see the painted signs in the windows in the fading light.

On the second-floor window, it said, "Klein and Levy, Tailors." Above that was a theatrical costumer, and on the top floor was a jeweler's. That jeweler's made sense out of it.

If Stockton had a key to the building, he probably worked with that jeweler. Dad would figure all that out.

I waited for the sound of shots, pretty scared Dad might get hurt. But nothing happened. Maybe Stockton would see he was cornered and just give in. I hoped so. At least they didn't have to evacuate the building. Late on Saturday, I supposed, it would be deserted.

After a while, I got tired of waiting. I chose a moment when no police officers were looking and moved quickly to the building entrance. Dad would be hopping mad when he saw me, but I was curious. I figured they had Stockton, and I wanted to see him.

They didn't have him.

There was a fat man in a vest in the lobby. He looked scared, and I guess he was the watchman. He kept saying, "I didn't see anybody."

Police officers were coming down the stairs and out of the old elevator, all shaking their heads.

My father was pretty angry. He said, "No one has anything?"

A police sergeant said, "Donovan said no one got out on the roof. All the doors and windows are covered."

"If he didn't get out," said my father in a low voice that carried, "then he's in the building."

"We can't find him," said the sergeant. "He's nowhere inside."

My father said, "It isn't a big building——"

"We had the watchman's keys. We've looked everywhere."

"Then how do we know he went into the building in the first place? Who saw him go in?"

There was a silence. A lot of police officers were milling about the lobby now, but no one said anything. So I spoke up. "I did, Dad."

Dad whirled and looked at me and made a funny sound in the back of his throat that meant I was in for it for still being there. "You said you saw him run into the alley," he said. "That's not the same thing."

"He didn't come out, Dad. There was no place else for him to go."

"But you didn't actually see him go in, did you?"

"He couldn't go up the side of the buildings. There wouldn't have been time for him to reach the roof——"

But Dad wasn't listening. "Did anyone actually see him go in?"

Of course no one said anything, and I could see my father was going to call the whole thing off, and then, when he got me home, I was going to get the talking-to of my life.

The thought of that talking-to must have stimulated my brain, I guess. I looked about the lobby desperately and said, "But, Dad, he did go into the building, and he didn't disappear. There he is right now. That man there." I pointed, and then I dropped down and rolled out of the way.

There wasn't any shooting. The man I pointed to was close to the door—he must have been edging toward it—and now he made a dash for it. He almost made it, but a police officer who had been knocked down grabbed his leg and then everyone piled on him. Later they had the jeweler, too.

I went home after Stockton was caught, and, when my father got home much later, he did have some things to say about my risking my life. But he also said, "You got onto that theatrical costume bit very nicely, Larry."

I said, "Well, I was sure he went into the building and was familiar with it. He could get into the costumer's if he had to, and they would be bound to have police uniforms. I figured that, if he could dump his jacket and pants and get into a uniform quickly, he could just walk out of the building."

Dad said, "You're right. Even after he got outside, he could pretend he was dealing with the crowd and then just walk away."

Mom said, "But how did you know which police officer it was, Larry? Don't tell me you know everyone by sight."

"I didn't have to, Mom," I said. "I figured if he got a police uniform at the costumer's, he had to work fast and grab any one he saw. And they wouldn't have much of an assortment of sizes anyway. So I just looked around for a police officer whose uniform didn't fit, and, when I saw one with trouser legs stopping above his ankles, I knew he was Stockton."

Developing Comprehension Skills

1. Why is Larry right there on the spot for this particular case? Why does he stay at the scene although he knows his father will be angry?

2. What are the clues that lead Larry to Stockton?

3. Why do you think the police officers did not note the same clues as Larry did?

4. Do you think Stockton could have been caught without Larry's help?

Reading Literature: Short Stories

1. **Appreciating Timing in a Detective Story.** After reading the end of "The Disappearing Man," you realize that the speaker noticed several seemingly unimportant things that he put together to solve the mystery. List them. Could all of the clues have been presented in the first paragraph? Would it have been a different story if they had? Would it have made a better story if it had been written that way? Why or why not?

2. **Analyzing the Plot.** Make a plot diagram for this story.

3. **Analyzing Relationships Between Characters.** Larry and his father obviously had a close relationship. Find at least three references Larry makes about his father that show the understanding between them.

Developing Vocabulary Skills

1. **Recognizing Standard and Nonstandard English.** Standard English is English that is understood by all speakers of English. It is acceptable at all times and in all places. It is the kind of English that is used in writing, speeches, and conversations with most people. All of the stories in this chapter are written in standard English.

   A second level of language, nonstandard English, is not acceptable at all times and places. One kind of nonstandard English that is sometimes acceptable is **slang.** If it is not overused, slang is acceptable in conversation, especially with close friends. Slang words and slang meanings for accepted words may be used by a small group of people or by many people for a short time. If the group stops using the word, it dies. Sometimes the word is accepted generally, and everyone begins to use it. At that point, the word is not considered slang anymore. It becomes part of standard English. Because slang is constantly changing, slang words are not always in the dictionary.

In the sentences below, identify the slang words or phrases. Use either the dictionary or context clues in the sentence to determine the meaning of the slang.

a. When you go to that theater, look at your seat carefully before you sit down. Some of the seats are so grungy you wouldn't want to touch them!

b. Stand up for yourself! Don't be a pushover!

c. In the shoot-out at the end of the western, the outlaw got the drop on the sheriff.

d. I can't buy your excuse for being late.

e. Ginny pretends to be friendly, but I've got her number. I wouldn't trust her with any of my secrets!

2. **Recognizing Formal and Informal Standard English.** The story of "The Disappearing Man" was written in the first-person point of view. Larry is speaking as though he were having a conversation with someone. He uses **informal standard English.** Compare the language in "The Disappearing Man" to that in "The Big Wave." Notice how casual Larry's language sounds when compared to the **formal standard English** of "The Big Wave."

Find another story in this chapter that is written in informal standard English. Find another written in formal standard English.

Developing Writing Skills

1. **Writing a Brief News Report.** Imagine that a radio news program reported the arrest of Stockton. Like a newspaper article, a radio news report must answer the five W questions:

Who?   Where?   When?   What happened?   Why?

Write a one-paragraph news report in which you answer all five questions. Use the information Larry gave in "The Disappearing Man." Make sure your sentences can be understood by someone hearing them read on the radio.

2. **Comparing Points of View.** "The Rocking Donkey" was written in the third-person point of view, while "The Disappearing Man" was written in the first-person point of view. Can you find some differences in the kinds of stories they are and the effects their authors wanted to have on readers? How do the different points of view help to make these differences clear?

3. **Writing Your Own Story.** Use the plot diagram you developed for the writing exercise following "The Rocking Donkey" (page 230, Developing Writing Skills, 2). Write your own story. It must be about one main character and must include all five parts of a plot. Make your story no less than ten paragraphs and no more than four pages long.

Developing Skills in Critical Thinking

Recognizing Deductive Reasoning. The kind of thinking Larry used in "The Disappearing Man" is called **deductive reasoning.** In deductive reasoning, you begin with a general statement that is always or almost always true, such as "All three-sided figures are triangles." Then you compare a specific case with the general rule and make a decision, for example, "That sign has three sides. Therefore, that sign is a triangle."

Larry began with the general statement, "All doors in New York are locked." He decided, therefore, that the door in the surrounded building was locked. Next, he realized that "To open a locked door, you need a key." Stockton opened the locked door, so Larry deduced that he had a key.

Here are three other general statements that Larry must have thought of as he unlocked the mystery. Read the general statement and figure out the specific statement that Larry deduced from it, using the rest of the information he had.

a. No one can carry materials (such as disguises) past police officers without being seen.

b. A person being chased doesn't have time to explore a new hiding place.

c. The police officers would have noticed anyone not in their group.

Review

Using Your Skills in Reading Short Stories

The following paragraph is the introduction of the short story "Charles" by Shirley Jackson. Read it carefully. Then answer these questions: From what point of view is the story being told? Who is the narrator? What have you learned about Laurie?

The day my son Laurie started kindergarten, he rejected corduroy overalls with bibs and began wearing blue jeans with a belt. I watched him go off the first morning with the older girl next door, seeing clearly that an era of my life was ended, my sweet-voiced nursery-school tot replaced by a long-trousered, swaggering character who forgot to stop at the corner and wave good-bye to me.

Using Your Comprehension Skills

Read the following poem from Chapter 5, "The Termite," by Ogden Nash. It contains at least two examples of cause and effect. Identify at least one effect and its cause. Then identify any clue words that helped you, and explain how they helped.

Some primal termite knocked on wood
And tasted it, and found it good,
And that is why your cousin May
Fell through the parlor floor today.

Using Your Vocabulary Skills

The following sentences are from poems you will read in Chapter 5. Each underlined word has more than one meaning and may be used as more than one part of speech. The possible parts of speech of the underlined word are listed after the sentence. If you were looking up the word in the dictionary, for which part of speech would you look?

1. I have nothing I <u>treasure</u> more.   noun, verb, adjective

2. The Barn Owl <u>blunders</u> on her way.   noun, verb, adjective

3. Every day that <u>dawns</u>, you must say to yourself, "I was born today!" noun, verb, adjective

4. He <u>clasps</u> the crag with crooked hands.   noun, verb

5. You gull up there, <u>dive</u> down!   noun, verb, adverb, preposition

Using Your Writing Skills

Choose one of the writing assignments below.

1. Choose, from any story in this chapter, the character whom you could picture the best. In one to three paragraphs, explain why you chose this character. Did the author describe him or her at length? Did the character's words or actions tell a great deal about him or her? Did you feel strongly about the character, either for or against? Use details from the story to support your statements.

2. You have learned that in the introduction to a short story, the writer usually describes the setting. Imagine that you are going to write a mystery story set in your own home or school. Write the introduction to your short story, concentrating only on the setting. Be as specific as possible. Provide details that describe the setting exactly. Use words that appeal to the senses.

Using Your Skills in Critical Thinking

You have learned that a generalization is a general statement about many specific things or events. You have also learned that some generalizations are not true. Of what use, then, are generalizations? Explain at least one way in which generalizations are helpful to us in our thinking or in explanations. Also, describe one way in which the use of generalizations might be harmful. (You may wish to review the use of generalizations in deductive reasoning. See Developing Skills in Critical Thinking on page 237.)

CHAPTER 5

Equinox, 1968, JOAN MIRÓ. Etching and aquatint, 41 1/16" × 29".
Collection, Museum of Modern Art, New York City.
Gift of Studebaker Worthington, Inc.

$\mathcal{R}$eading Literature: Poetry

What Is Poetry?

Poetry is a special way of using words. It appeals to your senses and your imagination. Poets choose words with particular meanings and sounds and combine them so as to create vivid pictures and feelings. Poets help you see your world in a new way.

The History of Poetry

Poetry is the oldest form of literature. In poetry, people of long ago were able to tell about and relive exciting experiences in their imagination. They could use the rhythm of words to make their poems music-like and easy to remember. Early songs, chants, prayers, and stories were all poems.

The ancient Greeks and Romans appreciated the beauty and power of carefully arranged words. Therefore, they wrote their plays in poetry. For thousands of years, stories about heroes and brave adventures, called **epics**, were told in poem form. In more recent times, William Shakespeare, perhaps the greatest English playwright, wrote his plays as poetry.

Poets pay attention to what is happening in the world. In their work, they show their feelings about current events and ideas. Because of this, styles in poetry change with the times. In some periods, poets have tried to be logical and controlled. At other times, they have been imaginative and free-thinking.

The Elements of Poetry

Rhythm. The pattern of stressed and unstressed beats in a poem is called **rhythm**. There are two types of rhythm: 1) regular, steady rhythm; and 2) free verse.

In words of more than one syllable, certain syllables are stressed. Others are not stressed. In a poem with **regular rhythm**, words are arranged to make a regular pattern of stressed and unstressed beats. An example is "One, two, buckle my shoe."

In **free verse**, words are arranged more freely. The pattern of beats is not regular. Every line of a free verse poem may have a different pattern of stressed and unstressed beats.

> Bring me all of your
> Heart melodies
> That I may wrap them.

Rhyme.   Words that **rhyme** end with the same sound. When rhyming words appear at the ends of lines, the rhyme is called **end rhyme**.

Sounds in a Poem.   To a poet, the sounds of words are just as important as their meanings. Poets choose words for special effects, including those you learned about in Chapter 3, such as alliteration, onomatopoeia, and rhyme.

Figurative Language.   As you learned in Chapter 3, **figurative language** is a way of speaking or writing that makes you look at familiar things in a new way. Types of figurative language in poetry include similes, metaphors, personification, and hyperbole.

How To Read a Poem

1. Read each poem aloud. Hearing the sounds of a poem makes the meaning clearer and adds to your enjoyment.
2. Decide who is speaking in the poem. Is the poet speaking? Is the poet imagining the words another person might say?
3. Take time to imagine the things or feelings the poet describes.
4. Give each poem a chance. You will like some poems more than others. Everyone does. But remember that each of these poems has something to give you, if you want to take it.

Comprehension Skills: Inferences and Outcomes

Making Inferences in Poetry

Most poets use as few words as possible. To understand poetry, you need to work with the clues that are given. In other words, you have to become skilled at making inferences.

Read these beginning lines from a poem about a close basketball game and its final tense seconds.

> With two 60's stuck on the scoreboard
> And two seconds hanging on the clock,
> The solemn boy in the center of eyes,
> Squeezed by silence,
> Seeks out the line with his feet,
> Soothes his hands along his uniform,

It's amazing how much you can learn from this short section of the poem. By building on the evidence in those six lines, you can answer all the following questions.

1. What's the score of the game? (The clues can be found in Line 1). *60–60*
2. How many seconds are left? (Line 2) *two seconds*
3. What are the fans doing? (Line 3) *watching the boy*
4. What is the atmosphere in the gym? (Line 4) *tense. The boy feels the silence pressing in on him from all sides.*
5. What is the boy about to do? (Line 5) *make a foul shot*
6. How does the boy feel? How do you know? (Line 6) *He's so nervous that his palms are damp. He has to wipe them off.*

After you have collected enough evidence and made logical inferences, you may use what you know to **draw a conclusion**. To do this, you study your evidence and decide what it means when taken as a whole.

Predicting Outcomes in Poetry

Some poems describe a situation and then invite you to figure out what might happen next. If you read carefully, you will usually find clues to help you. Combined with your common sense and knowledge from past experiences, they will point you in the right direction so that you can predict a logical outcome.

Even if you are reading a poem that tells a complete story, it's a good idea to think about what might happen next. When you do, you will discover that you have started reading more carefully just to find out if your guess is right or wrong.

Exercises: Understanding Inferences, Drawing Conclusions, and Predicting Outcomes

A. Which line of the following poem tells you that the eagle is perched on a high mountain?

He clasps the crag with crooked hands;
Close to the sun in lonely lands,
Ringed with the azure world, he stands.

B. Which conclusion can you draw about Abe Lincoln from this stanza of a poem about him? Remember that conclusions are based on more than one piece of evidence.

He liked telling stories,
He liked telling jokes.
"Abe's quite a character,"
Said quite a lot of folks.

a. Abe liked to tell jokes.
b. Abe was interesting and fun to be with.

C. Which sentence below tells what the eagle may do next?

He watches from his mountain walls,
And like a thunderbolt he falls.

a. He will attack a small animal below.
b. He will crash into the rocks below.

Vocabulary Skills: Context Clues

Using Context Clues

Do you take a dictionary along with you when you go to the movies? Do you keep a dictionary on your lap when you watch TV at home? You would never think of it. Yet, even without using a dictionary, you can probably define new words you have heard at the movies or on TV. You know that you can usually guess at the meaning of a new word if you pay attention to clues in the story.

Learning the meanings of new words that you read can be just as easy. All you need to do is know which clues to look for. Here are a few kinds of context clues that can help you.

Example Clues. Writers often explain unfamiliar words by examples. Some key words and phrases to look for in example clues are *for example, one kind, for instance, like, especially, and other,* and *such as.*

Jeff is fascinated by dangerous sea creatures, such as the stingray and the great white shark.

From this example clue, you can guess that a *stingray* is a dangerous sea creature. The key phrase is *such as.*

Comparison Clues. When writers want to relate similar ideas, they use comparison clues. Often you will find the meaning of an unfamiliar word in one of the related ideas. Some key words and phrases to look for are *in addition, also, too, moreover, besides, another, other, both, the same, and all.*

Lisa was ecstatic at winning first prize. Moreover, her parents and friends also felt joyful.

From this clue, you can guess that *ecstatic* means "joyful."

Contrast Clues. Contrast clues tell you that the writer is talking about opposite meanings. You can sometimes understand a new word after you know its opposite. Some key words and phrases are *although, but, however, on the other hand, as opposed to, unlike, different from, in contrast,* and *not the same.*

The grasshopper's frivolous attitude was very different from the practical, matter-of-fact attitude of the ant.

From this clue, you can guess that *frivolous* means "silly" or "not serious." The key phrase is *different from.*

Words in a Series. Writers sometimes use a series of words to explain a new word. They know that you may understand other words in the series. They hope that you will be able to transfer your knowledge of the known words to the unknown word.

The salesperson opened the cabinet. He showed his customer the necklaces, bracelets, brooches, and rings.

You can see that a *brooch* must be a type of jewelry because all the other items in the series are jewelry.

Exercise: Using Context Clues

Use context clues to figure out the meaning of each underlined word. Be prepared to tell why you believe that you are right. Also, identify the key words that helped you find the meaning.

1. Casey doffed his cap when the crowd cheered, unlike Jones who aways kept his cap on.

2. We studied moles and other small mammals that live underground.

3. You're not half as spry as I am. For instance, I can climb up the trees more quickly and gracefully than you can.

4. In addition to the tumult out on the playing field, there was also noisy confusion in the locker room.

5. Although he felt skittish inside, outwardly he acted calm.

Poems About Individual Growth

As you know, the **theme** of a piece of writing is the main idea that the writer wants to share with you. It is the meaning of the piece of writing. Every poem has a theme.

In this section, every poem is about individual growth. As you read, try to answer this question: Does this poem set goals for me?

Portrait of Mademoiselle Violette Heymann, 1909, ODILON REDON.
The Cleveland Museum of Art, Cleveland, Ohio, Honmun B. Hurlbut Collection.

The Dream Keeper

LANGSTON HUGHES

Have you ever given up a dream because someone told you it wasn't practical? Read to find out what Langston Hughes would like to do with that dream.

Bring me all of your dreams,
You dreamers,
Bring me all of your
Heart melodies
That I may wrap them
In a blue cloud-cloth
Away from the too-rough fingers
Of the world.

Developing Comprehension Skills

1. Why does the poet think our dreams need special care?
2. To whom is the poem addressed?
3. What does the poet offer to do? What do you think he means?
4. What do you think a heart melody is?

Reading Literature: Poetry

1. **Understanding Figures of Speech.** In lines 7 and 8 the poet uses a figure of speech, **personification**:

   > the too-rough fingers
   > Of the world

   What can a person's "too-rough" fingers do to a delicate object? In what way can the whole world be compared to a single person handling a dream?

2. **Identifying Sounds of Language.** This poem does not use rhymes or a regular rhythm to give a pattern to the poem. Instead, it uses repetition of letters at the beginning of words (alliteration), repetition of letters in other parts of words, and repetition of whole words. Find an example of each of these uses of language.

3. **Recognizing Special Terms.** This poem uses several terms that were made up just for the poem. We can understand these terms because each of them combines words we already know. The way in which the poet combined the words, however, gives them a fresh meaning. For example, the term "heart melodies" combines two ideas: things that are close to you personally, and songs that may bring beauty or happiness. What two ideas are combined in each of these terms: "cloud-cloth" and "dream keeper"? What do you think each term means? Could the poet have used different words and still expressed the same meaning and the same feeling?

4. **Identifying Theme.** In "The Dream Keeper," the poet is saying something about dreams. What general statement do you get from the poem? Do you think the poet is right?

The Duel

EMILY DICKINSON

Little David, the Bible says, killed the giant Goliath with just a small stone thrown by David's slingshot. As you read, find the answer to this question: Is the speaker in this poem as successful as David?

I took my power in my hand
And went against the world;
'Twas not so much as David had,
But I was twice as bold.

I aimed my pebble, but myself
Was all the one that fell.
Was it Goliath was too large,
Or only I too small?

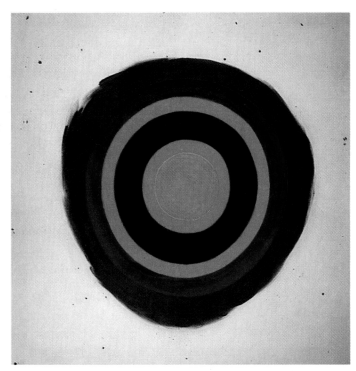

Song, 1958, KENNETH NOLAND. Whitney Museum of American Art, New York City. Gift of the Friends of the Whitney Museum of American Art.

Developing Comprehension Skills

1. This poem uses personification. The speaker pictures a duel between herself and another person, but what does the poem say her opponent really was?

2. What does the speaker mean by these lines?

   I aimed my pebble, but myself
   Was all the one that fell.

   What do you think the "pebble" might be? What is the speaker trying to do with it?

3. Which side won the duel? How do you know?

Reading Literature: Poetry

1. **Recognizing Allusions.** Frequently, writers refer, or **allude**, to other writings. These references are called **allusions**. When you know something about the work to which the writer alludes, you often understand more of what the writer means to say.

   Throughout "The Duel," the poet alludes to the Biblical story of David and Goliath. David was a prayerful person, who usually gave credit for his successes to God. How does that information affect the meaning of this poem?

2. **Identifying Rhythms.** Read "The Dream Keeper" and "The Duel" aloud. "The Dream Keeper" has an irregular rhythm. The accented syllables are not in any particular pattern, and the length of the lines varies. Does "The Duel" have a regular or an irregular rhythm?

3. **Identifying Mood.** As you learned in Chapter 4, the **mood** of a piece of writing is the feeling you get when reading it. Which of the following words best describes the mood of this poem? Be prepared to explain your choice.

   angry   puzzled   proud

4. **Understanding Theme.** Does this poem tell us not to fight against problems we see in the world? Is it telling us to give up without trying? What do you think it is suggesting?

The Courage That My Mother Had

EDNA ST. VINCENT MILLAY

What's the best thing we could inherit from our parents? Read to find out what this poet thinks.

The courage that my mother had
Went with her, and is with her still:
Rock from New England quarried;
Now granite in a granite hill.

The golden brooch my mother wore
She left behind for me to wear;
I have no thing I treasure more:
Yet, it is something I could spare.

Oh, if instead she'd left to me
The thing she took into the grave!—
That courage like a rock, which she
Has no more need of, and I have.

Developing Comprehension Skills

1. The mother in this poem has died and left a golden brooch, or pin, for her daughter. What does the speaker wish she had instead of the pin?

2. To what does the speaker compare her mother's courage?

3. Do you know from the poem where the mother's birthplace was? Which words tell you?

4. Why does the speaker regret that the mother took her courage "into the grave"?

Reading Literature: Poetry

1. **Recognizing Organization.** Prose writing is written in sentences, and the sentences are grouped in paragraphs. Each paragraph has a main idea. In poetry, the ideas may or may not be expressed in sentences. They are written in **lines**. The lines are grouped in **stanzas**—sets of two or more lines separated from other stanzas by a line of space. Often, there is a main idea in each stanza.

   How many stanzas are there in this poem? Are the lines in each stanza all about one main idea? If so, what is the main idea of each of the stanzas?

2. **Identifying Irony.** The term **irony** usually refers to a situation in which one thing seems to be true but actually the opposite is true. It can also refer to a situation in which one action seems right or needed, but it doesn't happen. This poem uses irony in the second sense. What is ironic in the situation that the speaker describes?

3. **Determining Theme.** A reader might say that this poem is talking about one woman's death and one daughter's feelings about her mother's death. However, most readers would feel that the poet is suggesting something more general. Think about the irony in this poem. Think about what you have received from your parents, grandparents, and other ancestors. Then decide on a general statement about life that this poem may be making.

All But Blind

WALTER de la MARE

Some animals, the poet points out, see very poorly. They are blinded by bright daylight. As you read, look for a comparison that the poet makes between these animals and another creature.

All but blind
  In his chambered hole
Gropes for worms
  The four-clawed Mole.

All but blind
  In the evening sky,
The hooded Bat
  Twirls softly by.

All but blind
  In the burning day
The Barn-Owl blunders
  On her way.

And blind as are
  These three to me,
So, blind to Someone
  I must be.

Developing Comprehension Skills

1. In the first stanza, the poet does not use the normal order of words in a sentence. Explain in your own words what he is saying.

2. The poem lists three examples of "all but blind" animals. Does their poor vision hurt these animals? Does it prevent them from doing what they need to do in order to survive?

3. In the last stanza, the person who is speaking compares himself to the three animals. In what way does he think he is like them? Who might the "Someone" be?

Reading Literature: Poetry

1. **Looking at Rhyme.** In each stanza of this poem, the second and the fourth lines rhyme. How does this affect the word order, especially in the first stanza?

2. **Recognizing Repetition of Words and Phrases.** The poet uses the word "blind" five times and the phrase "all but blind" three times. How does this repetition establish a pattern in the poem?

3. **Identifying Rhythm.** The **rhythm pattern** of a poem can be shown in writing. To do this, copy the poem, leaving extra space between lines. Then draw this mark, /, over each accented syllable and this mark, ⌣, over each unaccented syllable. Here is the first stanza of "All But Blind" with the rhythm marked:

   All but blind
      In his chambered hole
   Gropes for worms
      The four-clawed Mole.

   Figure out the rhythm pattern for the other three stanzas of the poem. One of the stanzas will be slightly different from this basic pattern. Which stanza has a different pattern? Can you think of any reason the poet would want it to sound different?

4. **Identifying Theme.** A poet expresses his or her personal beliefs in poetry. Not everyone will agree with what the poet says. What general statement about life is the writer of "All But Blind" making? Can you explain why some people will not agree with this statement?

Developing Vocabulary Skills

Using Context Clues. Read the following sentences. Each underlined word was taken from one of the first four poems of this chapter. You can determine the meaning of each word by using one of these types of clues: example, comparison, or contrast. Write the meaning of the word. Also, identify the type of clue that helped you find the meaning.

1. The duels between the knights were more serious than the hand-to-hand fights they had practiced as young squires.

2. Hard rocks like granite are made up of coarse grains and crystals.

3. The ancient Egyptians quarried huge blocks of limestone with copper chisels, unlike the later method of cutting stone with iron tools.

4. Emily blundered her way through the math test. However, she made no mistakes on the science quiz.

5. Marta wore several pieces of jewelry, including two bracelets, a necklace, and a brooch.

6. The mole's chambered hole had, for example, a room to eat in and a separate room to sleep in.

Developing Writing Skills

1. **Explaining Your Opinion.** Which of the four poems that you have read in this chapter do you like best? Do you like it for its sounds, for the pictures it brings to mind, for its ideas, or for some other reason? Tell your choice and explain your reason or reasons. Remember that every reader may make a different choice, or may base the choice on different reasons.

2. **Writing a Poem.** Three of the four poems you have read are organized in four-line stanzas. In two of the three poems, the second and fourth lines rhyme. The fourth poem was written in free verse, with no regular rhythm or rhyme. Choose one of these two forms, a four-line stanza with rhyme or a poem in free verse.

   Next, think about a good topic for a short poem. Your poem may have a serious theme, like the four poems in this section. It may have a lighter theme, if you prefer. Try to think of a topic you might discuss with your friends in conversation. Then turn it into a poem. Make your poem no longer than twelve lines long.

Developing Skills in Study and Research

Discovering the Quickest Way To Find Information. The major purpose of the card catalog is to direct library users to specific books. It is useful in other ways, too. Each card provides some important facts about the book and author listed. Sometimes you can get all the information you need from the card catalog itself, without going on to the books listed. This exercise will help you use the card catalog to its fullest.

First, look up one of these writers in the card catalog of your school or public library: Langston Hughes, Emily Dickinson, Edna St. Vincent Millay, Walter de la Mare. (They are the poets whose poems you have just read.) Use the information in the card catalog to answer the following questions:

1. Did the poet write complete books? List some titles.

2. Which of the poet's books are in this library?

3. Did the poet write anything that is not poetry? Give the title or titles.

4. When was the poet born? When did he or she die?

Next, choose a general encyclopedia in your school or local library. Look up the same poet. In the encyclopedia article for that writer, look for the answers to the four questions above.

Last, compare the information you got from each source. Which facts were you able to learn from both the card catalog and the encyclopedia? Which were in only one source? Which questions were answered more clearly or more completely in the encyclopedia?

Developing Skills in Speaking and Listening

Interpreting the Mood of a Poem. Before reading a poem aloud, you must understand its mood. You should read it over several times, asking yourself questions about the person making the statements in the poem. For example, for Langston Hughes's "The Dream Keeper," you might ask such questions as these:

What kind of person would care about the dreams of others? What kind of person would want to save those dreams, to wrap them up and protect them? If you were that person, what tone would you use to speak to dreamers? Would you use any gestures? Is there any place in the poem you should pause in order to make a point?

Prepare to read aloud one of the four poems you have read so far in this chapter. If you choose "The Dream Keeper," use the above questions. If you choose one of the others, think of similar questions for yourself. When you are ready, present the poem to a group. You may read it or, if you prefer, recite it from memory.

Ocean Park #114, 1979, RICHARD DIEBENKORN.
Private Collection, Toronto. Courtesy of M. Knoedler and Co., Inc., New York City.

Magic Words To Feel Better

NETSILIK ESKIMO

As you read this poem, decide what the speaker wants. The title gives you a clue.

SEA GULL
who flaps his wings
over my head
                in the blue air,

you GULL up there
dive down
            come here
take me with you
                in the air!

Wings flash by
my mind's eye
and I'm up there sailing
in the cool air,
            a–a–a–a–a–ah,
                        in the air.

Multi-Feathered Bird, 1961, KENOJUAK.
Reproduced with the permission of the West Baffin Eskimo Cooperative.

Developing Comprehension Skills

1. To whom is the speaker talking in the first stanza? In the second stanza? In the third stanza?

2. How does the speaker feel about the sea gull?

3. During the poem, the speaker changes the mood. Where does the change come? Explain the change.

4. Does the speaker actually fly at the end of this poem? If not, how does the speaker get the feeling of flying?

Reading Literature: Poetry

1. **Understanding the Shape of a Poem.** Sometimes the way a poem is printed adds to its message. How does this poem make the reader see that "in the air" is an important phrase?

2. **Recognizing Onomatopoeia.** The term **onomatopoeia** refers to words that sound like what they are describing, such as the *clop-clop* of horses' hooves. In this poem, the made-up word *a-a-a-a-ah* suggests what its stanza is describing. What action or feeling does it bring to your mind? If it were dropped from the stanza, what idea or feeling would the poem lose?

3. **Understanding Theme.** Explain how the title, "Magic Words To Feel Better," is right for this poem.

The Song by the Way

FRANCISCO A. de ICAZA

Imagine walking alone from town to town. What would you take along? Read to see what this person takes.

A solitary pilgrim I;
Through foreign lands I stray;
Yet am I not alone—my song
Goes with me all the way.

And if the night around be black,
I make it bright as day;
I sing, and then the song lights up
The darkness of the way.

I do not sigh for weariness
However far I stray;
The heavenly staff of song makes brief
The distance of the way.

Ah, sad indeed that pilgrim's lot
Who goes along all day,
Nor has, for comrade of his march,
A song along the way!

Shepherd Showing Travellers Their Way, 1857, JEAN FRANCOIS MILLET.
The Corcoran Gallery of Art. William A. Clark collection.

Developing Comprehension Skills

1. Who is speaking in this poem?

2. Name one difficulty the speaker faces and the thing that helps him through that difficulty.

3. The word *song* may refer only to a melody. However, can you think of some other things, such as "hopes," that it might stand for?

Reading Literature: Poetry

1. **Recognizing Rhyme and Rhythm.** Is the rhythm in this poem mostly regular or mostly irregular? What is somewhat unusual about the rhyming words in this poem? How do the patterns of rhythm and rhyme help to give the reader the idea of a long, steady hike?

2. **Understanding Metaphors.** This poem uses three different metaphors to show the importance of the speaker's song. In the second stanza, the speaker says the song "lights up the darkness," comparing it to the sun. In the third and fourth stanzas the speaker compares a song to two other things. What are those things? What does the speaker mean by each comparison?

I Was Born Today

AMADO NERVO

*When things don't work out,
wouldn't it be good sometimes
to start all over? Find out what
this poet has to say about
starting over.*

Every day that dawns, you must say
    to yourself,
"I was born today!
The world is new to me.
This light that I behold
Strikes my unclouded eyes for the
    first time;
The rain that scatters its crystal drops
Is my baptism!

"Then let us live a pure life,
A shining life!
Already, yesterday is lost. Was it bad?
    Was it beautiful?
. . . Let it be forgotten.
And of that yesterday let there remain
    only the essence,
The precious gold of what I loved
    and suffered
As I walked along the road . . .

"Today, every moment shall bring
    feelings of well being and cheer.
And the reason for my existence,

Take-Off, 1983, JOANNE CULVER.

My most urgent resolve,
Will be to spread happiness all over the world,
To pour the wine of goodness into the
        eager mouths around me . . .

"My only peace will be the peace of others;
Their dreams, my dreams;
Their joy, my joy;
My crystal tear,
The tear that trembles on the eyelash of another;
My heartbeat,
The beat of every heart that throbs
Throughout worlds without end!"

Every day that dawns, you must say to yourself,
"I was born today!"

Developing Comprehension Skills

1. What does the speaker tell you to do each day? What does he suggest you do about the past?

2. What does the speaker believe should be the attitude of every person toward other people?

3. The mood of this poem is very cheerful and optimistic. The poem asks the reader to "spread happiness" and to see each day as a new beginning. Would it be easy to put the ideas of this poem into practice? Give a reason for your opinion.

Reading Literature: Poetry

1. **Understanding Rhythm and Repetition.** In "I Was Born Today," the poet does not use rhyme or regular rhythm. Instead, he emphasizes important ideas by repeating them in slightly different words. For

example, in the first stanza, after stating "I was born today," he says "The world is new to me." Then he gives two examples of how it is new: he is seeing the light for the first time, and the rain is his baptism. For each of the phrases below, find another phrase that states almost the same idea:

a. a pure life
b. the reason for my existence
c. to spread happiness

2. **Making Inferences in Poetry.** Not every day is peaceful and joyful. Is there any indication in the poem that the speaker knows this? What lines in the poem suggest that the speaker has known unhappiness? Does the speaker realize that everyone is going to have bad days? What makes you think so?

3. **Recognizing Metaphors.** Gold ore is a combination of small particles of gold with large amounts of other, mostly worthless materials. The process of separating the gold from the other materials is called *refining.* In order to refine gold, the ore is crushed, heated, and treated with chemicals that pull the ore apart. In the second stanza of "I Was Born Today," find the metaphor that uses gold. What is being compared to gold? How is life like the process of refining gold?

4. **Understanding Theme.** What is the theme of this poem?

Developing Vocabulary Skills

Inferring Word Meaning from Context. Frequently you can figure out the meaning of a word from the sentence in which it appears, even though there are no specific context clues. This is called **inferring** the meaning. For example, read this sentence:

Joan's reason for being late seemed *plausible*, so the teacher excused her.

From the meaning of the sentence as a whole, you can guess that *plausible* means "believable" or "apparently acceptable."

The following sentences about the poems in this section use terms that may be new to you. Use the information in the sentence to find the meaning of each underlined word or phrase. On your paper, copy the underlined word or phrase and write the definition you have inferred from the sentence context.

1. The mole's eyes are so <u>myopic</u> that the poet calls the animal "all but blind."
2. In "The Dream Keeper," the poet <u>coined</u> the terms *cloud-cloth* and *heart-melodies.*
3. The living speaker had need of the courage that was <u>superfluous</u> to her dead mother.
4. A song cheered the traveler during his <u>peregrinations</u>.
5. The poem "Magic Words To Feel Better" <u>evokes</u> the feeling of flying or floating in the air.
6. In "I Was Born Today," the speaker expresses a desire for <u>empathy</u> with others when he says, "My only peace will be the peace of others; Their dreams, my dreams; Their joy, my joy."

Developing Writing Skills

1. **Comparing Moods.** Some of the selections in Poems About Individual Growth had a somewhat discouraged mood. Others had a very positive, enthusiastic mood. A few had a mood somewhere between these two feelings. Which poems would you place in each group? Explain your choices in a paragraph or more.

2. **Describing an Experience in a Poem.** "Magic Words" tells about a very simple experience. The speaker sees the soaring gull and feels like flying with it. In imagination, the speaker sails in the cool air.

   Think of some simple, natural thing that has cheered you up or made you feel excited. Write a poem about it. Speak to the animal or object in some part of the poem. End by telling how you feel.

Developing Skills in Study and Research

Using Sources. One of the poems in the group you have just read was by an Eskimo poet. Two of them were by poets from South America. Suppose you wanted to find out more about poems from other lands. How would you search for information or more poems? Choose either Eskimo poetry or poetry from South America, and answer both questions below.

1. How would you use the encyclopedia to find out more about the kind of poetry you chose? Tell at least two topics you might look up to

begin your search for information. Describe the sort of information you think you might find in these articles.

2. How would you use the card catalog to find out more about the kind of poetry you chose? List at least two different headings you might look up to find references to useful books. Tell what sort of material you might find listed under each heading.

Developing Skills in Speaking and Listening

Listening to Poetry. You have learned that in a poem every word is important. Therefore, when you listen to a poem, it is important to listen very carefully. This activity will help you think about and improve your listening habits.

Work in groups of three to five. Each group should choose one of the poems in this section, Poems About Individual Growth. One person in the group should prepare to read the entire poem; the other members should each choose and prepare one stanza.

Two or more groups should join to listen to each other's presentations. First, each poem should be read by the students who prepared one stanza each. Then have the entire group discuss these questions:

1. Does the speed at which poetry is read change with the reader?

2. What effect does a change in reading speed have on the listener?

3. Are there any skills that may help a listener adjust to different reading speeds?

4. Does hearing someone read a poem make it easier to understand the poem than just reading it silently? Why or why not?

Second, those students who prepared entire poems should present their poems. Then the entire group should discuss these questions:

5. Is it easier to listen to a poem of four or more stanzas when it is read by one person or when it is read by several persons? Are there some advantages to each way? What are those advantages?

6. Is it easier to listen to a short poem, of three stanzas or fewer, read by one person or by more than one person? What are the advantages and disadvantages of each way?

7. What should a listener do to develop listening skills for any of these situations?

Poems About Animals

Very often a poet invents a character as well as a poem. The poem sounds as if the character were talking, not the poet. The person speaking in any poem is called the **speaker**. When you read a poem, it is important for you to decide who the speaker is. It may be the poet. It may be an invented human character. It may even be an animal character!

Endangered Species: Bald Eagle, 1983, ANDY WARHOL.
Photograph by D. James Dee, Courtesy of Ronald Feldman Fine Arts, New York City.

Reading Literature: More About Poetry

More About the Elements of Poetry

You have already learned that a poem uses sounds and figures of speech to express its meaning. The information on these pages will help you see how a poet can make use of these elements.

The Shapes of Poems

Poems are organized according to **lines** rather than sentences. The lines are grouped in **stanzas** rather than paragraphs. The length of lines and of stanzas can vary, even within one poem.

Concrete Poems. Poets are very inventive. They think of every possible way to use words to get across their ideas. Sometimes they arrange their words to form a shape. That shape tells more about the subject of their poem. A poem whose shape reminds you of the subject of the poem is called a **concrete poem.** For example, a poem about a kite might be shaped like a kite.

Haiku. In this section, you will read two haikus. A *haiku* is a poem with seventeen syllables. Usually it has three lines, five syllables in the first line, seven in the second line, and five in the last line. Usually, a haiku is about one thing. It describes the thing so clearly that you can picture it in your mind. The haiku gives one, sensory image.

Rhyme Scheme

In poems with rhyme, the rhyming words usually form a pattern. This pattern is called **rhyme scheme.** It is possible to keep track of, or chart, the rhyme scheme of a poem. To do this, you label every line in the poem with a letter of the alphabet. Use the same letter for lines that end with words that rhyme. The rhyme scheme of the following poem has been labeled.

Lincoln was a long man. a
He liked the out of doors. b
He liked the wind blowing c
And the talk in country stores. b

Many different rhyme schemes are possible. Besides *a b c b,* some of the most common are these: *a a b b, a b a b, a b b a.*

Narrative and Lyric Poems

A poem can be either a narrative poem or a lyric poem. A **narrative poem** tells a story. Narrative poems are usually quite long. The epic poems of long ago that told of courageous adventures were narratives. So are a few of the poems you will read in the next section.

In a **lyric poem**, the poet expresses his or her personal emotions. A lyric poem seems almost like a song. It does not tell a story. Many examples of lyric poems are in this chapter.

Mood

The **mood** of a poem is the feeling the poem gives you. The mood is not created by accident. It is the result of the poet's efforts to choose the right words. The perfect word does two things: it communicates the meaning the poet has in mind; it stirs up in the reader the emotions and ideas the poet has in mind. That is why poets take into account both the **denotation** and the **connotation** of a word. The denotation of a word is its dictionary meaning. Its connotation consists of the thoughts and emotions it brings to your mind.

Poets can create a mood by the level of language they use. Informal language can give a casual, friendly, down-to-earth feeling. Formal language can make you feel serious and respectful.

Poem

WILLIAM CARLOS WILLIAMS

Imagine a cat walking on a narrow, cluttered shelf. As you read this poem, can you find ways in which the poem suggests the care with which the cat moves?

As the cat
climbed over
the top of

the jamcloset
first the right
forefoot

carefully
then the hind
stepped down

into the pit of
the empty
flowerpot.

Developing Comprehension Skills

1. What part of the cat moves first into the flowerpot? What part follows after?

2. Reading this poem is much like watching a film. It simply describes what happens. Why do you think anyone would write about something so simple?

Reading Literature: Poetry

1. **Understanding Rhythm.** This poem has no rhyming words and no regular rhythm. Two techniques the poet uses, however, give the poem a cat-like rhythm: short lines and repeated phrases.

   a. Read the poem aloud, pausing very briefly at the end of every line. What does the shortness of the lines tell about the way the cat is moving?

   b. Find the first verb, *climbed.* It is followed by a phrase that tells where, *over the top,* and one that gives an added detail, *of the jamcloset.* Where is this pattern repeated?

2. **Identifying Mood.** Does this poem show any particular feeling about the cat? What mood did you feel as you read the poem?

Catalog

ROSALIE MOORE

The title of this poem is a pun. Look up the meaning of the word catalog. Then read the poem and find the double meaning in its title.

Cats sleep fat and walk thin.
Cats, when they sleep, slump;
When they wake, stretch and begin
Over, pulling their ribs in.
Cats walk thin.

Cats wait in a lump,
Jump in a streak.
Cats, when they jump, are sleek
As a grape slipping its skin—
They have technique
Oh, cats don't creak.
They sneak.

Cats sleep fat.
They spread out comfort underneath
     them
Like a good mat,
As if they picked the place
And then sat;
You walk around one
As if he were the City Hall
After that.

If male,
A cat is apt to sing on a major scale;
This concert is for everybody, this
Is wholesale.
For a baton, he wields a tail.

(He is also found,
When happy, to resound
With an enclosed and private sound.)

A cat condenses.
He pulls in his tail to go under bridges,
And himself to go under fences.
Cats fit
In any size box or kit,
And if a large pumpkin grew under one,
He could arch over it.

When everyone else is just ready to go
     out,
The cat is just ready to come in.
He's not where he's been.
Cats sleep fat and walk thin.

Developing Comprehension Skills

1. What are some of the changes in a cat's shape that this poem describes? In what different ways does the cat move its tail?

2. Besides describing the appearance of a cat, this poem describes two of its sounds. Name them.

3. Why is a cat who has chosen its resting place compared to the City Hall?

4. Does the speaker seem to admire cats or dislike them? Explain your answer.

Reading Literature: Poetry

1. **Understanding Patterns of Rhyme.** Each stanza of this poem uses a different rhyme scheme. Which stanza matches each of the rhyme schemes shown below? Why do you suppose the poet did not stick to one pattern of stanza length and rhyme?

(a) a	(b) a	(c) a	(d) a	(e) a	(f) a	(g) a
b	b	b	a	b	b	a
a	a	a	a	b	b	b
c	a	c		c	b	a
a	a	c		b		a
d	a	d		b		
e		c		b		
a						

2. **Finding Alliteration.** There are several examples of alliteration in this poem. In a few stanzas, one particular sound appears repeatedly, both at the beginning of words and in other positions. The use of this single sound helps to hold the stanza together.

   Find at least two examples of alliteration—that is, the use of the same sound at the beginning of several words found close together. Also, identify one sound that is used several times in the same stanza, not only at the beginnings of words.

3. **Understanding Simile and Metaphor.** Find similes in stanzas 2 and 3 and a metaphor in stanza 4. In each comparison, identify the two things being compared to each other. In what way are the two things alike? How does each comparison add to the feelings you are getting about cats?

Sea Lions

VALERIE WORTH

Did you ever wonder how zoo animals like being in zoos? Read to find out how this poet might answer that question.

The satin sea lions
Nudge each other
Toward the edge
Of the pool until
They fall like
Soft boulders
Into the water,
Sink down, slide
In swift circles,
Twist together
And apart, rise again
Snorting, climb
Up slapping
Their flippers on
The wet cement.
Someone said
That in all the zoo
Only the sea lions
Seem happy.

Sea Lion. Photo Researchers, Inc., New York City.

Developing Comprehension Skills

1. Think of the sea lions you have seen in a zoo or on television. Why do you think the speaker calls them "satin"?

2. Identify the line that tells these two facts about the animals: they are heavy, and they are flexible.

3. Reread the last four lines of the poem. What has the rest of the poem said to support the statement in these lines?

Reading Literature: Poetry

1. **Understanding Sounds in a Poem.** In this poem, alliteration helps to suggest the movements of the sea lions. What sound do you hear at the beginning of words throughout the poem? Is it a hard sound or a soft sound? How does it relate to the sea lions' actions?

2. **Understanding Similes.** A simile says that two unlike things are alike in some way. Frequently, a good simile suggests several ways in which the two things are alike. For example, consider the simile in lines 5 to 7:

   They fall like
   Soft boulders
   Into the water.

   Comparing seals to boulders stresses the weight of the seals. It also stresses their size. It even suggests their color. In what way does it describe their movements?

Seal

WILLIAM JAY SMITH

The sea lions in Valerie Worth's poem moved softly and smoothly. Read William Jay Smith's poem. Pay special attention to the words that describe the seal's actions.

See how he dives
From the rocks with a zoom!
See how he darts
Through his watery room
Past crabs and eels
And green seaweed,
Past fluffs of sandy
Minnow feed!
See how he swims
With a swerve and a twist,
A flip of the flipper,
A flick of the wrist!
Quicksilver-quick,
Softer than spray,
Down he plunges
And sweeps away;
Before you can think,
Before you can utter
Words like "Dill pickle"
Or "Apple butter,"
Back up he swims
Past stingray and shark,
Out with a zoom,
A whoop, a bark;
Before you can say
Whatever you wish,
He plops at your side
With a mouthful of fish!

Developing Comprehension Skills

1. Read over the first eight lines and list all the words you can find that show movement. Is the seal moving rapidly or slowly?

2. Do you think the seal in this poem is swimming in a zoo pond or in the sea? Use phrases from the poem to support your answer.

3. Is the mood of "Seal" serious or light-hearted? Which words or phrases helped you decide?

Reading Literature: Poetry

1. **Understanding Concrete Poems.** A **concrete poem** uses shape to remind a reader of its subject. "Seal" is a concrete poem because the way it is printed on the page reminds the reader of something about the seal. Explain what you think it is.

2. **Understanding Rhyme.** What is the rhyme scheme of the first four lines of "Seal"? Is this rhyme scheme repeated anywhere else in the poem? If so, where?

   The poem is written as one long stanza. It could have had a more complicated rhyme scheme, as in the longer stanzas of "Catalog." Why do you think the poet kept to the rhyme scheme that you identified?

3. **Identifying Rhythm.** As you learned earlier in this chapter, the rhythm pattern of a poem can be shown in writing. Write the first eight lines of this poem, leaving space after every line. Then mark each stressed syllable with this accent, /, and each unstressed syllable with this accent, ⌣. (If you like, review Reading Literature 3, for "All But Blind," page 256.) You will find that the number and position of unstressed syllables vary. How many stressed syllables are there in every line?

Woodpecker

ISSA

This haiku distributes its seventeen syllables over four lines. It pictures one moment of a long day. However, can you tell what has been happening throughout the day?

Stubborn woodpecker
   Still hammering
    At twilight
At that single spot.

Developing Comprehension Skills

1. In your own words, tell what the poet describes in "Woodpecker."
2. This poem has only ten words. Three of them give clues about the woodpecker's actions during the day and the speaker's attitude toward the woodpecker. Identify the three words, and tell what you can infer from them.

Reading Literature: Poetry

Identifying Sensory Images. Usually, a haiku has three lines. Although this poem has four lines, its use of seventeen syllables shows that it is a haiku. It is also like other haiku in its presentation of a single sensory image. That is, it describes one experience so clearly that the reader imagines that he or she can see or hear or feel the thing described. To what sense does this haiku appeal? When you read it, do you imagine seeing, hearing, or feeling something?

Fall

As you read this haiku, decide which parts of it might be shown in a picture.

SALLY ANDRESEN

The geese flying south
In a row long and V-shaped
Pulling in winter.

The Twelve Months (detail), 1823—31,
KATSUSHIKA HOKUSAI. Freer Gallery of Art,
Smithsonian Institution, Washington, D.C.

Developing Comprehension Skills

1. To which of your senses does this poem appeal?

2. In order to understand this poem, you must know something about geese. What fact about geese explains why the poet says this flock is "Pulling in winter"?

Reading Literature: Poetry

1. **Examining Form.** How does the form of this haiku differ from the form of "Woodpecker"? Compare both the number of lines and the number of syllables per line.

   Basing your answer on these two haiku, would you say that rhyme is an important element in haiku poetry?

2. **Comparing Tone.** As you learned in Chapter 4, the **tone** of a piece of writing is the attitude the writer takes toward the subject. Both "Woodpecker" and "Fall" are about birds. Do the speakers in each poem take the same attitude toward birds? Give a reason from the haiku for your answer.

Developing Vocabulary Skills

Using Context Clues. In Chapter 1 you learned that an unfamiliar word can be figured out by finding a definition or restatement clue or a synonym. In this chapter you learned four other context clues: **example**, **comparison**, **contrast**, and **series**. Read the following sentences or groups of sentences. Each underlined word was used in one of the poems you have read. Figure out the meaning of the word by using context clues. Write the meaning of the word and the type of context clue you used to find the meaning.

1. In contrast to her day at the office, where she is constantly dealing with people, Mrs. Jordan enjoys a solitary evening at home.

2. Mr. Dexter often has lunch with his comrades at the university. He and his companions share their ideas and thoughts.

3. Jessica resolved not to quit the swim team, and she also decided to join the drama club.

4. The owner of this store buys his materials at wholesale prices. In other words, he buys them in large quantities at lower prices.

5. Large <u>boulders</u>, or rocks, slid from the steep mountain and blocked the highway.

6. The artist painted shades of blue, such as <u>azure</u>, in the background.

7. The snake-like <u>eel</u> is really a fresh- or salt-water fish.

8. Some people prefer the reserved <u>techniques</u> of a cat to the outgoing manners and style of dogs.

Developing Writing Skills

1. **Comparing Images.** You have just read two poems about cats, two about seals, and two about birds. Choose one of these pairs of poems. Compare the word pictures of the animals in the two poems. Did the animal move differently in each poem? Did it have a different personality? Did it affect the speaker in a different way?

   Imagine that you were a pet shop owner selling these animals. If you were to use one of the poems in an ad, which of the two poems would you expect to draw more customers?

   Write at least one paragraph comparing the poems.

2. **Writing a Haiku.** These two statements are true for every haiku: It presents a single sensory image, and it uses seventeen syllables. Think of experiences you have had. Try to remember something you saw clearly and vividly. You may remember a particular sound or touch or taste. Choose one of those sensations for the topic of your poem. Then list as many words and phrases as you can to describe it. Be as specific as possible.

   When you have listed all the words and phrases you can think of, choose the ones that describe the sensation best. Then write a haiku, using those words and phrases in your poem if you can. Remember that the number of syllables must be exactly seventeen. Make sure that the sensory image is clear.

Bee! I'm Expecting You!

EMILY DICKINSON

The following poem takes the form of a letter between two rather unusual friends. Read to find out who they are.

Bee! I'm expecting you!
Was saying Yesterday
To Somebody you know
That you were due—

The Frogs got Home Last Week—
Are settled, and at work—
Birds, mostly back—
The Clover warm and thick—

You'll get my Letter by
The seventeenth; Reply
Or better, be with me—
Yours, Fly.

Developing Comprehension Skills

1. Who is the speaker in this poem?
2. Who is being addressed and what does the speaker want him or her to do?
3. What season is celebrated in this poem?

Reading Literature: Poetry

1. **Identifying Rhyme.** In this poem, Emily Dickinson's rhyme scheme is not simple. Identify all the words that rhyme, either at the ends of lines or within one line.

2. **Recognizing Personification.** This poem personifies several animals and insects. Name them and the ways in which they are said to be like humans.

Flowers of Four Seasons (detail), 17th Century. SOSEN. The Philadelphia Museum of Art, Gift of Mrs. John C. Atwood.

The Eagle

As you read this poem, discover all the images that tell of the dignity and power of the eagle.

ALFRED, LORD TENNYSON

He clasps the crag with crooked hands;
Close to the sun in lonely lands,
Ringed with the azure world, he stands.

The wrinkled sea beneath him crawls;
He watches from his mountain walls,
And like a thunderbolt he falls.

Developing Comprehension Skills

1. At least three phrases tell you where the eagle of the poem is. Identify these phrases.

2. Explain this simile:

   And like a thunderbolt he falls.

3. Reread line 5. Can you suggest a cause-and-effect connection between that and line 6?

4. The poet uses many images in this poem to help us see the eagle as he does. Which one do you like best? Explain why.

Wallowa Lake, 1927–28, STEVE HARLEY. Abbey Aldrich Rockefeller Folk Art Center, Williamsburg, Virginia.

Reading Literature: Poetry

1. **Identifying Rhyme and Rhythm.** Copy the first stanza of this poem, leaving a line of space after each line. Mark the stressed and un-stressed syllables with these marks: ╱, ◡. Then write the rhyme scheme, using as many letters of the alphabet as you need.

2. **Recognizing Alliteration.** Which letter is used repeatedly at the beginning of words in stanza 1? How does it stress the harshness of the setting?

   Can you find examples of alliteration using other letters, also?

3. **Understanding Personification.** Some of the words used to describe the eagle make it seem almost human. What are some of the words? How does this personification make the eagle more interesting?

The Mountain and the Squirrel

RALPH WALDO EMERSON

This poem is very much like some of the fables you have read. Look for a moral stated in two words.

The mountain and the squirrel
Had a quarrel,
And the former called the latter "Little prig;"
Bun replied,
"You are doubtless very big;
But all sorts of things and weather
Must be taken in together
To make up a year,
And a sphere.
And I think it no disgrace
To occupy my place.
If I'm not so large as you,
You are not so small as I,
And not half so spry.
I'll not deny you make
A very pretty squirrel track.
Talents differ; all is well and wisely put;
If I cannot carry forests on my back,
Neither can you crack a nut!"

Ielerang or Javan Squirrel, 1850. Hand-colored lithograph from a drawing by Edward Lear. Field Museum of Natural History.

Developing Comprehension Skills

1. You will find three speakers in this poem. Identify each.

2. Read the first four lines carefully. Who is Bun?

3. Which of these words would you use to describe the squirrel?
   a. shy   b. self-confident   c. bold   d. overbearing

4. Identify the words of the poem that state its moral. Then explain the moral in your own words.

Reading Literature: Poetry

1. **Identifying Rhyme.** The rhyme scheme in this poem is unusual. Use letters of the alphabet to label the first eleven lines of the poem. Does every line rhyme with another line?

2. **Understanding Characters.** The squirrel tells the mountain:

   I'll not deny you make
   A very pretty squirrel track.

   Is the squirrel trying to insult the mountain or to compliment it? How do you think the mountain would react to the comment? Does the comment tell you anything about the squirrel's view of the world?

The Dog
(As Seen by the Cat)

OLIVER HERFORD

We usually think of dogs and cats as not getting along well with each other. Read this poem to get an insider's view of the relationship!

The dog is black or white or brown,
And sometimes spotted like a clown.
He loves to make a foolish noise,
And Human Company enjoys.

The Human People pat his head
And teach him to pretend he's dead,
And beg, and fetch, and carry, too;
Things that no well-bred Cat will do.

At Human jokes, however stale,
He jumps about and wags his tail,
And Human People clap their hands
And think he really understands.

They say "Good Dog" to him. To us
They say "Poor Kit" and make no fuss.
Why Dogs are "good" and Cats are "poor"
I fail to understand, I'm sure.

To Someone very Good and Just,
Who has proved worthy of her trust,
A Cat will sometimes condescend—
The Dog is Everybody's friend!

Developing Comprehension Skills

1. Who is the speaker in this poem?

2. The dog is compared to a clown. What other phrases show that the cat looks down on him?

3. If you believe this speaker, what kind of people would want cats for pets? What kind would like dogs?

4. In what tone of voice should the last two lines be read?

Reading Literature: Poetry

1. **Understanding Rhyme.** Write the rhyme scheme of the first stanza of this poem. Do all the stanzas use the same pattern?

2. **Making Inference.** This cat states its opinion of dogs quite clearly. The cat also suggests its opinion of humans. What is that opinion? What lines in the poem support your answer?

Developing Vocabulary Skills

Recognizing Context Clues. The following paragraph is about eagles. This is an example of a paragraph you may read in a textbook or a book about eagles. Read the paragraph and answer the four questions that follow.

> Eagles can be identified by three distinguishing habits. They are diurnal birds, as opposed to nocturnal fliers. That is, eagles fly and hunt for food by day, rather than by night as do the owls. An eagle is a raptorial bird, one who preys upon other birds and animals, seizing them in its talons and sometimes in its bill. Eagles are believed to mate for life, not a common occurrence among birds.

1. What phrase in the second sentence tells you that the sentence is a contrast statement?

2. The third sentence gives a clue to the meanings of the words *diurnal* and *nocturnal* found in the second sentence. What type of clue is it? What does each of the words mean?

3. In the fourth sentence what type of clue gives the meaning of a *raptorial* bird? What does the term mean?

4. The word *talons* is in the fourth sentence. Use the context of the sentence to infer what the word might mean. What is the exact meaning found in the dictionary?

Developing Writing Skills

1. **Analyzing a Poem.** What quality of eagles is most important in "The Eagle"? Write at least one paragraph explaining your opinion. Point out words or phrases from the poem that support your answer.

2. **Taking a Different Point of View.** Write one of these responses to poems you have read about animals.

   a. Imagine that you are the bee to whom the fly is writing in "Bee! I'm Expecting You!" Explain why you are late. Write in poetry, using four-line stanzas, or in prose.

   b. Imagine that you are the mountain in "The Mountain and the Squirrel." Add some lines to the poem, giving the mountain's point of view. You might comment on what a mountain is good for, or what a mountain can do that a squirrel cannot do.

   c. Imagine that you are a dog. Write an answer to the cat speaker in "The Dog (As Seen by the Cat)." Use examples of what cats and dogs do, and how they behave with humans, to make your points. Write in either prose or poetry.

Developing Skills in Critical Thinking

Identifying Slanted Language. Frequently a writer appears to be stating facts when he or she is actually expressing an opinion. The writer does not directly state that he or she likes or dislikes the thing being described. Instead, the writer uses words that make the thing look good or bad. For example, instead of saying that a person is *quiet*, the writer says the person is *dull*.

Reread "The Dog (As Seen by the Cat)." The cat looks down on the dog but never says so directly. The cat's slanted language, however, shows its opinion. Find four examples of language that is used to make the dog look inferior.

The Panther

OGDEN NASH

Perhaps you know the difference between leopards and panthers. See if you agree with Ogden Nash.

The panther is like a leopard,
Except it hasn't been peppered.
Should you behold a panther crouch,
Prepare to say Ouch.
Better yet, if called by a panther,
Don't anther.

Developing Comprehension Skills

1. Explain line 2 in your own words. Then explain line 6.

2. Is the poem serious or humorous? Refer to specific words and phrases in the poem that support your answer.

Reading Literature: Poetry

1. **Understanding the Poet's Choice of Words.** If a panther were to spring at you, you would probably not cry, "Ouch!" Why does the poet use this word instead of a more serious cry for help?

2. **Understanding Figurative Language.** The first line of the poem uses the word *like* to compare the two animals. Is this a simile? Explain your reasons.

The Termite

OGDEN NASH

*Do you know what instinct is?
This poem gives an example of
the results of termite instinct.*

Some primal termite knocked on wood
And tasted it, and found it good,
And that is why your Cousin May
Fell through the parlor floor today.

Developing Comprehension Skills

1. Explain in your own words why May fell through the floor.

2. Have you ever heard a superstitious person use the phrase "knock on wood"? That person may think that knocking on wood is a way to keep away bad luck. Why did the poet use that phrase in the poem? How does it affect your feelings toward the termite?

Reading Literature: Poetry

1. **Recognizing the Sounds of Language.** Rhyme and the repetition of the *t* sound and the *d* sound give shape to this poem. Write the rhyme scheme. Then list all the words that use the *t* sound and underline the letters that make the sound. Can you explain why those two sounds work well in this poem?

2. **Understanding Mood.** This poem discusses termites and a dangerous home accident. You might expect these topics to be discussed seriously. Is the poem serious? In what ways does it set its mood?

The Hippopotamus

OGDEN NASH

There is an old saying that beauty is in the eye of the beholder. In this poem, find out whose eye sees beauty in a hippo.

Behold the hippopotamus!
We laugh at how he looks to us,
And yet in moments dank and grim
I wonder how we look to him.
Peace, peace, thou hippopotamus!
We really look all right to us,
As you no doubt delight the eye
Of other hippopotami.

Hippopotamus from the Egyptian tomb of Senbi.
The Metropolitan Museum of Art, Gift of Edward S. Harkness, 1917.

Developing Comprehension Skills

1. The speaker addresses two audiences. Who are they and at what line does the change take place?

2. What does the speaker think hippos may feel about people? What line or lines make you think this?

Reading Literature: Poetry

Understanding Patterns of Rhythm. Certain rhythm patterns are used frequently in poems because they sound much like natural speech. One of these is iambic rhythm. **Iambic** rhythm alternates an unstressed beat and a stressed beat, shown this way: ∪ / ∪ / ∪ /. Is this poem mostly iambic or mostly some other pattern?

The Canary

OGDEN NASH

Most people think a canary is a pretty little bird that cheers us all with its song. Does this poet agree?

The song of canaries
Never varies,
And when they're moulting
They're pretty revolting.

Developing Comprehension Skills

1. What does the poet find "revolting" about canaries?

2. Do you think the poet likes the canaries' song? Give your reasons.

Reading Literature: Poetry

1. **Recognizing Rhythm.** Copy this poem, leaving space between the lines. Mark the stressed syllables. Is this poem mostly iambic or mostly another pattern? (If necessary, review page 295.)

2. **Understanding Mood.** The mood of this poem is critical and negative toward canaries. Write your own version of this poem, following these directions and keeping the same mood:

   a. Change the first line to read "A canary's song."

   b. Change the second line so that it rhymes with "song."

   c. Replace the last two lines with another statement critical of canaries. The ending words in the last two lines should rhyme.

The Purist

OGDEN NASH

This professor was an excellent scientist. Does he seem to be an excellent person?

I give you now Professor Twist,
A conscientious scientist.
Trustees exclaimed, "He never bungles!"
And sent him off to distant jungles.
Camped on a tropic riverside,

One day he missed his loving bride.
She had, the guide informed him later,
Been eaten by an alligator.
Professor Twist could not but smile.
"You mean," he said, "a crocodile."

Developing Comprehension Skills

1. List at least two phrases or words that describe the Professor.

2. In line 9, why did Professor Twist smile?

3. We can presume the professor has two loves. What were they and which was first in importance for him?

Reading Literature: Poetry

1. **Understanding Elements of Poetry.** Compare this poem to others by Ogden Nash, considering the following:

   a. rhyme scheme   b. mood

2. **Understanding Theme.** Most of the other poems by Ogden Nash in this book are humorous, with no particular message. It is possible, however, to find a rather serious message in this funny poem. Can you state that message, or theme, in your own words?

Developing Vocabulary Skills

Completing Analogies. As you learned in the vocabulary exercise for "The Bet" in Chapter 4 (page 172), an analogy consists of two pairs of related words that are related in the same way. Here is an example:

Herd is to cow as flock is to bird.

The first term in each pair, herd and flock, is the group name for the animal named in the second term, cow and bird. Other relationships include synonyms and antonyms.

Each incomplete analogy below uses words from the prose and poetry selections you have already read in this book. For each, choose the word that will complete the relationship. Be able to explain why you chose that word.

1. Weary is to tired as eager is to _____.
   zealous   valiant   tranquil   severe

2. Quack is to whinny as duck is to _____.
   bear   turkey   horse   dog

3. Venture is to hesitate as superintend is to _____.
   obey   direct   agree   tell

4. Cow is to hay as _____ is to wood.
   panther   termite   hippopotamus   canary

5. Friend is to loyal as enemy is to _____.
   slow   prophetic   vengeful   enthusiastic

6. Reed is to grass as stingray is to _____.
   seal   fish   glass   danger

7. Surrey is to horse as car is to _____.
   road   driver   tires   engine

8. Tremulous is to firm as monotony is to _____.
   treason   variation   rascal   vagabond

Developing Writing Skills

1. **Examining Humor in Poems.** All four poems by Ogden Nash in this text were funny. Can you explain, in one or more paragraphs, how his

rhymes helped create the humor? If you prefer, you can write about his rhythms or about his use of words that surprise the reader.

2. **Imitating a Poet.** The poetry of Ogden Nash is easy to imitate, especially with the regular rhythms used in "The Termite," "The Purist," and "The Hippopotamus." Think of some subjects you could use to make people laugh: joggers, TV watchers, video-game players, sports fans. Write a poem of at least four lines, using some of Ogden Nash's rhythm and rhyme patterns and his surprising mix of words.

Developing Skills in Study and Research

Becoming Familiar with Other Library Resources. A library contains more than books. In your school or local library, find the record and tape collection. Also, locate the section of the card catalog in which these resources are listed. Notice that some records are of music and some are of non-musical presentations, such as poetry readings.

Find out if your library has any records or tapes of any of the poems in this chapter. List the title of the record or tape, and the name of the person who did the reading.

Your library may have no records or tapes of poems in this book. However, it may have recordings of other poems by the poets you have read. If so, list those records and tapes.

Ogden Nash wrote funny poems to be read to the music of *Carnival of the Animals* by the French composer Emile Saint-Saens. Does your library have a recording of the music along with the poems? If so, list both the conductor and the narrator.

Developing Skills in Speaking and Listening

1. **Reading Humorous Poems.** Is there one Ogden Nash poem you liked best? Perhaps you have found another poem by the same author in another source. Prepare to read or recite your favorite Nash poem to your class. Remember that these funny poems are very short. Give your audience time to get the humor by using pauses or gestures.

2. **Changing the Interpretation of a Poem.** If you located "Carnival of the Animals" in the Study and Research activity above, you might want to listen to and copy some of the verses you like. Recite them with the record. Then prepare and recite your own interpretations, using different expression.

Poems About Sports

Most of us enjoy taking part in sports. We like the feelings that the activity and excitement give us. We also enjoy watching sports. The power and grace of an athlete are a pleasure to watch.

The poems in this section try to put into words what we feel or see in sports. As you read these poems, notice how the figures of speech make the sports action come alive.

Sandlot Game, 1964, RALPH FASANELLA. Private Collection.

The Base Stealer

ROBERT FRANCIS

As you read this poem, decide who is speaking. Is it the base stealer? Or is it someone watching the base stealer?

Poised between going on and back, pulled
Both ways taut like a tightrope-walker,
Fingertips pointing to opposites,
Now bouncing tiptoe like a dropped ball
Or a kid skipping rope, come on, come on,
Running a scattering of steps sidewise,
How he teeters, skitters, tingles, teases,
Taunts them, hovers like an ecstatic bird,
He's only flirting, crowd him, crowd him,
Delicate, delicate, delicate, delicate—now!

Developing Comprehension Skills

1. Who is the speaker in this poem, the base stealer or someone watching him? What makes you think as you do?

2. Find four similes in this poem. To what four different things is the base stealer compared?

3. Which of the four similes do you think pictures the action best? Why did you choose that one?

Reading Literature: Poetry

1. **Making Inferences in Poetry.** Do you think that the base stealer is experienced at stealing bases? Find two lines that you feel support your decision.

2. **Predicting Outcomes in Poetry.** Is it possible to make an accurate prediction about whether or not the base stealer succeeds? Why or why not?

3. **Understanding Rhythm.** This poem has been written in free verse, which means it has a free, or irregular, arrangement of stressed and unstressed beats. Copy the following lines and put an accent mark, ', over the syllables that are stressed. Notice how the rhythm of each line makes you feel the movement of the base stealer.

   How he teeters, skitters, tingles, teases,
   Delicate, delicate, delicate, delicate—now!

The Double-Play

ROBERT WALLACE

In this poem, things happen fast—too fast for the speaker to repeat a name, even when that person is involved in two actions. If you are unsure what or who is acting, go back to the last thing or person named.

The Wide Swing, about 1975,
HARVEY DINNERSTEIN.
Capricorn Galleries, Bethesda, Maryland.

In his sea lit
distance, the pitcher winding
like a clock about to chime comes down with

the ball, hit
sharply, under the artificial
banks of arc lights, bounds like a vanishing string

over the green
to the shortstop magically
scoops to his right whirling above his invisible

shadows
in the dust redirects
its flight to the running poised second baseman

pirouettes
leaping, above the slide, to throw
from midair, across the colored tightened interval,

to the leaning-
out first baseman ends the dance
drawing it disappearing into his long brown glove

stretches. What
is too swift for deception
is final, lost, among the loosened figures

jogging off the field
(the pitcher walks), casual
in the space where the poem has happened.

Developing Comprehension Skills

1. In your own words, describe the course of this double play.

2. In the sixth stanza, the speaker says the first baseman "ends the dance." Find another word or phrase that compares the action to a dance or the players to dancers.

3. Find the words listed below in the poem. What comparison do they suggest? In what ways is the comparison accurate?

   artificial   vanishing   magically
   invisible   disappearing   deception

1. **Making Inferences in Poetry.** Was this game played at night or during the day? What clues in the poem give you the answer?

2. **Understanding Rhythm.** This poem may be difficult to read because throughout most of the poem the rhythm is irregular. Why do you suppose the poet used this irregular rhythm?

   Reread the poem, listening for a break between the irregular rhythm and a regular rhythm at the very end. What is the effect of this change in rhythm?

3. **Recognizing Figurative Language.** Reading this poem is almost like watching a slow-motion instant replay. It draws your attention to little details that you do not ordinarily notice. Yet it does so in only a few words that suggest setting, action, and mood all at once. In your own words, explain each of these phrases:

   a. the pitcher winding
      like a clock about to chime
   b. the ball . . .
      bounds like a vanishing string
   c. the shortstop . . .
      whirling above his invisible
      shadows
      in the dust
   d. the running poised second baseman
   e. the leaning-
      out first baseman . . .
      drawing it disappearing into his long brown glove
   f. the loosened figures
      jogging off the field

4. **Recognizing Form.** This poem separates sharply into two parts: the action of the double play and the closing comments. There is a change in rhythm and a change in language, too. The first seven stanzas are full of details squeezed together, comparisons, and precise words. The last stanza, however, uses very ordinary language in a normal speaking tone. What detail about the players' actions does this stanza mention that makes the end of this inning like the end of a typical, ordinary inning?

Casey at the Bat

ERNEST LAWRENCE THAYER

This is one of the best known poems about sports that has ever been written. As you read, consider what it is that has made this poem so popular.

It looked extremely rocky for the Mudville nine that day;
The score stood two to four, with but an inning left to play.
So, when Cooney died at second, and Burrows did the same,
A pallor wreathed the features of the patrons of the game.

A straggling few got up to go, leaving there the rest,
With that hope which springs eternal within the human breast.
For they thought: "If only Casey could get a whack at that,"
They'd put even money now, with Casey at the bat.

But Flynn preceded Casey, and likewise so did Blake,
And the former was a pudd'n, and the latter was a fake.
So on that stricken multitude a deathlike silence sat;
For there seemed but little chance of Casey's getting to the bat.

But Flynn let drive a "single," to the wonderment of all.
And the much-despised Blakey "tore the cover off the ball."
And when the dust had lifted, and they saw what had occurred,
There was Blakey safe at second, and Flynn a-huggin' third.

Then from the gladdened multitude went up a joyous yell—
It rumbled in the mountaintops, it rattled in the dell;
It struck upon the hillside and rebounded on the flat;
For Casey, mighty Casey, was advancing to the bat.

The Autograph, 1980, OSCAR de MEJO.
20×16″ from the book, *My America,*
Harry N. Abrams, Inc., New York.

There was ease in Casey's manner as he stepped into his place,
There was pride in Casey's bearing and a smile on Casey's face;
And when responding to the cheers he lightly doffed his hat,
No stranger in the crowd could doubt 'twas Casey at the bat.

Ten thousand eyes were on him as he rubbed his hands with dirt,
Five thousand tongues applauded when he wiped them on his shirt;
Then when the writhing pitcher ground the ball into his hip,
Defiance glanced in Casey's eye, a sneer curled Casey's lip.

And now the leather-covered sphere came hurtling through the air,
And Casey stood a-watching it in haughty grandeur there.
Close by the sturdy batsman the ball unheeded sped;
"That ain't my style," said Casey. "Strike one," the umpire said.

From the benches, filled with people, there went up a muffled roar,
Like the beating of the storm waves on the stern and distant shore.
"Kill him! Kill the umpire!" shouted someone on the stand;
And it's likely they'd have killed him had not Casey raised his hand.

With a smile of honest charity great Casey's visage shone;
He stilled the rising tumult, he made the game go on;
He signaled to the pitcher, and once more the spheroid flew;
But Casey still ignored it, and the umpire said, "Strike two."

"Fraud!" cried the maddened thousands, and the echo answered "Fraud!"
But one scornful look from Casey and the audience was awed;
They saw his face grow stern and cold, they saw his muscles strain,
And they knew that Casey wouldn't let the ball go by again.

The sneer is gone from Casey's lips, his teeth are clenched in hate,
He pounds with cruel vengeance his bat upon the plate;
And now the pitcher holds the ball, and now he lets it go,
And now the air is shattered by the force of Casey's blow.

Oh, somewhere in this favored land the sun is shining bright,
The band is playing somewhere, and somewhere hearts are light;
And somewhere men are laughing, and somewhere children shout,
But there is no joy in Mudville: Mighty Casey has struck out.

Developing Comprehension Skills

1. How do you think the "patrons" or fans felt at the beginning of the poem? What is meant by, "A pallor wreathed (their) features"?

2. What caused the feelings of the crowd to change? Find the lines that are the first indication that their feelings have changed.

3. Why do you think Casey let the first two strikes go by?

4. The poem doesn't reveal what happened until the last two words. However, we begin to get the feeling that something went wrong in the line, "Oh, somewhere in this favored land the sun is shining bright." Explain why this line gives the reader that feeling.

Reading Literature: Poetry

1. **Identifying Rhythm and Rhyme Patterns.** Does this poem have a mostly regular rhythm or a mostly irregular rhythm?

   What is the rhyme scheme of the poem? Does every stanza follow the same pattern?

2. **Recognizing Hyperbole.** As you know, **hyperbole** is an extreme exaggeration that often brings to mind an absurd image. This poem has numerous examples of hyperbole, such as in stanzas 3 and 5:

   So on that stricken multitude a deathlike silence sat

   Then from the gladdened multitude went up a joyous yell—
   It rumbled in the mountaintops, it rattled in the dell;
   It struck upon the hillside and rebounded on the flat;
   For Casey, mighty Casey, was advancing to the bat.

   Find other examples of hyperbole in "Casey at the Bat."

3. **Examining Levels of Language.** One characteristic that makes this poem funny is its very serious tone, in contrast to its not very serious subject. In addition, it mixes slang terms, like "whack," and terms with special sports meanings, like "huggin' third," with rather formal terms, such as "stricken multitude." Make two lists. On the first, write at least five terms or phrases used in "Casey at the Bat" that are more formal than you would normally use in conversation. On the second, write at least five terms or phrases from the poem that are either slang or sports jargon.

Foul Shot

The following poem is not about just any foul shot. Read the first few lines carefully to find out what made this shot special.

EDWIN A. HOEY

With two 60's stuck on the scoreboard
And two seconds hanging on the clock,
The solemn boy in the center of eyes,
Squeezed by silence,
Seeks out the line with his feet,
Soothes his hands along his uniform,
Gently drums the ball against the floor,
Then measures the waiting net,
Raises the ball on his right hand,
Balances it with his left,
Calms it with fingertips,
Breathes,
Crouches,
Waits,
And then through a stretching of
    stillness,
Nudges it upward.

The ball
Slides up and out,
Lands,
Leans,
Wobbles,
Wavers,
Hesitates,
Exasperates,
Plays it coy
Until every face begs with
    unsounding screams—

And then
        And then
                And then,

Right before ROAR-UP,
Dives down and through.

Developing Comprehension Skills

1. There are four stanzas in this poem. The third stanza has only six words in it. What is the main idea of each stanza?

2. Give two meanings for this line: "The solemn boy in the center of eyes."

Reading Literature: Poetry

1. **Understanding Personification.** In this poem, the poet uses personification when he describes the ball. Find four words or phrases that suggest that the ball is a person.

2. **Understanding Concrete Poetry.** Many times the way the words are arranged in a poem helps to make the meaning of the poem clear. In two parts of "Foul Shot," there is only one word on each line. What effect does this have on the way you read the poem? What effect does it have on the feeling you get from the poem?

3. **Understanding Figurative Language.** This poem presents both the sights and sounds of a basketball game. Each phrase below mentions sound or the absence of sound. Explain both the sound and the feeling that the phrase expresses.

   a. Squeezed by silence   (stanza 1, line 4)
   b. through a stretching of stillness   (stanza 1, line 15)
   c. every face begs with unsounding screams   (stanza 2, line 10)
   d. Right before ROAR-UP   (stanza 4, line 1)

Developing Vocabulary Skills

Using Context Clues and Word Parts. Read the following sentences based on the poems you have just read. The meaning of each underlined word can be figured out by using context clues or word parts. Choose the correct answer. Then write the meaning of the word.

1. The base stealer teases, <u>taunts</u>, flirts as he skitters back and forth.

   a. restatement clue   b. comparison clue   c. words in a series

2. The shortstop scoops up the ball, and <u>redirects</u> its flight to the running second baseman.

   a. word parts   b. example clue   c. definition clue

3. The pitcher ground the ball into his hip and sent the leather-covered <u>sphere</u> hurtling through the air.

    a. words in a series   b. contrast clue   c. synonym

4. The sneer is gone from Casey's lips, his teeth are clenched in hate; he pounds with cruel <u>vengeance</u> his bat upon the plate.

    a. word parts   b. inference clue   c. contrast clue

5. The player leans, wobbles, <u>wavers</u>, and hesitates as he throws the ball.

    a. words in a series   b. comparison clue   c. example clue

Developing Writing Skills

1. **Evaluating a Poem.** Consider the four poems about sports that you have just read. Which one do you think did the best job of helping you experience the moment? Do not choose a poem just because you like the sport. Write a paragraph or more explaining why you chose the poem. Tell which figures of speech or sounds of language or sensory images meant the most to you.

2. **Using Specific Vocabulary.** "The Base Stealer," "The Double Play," and "Foul Shot" are all trying to do the same thing. They try to recreate the feeling of a specific moment in sports. You can do the same thing. First, think of the most exciting moment you have experienced in playing or watching a sport. Quickly list words and phases that describe the actions involved in the situation. Write every word that comes to mind as you relive the moment. Be as specific as possible. Also list any words that describe your feelings about the moment.

   Then, review your list. Choose the five best words or phrases. If you like, combine several separate words to form five strong phrases. Then use your five best phrases in a description of the moment. Write no more than ten lines or sentences in either poetry or prose.

Developing Skills in Speaking and Listening

Interpreting a Humorous Poem. "Casey at the Bat" provides an excellent opportunity for a dramatic reading. Practice reading this poem aloud. Your goal is to help your listeners experience the drama and emotion of that day. Sometimes silence in the right place adds to the drama. Look for places where pauses might be appropriate.

The Women's 400 Meters

LILLIAN MORRISON

This poem describes the racers as they prepare for and begin their run. Listen for the rhythm.

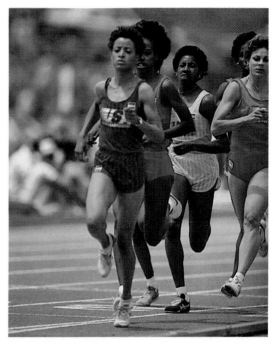

Photograph by John Kelly. The Image Bank, Chicago.

Skittish,
they flex knees, drum heels and
shiver at the starting line

waiting the gun
to pour them over the stretch
like a breaking wave.

Bang! they're off
careening down the lanes,
each chased by her own bright tiger.

Developing Comprehension Skills

1. What does "careening down the lanes" mean?

2. Explain the simile in lines 5 and 6. How are the runners like a wave?

3. Is the poet concerned with who will win this race? If not, what is she concerned with? Give a reason for your answer.

Reading Literature: Poetry

Appreciating Rhythm. Copy lines 5 and 9 on your paper, leaving space above each line. Mark each stressed beat with an accent, '. How many stressed beats do you find in line 5? How many are in line 9? How does the rhythm help to express the meaning of the line?

Poems About Sports 313

Skating

HERBERT ASQUITH

Have you ever watched an ice skater? Have you skated yourself? As you read this poem, watch for the ways the poem imitates the graceful movements of a good skater.

When I try to skate,
My feet are so wary
They grit and they grate;
And then I watch Mary
Easily gliding;
Skimming and curving,
Out and in,
With a turn of her head,
And a lift of her chin,
And a gleam of her eye,
And a twirl and a spin;
Sailing under
The breathless hush
Of the willows, and back
To the frozen rush
Out to the island
And round the edge,
Skirting the rim

Of the crackling sedge,
Swerving close
To the poplar root,
And round the lake
On a single foot,
With a three, and an eight,
And a loop and a ring;
Where Mary glides,
The lake will sing!
Out in the mist
I hear her now
Under the frost
Of the willow bow
Easily sailing,
Light and fleet,
With the song of the lake
Beneath her feet.

Developing Comprehension Skills

1. Is the speaker an experienced ice skater? Which lines in the poem give you the answer to that question?

2. Name three or more proofs that Mary is a good skater.

3. The speaker says that "Where Mary slides, The lake will sing." Is the lake making a sound? Is there any other kind of "song" to which this line could refer? Explain your opinion.

Reading Literature: Poetry

1. **Appreciating Rhyme.** Using letters of the alphabet, show the rhyme scheme of the first four lines of the poem. Then identify the rhyme in the next eleven lines the same way. Continue to use the same letter of the alphabet for the same rhyming sound.

   Examine the patterns of rhyme that you have found. Are the lines in this one long stanza grouped mostly in threes or in fours? Do you find a rhyme scheme repeating itself? Where is the rhyme different? Can you think of a reason why the poet used a different pattern of rhyme on certain lines?

2. **Recognizing Onomatopoeia.** This poem contrasts two kinds of skaters. It suggests the differences between them in the sounds of the words describing them.

   Find an example of alliteration in the first three lines. These lines describe the speaker's skating ability. What effect does the alliteration have on the description? Do the repeated sounds suggest any sound that the speaker's skates might make? If so, is the sound smooth or rough?

   Read over the rest of the poem. If possible, read it aloud. Note the number of times you hear each of these sounds, either at the beginning of a word or in any other position: *s, sh, z, l, r, w, th* as in *thick.* What effect do these sounds have on the description? What sorts of sounds do they suggest Mary's skates make?

Pole Vault

SHIRO MURANO

In a competition, an athlete concentrates on the track, mat, or other space in which he or she must perform. That space becomes the athlete's whole world. What is the horizon in the pole vaulter's small world?

He is running like a wasp,
Hanging on a long pole.
As a matter of course he floats in the sky,
Chasing the ascending horizon.
Now he has crossed the limit,
And pushed away his support.
For him there is nothing but a descent.

Oh, he falls helplessly.
Now on that runner, awkwardly fallen
   on the ground,
Once more
The horizon comes down,
Beating hard on his shoulders.

Developing Comprehension Skills

1. Restate line 7 in your own words.

2. At the beginning of the poem, the pole vaulter is aiming for his "horizon," the crossbar. Is he successful? Which lines led you to your answer?

3. Do you think this poem is only about the physical effort of the pole vaulter? Is there any way that a person's efforts in other parts of life could be like a pole vault contest?

Reading Literature: Poetry

Drawing Inferences in Poetry. Reread the last four lines of the poem. What do these lines tell you about this athlete? Has he failed to clear the crossbar on other jumps, too?

Sky Diving

RICHMOND LATTIMORE

*Not many of us will ever sky
dive, except in our imagination.
As you read "Sky Diving," try
to see and feel what the divers
are experiencing.*

They step from the high plane and begin
    to tumble
down. Below is the painted ground, above
is bare sky. They do not fumble
with the catch, but only fall; drop sheer;
    begin to move

in the breakless void; stretch and turn, freed
from pressure; stand in weightless air
and softly walk across their own speed;
gather and group, these dropping
      bundles, where

the neighbor in the sky stands, reach touch
and clasp hands, separate and swim
back to station (did swimmer ever
    shear such
thin water?) falling still. Now at last
    pull the slim

cord. Parasols bloom in the air, slow
the swift sky fall. Collapsed tents cover
the ground. They rise up, plain people now.
Their little sky-time is over.

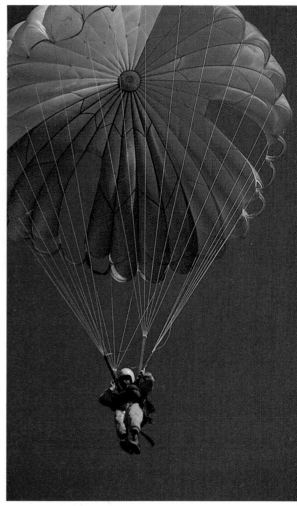

Freelance Photographers, New York.

Developing Comprehension Skills

1. What is meant by "the breakless void"?

2. How can you tell that these skydivers are experienced and have planned exactly what they will do as they fall?

Reading Literature: Poetry

1. **Recognizing Mood.** Which of these words would you use in describing the mood of this poem?

   excitement   wonder   danger   surprise   fear   delight

2. **Recognizing Rhyme and Rhythm.** Examine the way this poem looks, paying special attention to the ends of the lines. Does it look as if it has a strong, regular pattern of rhyme? Then reread the first two stanzas. Do you hear the rhymes clearly? Or do the rhymes blend in with the other words so that you hardly notice them? Reread the first two stanzas once more, listening for the rhythm. Is there a strong, steady rhythm, or an irregular rhythm?

   How do the patterns of rhyme and rhythm in this poem stress the meaning? How do they express the mood?

3. **Understanding Figurative Language.** Two metaphors are used to describe the parachutes. What are they? Why does the poet need two different metaphors? Are the parachutes in one metaphor different from the parachutes in the other?

Developing Vocabulary Skills

Choosing the Right Meaning for the Context. Read the following pairs of sentences. One sentence from each pair was drawn from the poems. Choose the correct meaning for the underlined word in each sentence.

1. Bob stretched his bubble gum until it broke.
2. The runners waited for the signal to pour them over the stretch.

   a. extend one's body or limbs; *stretch one's legs.*
   b. draw out to great length or size.
   c. a straight section of a race course or track.
   d. slang, a term of imprisonment; *served a two-year stretch.*

3. When I try to skate, my feet are so wary that they grit and grate.

4. His constant gum chewing grates on my nerves.

    e. a framework of iron to hold a fire.

    f. to have an annoying or unpleasant effect.

    g. to scrape or rub with rough or noisy friction; *to grate one's teeth.*

    h. to wear down or grind off in small pieces; *to grate cheese.*

5. The sky divers do not fumble with the catch, but only fall and drop sheer.

6. After the game, all of players dropped to their seats in sheer exhaustion.

    i. very thin; almost transparent; *a sheer blouse.*

    j. unmixed, complete; *There was sheer emptiness.*

    k. straight up and down; steep.

    l. swerve; turn aside; turn from a course.

7. This contract made ten years ago is now void.

8. The sky divers began to move in the breakless void.

    m. empty; vacant.

    n. something experienced as a loss; *When his friend moved, there was a void in his life.*

    o. an empty space.

    p. without force; not binding in law.

9. Don traced his descent from a family who came to America in the early years of our country.

10. For the pole vaulter there is nothing but a descent.

    q. coming or going down from a higher to lower place.

    r. a downward slope.

    s. deriving from a family line.

    t. a sudden attack.

Developing Writing Skills

1. **Analyzing Action Words in Sports Poems.** People who write about sports and athletes need to develop a good vocabulary in order to help other people share their excitement and enthusiasm. Choose any three poems in this section. List all the verbs you can find in these

three. Put the verbs into categories, such as active or passive, present tense or past tense. Study your lists and then write a paragraph or more in which you explain what you have discovered about writing sports poetry.

2. **Writing a Sports Poem.** You have been reading poems about athletes, their skill and their grace, their courage and determination.

Choose one sport you know something about, either through participation or by seeing it as a spectator. Make a list of at least ten words that you think best describe the sport. Include some words that show your attitude toward the sport, also.

Using these words as a starting place, try to write a poem in which you share just one feeling or idea about the subject you chose. Be sure you describe one event, and be sure you have included someone's feelings or attitude. The speaker may be either a participant or a spectator.

Developing Skills in Study and Research

Finding Biographies and Autobiographies. Find out how the biographies and autobiographies are grouped in your local or school library. On your paper, list the number or numbers assigned to biographies and autobiographies in the classification system used by your library. Then use the card catalog to locate a biography or autobiography of an author whose work you have read. Write on your paper the title, author, and the Dewey Decimal or other number assigned to the book.

Developing Skills in Critical Thinking

Classifying Poems. In this text, the poems have been grouped, or classified, according to themes or topics, including Individual Growth, Animals, Sports, and American History. The same poems could have been grouped according to other ideas, such as short poems and long poems, rhymed and unrhymed poems, humorous and serious poems. Choose your own system of classifying the poems you have read in this section, Poems About Sports, or in the first three sections of poetry. List the titles of your categories and, under each category title, the titles of the poems that fit in the category. Use two to four categories. Be sure to find a category for each poem in the group of poems you chose.

Poems About American History

The poems in this section are about people and events that happened in the past. Notice how the poets picture these people and events as clearly as if they were happening now. Notice, too, that each poet leaves us with a feeling about the person or event in the poem. Would you like to meet these people? Would you like to share in their adventures?

Three Flags, 1958, JASPER JOHNS. Encaustic on canvas, 30 ⅞ × 45 ½ × 5". Collection of Whitney Museum of American Art. 50th Anniversary gift of the Gilman Foundation, Inc., The Lauder Foundation, A. Alfred Taubman, (and purchase) Acq. #80.32.

Like Ghosts
of Eagles

The title of the poem is really a simile with the first word missing. Think carefully and decide who or what are "like ghosts of eagles."

ROBERT FRANCIS

The Indians have mostly gone
but not before they named the rivers
the rivers flow on
and the names of the rivers flow with them
    Susquehanna   Shenandoah

The rivers are now polluted plundered
but not the names of the rivers
cool and inviolate as ever
pure as on the morning of creation
    Tennessee   Tombigbee

If the rivers themselves should ever perish
I think the names will somehow somewhere hover
like ghosts of eagles
those mighty whisperers
    Missouri   Mississippi.

The Oxbow, 1836, THOMAS COLE. The Metropolitan Museum of Art. Gift of Mrs. Russell Sage, 1908.

Developing Comprehension Skills

1. This poem consists of three stanzas. Tell the main idea of each stanza in your own words. Be sure to mention the time about which each stanza speaks.

2. What changes in the rivers does the poet tell about? What has caused some of the changes? What might cause the final change?

3. The title is a simile. What does the poem compare to ghosts of eagles? What do the two things have in common?

4. Does the speaker in the poem have an opinion about the changes in the rivers? If so, what is the speaker's opinion? What is yours?

Reading Literature: Poetry

Looking for Cause and Effect. Does the speaker say there is any connection between the Indians going and the rivers being polluted? Did one event cause the other? Or is it possible that both events were caused by something else not mentioned in the poem?

The Flower-Fed Buffaloes

VACHEL LINDSAY

Keep "Like Ghosts of Eagles" in mind as you read this next poem. Look for ways in which the two poems are alike. Also look for ways in which they are different.

The flower-fed buffaloes of the spring
In the days of long ago,
Ranged where the locomotives sing
And the prairie flowers lie low:—
The tossing, blooming, perfumed grass
Is swept away by the wheat,
Wheels and wheels and wheels spin by
In the spring that still is sweet.
But the flower-fed buffaloes of the spring
Left us, long ago.
They gore no more, they bellow no more,
They trundle around the hills no more:—
With the Blackfeet, lying low,
With the Pawnees, lying low,
Lying low.

Herd of Buffalo (detail), 1862, WILLIAM JACOB HAYES.
The Denver Art Museum.

Developing Comprehension Skills

1. The speaker tells us that the buffalo, the grass, and the prairie flowers have gone. Tell in your own words what has taken their place.

2. Can you see any connection between the planting of wheat and the disappearance of buffalo?

3. The Blackfeet and Pawnees are native Americans. Like the buffalo, they are, the speaker says, "lying low." Tell what you think he means.

Reading Literature: Poetry

1. **Looking at Language.** Read again the first eight lines of the poem. Make a list of words the author uses to describe the locomotive and its movement. Do the words have pleasant or unpleasant sounds? Are these words intended to make the reader dislike the locomotive? Or do the words avoid giving the reader any strong feeling? Which line tells us the prairie spring has not completely changed?

2. **Appreciating Sound Patterns.** The poet repeats certain sounds frequently in this poem. Find at least three examples of each of the following sounds. (The same sound may be spelled different ways.)

   f   r   oa   l   s   w   m   oo

   What effect do these sounds have? Are they soft and flowing or harsh and disruptive?

3. **Identifying Rhyme Patterns.** "The Flower-Fed Buffaloes" makes use of rhyme. Use letters to identify the rhyme scheme.

4. **Recognizing Mood.** How would you describe the mood of this poem? Would you use any of the words listed below or others?

   sad   angry   happy   thoughtful   threatening   tired

Developing Vocabulary Skills

Using a Thesaurus. You have learned that you can use a dictionary to find the exact meaning. Some dictionaries will also list synonyms for a word. A **thesaurus** is another book to use when you need to find a synonym for a word.

To use a thesaurus, read the directions at the front of the book. Follow the directions to find the information about a word.

The entry words are grouped according to topic. After each entry word is a list of words that mean the same or almost the same thing. Most importantly, synonyms with different connotations, or feelings, are listed. The right synonym for any sentence will depend on the context of the sentence.

Reread the poem lines that contain the words listed below. Find each word in a thesaurus. Choose a synonym that could replace the word in the poem.

"Foul Shot"

1. soothes, line 6
2. crouches, line 13
3. exasperates, line 24

"Like Ghosts of Eagles"

4. perish, line 11
5. hover, line 12

"The Flower-Fed Buffaloes"

6. perfumed, line 5

Developing Writing Skills

1. **Comparing Poems.** Reread both "Like Ghosts of Eagles" and "The Flower-Fed Buffaloes." Make a list of ways in which the poems are alike. Make a separate list of ways they are different. Then write from one to three paragraphs comparing and contrasting the poems.

   Here are some features you might examine:

topic	rhythm	stanza form	theme
mood	rhyme	sound patterns	your reaction

2. **Writing About Change.** Both "Like Ghosts of Eagles" and "The Flower-Fed Buffaloes" were about change. They expressed some personal ideas and emotions about the subject. Think about changes in your life, both welcome and unwelcome. Then, either in prose or in poetry, describe your ideas or feelings about change. If you write prose, write no more than a paragraph. If you write a poem, it may be rhymed or unrhymed and no more than twelve lines long.

Developing Skills in Study and Research

Using Reference Sources: Maps and Dictionaries. Maps of different states and countries can be found in an **atlas.** Find in your library an atlas that includes a map of the United States as a whole. The atlas should also include maps of individual states or groups of states. The **index** of the atlas should include the names of the rivers listed in the poem "Like

Ghosts of Eagles." Using the index, locate each of those rivers on the maps. If you cannot find an atlas, find the rivers on a wall map, instead. On your paper, list the states through which each of the rivers flows.

There are many other rivers named by the native American Indians, and many states also bear Indian names. How can you find out which names came from the Indians? A dictionary can help you. Most desk dictionaries list not only a word and its meaning, but also the **origin**, or source, of the word. Usually the origin is shown after the pronunciation. If you look up *Susquehanna,* for example, you will find this:

[<Iroquoian tribal or stream name]

After *Shenandoah,* the dictionary may show some uncertainty:

[<AmInd. (? Iroquois)]

Using both the atlas and dictionary, find at least five names of states or rivers (not in the poem) from American Indian languages.

Developing Skills in Critical Thinking

Recognizing Generalizations. Imagine that you are discussing these poems with two other people. One of them says that life in America was better when the Indians were the only inhabitants because there was no pollution. The second person says that life is better now because we have so many modern conveniences.

Each of these statements is a **generalization**. A generalization is a general statement that describes all the items in a certain category. Some generalizations are always true, for example, "all triangles have three corners." Other generalizations are true only in certain cases. A generalization that is not always true is called a **faulty generalization**. An example is this statement: "Bike riders are careless in traffic." It is true that some bike riders do not follow traffic rules. However, there are other cyclists who follow the rules carefully.

Some faulty generalizations can be changed to be more accurate. For example, limiting the terms in the generalization about cyclists would make it true:

Some bike riders are careless in traffic.

Examine the two statements about life in the past and the present. Are they accurate or faulty generalizations? If they are faulty, how could they be changed and limited to be made accurate?

Benjamin Franklin
1706–1790

Ben Franklin was famous for many things. Two of his talents were writing and inventing. Keep these in mind as you read the poem.

STEPHEN VINCENT BENÉT
and ROSEMARY BENÉT

Ben Franklin munched a loaf of bread while walking down the street
And all the Philadelphia girls tee-heed to see him eat,
A country boy come up to town with eyes as big as saucers
At the ladies in their furbelows, the gempmun on their horses.

Ben Franklin wrote an almanac, a smile upon his lip,
It told you when to plant your corn and how to cure the pip,
But he salted it and seasoned it with proverbs sly and sage,
And people read "Poor Richard" till Poor Richard was the rage.

Ben Franklin made a pretty kite and flew it in the air
To call upon a thunderstorm that happened to be there,
—And all our humming dynamos and our electric light
Go back to what Ben Franklin found, the day he flew his kite.

Ben Franklin was the sort of man that people like to see,
For he was very clever but as human as could be.
He had an eye for pretty girls, a palate for good wine,
And all the court of France were glad to ask him in to dine.

But it didn't make him stuffy and he wasn't spoiled by fame
But stayed Ben Franklin to the end, as Yankee as his name.
"He wrenched their might from tyrants and its lightning from the sky."
And oh, when he saw pretty girls, he had a taking eye!

Developing Comprehension Skills

1. When Ben Franklin first came to town, what made the girls laugh at him?

2. When Franklin wrote his almanac, he wanted large numbers of people to read it. What did he put in it to "spice it up" and make it interesting?

3. The third stanza tells about a famous discovery. What was it?

4. Carefully reread the first and fourth stanzas. How has Ben Franklin changed?

5. Read the last two lines of the poem. What does each tell you? Explain how the two lines give two different sides of Franklin's personality.

Reading Literature: Poetry

1. **Recognizing Mood.** Would you say the mood of this poem is serious or light? Is it respectful or critical? Find some words and phrases in the poem that support your answer. Your examples should also show whether the level of language is formal or informal.

2. **Identifying Rhythm Patterns.** Choose any stanza of the poem and copy it, leaving space between lines. Mark the accents. You will find that the rhythm is very regular. How many syllables per line are stressed?

3. **Recognizing Narrative Poetry.** A poem that tells a story is called **narrative poetry**. A poem that emphasizes a mood or feeling, or shares one idea with the reader is called **lyric poetry**. Which kind of poem is "Benjamin Franklin"?

Paul Revere's Ride

HENRY WADSWORTH
LONGFELLOW

This long poem narrates the exciting events of the night of April 18, 1775. As you read, watch for words that make real for you the excitement of that long-ago night.

Listen, my children, and you shall hear
Of the midnight ride of Paul Revere,
On the eighteenth of April, in Seventy-five;
Hardly a man is now alive
Who remembers that famous day and year.

He said to his friend, "If the British march
By land or sea from the town tonight,
Hang a lantern aloft in the belfry arch
Of the North Church tower as a signal light,—
One, if by land, and two, if by sea;
And I on the opposite shore will be,
Ready to ride and spread the alarm
Through every Middlesex village and farm,
For the country folk to be up and to arm."

Then he said, "Good-night!" and with muffled oar
Silently rowed to the Charlestown shore.
Just as the moon rose over the bay,
Where swinging wide at her moorings lay
The Somerset, British man-of-war;
A phantom ship, with each mast and spar
Across the moon like a prison bar,
And a huge black hulk, that was magnified
By its own reflection in the tide.

Meanwhile, his friend, through alley and street,
Wanders and watches with eager ears.
Till in the silence around him he hears
The muster of men at the barrack door,
The sound of arms, and the tramp of feet,
And the measured tread of the grenadiers,
Marching down to their boats on the shore.

Then he climbed the tower of the Old North Church,
By the wooden stairs, with stealthy tread,
To the belfry-chamber overhead,
And startled the pigeons from their perch
On the sombre rafters, that round him made
Masses and moving shapes of shade,—
By the trembling ladder, steep and tall,
To the highest window in the wall,
Where he paused to listen and look down
A moment on the roofs of the town,
And the moonlight flowing over all.

Beneath, in the churchyard, lay the dead,
In their night-encampment on the hill,
Wrapped in silence so deep and still
That he could hear, like a sentinel's tread,
The watchful night-wind, as it went
Creeping along from tent to tent.
And seeming to whisper, "All is well!"
A moment only he feels the spell
Of the place and the hour, and the secret dread
Of the lonely belfry and the dead;
For suddenly all his thoughts are bent
On a shadowy something far away,
Where the river widens to meet the bay,—
A line of black that bends and floats
On the rising tide, like a bridge of boats.

The Paul Revere Event—Four Views (detail), 1968, LARRY RIVERS. Jason McCoy, Inc., New York City.

Meanwhile, impatient to mount and ride,
Booted and spurred, with a heavy stride
On the opposite shore walked Paul Revere.
Now he patted his horse's side,
Now gazed at the landscape far and near,
Then, impetuous, stamped the earth,
And turned and tightened his saddle-girth;
But mostly he watched with eager search
The belfry-tower of the Old North Church,
As it rose above the graves on the hill,

Lonely and spectral and sombre and still.
And lo! as he looks, on the belfry's height
A glimmer, and then a gleam of light!
He springs to the saddle, the bridle he turns,
But lingers and gazes, till full on his sight
A second lamp in the belfry burns!

A hurry of hoofs in a village street,
A shape in the moonlight, a bulk in the dark,
And beneath, from the pebbles, in passing, a spark
Struck out by a steed flying fearless and fleet:
That was all! And yet, through the gloom and the light,
The fate of a nation was riding that night;
And the spark struck out by that steed in his flight,
Kindled the land into flame with its heat.

He has left the village and mounted the steep,
And beneath him, tranquil and broad and deep,
Is the Mystic,[1] meeting the ocean tides;
And under the alders that skirt its edge,
Now soft on the sand, now loud on the ledge,
Is heard the tramp of his steed as he rides.

It was twelve by the village clock,
When he crossed the bridge into Medford town.
He heard the crowing of the cock,
And the barking of the farmer's dog,
And felt the damp of the river fog
That rises after the sun goes down.

It was one by the village clock,
When he galloped into Lexington.
He saw the gilded weathercock
Swim in the moonlight as he passed,
And the meeting-house windows, blank and bare,

---

1. The Mystic is a river that flows into Boston harbor.

Gaze at him with a spectral glare,
As if they already stood aghast
At the bloody work they would look upon.

It was two by the village clock,
When he came to the bridge in Concord town.
He heard the bleating of the flock,
And the twitter of birds among the trees,
And felt the breath of the morning breeze
Blowing over the meadows brown.
And one was safe and asleep in his bed
Who at the bridge would be first to fall,
Who that day would be lying dead,
Pierced by a British musket-ball.

You know the rest. In the books you have read,
How the British Regulars fired and fled,—
How the farmers gave them ball for ball,
From behind each fence and farm-yard wall,
Chasing the redcoats down the lane,
Then crossing the fields to emerge again
Under the trees at the turn of the road,
And only pausing to fire and load.

So through the night rode Paul Revere;
And so through the night went his cry of alarm
To every Middlesex village and farm,—
A cry of defiance and not of fear,
A voice in the darkness, a knock at the door,
And a word that shall echo forevermore!
For, borne on the night-wind of the Past,
Through all our history, to the last,
In the hour of darkness and peril and need,
The people will waken and listen to hear
The hurrying hoof-beats of that steed,
And the midnight message of Paul Revere.

Developing Comprehension Skills

1. Paul Revere and his friend agreed on signals. Tell in your own words what they were. Where was Paul to watch for the signals?

2. How did the British begin their move—by land or by sea?

3. What is meant by this line in stanza 2, line 6, on page 333: "The fate of a nation was riding that night"?

4. What is the purpose of this poem? Is it to teach history or to tell an exciting story? Do you believe it achieves its purpose?

Reading Literature: Poetry

1. **Recognizing Tone.** Compare the tone of the poem with that in "Benjamin Franklin." How does the poet feel about the subject? Does he provide any funny or informal pictures? Is the tone of the poem humorous? The poem about Franklin sketched his entire life and suggested his personality. This poem limits itself to one dangerous night in Revere's long life. Does this difference affect the tone?

2. **Understanding Rhythm.** Choose any four lines in the poem. Copy them, leaving space between lines, and mark the stressed syllables. Count the stressed syllables in each line. Are they close together or far apart? Would you describe the rhythm as slow or fast? How does the rhythm reflect the topic of the poem?

3. **Examining Form.** The length of stanzas and the pattern of rhyme change throughout this poem. Examine stanzas 1, 2, 4, 5, and 6. For each stanza, tell the following:

   a. the number of lines
   b. the rhyme scheme, using letters of the alphabet

Developing Vocabulary Skills

Using Inference To Determine Word Meaning. Sometimes the context clues in a sentence will provide a clear and fairly exact meaning for an unfamiliar word. Other times the clues can only steer you in the right direction—you can tell which meanings cannot fit, at least. Read each of the following excerpts from "Benjamin Franklin" and "Paul Revere's Ride." From the possible meanings below each sentence, choose the meaning for the underlined word that seems most reasonable to you.

1. A country boy come up to town with eyes as big as saucers
   At the ladies in their furbelows, the gempmun on their horses.

   a. saddles   b. gentlemen

2. And all our humming dynamos and our electric light
   Go back to what Ben Franklin found, the day he flew his kite.

   a. a person who hums
   b. a machine that makes a humming sound

3. He wrenched their might from tyrants.

   a. took   b. used a wrench

4. Just as the moon rose over the bay,
   Where swinging wide at her moorings lay
   The Somerset, British man-of-war.

   a. a tract of open land with poor drainage
   b. something by which a ship is fixed in place, such as a cable.

5. In the silence around him he hears
   The muster of men at the barrack door,
   The sound of arms, and the tramp of feet,
   And the measured tread of the grenadiers.

   a. soldiers   b. weapons

6. He could hear, like a sentinel's tread,
   The watchful night-wind, as it went
   Creeping along from tent to tent.

   a. one who keeps watch   b. the wind

Developing Writing Skills

1. **Expressing Your Opinion.** "Casey at the Bat," "Benjamin Franklin," and "Paul Revere's Ride" are narrative poems, poems that tell stories. Almost every other poem in this chapter is a lyric poem, a poem that shares one idea or feeling. Which type of poetry do you prefer? Or do you enjoy both kinds, for different reasons? Write a paragraph or more explaining how you feel about the two types of poetry. Give reasons for your opinions.

2. **Using the First-Person Point of View.** Write a short poem of four to twenty lines, rhymed or unrhymed, from the point of view of Paul

Revere's friend. The poem may use any tone you like. It may include ideas and events that are not in "Paul Revere's Ride," perhaps even made-up events. Here are three possible ideas for your poem:

a. A suspense-filled poem about sneaking up to the window of the British officers' meeting room to listen to their plans.
b. A humorous poem about being jealous of Paul for getting a long poem written about him, while your name isn't mentioned.
c. A proud or bragging poem about your part in the adventure.

Developing Skills in Critical Thinking

Evaluating Historical Accuracy. The poem about Paul Revere focuses on one single act performed by one man. In the history of the long War for Independence, it was a small event. Longfellow made it famous by his poem. Did the poet stick to the facts or did he make the event more dramatic than it really was? Did he report some events inaccurately because of the rhyme or rhythm?

How would you find out how accurate his version really is? Using the card catalog and then the indexes of the books listed in the catalog, locate at least three reference books in your library that will give you information about that time in United States history. Remember that you can use biographies as well as more general reference sources.

Developing Skills in Speaking and Listening

Interpreting a Narrative Poem. "Paul Revere's Ride" can be an enjoyable poem to read aloud. Work with a group of your classmates to prepare a reading for the students in another class.

Remember that you can't read a poem well until you understand and feel exactly what the speaker is telling. The group should first take the time to discuss the events in the poem. They should decide which parts should sound loud or soft, slow or fast. Then, work together to decide how the speakers will take turns. Will each person in the group speak one or more stanzas alone or will small groups speak together? Next, the group members should decide who will read what parts. Each member should practice his or her own parts. Last, the group members should practice the poem all together once or twice. Then they can present it to an audience.

Western Wagons

STEPHEN VINCENT BENÉT
and ROSEMARY BENÉT

This poem captures the spirit of the men and women who settled the American West in the mid- to late 1800's. Did they consider themselves heroic? As you read, decide whether you would want to join them.

They went with ax and rifle, when the trail was still to blaze,
They went with wife and children, in the prairie-schooner days,
With banjo and with frying pan—Susanna, don't you cry!
For I'm off to California to get right out there or die!

We've broken land and cleared it, but we're tired of where we are.
They say that wild Nebraska is a better place by far.
There's gold in far Wyoming, there's black earth in Ioway,
So pack up kids and blankets, for we're moving out today!

The cowards never started and the weak died on the road,
And all across the continent the endless campfires glowed.
We'd taken land and settled—but a traveler passed by—
And we're going West tomorrow—Lordy, never ask us why!

We're going West tomorrow, where the promises can't fail.
O'er the hills in legions, boys, and crowd the dusty trail!
We shall starve and freeze and suffer. We shall die, and tame the lands.
But we're going West tomorrow, with our fortune in our hands.

Settlers moved West in great numbers after the Homestead Act of 1862. Denver Public Library.

Developing Comprehension Skills

1. According to the poem, why did the pioneers move west? Give two reasons.

2. What kind of people were the pioneers as described in the poem? Do you consider them likable? Were they brave or foolhardy or both?

Reading Literature: Poetry

1. **Identifying Speakers.** In the first stanza of the poem, a speaker is telling about the pioneers: "they" went, the speaker says. Who is the speaker in the other three stanzas?

2. **Recognizing Irony.** Read again the last stanza. The speaker says that in the West "promises can't fail." Just two lines further, however, the speaker says that pioneers will die. Why might a pioneer say the promises can't fail even though death is always a possibility?

3. **Understanding Mood.** We know that the kinds of people this poem is about succeeded in settling the West. Does the mood of this poem give you an indication of why they succeeded? Explain.

Abraham Lincoln
1809—1865

STEPHEN VINCENT BENÉT
and ROSEMARY BENÉT

Today, the name of Abraham Lincoln is one of the most respected in the history of this country. This poem gives us a view of the man before he became President. Was he always highly respected?

Lincoln was a long man.
He liked out of doors.
He liked the wind blowing
And the talk in country stores.

He liked telling stories,
He liked telling jokes.
"Abe's quite a character,"
Said quite a lot of folks.

Lots of folks in Springfield
Saw him every day,
Walking down the street
In his gaunt, long way.

Shawl around his shoulders,
Letters in his hat.
"That's Abe Lincoln."
They thought no more than that.

Knew that he was honest,
Guessed that he was odd,
Knew he had a cross wife
Though she was a Todd.

Knew he had three little boys
Who liked to shout and play,
Knew he had a lot of debts
It took him years to pay.

Knew his clothes and knew his house.
"That's his office, here.
Blame good lawyer, on the whole,
Though he's sort of dear.

"Sure, he went to Congress, once.
But he didn't stay.
Can't expect us all to be
Smart as Henry Clay.

"Need a man for troubled times?
Well, I guess we do.
Wonder who we'll ever find?
Yes—I wonder who."

That is how they met and talked,
Knowing and unknowing.
Lincoln was the green pine.
Lincoln kept on growing.

Abraham Lincoln, 1887,
Artist believed to be ROBERT KRINER. Wood Carving,
Collection of Allan L. Daniel. Courtesy of E. P. Dutton, Inc.

Developing Comprehension Skills

1. Did the people of Springfield see Abraham Lincoln as a great man? Explain your answer in your own words.

2. Why did the people think Lincoln didn't stay in Congress?

Reading Literature: Poetry

1. **Recognizing Metaphor.** A metaphor compares two unlike things without using "like" or "as." Find a metaphor in this poem and tell what two things or persons are compared. Explain how they are alike.

2. **Predicting Outcomes.** Does this poem lead you to believe that Abe Lincoln will be the "man for troubled times" the people in Springfield say is needed? Support your answer with evidence from the poem.

Women

ALICE WALKER

"Women" tells about the black
women of the past who worked
for a better future for their
children. How does the speaker
feel toward these women?

They were women then
My mama's generation
Husky of voice—Stout of
Step
With fists as well as
Hands
How they battered down
Doors
And ironed
Starched white
Shirts
How they led
Armies
Headragged Generals
Across mined
Fields
Booby-trapped
Ditches
To discover books
Desks
A place for us
How they knew what we
Must know
Without knowing a page
Of it
Themselves.

Mrs. Lucy Jefferson of Fort Scott, Kansas, 1949.
Copyright © 1949. GORDON PARKS

Developing Comprehension Skills

1. How many stanzas do you find in this poem?

2. What quality does the speaker imply is part of these women when she describes them in these words: "Husky of voice—Stout of Step, With fists as well as Hands"?

3. Why did the women "batter" down doors? Did they literally break down a door? Think of what we mean when we say someone "broke into" some group or organization.

4. The women generals led the armies across "mined fields" to discover books and desks. From what you know of the history of minorities in this country, what do you suppose might be represented by the term "mined fields"?

Reading Literature: Poetry

1. **Understanding Metaphor.** Reread the last five lines of the poem. Does the word "page" stand for what can be learned from a book? Or is the speaker referring to something broader? Explain your answer.

2. **Recognizing Rhythm and Rhyme.** Look at the pattern of this poem. Look for rhyme or regular rhythm. What kind of poem is this?

3. **Identifying Tone.** How would you describe the attitude of the poet towards the women about whom she is writing?

America the Beautiful

KATHARINE LEE BATES

Since this poem is usually sung, you probably think of it with its melody. This time, treat it as a poem rather than a song. As you read it, try to picture its images.

O beautiful for spacious skies,
  For amber waves of grain,
For purple mountain majesties
  Above the fruited plain!
    America! America!
  God shed His grace on thee
And crown thy good with brotherhood
  From sea to shining sea!

O beautiful for pilgrim feet,
  Whose stern, impassioned stress
A thoroughfare for freedom beat
  Across the wilderness!
    America! America!
  God mend thine every flaw,
Confirm thy soul in self-control,
  Thy liberty in law!

O beautiful for heroes proved
  In liberating strife,
Who more than self their country loved,
  And mercy more than life!
    America! America!
  May God thy gold refine
Till all success be nobleness
  And every gain divine!

O beautiful for patriot dream
  That sees beyond the years
Thine alabaster cities gleam
  Undimmed by human tears!
    America! America!
  God shed His grace on thee
And crown thy good with brotherhood
  From sea to shining sea!

The Grand Canyon of the Yellowstone, 1893–1901, THOMAS MORAN. National Museum of American Art, Smithsonian Institution, Washington, D.C. Gift of George G. Pratt.

Developing Comprehension Skills

1. In the third stanza, what kind of wars did the heroes fight? In the final stanza, what kind of society do the patriots dream about?

2. This poem answers the question, "Why is America beautiful?" with four different reasons. What are the four qualities of America and Americans that the speaker considers beautiful?

3. In addition to being a poem and a song, "America the Beautiful" could also be considered something else. Look at the last three lines of each stanza. What else could this piece of writing be called?

4. List three qualities the poet wishes for America.

Reading Literature: Poetry

1. **Finding Figurative Language.** Explain what is meant by each of these phrases:

   a. A thoroughfare for freedom
   b. May God thy gold refine
      Till all success be nobleness

2. **Identifying Rhyme Scheme.** Each stanza contains the same rhyme scheme. Using letters, tell what it is. (In stanza one, consider the words "skies" and "majesties" as rhymes.)

3. **Recognizing Internal Rhyme.** When two words in the same line rhyme, the poet is using **internal rhyme**. Find four examples of internal rhyme in this poem. What pattern do you notice?

4. **Understanding Mood.** What feeling do you get reading this poem? Write a list of the words that give you this feeling.

Developing Vocabulary Skills

Putting Context Clues into Use. Without using a dictionary, determine the meanings of the underlined words in the following excerpts from poems in this section. Use all types of context clues and also word parts. Write your meaning on your paper. Then look up the word in the dictionary. Copy the dictionary definition after yours.

1. The rivers are now polluted plundered
   but not the names of rivers
   cool and inviolate as ever
   pure as on the morning of creation.

2. Lots of folks in Springfield
   Saw him every day,
   Walking down the street
   In his gaunt, long way.

3. God mend thine every flaw,
   Confirm thy soul in self-control,
   Thy liberty in law.

4. A hurry of hoofs in a village street,
   And beneath, from the pebbles, in passing, a spark
   Struck out by a steed flying fearless and fleet.

5. A cry of defiance and not of fear.

6. O beautiful for heroes proved
   In liberating strife,
   Who more than self their country loved,
   And mercy more than life!

Developing Writing Skills

1. **Comparing Poems.** Six of the poems in this section are concerned with heroes and heroines. However, only "America the Beautiful" uses the term "heroes."

   Choose two of the other poems: "Benjamin Franklin," "Paul Revere's Ride," "Western Wagons," "Abraham Lincoln," or "Women." Then write two or more paragraphs comparing how the poems present their heroes or heroines. Consider questions such as these: Does each poem tell about a short period of the person's life or the whole life? Does it picture one heroic act or an average day? Does it describe specific places and actions or suggest the person's activities in a very general way? Is the tone of each poem admiring, amused, matter-of-fact, or something else? What quality or qualities of the hero or heroine does each poem concentrate on?

2. **Writing About Heroes and Heroines.** Think about your heroes and heroines. Is there one man or woman whom you feel is great? What makes that person great? Is it courage, intelligence, humor, or some special talent? Or is there a group of people you admire greatly? What do these people have in common that makes them heroic in your eyes? Write from one to three paragraphs of prose or a short poem (eight to forty lines long) about your heroes or heroines.

Developing Skills in Critical Thinking

Defining Terms. In order to communicate clearly with other people, both you and the other people should understand words in the same way. It is important to agree on what the words, or terms, mean. The process of stating what you mean by certain words is called **defining your terms**. Heroism, for example, can mean different things to different people. Perhaps you and others in your class wrote about heroes and heroines for the second writing activity above. If so, each of you probably wrote about different people and different heroic qualities. Choose one of the terms below. Look it up in a dictionary and discuss it with at least three other people, either separately or in one group meeting. Try to form a definition of the term that is acceptable to all of you. Your definition may not disagree with the dictionary meaning. Write a paragraph or more to explain the meaning you have agreed on.

      honesty   fairness   beauty   leadership   trust   humor

Using Your Skills in Reading Poems

Read the following part of the poem "City," by Langston Hughes. Then follow these directions.

1. Using letters of the alphabet, write the rhyme scheme of the poem.
2. Identify the type of rhythm used in the poem. Is it a regular, steady rhythm or free verse?
3. Identify one metaphor used in the poem. To what is the city being compared? How are the two things alike?

> In the morning the city
> Spreads its wings
> Making a song
> In stone that sings.

Using Your Comprehension Skills

Read these paragraphs from a selection in Chapter 6. Then explain Betty Marie's inner struggle. What decision must she make? Next, predict the outcome of her struggle. What do you think Betty Marie will choose? What evidence in the paragraph did you use to come to your conclusion?

> In high school, Betty Marie's favorite subject was writing. Once she wrote about trying to decide between music and dancing. At fifteen, she was performing at the piano and studying ballet with a great Russian teacher, Mme. Bronislava Nijinska.
>
> Mme. Nijinska was also a choreographer—a person who makes up dances. She gave Betty Marie a leading part in one of her ballets. The performance took place before an enormous audience. As she danced, Betty Marie felt strong and free. Afterward, everyone told her how well she had done.

Using Your Vocabulary Skills

Read the following sentences from selections in Chapter 6. Use context clues to figure out the meaning of each underlined word. Write the meaning in your own words. Then tell which type of context clue you used: example, comparison, contrast, or words in a series.

1. Hjalmar's horse needed an <u>incentive</u> to act up, but all I had to do to my horse was to say "People"; she would dance from one side of the street to the other.
2. There I had my first lessons in the <u>beneficence</u> of nature. But I also had an experience which taught me that nature is not always kind.
3. He had survived against floods, forest and prairie fires, snake-bites, chills, fevers, <u>ague</u>, malaria.
4. The youth found a job on a boat, a <u>square-rigger</u> with tall white sails destined for Hong Kong.

Using Your Writing Skills

Choose one of the writing assignments below. Follow the directions carefully.

1. Select the poem in this chapter that you liked best. Write one clear paragraph reporting your choice. In your paragraph, give three reasons for your choice, in increasing order of importance.
2. Write a poem about a game or a hobby. Use free verse or a regular rhythm and rhyme scheme. Your tone may be serious or humorous. Make your poem no longer than twelve lines. Be sure to include some figurative language in it.

Using Your Skills in Study and Research

Imagine that you have been asked to put together a collection of poems on nature and the seasons. Explain how you would locate in a library some poems you might consider. Explain, also, how you would find poems on these topics in a poetry anthology. Last, tell how you would look for information on the writers of your poems.

CHAPTER 6

Nonfiction

Icon-Ero, 1980, ED PASCHKE.
Courtesy of Phyllis Kind Gallery,
New York and Chicago.

Reading Literature: Nonfiction

What Is Nonfiction?

Nonfiction is writing that tells about real people, places, and happenings. It is based on facts. In this important way it is different from fiction, which comes from the writer's imagination.

The History of Nonfiction

Nonfiction has existed as long as people have had news to tell or important facts to remember. Before writing was invented, listeners had to depend on the memory and accuracy of the person reporting the news or facts. The first purpose of writing was to put the facts in a more permanent form.

Nonfiction consists of every kind of writing that people have done that has not come from their imaginations. Whenever people have needed to record, explain, describe, or inform, they have written nonfiction. Here are some categories of nonfiction:

1. Records of the lives, achievements, words, and personalities of famous and not-so-famous people
2. Records of a person's own life and achievements
3. True adventure stories telling of remarkable experiences
4. Records of journeys, including the sights, the events, and the people the traveler met
5. Letters communicating news and private thoughts
6. Memorable speeches first delivered by talented speakers
7. Essays telling personal thoughts and opinions
8. Reports concerning theories and information from research
9. Newspaper and magazine articles recording important events and passing on timely information
10. Special reports and documentaries for television and radio

The Elements of Nonfiction

Point of View. Some works of nonfiction are written from the **first-person point of view**. Autobiographies, letters, speeches, and essays are usually written in this way. Other works are written from the **third-person point of view**. In those cases, writers simply report the facts. They are not part of the action.

Organization. Like short stories and legends, some forms of nonfiction are organized according to **chronological order**. That is, they tell about events in the order in which they happen. These include autobiographies, biographies, anecdotes, and any other forms that tell of people's lives or of events.

Other forms of nonfiction are organized according to **logical order**. In logical order, ideas are arranged so as to explain or prove a statement, or to lead to a certain conclusion. Forms of nonfiction that discuss ideas use logical order. These include essays, letters, and speeches.

Tone. The **tone** of a piece of writing is the way in which the writer lets you know his or her attitude toward a subject. In some cases, the writer may want you to take the subject seriously. The tone could be, for example, admiring or angry. The piece could, on the other hand, be written with a carefree tone that asks you to relax and enjoy it. To understand the meaning of a piece of writing, the reader must be aware of its tone.

How To Read Nonfiction

1. Decide who is speaking. Is the piece written from the first-person or the third-person point of view?
2. Use information in the title. Some titles tell the topic of the piece or its main idea. Others give clues about the tone.
3. Learn what you can about when and where the events take place. The setting affects the events.
4. Make use of your own experience with the topic. What you know will help you understand what you read.

Comprehension Skills: Connotations, Denotations

Identifying Opinions and Slanted Writing

When people feel strongly about a topic, they often include their opinions in their writing. Sometimes they identify their opinions. Other times, though, they mix their opinions with the facts. As a reader, you must be alert to the ways in which writers try to persuade readers to agree with their opinions.

Fact and Opinion. An opinion is one person's belief. It may or may not be based on facts. Opinions are often stated as if they were facts. For example, "February is the shortest month" is a fact. "February is the worst month" is an opinion.

If a statement is really a fact, it can be proved to be true. You can check it in a source such as an encyclopedia. Sometimes you can observe that it is true by using what you see around you.

Slanted Writing. Sometimes it may seem as if the writer is reporting only the facts. Even facts, however, can be presented so that they favor one side of an issue. A writer who enjoys football, for example, may report only the exciting moments of a particular game. A writer who does not care for the sport may report that the weather that day was cold and wet, that the crowd was unruly, and that several players were injured.

When writing "leans" to one side of an argument, or shows only one view of an event, the writer has used **slanted writing**. Slanted writing is also called **biased writing**.

Connotation and Denotation. The **denotation** of a word is its dictionary meaning. Its **connotation** is the combination of ideas and emotions that the word beings to your mind. Writers can slant their writing by choosing words that have the connotations they want.

Connotations can be positive (good), negative (bad), or neutral (neither good nor bad). Even when words are close in meaning, their connotations can differ widely. The underlined words in the following sentences are similar in denotative meaning. Notice how the picture in your mind changes with each sentence.

1. The crowd left the auditorium.   (Neutral)
2. The crowd filed out of the auditorium.   (Positive)
3. The crowd escaped from the auditorium.   (Negative)

Exercises: Identifying Opinions and Slanted Writing

A. Decide which sentences are facts and which are opinions.

1. I was born on June 27, 1880, in Tuscumbria, Alabama.

2. December goes by too quickly.

3. Abraham Lincoln was our sixteenth president.

4. Training a horse takes care and effort.

5. April just isn't April without robins.

B. Match each sentence with a positive slant to a similar sentence with a negative slant.

Sentences with a Positive Slant

1. The explorers were brave.

2. Abe was so interested that he studied for hours.

3. The general avoided risking the lives of his men needlessly.

4. Maria devoted all her time to her favorite activity, dancing.

5. Helen's teacher was young, lively, and enthusiastic.

Sentences with a Negative Slant

1. The general stubbornly refused to attack.

2. Helen's new teacher was inexperienced.

3. It took Abe hours to understand even the simplest ideas.

4. The explorers took foolish chances.

5. Maria never did anything but dance.

Vocabulary Skills: Reference Sources

Using Reference Sources

When you come across an unfamiliar word, you should first try to figure out its meaning from context clues or word parts. If those approaches don't help, turn to a reference source. Three reference sources you should become familiar with are the dictionary, the glossary, and the encyclopedia.

The Dictionary. The **dictionary** lists words in alphabetical order and gives you useful information about them. Each word that is listed is called an **entry word**. For each entry word, the dictionary gives some or all of the following information.

1. **How to divide the word into syllables.** The syllables may be separated by a space or by a centered dot: for est, for•est.

2. **How to pronounce the word.** The pronunciation is usually given in parentheses: (fôr′ist). The **respelling** identifies the sounds in the word. Each dictionary has a pronunciation key that helps you pronounce each sound correctly. **Accent marks** (′) within a respelling show which syllables to stress.

3. **The part of speech of the word.** The **parts of speech** are abbreviated as follows:

n.	noun	*pro.*	pronoun	*prep.*	preposition
v.	verb	*adv.*	adverb	*conj.*	conjunction
		adj.	adjective	*interj.*	interjection

4. **The origin of the word.** The word may have come into our language in one of a number of different ways. Its **origin**, or source, is printed in brackets such as these: { }.

5. **The definition of the word.** If there is more than one **definition**, each meaning is assigned a number. Often a sample phrase or sentence will show you how to use the word.

The Glossary.   A **glossary** of a book lists all the words in that book that may be new or unfamiliar. There is usually a glossary at the back of a nonfiction book. The glossary lists words in alphabetical order and gives pronunciations and definitions.

The Encyclopedia.   When you need more information than just the definition or the pronunciation of a word, it sometimes helps to look the word up in an encyclopedia. There may be an article to explain that term, or a cross-reference to an article that does. Like dictionary entries, encyclopedia articles are listed in alphabetical order. Each article is a short factual report.

Exercises: Using Reference Sources

A.   Use this dictionary entry to answer the questions below.

en•gaged (in gājd′), *adj.* {Fr. and OFr. engager} **1.** pledged. **2.** pledged in marriage. **3.** occupied; employed; busy. **4.** involved in combat, as troops. **5.** attached to or partly set into (a wall, etc.): as engaged columns. **6.** interlocked; meshed; in gear.

1. How is engaged divided into syllables?
2. Is the accent on the first or the second syllable?
3. What part of speech is engaged?
4. Which meaning is used in each of these sentences?
   a. Now we are engaged in a great civil war.
   b. His telephone is engaged at this moment.
   c. The couple was engaged for six months before the wedding.

B.   Copy these sentences, filling in each blank correctly.

1. A _____ lists words in alphabetical order and gives pronunciations, parts of speech, origins, and meanings.
2. An _____ gives a short report to explain each entry word.
3. A _____ lists and defines the new or unfamiliar words in a particular book in alphabetical order.

Autobiographies

An **autobiography** is the story a person writes about his or her own life. It may tell a person's whole life story up to that point or only parts of it. It is written from the first-person point of view.

An autobiography can give you information you cannot find anywhere else. You learn about the subject's personal feelings and reasons for certain actions. You also get a glimpse of how the person thought and expressed himself or herself.

Rhododendron Bower, 1920, CHARLES C. CURRAN.
Courtesy of Fred and Maureen Radl, Cragsmoor, N.Y.

I Get a Colt To Break In

LINCOLN STEFFENS

This selection describes an enjoyable time in Lincoln Steffens' boyhood. It also tells some of his private thoughts and feelings. What are some of these thoughts and feelings? Do you agree with him?

Colonel Carter gave me a colt. I had my pony, and my father meanwhile had bought a pair of black carriage horses and a cow, all of which I had to attend to when we had no "man." My hands were pretty full, and so was the stable. But Colonel Carter seemed to think that he had promised me a horse. He had not; I would have known it if he had. No matter. He thought he had, and maybe he did promise himself to give me one. That was enough. The kind of man that led immigrant trains across the continent and delivered them safe, sound, and together where he promised, would keep his word. One day he drove over from Stockton, leading a two-year-old which he brought to our front door and turned over to me as mine. Such a horse!

She was a cream-colored mare with a black forelock, mane, and tail and a black stripe along the middle of her back. Tall, slender, high-spirited, I thought then—I think now that she was the most beautiful of horses. Colonel Carter had bred and reared her with me and my uses in mind. She was a careful cross of a mustang mare and a thoroughbred stallion, with the stamina of the wild horse and the speed and grace of the racer. And she had a sense of fun. As Colonel Carter got down out of his buggy and went up to her, she snorted, reared, flung her head high in the air, and, coming down beside him, tucked her nose affectionately under his arm.

"I have handled her a lot," he said. "She is as kind as a kitten, but she is as sensitive as a lady. You can spoil her by one mistake. If you ever lose your temper, if you ever abuse her, she will be ruined for ever. And she is unbroken. I might have had her broken to ride for you, but I didn't want to. I want you to do it. I have taught her to lead, as you see; had to, to get her over here. But here she is, an unbroken colt; yours. You take and you break her. You're only a boy, but if you break this colt right, you'll be a man—a young man, but a man. And I'll tell you how."

Now, out west, as everybody knows, they break in a horse by riding him in his wild state, lassoing, throwing, and saddling him; then they let him up, frightened and shocked, with a yelling broncho-buster astride of him. The wild beast bucks, the cowboy drives his spurs into him, and off they go, jumping, kicking, rearing, falling, till by the weight of the man, the lash, and the spurs, the horse is broken—in body and spirit. This was not the way I was to break my colt.

"You must break her to ride without her ever knowing it," Colonel Carter said. "You feed and you clean her—you, not the stable man. You lead her out to water and to walk. You put her on a long rope and let her play, calling her to you and gently pulling on the rope. Then you turn her loose in the grass lot and, when she has romped till tired, call her. If she won't come, leave her. When she wants water or food, she will run to your call, and you will pet and feed and care for her." He went on for half an hour, advising me in great detail how to proceed. I wanted to begin right away. He laughed. He let me lead her around to the stable, water her, and put her in the stable and feed her.

There I saw my pony. My father, sisters, and Colonel Carter saw me stop and look at my pony.

"What'll you do with him?" one of my sisters asked. I was bewildered for a moment. What should I do with the little red horse? I decided at once.

"He's yours," I said to my sisters.

"No," said Colonel Carter, "not yet. You can give your sisters the pony by and by, but you'll need him till you have taught the colt to carry you and a saddle—months; and you must not hurry. You must learn patience, and you will if you give the colt time to learn it, too. Patience and control. You can't control a horse unless you can control yourself."

He went off downtown with my father, and I started away with my colt. I fed, I led, I cleaned her, gently, as if she were made of glass; she was playful and willing, a delight. When Colonel Carter came home with my father for supper, he questioned me.

"You should not have worked her today," he said. "She has come all the way from Stockton and must be tired. Yes, yes, she would not show fatigue; too fine for that, and too young to be wise. You

have got to think for her." He went on to draw on my imagination a centaur; the colt as a horse's body—me, a boy, as the head and brains of one united creature. I liked that. I would be that. I and the colt: a centaur.

After Colonel Carter was gone home, I went to work on my new horse. The old one, the pony, I used only for business: to go to fires, to see my friends, run errands, and go hunting. But the game that had all my attention was the breaking in of the colt, the beautiful cream-colored mare, who soon knew me—and my pockets. I carried sugar to reward her when she did right, and she discovered where I carried it; so did the pony, and when I was busy they would push their noses into my pockets, both of which were torn down a good deal of the time. But the colt learned. I taught her to run around a circle, turn and go the other way at a signal. My sisters helped me. I held the long rope and the whip (for signaling), while one of the girls led the colt. One would lead the colt round and round till I snapped the whip; then she would turn, turning the colt, till the colt did it all by herself. The colt was very quick. She shook hands with each of her four feet. She let us run under her, back and forth. She was slow only to carry me. Following Colonel Carter's instructions, I began by laying my arm or a saddle strap over her back. If she trembled, I drew it slowly off. When she could abide it, I tried buckling it, tighter and tighter. I laid over her, too, a blanket, folded at first, then open, and, at last, I slipped up on her myself, sat there a second, and, as she trembled, slid off. My sisters held her for me, and when I could get up and sit there a moment or two, I tied her at a block, and we, my sisters and I, made a procession of mounting and dismounting. She soon got used to this and would let us slide off over her rump, but it was a long, long time before she would carry me.

That we practiced by leading her along a high curb where I could get on as she walked, ride a few steps, and then, as she felt me and crouched, slip off. She never did learn to carry a girl on her back; my sisters had to lead her while I rode.

While we were breaking in the colt, a circus came to town. The ring was across the street from our house. Wonderful! I lived in that circus for a week. I saw the show but once, but I marked the horse-trainers, and in the mornings when they were not too busy I told them about my colt, showed her to them, and asked them how to train her to do circus tricks. With their hints I taught the colt to stand up on her hind legs, kneel, lie down, and balance on a small box. This last was easier than it looked. I put her first on a low, big box and taught her to turn on it; then got a little smaller box upon which she repeated what she did on the big one. By and by we had her so that she would step on a high box so small that her four feet were almost touching, and there also she would turn.

The circus man gave me one hint that was worth all the other tricks put together. "You catch her doing something of herself that looks good," he said, "and then you keep her at it." It was thus that I taught her to bow to people. The first day I rode her out on to the streets was a proud one for me and for the colt, too, apparently. She did not walk, she danced; perhaps she was excited, nervous; anyhow I liked the way she threw up her head, champed at the bit, and went dancing, prancing down the street. Everybody stopped to watch us, and so, when she began to sober down, I pick her up again with heel and rein, saying, "Here's people, Lady," and she would show off to my delight. By constant repetition I had her so trained that she would singlefoot, head down, along a country road till we came to a house or a group of people. Then I'd say, "People, Lady," and up would go her head, and her feet would dance.

But the trick that set the town talking was her bowing to anyone I spoke to. "Lennie Steffens' horse bows to you," people said, and she did. I never told how it was done; by accident. Dogs used to run out at us, and the colt enjoyed it; she kicked at them sometimes with both hind hoofs. I joined her in the game, and being able to look behind more conveniently than she could, I watched the dogs until they were in range, then gave the colt a

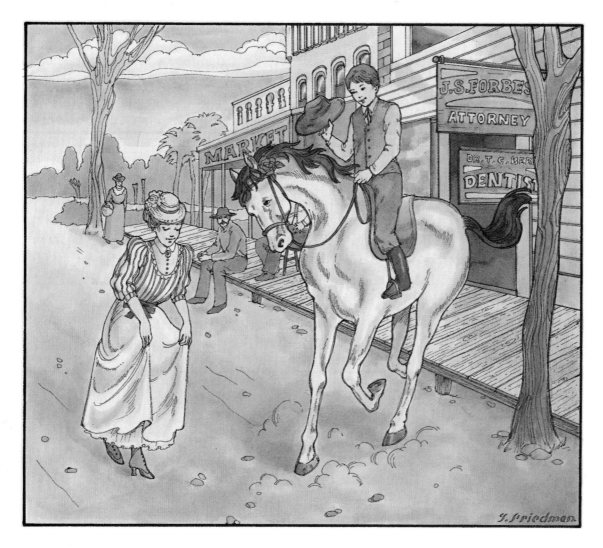

signal to kick. "Kick, gal," I'd say, and tap her ribs with my heel. We used to get dogs together that way; the colt would kick them over and over and leave them yelping in the road. Well, one day when I met a girl I knew, I lifted my hat, probably muttered a "Good day," and I must have touched the colt with my heel. Anyway, she dropped her head and kicked—not much; there was no dog near, so she had responded to my unexpected signal by what looked like a bow. I caught the idea and kept her at it. Whenever I wanted to bow to a girl or anybody else, instead of saying "Good day," I muttered "Kick, gal," spurred her lightly, and—the whole centaur bowed and was covered with glory and conceit.

Yes, conceit. I was full of it, and the colt was quite as bad. One day my chum Hjalmar came into town on his Black Bess, blanketed. A great fistula had been cut out of her shoulder, and she had to be kept warm. I expected to see her weak and dull, but no, the good old mare was champing and dancing, like my colt.

"What is it makes her so?" I asked, and Hjalmar said he didn't know, but he thought she was proud of her blanket. A great idea. I had a gaudy horse blanket. I put it on the colt and I could hardly hold her. We rode down the main street together, both horses and boys so full of vanity that everybody stopped to smile.

We pranced, the black and the yellow, all the way down J Street, up K Street, and agreed that we'd do it again, often. Only, I said, we wouldn't use blankets. If the horses were proud of a blanket, they'd be proud of anything unusually conspicuous. We tried a flower next time. I fixed a big rose on my colt's bridle just under her ear and it was great—she pranced downtown with her head turned, literally, to show off her flower. We had to change the decoration from time to time, put on a ribbon, or a bell, or a feather, but really, it was not necessary for my horse. Old Black Bess needed an incentive to act up, but all I had to do to my horse was to pick up the reins, touch her with my heel, and say, "People"; she would dance from one side of the street to the other, asking to be admired. As she was. As we were.

I would ride down to my father's store, jump off my prancing colt in the middle of the street, and run up into the shop. The colt, free, would stop short, turn, and follow me right up on the sidewalk, unless I bade her wait. If anyone approached her while I was gone, she would snort, rear, and strike. No stranger could get near her. She became a frightened, frightening animal, and yet when I came into sight she would run to me, put her head down, and as I straddled her neck, she would throw up her head and pitch me into my seat, facing backward, of course. I whirled around right, and off we'd go, the vainest boy and the proudest horse in the state.

"Hey, give me a ride, will you?" some boy would ask. "Sure," I'd say, and jump down and watch that boy try to catch and mount my colt. He couldn't. Once a cowboy wanted to try her, and he caught her; he dodged her forefeet, grabbed the reins, and in one spring was on her back. I never did that again. My colt reared, then bucked, and, as the cowboy kept his seat, she shuddered, sank to the ground, and rolled over. He slipped aside and would have risen with her, but I was alarmed and begged him not to. She got up at my touch and followed me so close that she stepped on my heel and hurt me. The cowboy saw the point.

"If I were you, kid," he said, "I'd never let anybody mount that colt. She's too good."

That, I think, was the only mistake I made in the rearing of Colonel Carter's gift-horse. My father differed from me. He discovered another error or sin, and thrashed me for it. My practice was to work hard on a trick, privately, and when it was perfect, let him see it. I would have the horse out in our vacant lot doing it as he came home to supper. One evening, as he approached the house, I was standing, whip in hand, while the colt, quite free, was stepping carefully over the bodies of a lot of girls, all my sisters and all their girl friends. My father did not express the admiration I expected; he was frightened and furious. "Stop that," he called, and he came running around into the lot, took the whip, and lashed me with it. I tried to explain; the girls tried to help me explain.

I had seen in the circus a horse that stepped thus over a row of prostrate clowns. It looked dangerous for the clowns, but the trainer had told me how to do it. You begin with logs, laid out a certain distance apart; the horse walks over them under your lead, and whenever he touches one you scold him. By and by he will learn to step with such care that he never trips. Then you substitute clowns. I had no clowns, but I did get logs, and, with the girls helping, we taught the colt to step over the obstacles even at a trot. Walking, she touched nothing. All ready thus with the logs, I had my sisters lie down in the grass, and again and again the colt stepped over and among them. None was ever touched. My father would not listen to any of this. He just walloped me, and, when he was tired or satisfied and I was in tears, I blubbered a short excuse:

"They were only girls." And he whipped me some more.

My father was not given to whipping; he did it very seldom, but he did it hard when he did it at all. My mother was just the opposite. She did not whip me, but she often smacked me, and she had a most annoying habit of thumping me on the head with her thimbled finger. This I resented more than my father's thorough-going thrashings, and I can tell why now. I would be playing Napoleon and, as I was reviewing my Old Guard, she would crack my skull with that thimble. No doubt I was in the way; it took a lot of furniture and sisters to represent properly a victorious army; and you might think as my mother did that a thimble is a small weapon. But imagine Napoleon at the height of his power, the ruler of the world on parade, getting a sharp rap on his crown from a woman's thimble. No. My father's way was more appropriate. It was hard. "I'll attend to you in the morning," he would say, and I lay awake wondering which of my crimes he had discovered. I know what it is to be sentenced to be shot at sunrise. Also, it hurt in the morning when he was not angry but very fresh and strong. You see, he walloped me in my own person; he never shamed Napoleon or my knighthood, as my mother did. I learned something from his discipline, something useful.

I learned what tyranny is and the pain of being misunderstood and wronged, or, if you please, understood and set right. They are pretty much the same. He and most parents and teachers do not break in their children as carefully as I broke in my colt. They haven't the time that I had, and they have not some other incentives I had. I saw this that day when I rubbed my sore legs. He had to explain to my indignant mother what had happened. When he had told it his way, I gave my version: how long and cautiously I had been teaching my horse to walk over logs and girls. Having shown how sure I was of myself and the colt, while my mother was boring into his silence with one of her reproachful looks, I said something that hit my father hard.

"I taught the colt that trick, I have taught her all that you see she knows, without whipping her. I have never struck her; not once. Colonel Carter said I mustn't, and I haven't."

And my mother, backing me up, gave him a rap: "There," she said, "I told you so." He walked off, looking like a thimble-rapped Napoleon.

Developing Comprehension Skills

1. Why did Colonel Carter give Lennie a colt?

2. How did Lennie teach the colt to balance and turn on a small box?

3. On page 360, paragraph 2, you learned how most horses were broken to ride in the Old West. Compare that way of breaking a horse to the way Colonel Carter told Lennie to break his new colt. What is the difference in the trainers' attitudes? How does the effect on the horse differ?

4. Lennie's father whipped him for having his colt step over his sisters. Lennie defended himself by saying, "They were only girls." On the next page (page 365), Lennie described how it shamed him to get "a sharp rap on his crown from a woman's thimble." From these two examples, what can you tell about Lennie's attitude toward girls and women when he was young?

5. The author describes three ways of training children or horses. One is his mother's way of training him, one his father's way, and the third one is the way he himself trained his colt. Tell which way you think is

the best of these three ways for raising children. Give your reasons for answering the way you do.

Reading Literature: Nonfiction

1. **Identifying Point of View.** Is this story told from the first-person or the third-person point of view? How does the point of view help you know whether the story is from a biography or an autobiography?

2. **Examining Nonfiction Writing.** This selection is presented in the nonfiction chapter, so you know it is based on real happenings. Can you tell from the selection itself that it is nonfiction rather than fiction? Are there similarities? Are there differences? What are they?

3. **Distinguishing Fact and Opinion.** In telling about his parents' ways of disciplining him, Lennie says, "My father's way was more appropriate." Is this a fact or an opinion? How can you tell?

4. **Describing Tone.** In the introduction to this chapter, you read that nonfiction writing can have different tones. The tone can be serious—admiring, for instance, or angry. Or it can be carefree, asking the reader just to relax and enjoy it. How would you describe the tone of this selection? Give examples from the story to support your answer.

Developing Vocabulary Skills

1. **Choosing the Correct Respelling.** You know that the dictionary and glossary show how words are pronounced. The words are respelled with special symbols to stand for certain sounds. The pronunciation key in the dictionary or glossary explains these respelling symbols by using key words. Here is the pronunciation key from the glossary of this text.

   at, āte, fär; pen, ēqual; sit, mīne; sō, côrn, join,
   took, fool, our; us, turn; chill, shop, thick, they,
   sing; zh *in* measure; 'l *in* idle;
   ə *in* alive, cover, family, robot, circus.

   Use the key to help you pronounce each respelling in the following list. Then read the following sentences from or about the story. Choose the respelling of the word that would make sense in each sentence. Write both the respelling and the word that the respelling stands for.

(1) sen′ sə tiv   (3) stal′ yən   (5) sen′ tor
(2) sub′ stə tüt   (4) pā′ shəns   (6) shug′ ər

a. The horse was a cross of a mustang mare and a thoroughbred _____.
b. The horse and I were like one united creature. We were a _____.
c. "She is a very _____ horse and if you lose your temper and abuse her, she will be ruined forever," he warned.
d. "Training the pony will take much _____," said Colonel Carter.
e. Lennie carried _____ to reward Lady when she did right.
f. The circus trainer told him to begin training the horse to step over logs, and then _____ people.

2. **Accent Marks and the Schwa Sound.** Each of the words above has one accent mark. The respellings of some of the words found in the story have more than one accent. Here is an example:

ad′ mə rā′ shən

The heavy, dark accent is called the **primary accent**. That syllable gets the most stress. The lighter accent is called the **secondary accent**. That syllable gets a lighter stress.

Look again at the words in the exercise above. In some of them you see this symbol: ə. This is called the **schwa**. It represents the sound of the vowel heard in the unaccented syllable.

Find these words in the dictionary. Write them in syllables. Mark the primary and secondary accents. Underline any syllables that have a schwa sound.

a. decoration   c. bewilder   e. repetition
b. continent   d. attention   f. convenient

Developing Writing Skills

1. **Understanding the Author's Purpose.** This is mostly a story about breaking a colt. However, at the end of the story, Lincoln Steffens also tells his feelings about how to discipline a child. Write a paragraph explaining how he felt about this subject. Include what he thought of his mother's method and his father's method. Why did he tell his parents how he taught his colt to step over the girls?

2. **Inferring from Indirect Description.** In this selection, the author does not describe himself directly. The reader learns about him from his words and actions. Write a paragraph describing in your own words what Lincoln Steffens was like when he was a boy. Use passages from the story to explain and support your description.

3. **Writing an Autobiography.** Lincoln Steffens was proud of his accomplishment in training his colt. Write a story about something you have done that you are proud of. Your story should be at least two paragraphs long.

Developing Skills in Study and Research

Taking Notes. Do you have a favorite animal? Go to the library. Use the card catalog to find at least one book on how to train one animal. Write notes on what the book says about one important part of training, for instance, how to train the animal to do tricks. Be sure to record the name of your book, the author, and the chapter and page from which you take your notes. You may also take notes on notebook paper. Be sure to include all of the information asked for here.

Developing Skills in Critical Thinking

Understanding Connotation. In the introduction to this chapter, you learned that the connotation of words can be positive (good), negative (bad), or neutral. In the following sentence from the story, the author tells us that he learned about being bossed around. He also tells how bad it feels to be misunderstood. Read the sentence. One part of it is written with a positive slant and the other part with a negative slant. Tell which part of the sentence is positive and which is negative. Then tell what the author means in this sentence:

I learned what tyranny is and the pain of being misunderstood and wronged, or, if you please, understood and set right; they are pretty much the same.

From
The Story of My Life

HELEN KELLER

Helen Keller's childhood was very different from yours. See how her autobiography can help you understand an experience you have not had yourself.

Helen Keller at age seven. Photograph by Ira F. Collins. American Foundation for the Blind.

I was born on June 27, 1880, in Tuscumbia, a little town of northern Alabama. The beginning of my life was simple and much like every other little life. I came, I saw, I conquered, as the first baby in the family always does.

I am told that while I was still in long dresses I showed many signs of an eager, self-asserting disposition. Everything that I saw other people do I insisted upon imitating. At six months, I could pipe out "How d'ye," and one day I attracted everyone's attention by saying "Tea, tea, tea" quite plainly. Even after my illness I remembered one of the words I had learned in these early months. It was the word "water," and I continued to make some sound for that word after all other speech was lost. I ceased making the sound "wah-wah" only when I learned to spell the word.

They tell me I walked the day I was a year old. My mother had just taken me out of the bathtub and was holding me in her lap, when I was suddenly attracted by the flickering shadows of leaves that danced in the sunlight on the smooth floor. I slipped from my mother's lap and almost ran toward them. The impulse gone, I fell down and cried for her to take me up in her arms.

These happy days did not last long. One brief spring, musical with the song of robin and mocking-bird, one summer rich in fruit and roses, one autumn of gold and crimson sped by and left their gifts at the feet of an eager, delighted child. Then, in the dreary month of February, came the illness that closed my eyes and ears and plunged me into the unconsciousness of a new-born baby. They called it acute congestion of the stomach and brain. The doctor thought I could not live. Early one morning, however, the fever left me, as suddenly and mysteriously as it had come. There was great rejoicing in the family that morning, but no one, not even the doctor, knew that I should never see nor hear again.

Night

I cannot recall what happened during the first months after my illness. I only know that I sat in my mother's lap or clung to her dress as she went about her household duties. My hands felt every object and observed every motion, and in this way I learned to know many things. Soon I felt the need of some communication with others and began to make crude signs. A shake of the head meant "No" and a nod, "Yes;" a pull meant "Come" and a push, "Go." Was it bread that I wanted? Then I would imitate the acts of cutting the slices and buttering them. If I wanted my mother to make ice cream for dinner, I made the sign for working the freezer and shivered, indicating cold. My mother, moreover, succeeded in making me understand a good deal. I always knew when she wished me to bring her something, and I would run upstairs or anywhere else she indicated. Indeed, I owe to her loving wisdom all that was bright and good in my long night.

I understood a great deal of what was going on about me. At five I learned to fold and put away the clean clothes when they were brought in from the laundry, and I knew my own from the rest. I knew by the way my mother and aunt dressed when they were going out, and I always begged to go with them. I was always sent for when there was company, and when the guests took their leave, I waved my hand to them, I think with a vague remembrance of the meaning of the gesture.

I do not remember when I first realized that I was different from other people; but I knew it before my teacher came to me. I had noticed that my mother and my friends did not use signs as I did when they wanted anything done, but talked with their mouths. Sometimes I stood between two persons who were conversing and touched their lips. I could not understand and was vexed. I moved my lips and gestured frantically without result. This made me so angry at times that I kicked and screamed until I was exhausted.

I think I knew when I was naughty, for I knew that it hurt Ella, my nurse, to kick her, and when my fit of temper was over I had a feeling similar to regret. But I cannot remember any instance in which this feeling prevented me from repeating the naughtiness when I failed to get what I wanted.

Many incidents of those early years are fixed in my memory, isolated, but clear and distinct, making the sense of that silent, aimless, dayless life all the more intense.

One day I happened to spill water on my apron, and I spread it out to dry before the fire which was flickering on the sitting-room hearth. The apron did not dry quickly enough to suit me, so I drew nearer and threw it right over the hot ashes. The fire leaped into life; the flames encircled me so that in a moment my clothes were blazing. I made a terrified noise that brought Viny, my old nurse, to the rescue. Throwing a blanket over me, she almost suffocated me, but she put out the fire. Except for my hands and hair I was not badly burned.

About this time I found out the use of a key. One morning I locked my mother up in the pantry, where she was obliged to remain three hours, as the servants were in a detached part of the house. She kept pounding on the door, while I sat outside on the porch steps and laughed with glee as I felt the jar of the pounding. This most naughty prank of mine convinced my parents that I must be taught as soon as possible.

The Search for Help

Meanwhile the desire to express myself grew. The few signs I used became less and less adequate, and my failures to make myself understood were invariably followed by outbursts of passion. I felt as if invisible hands were holding me, and I made frantic efforts to free myself. I struggled—not that struggling helped matters, but the spirit of resistance was strong within me; I generally broke down in tears and physical exhaustion. If my mother happened to be near, I crept into her arms, too miserable even to remember the cause of the tempest. After awhile, the need of some means of communication became so urgent that these outbursts occurred daily, sometimes hourly.

My parents were deeply grieved and perplexed. We lived a long way from any school for the blind or the deaf, and it seemed unlikely that anyone would come to such an out-of-the-way place as Tuscumbia to teach a child who was both deaf and blind. Indeed, my friends and relatives sometimes doubted whether I could be taught. My mother's only ray of hope came from Dickens's "American Notes." She had read his account of

Laura Bridgman, and she remembered vaguely that Laura was deaf and blind, yet had been educated. But she also remembered with a hopeless pang that Dr. Howe, who had discovered the way to teach the deaf and blind, had been dead many years. His methods had probably died with him; and, if they had not, how was a little girl in a far-off town in Alabama to receive the benefit of them?

When I was about six years old, my father heard of an eminent eye doctor in Baltimore, who had been successful in many cases that had seemed hopeless. My parents at once determined to take me to Baltimore to see if anything could be done for my eyes.

When we arrived in Baltimore, Dr. Chisholm received us kindly, but he could do nothing. He said, however, that I could be educated. He advised my father to consult Dr. Alexander Graham Bell, of Washington, who would be able to give him information about schools and teachers of deaf or blind children. Acting on the doctor's advice, we went immediately to Washington to see Dr. Bell, my father with a sad heart and many misgivings, I wholly unconscious of his anguish, finding pleasure in the excitement of moving from place to place. Child as I was, I at once felt the tenderness and sympathy which endeared Dr. Bell to so many hearts. He held me on his knee while I examined his watch, and he made it strike for me. He understood my signs, and I knew it and loved him at once. But I did not dream that that interview would be the door through which I should pass from darkness into light, from isolation to friendship, companionship, knowledge, love.

Dr. Bell advised my father to write to Mr. Anagnos, director of the Perkins Institution in Boston, the scene of Dr. Howe's great labors for the blind, and ask him if he had a teacher able to begin my education. This my father did at once. In a few weeks there came a kind letter from Mr. Anagnos with the comforting assurance that a teacher had been found. This was in the summer of 1886, but Miss Sullivan did not arrive until the following March.

Miss Sullivan Comes

The most important day I remember in all my life is the one on which my teacher, Anne Mansfield Sullivan, came to me. I am filled with wonder when I consider the immeasurable contrasts between the two lives that it connects. It was the third of March, 1887, three months before I was seven years old.

On the afternoon of that eventful day, I stood on the porch, expectant. I guessed vaguely from my mother's signs and from the hurrying to and fro in the house that something unusual was about to happen, so I went to the door and waited on the steps. The afternoon sun penetrated the mass of honeysuckle that covered the porch and fell on my upturned face. My fingers lingered almost unconsciously on the familiar leaves and blossoms that had just come forth to greet the sweet southern spring. I did not know what the future held of marvel or surprise for me. Anger and bitterness had preyed upon me continually for weeks and a deep languor had followed this passionate struggle.

Have you ever been at sea in a dense fog, when it seemed as if a tangible white darkness shut you in, and the great ship, tense and anxious, groped her way toward the shore with plummet and sounding-line, and you waited with beating heart for something to happen? I was like that ship before my education began, only I was without compass or sounding-line and had no way of knowing how near the harbor was. "Light! give me light!" was the wordless cry of my soul, and the light of love shone on me in that very hour.

I felt approaching footsteps. I stretched out my hand as I supposed to my mother. Someone took it, and I was caught up and held close in the arms of her who had come to reveal all things to me and, more than all things else, to love me.

The morning after my teacher came, she led me into her room and gave me a doll. The little blind children at the Perkins Institution had sent it and Laura Bridgman had dressed it; but I did not know this until afterward. When I had played with it a little while, Miss Sullivan slowly spelled into my hand the word "d-o-l-l." I was at once interested in this finger play and tried to imitate it. When I finally succeeded in making the letters correctly, I was flushed with childish pride and pleasure. Running downstairs to my mother, I held up my hand and made the letters for doll. I did not know that I was spelling a word or even that words existed; I was simply making my fingers go in monkey-like imitation. In the days that followed, I learned to spell in this uncomprehending way a great many words, among them *pin*, *hat*, *cup*, and a few verbs like *sit*, *stand*, and *walk*. But my teacher had been with me several weeks before I understood that everything has a name.

One day, while I was playing with my new doll, Miss Sullivan put my big rag doll into my lap also, spelled "d-o-l-l" and tried to make me understand that "d-o-l-l" applied to both. Earlier in the day we had had a tussle over the words "m-u-g" and "w-a-t-e-r." Miss Sullivan had tried to impress it upon me that "m-u-g" is *mug* and that "w-a-t-e-r" is *water*, but I persisted in confusing the two. In despair she had dropped the subject for the time, only to renew it at the first opportunity. I became impatient at her repeated attempts and, seizing the new doll, I dashed it upon the floor. I was keenly delighted when I felt the fragments of the broken doll at my feet. Neither sorrow or regret followed my passionate outburst. I had not loved the doll. In the still, dark world in which I lived there was no strong sentiment or tenderness. I felt my teacher sweep the fragments to one side of the hearth, and I had a sense of satisfaction that the cause of my discomfort was removed. She brought me my hat, and I knew I was going out into the warm sunshine. This thought, if a wordless sensation may be called a thought, made me hop and skip with pleasure.

We walked down the path to the well-house, attracted by the fragrance of the honeysuckle with which it was covered. Some one was drawing water, and my teacher placed my hand under the spout. As the cool stream gushed over one hand, she spelled into the other word *water*, first slowly, then rapidly. I stood still, my whole attention fixed upon the motions of the fingers. Suddenly I felt a misty consciousness as of something forgotten—a thrill of returning thought; and somehow the mystery of language was revealed to me. I knew then that "w-a-t-e-r" meant the wonderful cool something that was flowing over my hand. That living word awakened my soul, gave it light, hope, joy, set it free! There were barriers still, it is true, but barriers that could in time be swept away.

I left the well-house eager to learn. Everything had a name, and each name gave birth to a new thought. As we returned to the house, every object which I touched seemed to quiver with life. That was because I saw everything with the strange,

Helen Keller and Annie Sullivan, 1890.
American Foundation for the Blind.

new sight that had come to me. On entering the door, I remembered the doll I had broken. I felt my way to the hearth and picked up the pieces. I tried vainly to put them together. Then my eyes filled with tears; for I realized what I had done. For the first time I felt repentance and sorrow.

I learned a great many new words that day. I do not remember what they all were; but I do know that *mother, father, sister, teacher* were among them—words

I left the well-house eager to l(ea)r n . Every th ing

had a name, and each name gave birth to a

new th ou gh t . As we r e t u r n ed to the h ou s e ,

ever y object I t ou ch ed s e e m ed to q u iv er with l i f e .

Above is the Braille writing for the last three sentences in column one on page 375. Helen Keller wrote her autobiography this way. The dots are raised on paper with a special machine much like a typewriter. The writing is read by touch.

that were to make the world blossom for me, "like Aaron's rod, with flowers." It would have been difficult to find a happier child than I was as I lay in my crib at the close of that day and lived over the joys it had brought me, and for the first time longed for a new day to come.

Nature

I recall many incidents of the summer of 1887 that followed my soul's sudden awakening. I did nothing but explore with my hands and learn the name of every object that I touched; and the more I handled things and learned their names and uses, the more joyous and confident grew my sense of kinship with the rest of the world.

When the time of daisies and buttercups came, Miss Sullivan took me by the hand across the fields, where men were preparing the earth for the seed, to the banks of the Tennessee River. There, sitting on the warm grass, I had my first lessons in the beneficence of nature. I learned how the sun and the rain make to grow out of the ground every tree that is pleasant to the sight and good for food; how birds build their nests and live and thrive from land to land; how the squirrel, the deer, the lion, and every other creature finds food and shelter. As my knowledge of things grew, I felt more and more the delight of the world I was in. Long before I learned to do a sum in arithmetic or describe the shape of the earth, Miss

Sullivan had taught me to find beauty in the fragrant woods, in every blade of grass, and in the curves and dimples of my baby sister's hand. She linked my earliest thoughts with nature, and made me feel that "birds and flowers and I were happy peers."

But about this time I had an experience which taught me that nature is not always kind. One day my teacher and I were returning from a long ramble. The morning had been fine, but it was growing warm and sultry when at last we turned our faces homeward. Two or three times we stopped to rest under a tree by the wayside. Our last halt was under a wild cherry tree a short distance from the house. The shade was grateful, and the tree was so easy to climb that with my teacher's assistance I was able to scramble to a seat in the branches. It was so cool up in the tree that Miss Sullivan proposed that we have our luncheon there. I promised to keep still while she went to the house to fetch our lunch.

Suddenly a change passed over the tree. All the sun's warmth left the air. I knew the sky was black, because all the heat, which meant light to me, had died out of the atmosphere. A strange odor came up from the earth. I knew it, it was the odor that always precedes a thunderstorm, and a nameless fear clutched at my heart. I felt absolutely alone, cut off from my friends and the firm earth. The immense, the unknown, enfolded me. I remained still and expectant; a chilling terror crept over me. I longed for my teacher's return; but above all things I wanted to get down from that tree.

There was a moment of sinister silence, then a multitudinous stirring of the leaves. A shiver ran through the tree, and the wind sent forth a blast that would have knocked me off had I not clung to the branch with might and main. The tree swayed and strained. The small twigs snapped and fell about me in showers. A wild impulse to jump seized me, but terror held me fast. I crouched down in the fork of the tree. The branches lashed about me. I felt the intermittent jarring that came now and then, as if something heavy had fallen and the shock had traveled up till it reached the limb I sat on. It worked my suspense up to the highest point, and just as I was thinking the tree and I should fall together, my teacher seized my hand and helped me down. I clung to her, trembling with joy to feel the earth under my feet once more. I had learned a new lesson—that nature "wages open war against her children, and under softest touch hides treacherous claws."

After this experience, it was a long time before I climbed another tree. The mere thought filled me with terror. It was the sweet allurement of the mimosa tree in full bloom that finally overcame my fears. One beautiful spring morning when I was alone in the summer-house reading, I became aware of a wonderful, subtle fragrance in the air. I started up and instinctively stretched out my hands. It seemed as if the spirit of spring had passed through the summer-house. "What is it?" I asked, and the next minute I recognized the odor of the mimosa blossoms. I felt my way to the end of the garden, knowing that the mimosa tree was near the fence, at the turn of the path. Yes, there it was, all quivering in the warm sunshine, its blossom-laden branches almost touching the long grass. Was there ever anything so exquisitely beautiful in the world before! Its delicate blossoms shrank from the slightest earthly touch; it seemed as if a tree of paradise had been transplanted to earth.

I made my way through a shower of petals to the great trunk and for one minute stood irresolute; then, putting my foot in the broad space between the forked branches, I pulled myself up into the tree. I had some difficulty in holding on, for the branches were very large and the bark hurt my hands.

I had a delicious sense that I was doing something unusual and wonderful, so I kept on climbing higher and higher, until I reached a little seat which somebody had built there so long ago that it had grown part of the tree itself. I sat there for a long, long time, feeling like a fairy on a rosy cloud. After that I spent many happy hours in my tree of paradise, thinking fair thoughts and dreaming bright dreams.

Love

I had now the key to all language, and I was eager to learn to use it. Children who hear acquire language without any particular effort; the words that fall from others' lips they catch on the wing, as it were, delightedly, while the little deaf child must trap them by a slow and often painful process. But whatever the process, the result is wonderful. Gradually, from naming an object, we advance step by step until we have traversed the vast distance between our first stammered syllable and the sweep of thought in a line of Shakespeare.

At first, when my teacher told me about a new thing, I asked very few questions. My ideas were vague, and my vocabulary was inadequate; but as my knowledge of things grew and I learned more and more words, my field of inquiry broadened, and I would return again and again to the same subject, eager for further information. Sometimes a new word revived an image that some earlier experience had engraved on my brain.

I remember the morning that I first asked the meaning of the word "love." This was before I knew many words. I had found a few early violets in the garden and brought them to my teacher. She tried to kiss me, but at that time I did not like to have anyone kiss me except my mother. Miss Sullivan put her arm gently round me and spelled into my hand, "I love Helen."

"What is love?" I asked.

She drew me closer to her and said, "It is here," pointing to my heart, whose beats I was conscious of for the first time. Her words puzzled me very much because I did not understand anything unless I touched it.

I smelled the violets in her hand and asked, half in words, half in signs, a question which meant, "Is love the sweetness of flowers?"

"No," said my teacher.

"Is this not love?" I asked, pointing the direction from which the heat came. "Is this not love?"

It seemed to me that there could be nothing more beautiful than the sun, whose warmth makes all things grow. But Miss Sullivan shook her head, and I was greatly puzzled and disappointed. I thought it strange that my teacher could not show me love.

A day or two afterward, I was stringing beads of different sizes in symmetrical groups—two large beads, three small ones, and so on. I had made many mistakes, and Miss Sullivan had pointed them out again and again with gentle patience.

Finally I noticed a very obvious error in the sequence, and for an instant I concentrated my attention on the lesson and tried to think how I should have arranged the beads. Miss Sullivan touched my forehead and spelled with decided emphasis, "Think."

In a flash I knew that the word was the name of the process that was going on in my head. This was my first conscious perception of an abstract idea.

For a long time I was still—I was not thinking of the beads in my lap, but trying to find a meaning for "love" in the light of this new idea. The sun had been under a cloud all day, and there had been brief showers; but suddenly the sun broke forth in all its southern splendor.

Again I asked my teacher, "Is this not love?"

"Love is something like the clouds that were in the sky before the sun came out," she replied. Then in simpler words than these, which at that time I could not have understood, she explained: "You cannot touch the clouds, you know; but you feel the rain and know how glad the flowers and the thirsty earth are to have it after a hot day. You cannot touch love either; but you feel the sweetness that it pours into everything. Without love you would not be happy or want to play."

The beautiful truth burst upon my mind—I felt that there were invisible lines stretched between my spirit and the spirits of others.

From the beginning of my education Miss Sullivan made it a practice to speak to me as she would speak to any hearing child; the only difference was that she spelled the sentences into my hand instead of speaking them. If I did not know the words and idioms necessary to ex-

Iris and Wild Roses, 1887, JOHN LA FARGE. The Metropolitan Museum of Art, Gift of Priscilla A.B. Henderson, 1950.

numberless idioms and expressions used in the simplest daily intercourse. The little hearing child learns these from constant repetition and imitation. The conversation he hears in his home stimulates his mind and suggests topics and calls for the spontaneous expression of his own thoughts. This natural exchange of ideas is denied to the deaf child. My teacher, realizing this, determined to supply the kinds of stimulus I lacked. This she did by repeating to me as far as possible, verbatim, what she heard, and by showing me how I could take part in the conversation. But it was a long time before I ventured to take the lead and still longer before I could find something appropriate to say at the right time.

The deaf and the blind find it very difficult to acquire the amenities of conversation. How much more this difficulty must be augmented in the case of those who are both deaf and blind! They cannot distinguish the tone of the voice or, without assistance, go up and down the gamut of tones that give significance to words; nor can they watch the expression of the speaker's face, and a look is often the very soul of what one says.

press my thoughts she supplied them, even suggesting conversation when I was unable to keep up my end of the dialog.

This process was continued for several years; for the deaf child does not learn in a month, or even in two or three years, the

Developing Comprehension Skills

1. How did Helen Keller become deaf and blind?

2. Here are five quotations from the story. Tell if each one is a fact or an opinion:

   a. I was born on June 27, 1880, in Tuscumbia.
   b. I owe to her loving wisdom all that was bright and good in my long night.
   c. One morning I locked my mother up in the pantry.
   d. Dr. Bell advised my father to write to Mr. Anagnos.
   e. It would have been difficult to find a happier child than I was as I lay in my crib at the close of that eventful day.

3. How did Helen learn that everything has a name? Compare this with how children who are not deaf and blind learn the same thing.

4. Do you think a blind person can understand how things look? Give examples from the story to support your opinion.

5. Helen describes how she used to have temper tantrums when she was very young. What does she say caused her to act that way? Now imagine that she had never been educated and did not write her autobiography. What do you suppose her parents would think caused her temper tantrums?

Reading Literature: Nonfiction

1. **Understanding Elements of Autobiography.** Autobiographies give you information you cannot get anywhere else. Give one example from the story for each of these categories:

   a. the reasons why Helen acted in a particular way
   b. one of Helen's personal, secret feelings

2. **Understanding the Author's Purpose.** Helen Keller did not have sight or hearing, two senses that most of us take for granted. How does her autobiography help you understand what it is like to be deaf and blind? What are some of the problems shared by deaf and blind people with people who do not have these handicaps? What are some of the additional problems faced by deaf and blind people? Refer to the selection to support your answer.

3. **Identifying Tone.** You have now read two selections of autobiography. Are the tones of the two selections alike or different? Give examples to support your answer.

4. **Understanding Literature as a Reflection of Culture.** Literature often reflects the culture of the time and place in which it was written. Name at least two things you learned about life a hundred years ago from this story.

5. **Recognizing Personal Style.** Every person who writes frequently will develop a personal style. The language in that person's writing becomes different from everyone else's. Even though the writer might not sign every page of his or her writing, a good reader could tell whether two pages were by the same person.

   One of the marks of Helen Keller's style is the frequent use of paired words or phrases. Here are some examples:

   > Then, in the dreary month of February, came the illness that closed my eyes and ears and plunged me into the unconsciousness of a new-born baby.

   > They called it acute congestion of the stomach and brain.

   > Early one morning, the fever left me as suddenly and mysteriously as it had come.

   > My hands felt every object and observed every motion.

   > My parents were deeply grieved and perplexed.

   Identify at least five other sentences in which you find paired words or phrases.

Developing Vocabulary Skills

Recognizing Base Words and Affixes. Several words found in the story of Helen Keller contain some of the affixes you learned in Chapter 2 on page 66. Other words contain the same letters as an affix, but the letters are part of the base word. They cannot be separated from the base word. For example, in the word *rewrite*, *re* is a prefix. However, in *read*, *re* is part of the base word.

Each of the following words contains the letters of an affix. If the letters are an affix added to a base word, write the meaning of the word. Use the affix as a clue to meaning. If the letters are part of the base word, write the dictionary or glossary definition.

1. disposition
2. image
3. unconciousness
4. discomfort

5. immeasurable
6. invisible
7. renew
8. impatient

Developing Writing Skills

1. **Comparing Two Autobiographies.** "The Story of My Life" and "I Get a Colt To Break in" are both selections of autobiography. Write a paragraph comparing the two. What are some things they have in common? What are some differences? You may write about the whole selection, or you may choose to compare just the two main characters, the author's purposes, or the tone of the two selections.

2. **Writing a Description.** Helen Keller describes vividly how she felt sitting in a tree during a thunderstorm. Write a description of something that made you feel frightened or helpless. Use specific details and descriptive words to tell your readers what it was like. Appeal to as many senses as you can, including sight, sound, touch, and smell.

Developing Skills in Critical Thinking

Analyzing Slanted Writing. Helen Keller used words and phrases with a positive connotation to describe herself as a child. Find two examples of descriptions that are slanted to make little Helen seem good or cute. Rewrite the sentences with a neutral connotation (neither good nor bad). Do you think Helen Keller was unfair to write about herself with a positive slant? If some writing is slanted, does that mean it is not true?

Developing Skills in Speaking and Listening

Understanding and Using Gestures. At the beginning of her autobiography, Helen Keller describes several ways she communicated before she knew any language. People who can see and hear often use "body language," too. Observe yourself and your friends and family for a few days. Take notes on ways you notice people communicating without language. Then show the class some of the things you noticed. See if your classmates can tell what you mean by your motions.

Biographies

A **biography** is a true story of a real person's life. Unlike the autobiography, it is written by another person, usually from the third-person point of view.

Biographers research their subjects thoroughly. They read everything written about them or by them. Then, in writing about a subject, the biographer tells both the good qualities of that person and some of the less admirable ones. Wherever possible, the writer uses the subject's own words.

The Firebird, Sketch for the Curtain for Stravinsky's Ballet, 1945, MARC CHAGALL.
Private Collection. Courtesy of Crown Publishers, QLP series, New York.

Peculiarsome Abe

CARL SANDBURG

In this selection from a biography of Abraham Lincoln, you will learn about Abe's boyhood. As you read, see if you can tell why its title is "Peculiarsome Abe."

The farm boys in their evenings at Jones's store in Gentryville talked about how Abe Lincoln was always reading, digging into books, stretching out flat on his stomach in front of the fireplace, studying till midnight and past midnight, picking a piece of charcoal to write on the fire shovel, shaving off what he wrote, and then writing more—till midnight and past midnight. The next thing Abe would be reading books between the plow handles, it seemed to them. Once, trying to speak a last word, Dennis Hanks said, "There's suthin' perculiarsome about Abe."

He wanted to learn, to know, to live, to reach out; he wanted to satisfy hungers and thirsts he couldn't tell about, this big boy of the backwoods. Some of what he wanted so much, so deep down, seemed to be in the books.

This was one thing meant by Dennis when he said there was "suthin' peculiarsome" about Abe. It seemed that Abe made the books tell him more than they told other people. All the other farm boys had gone to school and read "The Kentucky Preceptor," but Abe picked out questions from it, such as "Who has the most right to complain, the Indian or the Negro?" Abe would talk about it, up one way and down the other, while they were in the cornfield pulling fodder for the winter. When Abe got hold of a storybook and read about a boat that came near a magnetic rock, and how the magnets in the rock pulled all the nails out of the boat so it went to pieces and the people in the boat found themselves floundering in water, Abe thought it was funny and told it to other people. After Abe read poetry, especially Bobby Burns's poems, Abe began writing rhymes himself. When Abe sat with a girl, with their bare feet in the creek water, and she spoke of the moon rising, he explained to her it was the earth moving and not the moon—the moon only seemed to rise.

Boyhood of Lincoln, 1868,
EASTMAN JOHNSON. Oil on canvas.
The University of Michigan Museum of Art;
bequest of Henry C. Lewis.

He liked to explain to other people what he was getting from books; explaining an idea to some one else made it clearer to him. The habit was growing on him of reading out loud; words came more real if picked from the silent page of the book and pronounced on the tongue; new balances and values of words stood out if spoken aloud. When writing letters for his father or the neighbors, he read the words out loud as they got written. Before writing a letter, he asked questions such as: "What do you want to say in the letter? How do you want to say it? Are you sure that's the best way to say it? Do you think we can fix up a better way to say it?"

As he studied his books, his lower lip stuck out, Josiah Crawford noticed it was a habit and joked Abe about the "stuck-out lip." This habit too stayed with him.

What he got in the schools didn't satisfy him. He went to three different schools in Indiana, two in Kentucky— altogether about four months of school. He learned his A,B,C's, how to spell, read, write. And he had been with the other barefoot boys in butternut jeans learning "manners" under the school teacher, Andrew Crawford, who had them open a door, walk in, and say, "Howdy do?" Yet what he tasted of books in school was only a beginning, only made him hungry and thirsty, shook him with a wanting and a wanting of more and more of what was hidden between the covers of books.

He kept on saying, "The things I want to know are in books; my best friend is the man who'll git me a book I ain't read." He said that to Pitcher, the lawyer over at Rockport, nearly twenty miles away, one fall afternoon, when he walked from Pigeon Creek to Rockport and borrowed a book from Pitcher. Then when fodder-pulling time came a few days later, he shucked corn from early daylight till sundown along with his father and Dennis Hanks and John Hanks, but after supper he read the book till midnight, and at noon he hardly knew the taste of his corn-bread because he had the book in front of him. It was a hundred little things like these which made Dennis Hanks say there was "suthin' peculiarsome" about Abe.

Besides reading the family Bible and figuring his way all through the old arithmetic they had at home, he got hold of "Aesop's Fables," "Pilgrim's Progress," "Robinson Crusoe," and Weems's "The Life of Francis Marion." The book of fables, written or collected thousands of years ago by the Greek slave known as Aesop, sank deep in his mind. As he read through the book a second and third time, he had a feeling there were fables all around him, that everything he touched and handled, everything he saw and learned had a fable wrapped in it somewhere.

The style of the Bible, of Aesop's fables, the hearts and minds back of those books, were much in his thoughts. His favorite pages in them he read over and over. Behind such proverbs as, "Muzzle not the ox that treadeth out the corn," and "He that ruleth his own spirit is greater than he that taketh a city," there were the music of simple wisdom and the mysteries of common everyday life that touched deep spots in him.

Book talk was a comfort against the same thing over again, day after day, so many mornings the same kind of water from the same spring, the same fried pork and corn-meal to eat, the same drizzles of rain, spring plowing, summer weeds, fall fodder-pulling, each coming every year, with the same tired feeling at the end of the day, so many days alone in the woods or the fields or else the same people to talk with, people from whom he had learned all they could teach him. Yet there ran through his head the stories and sayings of other people, the stories and sayings of books, the learning his eyes had caught from books; they were a comfort; they were good to have because they were good by themselves; and they were still better to have because they broke the chill of the lonesome feeling.

Already, Abe knew more than his father; he was writing letters for the neighbors; they hunted out the Lincoln farm to get young Abe to find his bottle of ink with blackberry brier root and copperas in it, and his pen made from a turkey buzzard feather, and write letters. Abe had a suspicion sometimes his father was a little proud to have a boy that could write letters, and tell about things in books, and outrun and outwrestle and rough-and-tumble any boy or man in Spencer County. Yes, he would be different from his father; he was already so; it couldn't be helped.

In growing up from boyhood to young manhood, he had survived against lonesome, gnawing monotony and against floods, forest and prairie fires, snake-bites, horse-kicks, ague, chills, fever, malaria, "milk-sick."

A comic outline against the sky he was, hiking along the roads of Spencer and other counties in southern Indiana in those years when he read all the books within a fifty-mile circuit of his home. Stretching up on the long legs that ran from his moccasins to the body frame with its long, gangling arms, covered with linsey-woolsey, then the lean neck that carried the head with its surmounting coonskin cap or straw hat—it was, again, a comic outline—yet with a portent in its shadow. His laughing "Howdy," his yarns and drollery, opened the doors of men's hearts.

Developing Comprehension Skills

1. How much time did Abe Lincoln spend in school? Was this because he did not like school? How do you know?

2. Why did Abe like to read?

3. Explain why "Peculiarsome Abe" is a good title for this biography.

4. The story says that Abe was bored with "the same people to talk with, people from whom he had learned all they could teach him." The phrase "all they could teach him" is a generalization. Do you think it was true in all cases? If not, can you limit the statement in some way to make it true?

Reading Literature: Nonfiction

1. **Identifying Biography.** Name one way you can tell that this is a biography and not an autobiography.

2. **Analyzing the Author's Viewpoint.** Most modern biographies tell both the good qualities of the person they are describing and some of the bad ones. Does this biography show both sides? Explain your answer.

3. **Understanding Elements of Biography.** Find at least one small detail about Abe that helps the reader see him as a real person.

4. **Understanding the Setting.** What is the importance of the setting of Abe's early life? How would his youth have been different in another setting?

5. **Recognizing Persuasive Writing.** A biography tells us something about what life was like at the time and place the main character lived. It can also help persuade a reader to have a certain opinion about the person and the times. Does this biography give you a certain opinion about Abe Lincoln? Explain your answer.

Developing Vocabulary Skills

Identifying Dictionary Terms. Review the information about the dictionary on page 356 and the study questions for Developing Vocabulary Skills on pages 367 and 368. Then match each of the following dictionary terms in column A with the definitions in column B. Write the letter on your paper.

A

1. entry words
2. respelling
3. pronunciation key
4. syllable
5. primary accent
6. secondary accent
7. schwa sound
8. homographs
9. multiple meanings

B

a. A list of sample words that show the symbols used in identifying sounds in words
b. The heavy mark that indicates which syllable has the strongest stress
c. The symbol that represents the vowel sound heard in an unaccented syllable
d. Entry words that are spelled the same but have two different meanings, and may be pronounced differently
e. More than one definition
f. The lighter mark on a syllable that has a lighter stress
g. All the words entered in alphabetical order in a dictionary or glossary
h. The pronunciation of a word shown in parentheses immediately after an entry word
i. A part of a word that consists of one vowel sound alone or with one or more consonant sounds

Developing Writing Skills

1. **Learning About Human Experience Through Literature.** Nonfiction writing can play a valuable role by reflecting the culture, or way of life, of a certain time and place. Write a paragraph telling what you learned from reading this selection about life in Indiana in Abe Lincoln's time. What things were different from our times? What were the same?

2. **Writing Biography.** This biography tells the reader what life was like when Abe was growing up. It describes the kinds of things people did and how they lived. Try writing a short biography of someone you know, someone your age or a little older. The person you choose must be someone you can interview.

Before you interview your subject, prepare questions you wish to ask him or her. Include questions about such facts as the subject's birth date, schools he or she has attended, and jobs or hobbies he or she has had. Also include questions about feelings and opinions, such as favorite songs or sports or classes, or most important memories. Write out the questions so that you won't forget them as you talk with your subject.

During the interview, take notes on the subject's answers. Write down the main ideas, not every word.

After the interview, use your questions and the subject's answers to write about that person's life. Be sure to include details of daily life as in Carl Sandburg's biography of Lincoln. Write so that someone reading your biography a hundred years from now could learn something about life in the twentieth century. Your biography should be at least eight paragraphs long.

Developing Skills in Study and Research

Scanning for Specific Information. Many biographies have been written about Abe Lincoln besides Carl Sandburg's. Go to the library and find at least three of them. On your paper, write the author and title of each biography you have chosen. Then look inside the books. Skim the table of contents and index. Examine the bibliography, if there is one, to see how many books the author referred to in writing the book. Read a few sample pages of each book to see if the writing is slanted. Does the author quote from reference sources to let you know where he or she got the information? Or does the writer just tell the story? Does the writer tell about the character's personal thoughts without telling how he or she found out that the character thought that way? Does the writer include personal opinions? If a writer does not identify sources for information, but does give personal opinions, you have a clue that the writing is slanted.

After you have examined the table of contents, index, and bibliography, and have read to discover slanted writing, put the three books in order. The first book on your list should be the one that you think would have the most accurate information about Abe. The last book on the list should be the one you consider the least accurate. Write a few brief notes about each book to explain your ranking.

Matthew A. Henson

LANGSTON HUGHES

To reach the North Pole, Robert Peary and Matt Henson faced bitter cold, starvation, and other dangers. Look for clues that suggest why Matt Henson was willing to take such great risks.

Portrait of Matthew Henson. The Bettmann Archive, Inc. New York City.

The North Pole was discovered on April 6, 1909, by Rear Admiral Robert E. Peary of the United States Navy. With Admiral Peary at the North Pole was Matthew Henson. In fact, Henson was the trail breaker for Peary's expedition and, as such, went ahead first to the Pole, reaching it some forty-five minutes before the Admiral himself. So Henson was actually the very *first* person to stand at the top of the world.

At the Pole, the latitude is 90 degrees North and from there all directions are South. In Admiral Peary's Log Book his arrival at the North Pole is recorded thus: "Arrived here today, 27 marches from Cape Columbia, I have with me five men, Matthew Henson, colored, Ootah, Eginwah, Seegloo, and Ookeah, Eskimos; five sledges and thirty-eight dogs. The expedition under my command has succeeded in reaching the POLE . . . for the honor and prestige of the United States of America." To Henson then, his only English speaking companion, Peary is reported to have said, "This scene my eyes will never see again. Plant the Stars and Stripes over there, Matt—at the North Pole."

Born on a farm in Charles County, Maryland, the year after the close of the War Between the States, Matthew Alexander Henson had a harsh childhood. When he was two years old, his mother died and his father married again. Matt was only eight when his father died, too. His stepmother was not kind to him. She made him work very hard, would not allow him to go to school, and often whipped him severely. When he was eleven years old, in the middle of the winter, Matt decided to run away. While everyone else was asleep in the house, in the dark of night he started out on foot, heading toward Washington. There, a kind woman who ran a small lunch room took him in, fed him, and gave him a job as her dishwasher at a dollar and a half a week. For a number of years he was happy, until the urge came over him to travel further. Matt had heard that in Baltimore there were docks and great ships that sailed away into all the waters of the world. Young Henson wanted to be a sailor.

Life at Sea

Matt was lucky. After walking from Washington to Baltimore, it was not long before the thirteen-year-old youth found a job on a boat, a square-rigger with tall white sails destined for Hong Kong, a port halfway around the world. Matt was signed on as a cabin boy. Added to this good fortune was the fact that the *Katie Hines* was in command of a kind-hearted captain who took an interest in the brave youngster who could hardly read or write. The captain decided to teach him to read and write before the ship got back to Baltimore. In those days it was a voyage of many months to China. Every day the captain gave Matt a private class in his cabin. In this way, Matt acquired the groundwork of a good education on a windjammer rocking and rolling through the troughs of the sea.

For five years Matt Henson sailed on the *Katie Hines*, learning seamanship, learning from books, learning from people of all nationalities, and growing into a man. One entire winter the ship was locked in by ice at the Russian harbor of Murmansk. Matt learned to speak Russian, hunt wolves, and drive sleighs. Later he saw the pagodas of Japan, the gypsies of Spain, the palm trees of the West Indies, and the great rivers of Africa. Matt picked up a smattering of many languages, and some he learned well. He acquired a knowledge and understanding of strange peoples and strange ways, and he learned to take foreign customs in his stride and to mingle in a friendly way with everybody. This ability to get along with strangers and live with folks whose language he did not speak stood him in good stead later in life, for it was his destiny to become an explorer.

The good captain of the *Katie Hines*, who introduced the world to Matt, died when Matt was seventeen. His ship had just left Jamaica heading through the Caribbean for Baltimore. With the Captain in his cabin when he died was the boy he had guided toward manhood, young Matthew Henson. The master of the ship was buried at sea.

Matt did not sail on the *Katie Hines* again. He shipped instead on a fishing boat, but quit when it reached Newfoundland. In Boston and other cities along the coast as far as New York, young Henson worked at various jobs ashore—nightwatchman, ditch digger, coachman.

Matt Works for Robert Peary

When he was nineteen, Matt Henson went back to Washington again. There, two years later, working as a stockroom clerk in a men's furnishing store, he met young Robert Peary, a civil engineer for the Navy, who came in to the store to buy a sun helmet for use in the tropics. Peary offered Matt Henson a job as his personal attendant on a surveying trip to Nicaragua for the government. Henson did not like the idea of being anyone's man-servant, but he felt intuitively that the job might lead to something better. Having adventure in his blood, he accepted it. In no time at all, Peary recognized in the youth qualities of value far beyond those of a personal servant, so he promoted him to his surveying crew as a field helper. For twenty-three years thereafter, Henson was associated with Peary in his work and his trips.

Peary was not a rich man so he could not always personally afford to pay Henson for his services. But on their return from Central America, a job was secured for Henson on government pay as a messenger in Peary's office at the Navy Yard in Philadelphia. About a year later, Peary told young Henson about a proposed expedition to Greenland. He intended to explore the northern icecaps, and he said he desired very much to take Matt along. But since the trip had very meager backing, there was no money to pay for Henson's services. Matt Henson volunteered to go without pay. In this he was joined by a number of other adventurers.

First Trip to the Arctic

In 1888 the party set out for Baffin Bay.[1] In spite of the fact that Peary suffered a broken leg shortly after his arrival in Greenland, he and the whole party elected to allow their ship to depart, leaving them isolated for a year at the foot of a glacier they hoped to cross.

Matt built a house for Peary, his wife, and the rest of the party and aided in the construction of sledges for their inland trips. From the Eskimos, he learned how to handle a team of eight to sixteen dogs to pull sledges across the ice. Matt's light

---

1. **Baffin Bay.** A body of water on the southwestern coast of Greenland. It separates Canada's Baffin Islands from Greenland. It is the farthest north a ship can go and tie up to land.

tan skin at first caused the Eskimos to think him one of them. In short order, he had established friendly relations with the native peoples and soon began to learn their language. That winter they taught him a great many things useful to know in the frozen North, especially how to hunt, trap, and fish for food.

Since Henson put his newly acquired knowledge at the disposal of the entire party of explorers, he became a most valuable man to Peary's expedition. Lieutenant Peary realized his value and respected Henson accordingly. Matt, in turn, sympathized deeply with Peary's aims and marvelled at his determination. Soon between the two men there sprang up a relationship of mutual admiration and dependence. When the party set out in the face of stinging sleet through sub-zero weather to conduct its explorations, Matt was considered one of the most important men in the group. By then, on the part of others, his race had been entirely forgotten. Here in the frozen North, no one thought of color lines. In the primitive Arctic, a man was a man—and that was that.

When the expedition returned to New York in 1892, Peary told Matt Henson, "We are going back to the Arctic again—but next time, all the way to the North Pole." At the turn of the century, no one knew what lay at either the North Pole or the South Pole. At the earth's axis would there be snow-covered land, or only drifting ice floes impossible of crossing? No-

body could tell. And how could a man reach the North Pole? By land or by sea? No one knew. In those days there were no radios to keep up communications with the rest of the world. There were no airplanes to survey terrain from the air, or to drop food if explorers were stranded, or to effect a quick rescue if they were isolated. To make an attempt to reach the North Pole was considered by most people to be a foolhardy adventure indeed, but Henson and Peary both wanted to attempt it.

Second Trip to the Arctic

In 1895 a party of eleven men and two women again headed for Greenland, with Peary intending to go further North this time. After a year of Arctic hardships and frustrations, all but two of the men returned to the United States. Only Matt Henson and one other, Hugh Lee, stuck by Peary, electing to remain another year, sticking out a second winter that they might go forward in the spring. Peary's first attempt that year to reach the Pole had been unsuccessful, and their supplies were buried in a frozen drift of snow and ice. In April, the party made another attempt in the face of icy winds that bore down from the North under the cold but continuous glare of a twenty-four-hour sun on blindingly white snow. In their three dog-sledges, the men often lost contact in the swirling blizzards through which they travelled. It was slow and dangerous going over ice that might split and isolate one dog team from another.

At one time Lee was lost. Peary and Henson made camp trusting he would catch up to them, but he did not. To keep warm while waiting and hoping, the two men slept huddled in furs as close together as they could, that their body heat might keep each other from freezing. After three days, Henson went in search of the third man and, luckily, found him. Lee was almost frozen on the top of his dog sledge, though still alive. Henson rescued him and treated him for frostbite and extreme exposure.

When their food supply got so low the men could not share any of it with the dogs, they would each day kill a dog and feed that one to the other animals. Finally, the men were reduced to eating dogs themselves. After a month, however, the three pioneers had covered six hundred miles. They were too exhausted by then and their supplies too low to hope to go any further and expect to make the long trek back to civilization alive. Besides, scurvy, the dreaded disease caused by malnutrition, set in. They had failed.

Nevertheless they brought back to New York from the Greenland coast two large meteorites of scientific interest, leaving behind one of many tons that was too large to be loaded aboard their small ship. In 1897 they secured a larger ship and stronger tackle, sailed again to Green-

land, and this time brought back to New York the largest meteorite in the world. This gained Peary wide newspaper publicity as well as a profitable lecture tour. Matt, meanwhile, was employed by the American Museum of Natural History as an assistant in the mounting of Arctic animals and arranging true-to-nature panoramas of the beasts and backgrounds of the far North.

Later Trips to the Arctic

In England, Peary's lectures and interviews were so successful that a publisher presented him with a ship, the *Windward*, especially equipped for Arctic travel. On his return to America, he immediately began to plan another Polar search, this time working out details most carefully in advance, selecting a full complement of assistants to cover each lap, and preparing to spend at least four years on the expedition. He alerted Matt to be ready to accompany him.

Off again in 1898, Peary and Henson steamed past the Statue of Liberty, but ice prevented the *Windward* from penetrating as far north as Peary had hoped. They got only to Cape d'Urville on Ellesmere Island. From there, Peary decided to go by sledge overland to Fort Conger, deserted fifteen years before by another exploring party that had left behind a large stock of supplies. This trip to Conger was one of two hundred and fifty miles

Icebergs, 1861, FREDERICK CHURCH. The Dallas Museum of Fine Arts, anonymous gift. Photograph by David Wharton.

through deep snowdrifts over mountains of ice, but Matt and Peary, with a group of Eskimos, got there. On arrival, Peary's feet were frozen so badly that some of his toes snapped off as his shoes were removed. For three months at Conger, Matt cared for Peary, treating his frozen feet and trying to prevent gangrene from setting in. When they could travel again, they returned to Cape d'Urville where all of Peary's remaining toes, except one on either foot, had to be amputated. This great misfortune left him a partial cripple for life. Convalescence did not keep him

from remaining for two years more in Greenland, but again he failed on this trip to reach the Pole. At Etah, Matt and Peary passed many months alone, except for the Eskimos, and they were the first to define for map makers the northern rim of Greenland. When they returned to New York in 1902, they had added to the geographical knowledge of the world by this major exploration.

Over a period of many years, from youth to middle-age, the still determined Robert Peary made a total of eight unsuccessful attempts to reach the Pole, and, on all but one, Matt Henson accompanied him. Henson became an expert in his knowledge of the Arctic and its winds and weather. In the frozen North, far away from the centers of civilization, he developed into a sort of Jack-of-all-trades since there was nothing Matt would not do to be of value to himself or his party. He learned to harpoon walrus; to hunt reindeer, bear, and musk-oxen; to skin and stuff animals; to cook over a hole in the ice; and to build igloos as an ice shelter against zero gales. He could not only build a boat but navigate it. He could interpret for the white men and the Eskimos. He was so good at manipulating heavily loaded dog sledges, even in blizzards of 50 degrees below, that Peary once said of Henson, "He is a better dog driver and can handle a sledge better than any man living except some of the best Eskimo hunters themselves." With the Eskimos no one could form closer friendships or achieve cooperation more quickly than could Henson. He not only learned to speak their language but to understand their jokes, eat their food, and wear their clothes. He adopted an orphan Eskimo boy, Kudlooktoo. And once when Henson slipped on an ice floe and went into the freezing water, it was an Eskimo who saved his life.

On the expedition begun in 1905, they went by ship as far as Cape Sheridan, then by sledge and on foot across the ice of the Polar Sea. That year Peary and Matt Henson reached a new farthest North, 87°6″, only 175 miles from the Pole. Here again they were stymied by all the conditions that make travel in the Land of the Midnight Sun excessively difficult—the breaking ice floes, the towering cliffs of frozen snow, the swirling blizzards and the terrors of complete isolation. With supplies gone, dogs emaciated and the Eskimos exhausted, for days they faced death on floating ice fields as they tried to make their way back to their base camp. Again defeated, Matt and Peary reached New York on Christmas Eve, 1906.

Success at Last

In 1907, Henson got married, but marriage did not keep Matt at home. The call came again to seek, with the undaunted Peary, a foothold at the top of the world. Two more determined men than Peary and Henson have never been known in the annals of exploration. One disappointment after another plus the ridicule of the press of the world at his continual failures only made Peary more firm in his ambition to reach 90 degrees North, where no person had ever stood before. On each expedition his accompanying members changed, but Matt Henson remained with him. Henson was forty-two years old when again he left the United States on July 8, 1908, once more heading for familiar Cape Sheridan. This time President Theodore Roosevelt came aboard their ship in New York Harbor to see the expedition off and to cheer its departure.

Leaving the ship at Cape Sheridan, the party travelled overland ninety-three miles across the snow to Cape Columbia where a base was established. From here, it was four hundred uncharted miles across seas of ice to the Pole. The temperature was so cold that often the men's beards were frozen stiff from the moisture from their breath. Eighteen years of determination lay behind Peary when on February 28, 1909 he began another attempt to reach the Pole.

The party got off to a good start. But in March a great lead of water that they could not cross—an Arctic river between the ice—stopped their progress and made it appear they might never get further. Fortunately, after a week of waiting, the weather went even further below zero. Then the water froze, permitting lightly loaded sledges to cross and re-cross, conveying supplies to the other side. When they were a hundred and thirty miles from the Pole, the last of the supporting parties turned back. Now Peary and Henson were left alone with four Eskimos, five sledges, and a group of huskies for their final dash northward, destined, if successful, to make history. Matt was to blaze the trail, Peary to follow.

A gruelling trail it was, over a white wilderness of snow and ice, but they pushed forward. "Day and night were the same," wrote Henson later in his autobiography, *A Negro at the North Pole*. "My thoughts were on the going and the getting forward and on nothing else. The wind was from the southeast and seemed to push us on and the sun was at our backs, a ball of livid fire rolling its way above the horizon in never ending day." But on this last lap, he continued, "As we looked at each other we realized . . . the time had come for us to demonstrate that we were the men who, it had been ordained, should unlock the door which held the mystery of the Arctic."

By April 5 they were thirty-five miles from the Pole. Peary with his mutilated feet was then fifty-three years old, and Matt was not young either. Could it be that at last their dream of so many years would come true? Henson and Peary could not sleep from the excitement of it. A part of Matt's job as trailblazer was to build an igloo of ice at each stopping point so that when Peary got there they could rest until time to start again. On the day when Henson, forging ahead, finally arrived at a point where North no longer existed, he knew he had reached the Pole. With Ootah's assistance, there he began to build an igloo. Forty-five minutes later, with Eskimos and a team of dogs, Peary arrived. To Matt Henson, Peary gave the honor of planting the American flag at the North Pole while he stood in salute. It was April 6, 1909.

Eleven years later Admiral Peary died, but Matt Henson lived to be eighty-eight years old. He passed away in New York City in 1955. In tribute to his long series of explorations, Matt Henson received a Congressional Medal, a gold medal from the Chicago Geographical Society, and a loving cup from the Bronx Chamber of Commerce. A building has been named after him at Dillard University. On the occasion of the forty-fifth Anniversary of the Discovery of the North Pole, President Eisenhower honored Matt Henson at the White House.

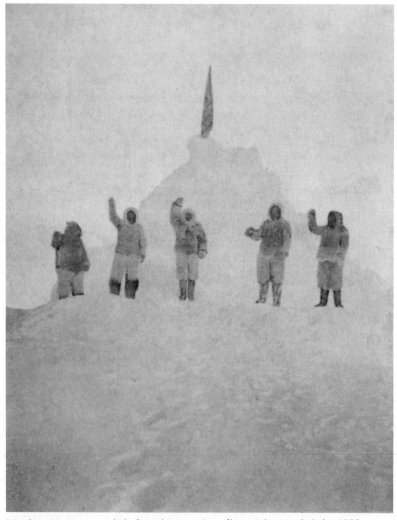

Matthew Henson stands before the American flag at the North Pole, 1909.
The Bettmann Archive, Inc. New York City.

Developing Comprehension Skills

1. How did Matt happen to learn to read and write aboard a ship?

2. A good biography should make its subject seem real. Name two or three small details in this biography that made Matt seem real to you.

3. Do you think that the way Matt grew up helped him become an explorer as an adult? Give a reason for your answer.

4. What would happen if a child living today tried to do what Matt did when he was a boy?

5. Do you think life was better for a child growing up in the 1860's and '70's or in the 1980's? Give some reasons for your answer.

Reading Literature: Nonfiction

1. **Learning About Human Experience Through Literature.** Nonfiction writing is an important way of recording human experience. In this biography, you learned about the life of Matt Henson. What other important experience did you learn about? In what other ways might you learn about the same topic? Do you think reading a biography is as good a way to learn as these other ways, or better, or worse? Give a reason for your answer.

2. **Comparing Two Characters.** Compare what you have learned about Matt Henson and about Abe Lincoln when they were boys. How were they different? How were they similar? Give at least two answers for each question.

3. **Comparing Biographies.** The biography of Matt Henson covers most of his life. That of Abe Lincoln covers only part of his boyhood. How does this difference affect the two biographies? Does it affect how well you get to know the subject (main character)? How does it affect the author's choice of events? Which approach do you think works better in helping you know about the subject of the biography? Or do you feel that the approaches are equally good? Give a reason for your answer.

4. **Comparing Autobiography and Biography.** Consider the two autobiographies and two biographies you have read. An autobiography can tell you some things that a biography cannot tell as accurately and completely. A biography can tell other things that an autobiography

cannot tell as accurately and completely. Find evidence in the four selections to prove each of these statements.

5. **Evaluating an Opinion.** Read this sentence from the biography: "A kind woman who ran a small lunchroom took him in, fed him, and gave him a job as her dishwasher." Calling the woman "kind" is an opinion. From the information in the rest of the sentence, do you think the opinion is based on facts? Give a reason for your answer.

Developing Vocabulary Skills

Reviewing Ways To Find Correct Meanings. You have learned these methods for figuring out the meaning of an unfamiliar word:

a. Word Parts. Knowing the meaning of affixes and how they change the meaning of a base word.

b. Context Clues. Considering the sentence or paragraph in which a specific word appears. Frequently, context clues give the information you need to understand the use of the word.

c. Dictionary and Glossary. Finding the exact meaning of a word in a dictionary or glossary.

Read these sentences about events in Matthew Henson's life. Decide which method you want to use for figuring out the meaning of each underlined word. On your paper, write the meaning of the word. Also write which of the methods you used to find the meaning.

1. Later he saw the pagodas of Japan, the gypsies of Spain, and the palm trees of the West Indies.

2. The men were too exhausted to go any further. Besides, scurvy, the dreaded disease caused by malnutrition, set in.

3. It was not long before young Henson found a job on a boat, a square-rigger with tall white sails destined for Hong Kong.

4. Peary's first attempt to reach the pole had been unsuccessful.

5. The men faced the cold but continuous glare of a twenty-four-hour sun on blindingly white snow.

6. With supplies gone, dogs emaciated, and the Eskimos exhausted, they faced death on floating ice fields.

7. Peary's toes, except one on either foot, had to be amputated.

8. Matt worked in the American Museum of Natural History arranging true-to-nature panoramas. These pictures depicted the beasts and backgrounds of the far North.

Developing Writing Skills

1. **Analyzing a Character.** After reading this biography, what kind of a person do you think Matt Henson was? Write a paragraph describing Matt's character and personality. Use details from the story to support what you write.

2. **Writing About Courage.** Think about a time when you had to show courage. You may have been frightened when you learned to swim. Perhaps large dogs or other animals upset you. You may have been lost in a strange place. How did you face your problem? Write one or more paragraphs explaining how you showed courage.

Developing Skills in Study and Research

1. **Reading a Map.** Find and examine a map that shows the area of the North Pole. Look at the **legend**, the box that explains the symbols used on the map. How does the map show land and water? Is the North Pole on land or is it a sea covered by ice? Now look at the distance scale in the legend. Using your finger or a ruler, estimate how far the North Pole is from Ellesmere Island, one of Henson's stops.

2. **Using Two Reference Materials.** Locate magnetic north on a map of the North Pole. Is magnetic north the same as the North Pole? Now look up *magnetic north* in an encyclopedia, dictionary, or atlas. On your paper, write what the term means. Also write how and where you found the meaning.

Developing Skills in Speaking and Listening

Introducing a Guest Speaker. Imagine that you are the chairperson of an explorer's club in 1909. Your club has invited Matt Henson to speak and receive an award. You are given the job of presenting the award and telling Matt why the club thinks he deserves it. Write your speech and practice it. Then present it before a group. Be sure to speak loudly enough for everyone to hear. Give your audience the feeling that you really admire Matt and want him to know it.

Maria Tallchief

TOBI TOBIAS

Like most people, Maria Tallchief had to make some important decisions during her life. As you read her biography, look for the moments when she had to make choices. Can you predict her decisions?

In the Osage language, *Ki He Kah Stah* means "the tall chiefs." One of America's greatest ballerinas comes from the native American family with this name. Elizabeth Marie Tallchief was born on January 24, 1925, in Fairfax, Oklahoma, a small town on the Osage reservation in southwestern United States. Her father was a full-blooded Osage; his father had been chief of the tribe. Her mother came from Scottish and Irish people.

Betty Marie's father was an easygoing man. He did not have to work at a regular job because oil had been discovered on the Osage reservation. The tribal council sold this oil and each member of the Osage shared in the profits. Mr. Tallchief loved the outdoors and a relaxed, comfortable life. Gerald, Betty Marie's older brother, was like him.

Mrs. Tallchief was different. She was strict and full of energy. She had great plans for Betty Marie and for her other daughter, Marjorie, who was two years younger. She wanted them to study music and dancing, and she expected them to work hard at everything they did.

Betty Marie was only three when she started taking piano lessons, but she learned music quickly and easily. Mrs. Tallchief dreamed that one day her daughter would play in concerts all over the world.

By the next year, Betty Marie was dancing too. She had ballet lessons with a teacher who came to Fairfax once a week. This teacher did not realize that ballet dancing should be taught slowly and carefully. She showed Betty Marie how to jump and leap and spin like a circus acrobat. She put her in toe shoes and taught her to dance on the tips of her toes. She had Betty Marie on stage when she was only five years old.

When Marjorie began taking lessons and performing with her sister, Mrs. Tallchief decided that the family should move to Los Angeles, where the girls could find better music and dancing teachers. Mr. Tallchief liked the idea. In California's sunshine, he said, he could play golf all year long.

At first Betty Marie felt strange and lonely in her new home. She was glad to settle down to the things she knew best— school, music, and dancing. The sisters went to a fine teacher, Ernest Belcher, for ballet lessons. The first time the eight-year-old Betty Marie danced for Mr. Belcher, he was horrified. "If you really want to dance," he said, "you will have to start all over again, from the beginning. No toe shoes, no fancy tricks, no performing. I'm surprised that your back and feet haven't been ruined by all this nonsense."

Betty Marie felt very disappointed but she was used to doing as she was told. She always tried to please her mother and her teachers. She wasn't afraid of any amount of hard work, either, and she loved to dance. So she began again, this time in the right way, with the simplest exercises and steps.

Mrs. Tallchief still wanted her daughter to become a concert pianist. She felt that dancing was wonderful, as long as it didn't keep Betty Marie away from her music. Betty Marie tried to be perfect in both. Every day she practiced the piano for several hours and went to a two-hour ballet class. She did well in her school-work too and even found time to have fun with her friends. At home her mother

taught her to cook and sew. But she had no time for dreaming, no time for just doing nothing.

To celebrate her twelfth birthday, Betty Marie gave a concert. For the first half she played the piano, and for the second half she danced. That concert, she said, showed how she felt inside. She was split in half between the two things she loved most. One day she would have to choose between them. In high school, Betty Marie's favorite subject was writing. Once she wrote about trying to decide between music and dancing. At fifteen, she was both performing at the piano and studying ballet with a great Russian teacher, Mme. Bronislava Nijinska.

Mme. Nijinska was also a choreographer—a person who makes up dances. She gave Betty Marie a leading part in one of her ballets. The performance took place before an enormous audience. As she danced, Betty Marie felt strong and free. Afterward, everyone told her how well she had done. Now she realized that, more than anything else, she wanted to be a dancer.

Betty Marie grew to be tall and slim, with a lovely, strong body. Her face was beautiful. She had olive skin, mysterious dark eyes, high cheekbones, a wide, well-shaped mouth, and a cloud of dark hair. She was a quiet, serious girl and, even more than most dancers, a hard worker.

When she was seventeen, Betty Marie finished high school and went to New

York City, hoping to find a job in a ballet company. Sergei Denham, the director of the famous Ballet Russe de Monte Carlo, had seen and liked her dancing when she was a student in California. Now he said he would try her out in his company.

Betty Marie went on tour with the Ballet Russe. The company traveled from city to city, giving performances. Betty Marie danced so well that people began to notice her. Soon she had some solo parts.

Ballet life was often hard, though, and Betty Marie was sometimes unhappy. She kept to herself at first, and many people in the company thought she was unfriendly. Some of them were jealous because she was doing so well. She missed her family and wrote long letters home.

When Mr. Denham asked her to stay on in the company, he said that she must have a beautiful stage name. So Betty Marie became Maria. She refused to

The Entrance of the Masked Dancers, 1879, EDGAR DEGAS. Sterling and Francine Clark Art Institute, Williamstown, Massachusetts.

change Tallchief, though. She was proud of her native American family name.

Then George Balanchine, a well-known choreographer, joined the Ballet Russe. Maria caught his eye at once. Her dancing was fast and brilliant. She could jump up and cross her long legs together four times in the air. She could turn in the air and land on the points of her strong toes. Her balance was sure. Her leaps were sharp and high. Her turns were quick and powerful.

Day after day, Mr. Balanchine worked with Maria. He was a gentle, patient teacher, but he often asked her to perform steps that seemed impossible. She tried over and over again, until she could do what he wanted. Soon she was dancing better than ever before.

When Maria was twenty-one, she and Mr. Balanchine married. The next year she and her husband went to France to work with the Paris Opéra Ballet. Maria was the first American to dance with this company in more than a hundred years. The French people loved her. When she came out to bow, they greeted her with applause and bouquets of flowers.

Then Mr. Balanchine went back to work at his own studio in New York, the School of American Ballet. He formed a company called Ballet Society with the dancers he had trained there. In time this group would grow into the New York City Ballet and become one of the best companies in the world. Maria joined this company as its leading dancer when she was twenty-two.

In the years that followed, George Balanchine made great changes in ballet. He took old ballets and old steps and made them new and different. He tried out new ways of moving and new ways of making dances. Many people called him a genius.

Mr. Balanchine created marvelous ballets for Maria. In one of them, *Firebird*, she danced the part of a beautiful, wild bird with magic powers. Mr. Balanchine gave her very difficult steps that made the audience gasp with wonder and surprise. Maria flashed across the stage, she flew, she whirled, she slashed through space like a flaming arrow. *Firebird* proved that Maria was truly a ballerina. She was not just a fine dancer but one of the best in the world.

Maria was a very musical dancer. Her years of study at the piano had taught her to love and understand music, and this helped her to work well with Mr. Balanchine. Some of his greatest ballets had no story, no elaborate scenery or costumes. They were just movements to music. Maria's dancing in ballets like *Serenade*, *Concerto Barocco*, *The Four Temperaments*, and *Symphony in C* helped to make the New York City Ballet famous.

Still, Maria's life was almost all hard work. Every morning she took a long ballet class. In the afternoon she rehearsed with the company, went to costume fittings, saw reporters and photographers, and practiced by herself. When evening came, she did her warm-up exercises, put on her stage make-up and costume, and went out on the stage to perform. She had little time to rest and no time for anything outside of ballet. Like most dancers, though, Maria loved her work.

Maria won many honors for her dancing. One came from her hometown. Thousands of people gathered in Fairfax for the celebration. Among them were the leaders of the Osage, the governors of Oklahoma, and Maria's mother and father. There were speeches, songs, dancing, and feasting. The Osage wore native dress and performed a special ceremony that made Maria a princess of the Osage tribe.

Maria's ballet career was a success, but her marriage to Mr. Balanchine had become very unhappy. She wanted to have children, but her husband could not agree. He thought a ballerina should give her whole life to dancing. After several years their marriage ended. Then, when she was thirty-one, Maria married Henry D. Paschen, Jr., an engineer who worked in Chicago. Three years later she became the mother of a little girl whom she named Elise Maria.

In her years with the New York City Ballet, Maria often went on tour with the company. She traveled with other companies, too, as a guest ballerina. She danced in most of the big cities of the United States and Europe. Working with these other groups, Maria performed parts that have made ballerinas famous throughout history. She danced in ballets that the New York City company never presented. She also met new partners who were excellent dancers and who knew exactly how to make a ballerina look her best.

Soon Maria began to see that the New York City Ballet was not the right place for her any more. She felt that a ballerina should have roles that make her look like a star. She wanted to have partners who were stars too. In the New York City Ballet, Mr. Balanchine's choreography was the most important thing. No matter how good they were, the dancers took second place.

Finally Maria decided to join American Ballet Theatre. She toured with this company as its prima, or first, ballerina, for several years and appeared with other companies as well. By the time she was thirty-five, Maria was called America's greatest ballerina. But she was facing a hard question. What should she do next? What would be best for her, as a dancer and as a person?

She could go back to the New York City Ballet. But she felt she did not belong there any more. She could go on dancing with other companies, but these groups were almost always on tour. Maria was tired of traveling all the time. She was tired of dancing the same parts over and over again. Maria Tallchief was one of the

Maria Tallchief and Erik Bruhn, dancing the *Flower Festival at Benzano* ballet. Photograph by Jack Mitchell.

finest dancers in the history of ballet. Yet the ballet world did not seem to have a place for her.

She had a third choice, though, and now she turned to it. She had once said, "Marriage and dancing are both very important but it is better to take them one at a time." In 1966, when she was forty-one, Maria made her decision. She "hung up her toe shoes," as people in ballet say, and went home to her family in Chicago.

Although Maria left the stage, she did not leave the dance world. She began teaching young people and, in 1980, formed her own dance company, the Chicago City Ballet. Her sister, Marjorie, who also had a fine career as a ballerina, now heads the company's school. Maria has many duties as an artistic director but she likes to think of herself simply as a teacher, passing on what she has learned to a new generation of dancers.

Developing Comprehension Skills

1. Maria started playing piano and dancing while very young. Who was responsible for her starting out so young?

2. Young Maria was very good at both piano and ballet. As she grew up, she had to make a choice between them. Tell how you know that at first she did not know which she would pick. What caused her to choose ballet?

3. Find an idea about Maria that the author repeats over and over again in this biography. Do you think that the idea reflects the facts? Give a reason for your answer.

4. Mr. Balanchine did not want Maria to have children. He thought children would distract her from dancing. Later, Maria had a child. She continued to dance for seven more years, and after that she became a ballet teacher. What do you think of Mr. Balanchine's objections? How did Maria's actions conflict with his ideas? Do you think that taking on the responsibility for a child means that a man or woman cannot perform well in his or her career? Give reasons for your answer.

Reading Literature: Nonfiction

1. **Analyzing Organization:** Most biographies are organized in one of two ways. They are either related in simple, chronological (time) order, or told in terms of cause and effect. "Maria Tallchief" is mainly organized in chronological order, but there are also some examples of cause and effect. Find one of these and tell how the cause and effect relationship affects the author's choice of events and the order in which they are told.

2. **Describing the Tone.** The **tone** of a piece of writing lets you know how the author feels about his or her subject. Some words to describe tone include *serious, admiring, angry, sad, carefree, amused.* How would you describe the tone of "Maria Tallchief"? Refer to the selection to explain your answer.

3. **Identifying Faulty Generalizations.** As you remember, a generalization is faulty if it can be disproven in even one case. Words like *all, always,* and *every* are clues that you may have a faulty generalization.

Words like *most* and *almost* usually indicate the generalization is not faulty. Read the following sentences from the story. Decide whether each one is or is not a faulty generalization. Think about whether each statement includes too much to be true. For each sentence, explain why you decided as you did.

a. Maria's life was almost all hard work.
b. Like most dancers, Maria loved her work.
c. Like most women, she wanted to have children.
d. These groups were almost always on tour.

4. **Understanding the Effect of Connotations.** The following sentences from "Maria Tallchief" include words with positive connotations. Identify each word that suggests a strong, favorable feeling. If the author had used only neutral words, would the sentences be more accurate or less accurate? Would they be more or less interesting?

a. She slashed through space like a flaming arrow.
b. They greeted her with applause.
c. Mr. Balanchine created marvelous ballets for Maria.

5. **Identifying Elements of Biography.** Three thousand years ago, biographers told only about a person's great deeds and heroic qualities. Today, biographers tell both the great and the small, the good and the bad, the successful and difficult times of a person's life. If Maria's biography were written by a 3000-year-old-biographer, what parts of this biography do you think would be left out?

Developing Vocabulary Skills

Using Glossaries in Other Textbooks. Most of the textbooks you use in your classes contain a glossary. The glossary in the back of this book contains words that are used in the selection. Your math, social studies, geography, and science books also have glossaries. The glossary of each text contains vocabulary words on that subject. Several words that are used in the selections in this book might also be found in one of your other textbooks. Decide in which of your textbooks you might find each word listed. Then look the word up in that textbook's glossary. If you cannot find the word in the glossary of any other textbook, look it up in the glossary of this text. Write the meaning of each word and tell where you found it.

1. monarch   6. granite   11. allies
2. immigrant   7. continent   12. dynamo
3. sphere   8. terrain   13. irrigate
4. meteorite   9. autocratic   14. symmetrical
5. primitive   10. magnify

Developing Writing Skills

1. **Comparing Writing Styles.** The author of "Maria Tallchief" wanted to give the reader a certain impression of her subject. To do this, she used much descriptive language, emotional appeal, and repetition of certain ideas. Write a paragraph or two comparing this approach with the way the biography of Matt Henson was written. Which style of writing made you feel more as if you knew the person? If possible, quote passages from the selections to make your opinions clear.

2. **Presenting Your Opinion.** Abe Lincoln and Matt Henson were both historical figures. Maria Tallchief achieved fame in a cultural field. Is it important to write about achievements in cultural fields? Write at least one paragraph stating your opinion about this question and giving reasons for your opinion.

Developing Skills in Study and Research

Using the Readers' Guide. Many newspaper and magazine articles have been written about Maria Tallchief. The names of these articles and the periodicals (newspaper or magazine) in which they were published are listed in the *Readers' Guide to Periodical Literature*. A new volume of the *Guide* is printed almost every month. This keeps the *Guide* up-to-date. At the end of the year, all the listings for the year are joined in one large volume.

In each volume of the *Readers' Guide*, each article is listed under the subject of the article. The subjects are in alphabetical order. The same article may be listed under several subjects. At the beginning of each volume is an explanation of the abbreviations used in the entries, for example, for the titles of the magazines.

Find a recent volume of the *Readers' Guide* in your school or public library. Look under the subject "ballet" or "dance." See if you can find any entries for articles about Maria or Marjorie Tallchief or George Balanchine. Choose one. If there is none, choose any article about ballet.

On your paper, write the volume of the *Readers' Guide* in which you found the entry. Compare the abbreviations used in the entry with the code to abbreviations at the front of the volume. Then write the following information:

a. the name of the article
b. the name of the periodical the article is in
c. the month or volume number of that issue of the magazine
d. the pages the article appears on

You do not need to find the article itself.

Developing Skills in Critical Thinking

Identifying Unstated Opinions. An author can express an opinion by stating it directly. For example, the author could write, "Vince is a good fielder, but he doesn't hit well under pressure." An author can also express an opinion without stating it directly.

There are two ways the author can express an unstated opinion. First, he or she can simply leave out information. For example, instead of saying that Vince is a weak hitter in tight situations, his biographer may report only his fielding averages and not mention his batting average or, especially, his runs batted in. Second, the writer may include some information on the topic and imply things that are not said. For example, Vince's biographer might report, "The manager surprised everyone by leaving Vince in the lineup going into the tenth inning."

When the writer presents opinions indirectly, the reader may not think about these opinions. Still, he or she may accept the opinions without thinking.

Read the following opinions. Which one is implied, that is, meant but not stated, in "Maria Tallchief"? Find passages in the selection that support the unstated opinion. Which opinions are not supported?

1. Maria made a bad choice when she decided to have a baby.

2. Maria's mother was important in encouraging her career, but her father was not.

3. Maria and her sister did not get along well because they were jealous of each other.

Humorous Sayings, Writings, and Anecdotes

Abraham Lincoln must have been a witty man. We know this because so many of his sayings have been remembered for so long. Some of his sayings stand alone. Others can be better appreciated when they are part of a short account of some happening in Lincoln's life. Such an account is called an **anecdote**. The sayings, writings, and anecdotes in this section give a good picture of Lincoln's personality.

Long Abraham Lincoln a Little Longer,
F. BELLEW. Reprinted from *Harper's Weekly,*
November 26, 1864. Culver Pictures, Inc., New York City.

Abraham Lincoln Is My Name

When Abe wrote this poem, he was about the same age as he was in the biography you read. See what you learn about his personality by reading his poem.

ABRAHAM LINCOLN

Abraham Lincoln is my nam
And with my pen I wrote the same
I wrote in both hast and speed
and left it here for fools to read

Abraham Lincoln his hand and pen
he will be good but god knows When

Developing Comprehension Skills

1. What did Abe write with his pen?

2. How can you tell this poem was written by a young person?

3. What makes this poem funny? Explain your answer.

Reading Literature: Nonfiction

Combining Information from Two Sources. Think about what you learned in the biography of Abraham Lincoln about his schooling. Then proofread this poem, written when Abe was a teenager. Several words are misspelled and some capitalization is incorrect. Why did Abe make these mistakes? Was he just careless or did he have better reasons? Would it be acceptable if you wrote that way?

Lawyer Lincoln Turns Down a Case

ABRAHAM LINCOLN

Lincoln wrote this note when he was a lawyer. A man had died, leaving a widow, six children, and a debt of $600. A second man asked Lincoln to help him collect the debt. What advice did Lincoln give?

Yes, we can doubtless gain your case for you; we can set a whole neighborhood at loggerheads; we can distress a widowed mother and her six fatherless children, and thereby get for you six hundred dollars to which you seem to have a legal claim, but which rightfully belongs, it appears to me, as much to the woman and her children as it does to you. You must remember, however, that some things legally right are not morally right. We shall not take your case, but we will give you a little advice for which we will charge you nothing. You seem to be a sprightly, energetic man. We would advise you to try your hand at making six hundred dollars in some other way.

Abraham Lincoln. Library of Congress.

Developing Comprehension Skills

1. What did the man want to hire Lincoln to do?

2. Why didn't Lincoln want to take the case?

3. How can something be legally right but not morally right?

Reading Literature: Nonfiction

1. **Learning About a Character.** This note gives a reader insight into Abe's personality. What quality or qualities do you become aware of?

2. **Recognizing Sentence Patterns.** This paragraph is made up of five sentences. The first sentence is as long as the other four combined. This sentence is also complex; that is, it is really made up of several smaller sentences. Why do you think Lincoln joined these sentences in one sentence? Try to imagine Lincoln reading this sentence to the man. What tone of voice do you think he would use?

    The second sentence is short and direct. Following such a long first sentence, what is the effect of a short sentence here? What tone of voice do you imagine Lincoln using for this sentence?

Lawyer Lincoln Answers an Inquiry

ABRAHAM LINCOLN

Someone asked Lincoln how a neighbor of his stood in terms of money and possessions. Lincoln's answer tells you something about what he thought of the question.

First of all, he has a wife and a baby; together they ought to be worth $500,000 to any man. Secondly, he has an office in which there is a table worth $1.50, and three chairs, worth, say $1.00. Last of all, there is in one corner a large rathole, which will bear looking into.

Respectfully,
A. Lincoln

Developing Comprehension Skills

1. Was Lincoln's neighbor rich? Give a reason for your answer.

2. Money was worth more a hundred years ago. If we suppose that a penny in Lincoln's time bought what a dime will buy now, then Lincoln placed the value of the man's wife and baby at about five million dollars in today's money. What did he mean by saying the wife and baby were worth that much money?

3. What did Lincoln think of the question about the financial standing of his neighbor? Do you agree with him?

Reading Literature: Nonfiction

1. **Analyzing the Organization.** In answering the question about his neighbor's finances, Lincoln lists three possessions. The first is priceless, the second is worth a moderate amount of money, and the third is worthless—in fact, ridiculous. Why did Lincoln name those three items in this order? How does the order help make Lincoln's point? How does it make the writing funny?

2. **Learning about Lincoln Through His Writing.** What can you learn about Lincoln from this note that you might not learn from someone else writing about Lincoln?

Appliqué Quilt commemorating the Century of Progress Exhibition of 1933. America Hurrah, New York City.

On Political Skill

ABRAHAM LINCOLN

Abraham Lincoln, asked what he thought was the best attribute for a politician, said he thought it "would be the ability to raise a cause which would produce an effect and then fight the effect."

Developing Comprehension Skills

1. The quote deals with cause and effect. Here is an example of the kind of cause and effect Lincoln had in mind.

   Cause: A person holds a lighted match next to a pile of newspapers

   Effect: The newspapers burn up.

   In your own words, say what Lincoln meant by this quote.

2. What did Lincoln think of politicians?

Reading Literature: Nonfiction

1. **Appreciating Humor.** One thing which makes this quote humorous is the way it is worded. What is funny about the wording?

2. **Understanding Irony.** As you may remember, **irony** results when something happens that contradicts what was expected to happen. Often irony is humorous. After reading this quote, do you think it was ironic that Lincoln later went into politics himself? Explain your answer.

On Fooling the People

Lincoln made this statement shortly before he was elected President. People all over the world have repeated it.

ABRAHAM LINCOLN

You can fool all of the people some of the time, and some of the people all of the time, but you cannot fool all the people all of the time.

Developing Comprehension Skills

1. From reading this statement, do you think Lincoln thought it was a good idea to try to fool people? Give a reason for your answer.

2. What can you learn from this statement about Lincoln's attitude toward people?

Reading Literature: Nonfiction

1. **Understanding the Effect of Literary Style.** One reason this quote has been repeated through the years is its message. Another reason is the way it was written, or its **style**. Identify how Lincoln used repetition of words and balance of ideas. Do you suppose these techniques have contributed to the popularity of this saying? Explain your answer.

2. **Applying Lincoln's Ideas.** According to this saying, Lincoln thought it was wrong for leaders to try to fool people. Do you think his ideas still apply today? Are there any modern leaders who should be reminded of this warning?

On Meeting Harriet Beecher Stowe

ABRAHAM LINCOLN

Harriet Beecher Stowe wrote a novel about slavery, Uncle Tom's Cabin. After reading this book, many Northerners wanted to fight to abolish (get rid of) slavery. What did President Lincoln think of Mrs. Stowe?

So you're the little woman who wrote the book that made this great war!

Developing Comprehension Skills

1. What did President Lincoln mean when he said "this great war"? Did he mean the war was wonderful?

2. Do you think Lincoln really felt that Mrs. Stowe made the war? Give a reason for your answer.

Reading Literature: Nonfiction

1. **Appreciating Contrast.** Humor is often developed by making contrasts. For example, the comedians Laurel and Hardy made good use of the contrast between Hardy's round shape and Laurel's thin shape. What contrast does Lincoln make in this quote? In your opinion, does this make the quote humorous?

2. **Recognizing Style.** Compare this quote to Lincoln's other short sayings in this section. Consider such techniques as sentence patterns, balance of ideas, repetition of words, and development from unimportant to important details (or the opposite). Does the style of this saying have anything in common with the other sayings?

   Imagine that Lincoln had said only "So this whole war is your fault!" Would his words have been remembered?

What Must God Think?

Lincoln wrote this during the Civil War, also called the War Between the States. Does it apply only to that war? Or is it true of every war?

ABRAHAM LINCOLN

We, on our side, are praying to Him to give us victory, because we believe we are right; but those on the other side pray to Him, look for victory, believing they are right. What must He think of us?

Developing Comprehension Skills

1. What are both sides praying for?

2. If Lincoln answered his own question ("What must He think of us?"), what do you think he would say? Give a reason for your answer, based on this paragraph.

Reading Literature: Nonfiction

1. **Understanding Irony.** This paragraph can be read seriously. However, suppose you read it as ironic humor. What does it tell you about Lincoln's personality? Does it tell anything about his opinion of human nature?

2. **Appreciating Theme.** Some things are written or said to apply only to a specific time and place. Other writings and sayings can apply to similar situations at any time. In which category would you place this saying by Lincoln? How does this help make Lincoln's words worth remembering?

Developing Vocabulary Skills

Recognizing Confusing Words. Some of the words in the selections you have read are often confused with other words. They look very much alike and may have similar meanings. Read the following list of words. Match each word with its respelling. Then read the sentences below. Choose the correct word to fill in each blank. Write the part of speech of each word as it is used in the sentence. You may use a dictionary if you need to.

a.	advice	(1)	i fekt′
b.	advise	(2)	ək sept′
c.	effect	(3)	əd vīz′
d.	affect	(4)	ek sept′
e.	except	(5)	əd vīs′
f.	accept	(6)	ə fect′

1. Abraham Lincoln thought that a good politician should be able to raise a cause which would produce an _____.

2. Exercise can _____ the way we feel.

3. Dr. Chisholm did _____ my father to consult Dr. Alexander Graham Bell.

4. Acting on the doctor's _____, we immediately took a train to Washington.

5. At that time I did not like to have anyone kiss me _____ my own mother.

6. Having adventure in his blood, Henson did _____ Peary's offer for the job.

7. Peary once said of Henson, "He is a better dog driver than any man living _____ for some of the best Eskimo hunters themselves."

8. We would _____ you to try your hand at making six hundred dollars in some other way.

Developing Writing Skills

1. **Identifying Humor.** Choose a saying that you think is funny. Write a paragraph telling why you think your choice is humorous.

2. **Writing Humor.** In the humorous sayings and writings you have read, Lincoln used several means of making his statements funny. Sometimes he made a funny contrast. Sometimes irony made the writing funny. At other times there was a build-up of details. Using these or other techniques, write a humorous paragraph about some event in the news or in your own life.

Developing Skills in Study and Research

Using Library Skills. Other people besides Abe Lincoln have made humorous statements. Go to your library to find some books containing humorous quotations. First, you will need to find out how collections of quotations are listed. Make use of the card catalog. If necessary, ask the librarian for help. Once you have found several books of humorous quotations and sayings, write down their titles and authors. Explain briefly how you found the books.

Now read at least one short passage from one of the books you found. Be ready to explain whether you thought it was humorous, and to tell why or why not.

Developing Skills in Speaking and Listening

Performing a Humorous Saying. Most of these sayings and writings have a serious side as well as a humorous side. They were said for a reason. Choose one of the sayings and memorize it. Practice saying it so that your audience will understand the serious part of it but will also see the humor. As you practice, consider these questions: What should the **pitch** of your voice be? Should the whole saying be said at the same level, or should your voice go up and down with the meaning? What **pace**, or speed, should you use? Can you make **eye contact** with your audience? Is there **feeling** in your voice?

Horse Trade

BEATRICE SCHENK de REGNIERS

Before there were cars, horses provided the fastest transportation. A horse trade was an important event. What can you learn about Abraham Lincoln from this anecdote?

Lincoln and the judge were joking about who could make the better horse trade. At last they agreed to meet in the morning to swap horses. Lincoln would not see the judge's horse beforehand. And the judge would not see Lincoln's horse.

The next morning a crowd gathered. Who would get the better of the trade?

The judge came first, dragging behind him the oldest, sorriest, boniest nag that ever managed to stand on four feet.

While the crowd was still laughing, Lincoln came along, carrying a carpenter's wooden saw horse. For a full minute Lincoln stared at the judge's horse without saying a word.

"Judge," said Lincoln at last, "this is the first time I ever got the worst of it in a horse trade."

Developing Comprehension Skills

1. Lincoln brought a horse to the horse trade. Was it the kind of horse that everyone expected?
2. Why did Lincoln decide that he had gotten the worst of the trade?

Reading Literature: Nonfiction

Inferring Character Traits. Lincoln's sense of humor comes through in his bringing a saw horse to the trade. He is playing a joke on the judge. After it is all over with, at whom else is he laughing? What does this tell you about his personality?

Here is a funny story about Abraham Lincoln. Can you explain what is funny about it?

No Trouble

BEATRICE SCHENK de REGNIERS

Lawyer Lincoln, so they say, was walking along a dusty road. Along came a farmer driving his wagon to town.

Lincoln. Would you be good enough to take my overcoat to town for me?

Farmer. Glad to. But how will you get it back again?

Lincoln. No trouble at all. I'm going to stay right inside it!

Developing Comprehension Skills

1. What was "no trouble"?
2. What was Lincoln really asking the farmer?

Reading Literature: Nonfiction

1. **Understanding Tone.** What is the tone of this anecdote; that is, what is the attitude of the author?

2. **Applying Your Knowledge.** From your knowledge of Abraham Lincoln, do you think this occurrence really happened, or that he made up this story, or that someone else invented it about him? Give a reason for your answer.

The Longest Leg

BEATRICE SCHENK de REGNIERS

As you read this anecdote, consider two questions: Do you think this event really happened? Do you think Mr. Lincoln was being rude?

One day a man came to Abraham Lincoln's law office. He saw Lincoln sitting with one leg stretched across the desk.

"Why Mr. Lincoln," said the man, "that's the longest leg I've ever seen!"

"Here's another just like it," said Lincoln. And he put his other leg across the desk.

Abraham Lincoln, 1838–39, WILLIAM NORRIS.
Wood carving from a single log. Abbey Aldrich Rockefeller
Folk Art Center, Williamsburg, Virginia.

Developing Comprehension Skills

1. Why do you think the man commented on Abe's leg?

2. In Lincoln's time, as today, putting your leg on your desk would be considered impolite or undignified. What does this story show about Lincoln's attitude toward rules of polite behavior? Give a reason for your answer.

Reading Literature: Nonfiction

1. **Comparing Types of Nonfiction.** The sayings of a famous person are usually brief quotes by that person about specific topics. Anecdotes are humerous stories about the person. In what ways is this anecdote like the legends or short stories you have read? What elements do they have in common?

2. **Understanding the Role of Setting.** What is the setting of this anecdote? Would it matter if the event took place somewhere other than in Lincoln's own office?

3. **Analyzing the Tone.** Judging from his words, what do you think was the attitude of the man coming to Lincoln's office? Was he shocked? Was he kidding or criticizing? What was the tone of Lincoln's response? Was he being rude? Give reasons for your answers.

A Lincoln Riddle

BEATRICE SCHENK de REGNIERS

Now you will read two riddles. We are not sure if Lincoln made them up, but he did use them. As you read this first riddle, see what it tells you about Mr. Lincoln.

Lincoln. If you call a sheep's tail a leg, how many legs will a sheep have?

Man. Five legs, of course.

Lincoln. Wrong. A sheep has four legs. Even if you call a tail a leg, it is still a tail.

Lincoln used this riddle to help him win an argument. Lincoln was trying to explain that just *saying* a thing is true does not make it true.

Developing Comprehension Skills

1. What kind of argument do you suppose Lincoln was having when he used this riddle? Give a reason for your answer.

2. Why would Lincoln or anyone else like to use humor in an argument?

Reading Literature: Nonfiction

Recognizing How Literature Reflects Its Time. The example Lincoln used in this riddle, sheep, is a reflection of his environment. In modern times, we might use a different example. What does the example used tell you about his environment?

Another Riddle

BEATRICE SCHENK de REGNIERS

Read the first part of this riddle. Then stop and see if you can answer it yourself before you read the answer.

Lincoln may have heard this riddle when he was a boy in Indiana. He used it when he was President to show that the right answer in arithmetic can sometimes be the wrong answer when you are dealing with pigeons or people:

Lincoln. If there be three pigeons on the fence, and you fire and kill one, how many will there be left?

Answer. Two?

Lincoln. No. There will be none left. For the other two birds, frightened by the shot, would have flown away.

Developing Comprehension Skills

1. The answer to the question in this riddle seems simple: three pigeons take away one pigeon leaves two pigeons. The simple answer is not correct, however, because an important fact has been left out of the question. What fact was left out?

2. Why do you think Lincoln used a riddle about pigeons and not about people?

Reading Literature: Nonfiction

Comparing Types of Literature. Sometimes an anecdote can be like a fable. It can teach a lesson and have a moral. "Another Riddle" is an example of this kind of anecdote. Identify the moral of this riddle.

Lincoln Tells a Story About the King, the Farmer, and the Donkey

BEATRICE SCHENK de REGNIERS

Abraham Lincoln was a humorous man. Yet he had a serious job, and there was a war going on. See how he used his sense of humor to help solve a real problem.

One day President Lincoln found twenty men in his office waiting to see him. They all wanted jobs in the government. And they all had letters and other papers with them saying what smart men they were—what good work they could do.

These men didn't seem to understand that the President did not have time to give to the many, many people who came to him for jobs. There was a civil war going on. How could the President turn these job-hunters away without hurting their feelings? Maybe he could do it with a story.

"Gentlemen," said President Lincoln, "let me tell you a story I read long ago."

There was once a King who wanted to go hunting. He called the man who was Chief Weatherman and Court Minister.

"Tell me," said the King, "will it rain today?"

"No, your Majesty," said the Chief Weatherman and Court Minister. "The weather is clear. It won't rain. Good hunting to you!"

The King set out with his hunting party. On the way they met a farmer riding on a donkey. "Don't try to go hunting today, Your Majesty," said the farmer. "It is going to rain."

The King laughed and rode on. Surely the Court Minister knew better than a simple farmer!

But just as the King reached the forest, it began to rain. Oh, how it poured! The King and everyone with him were soaked to the skin.

When the King got home, he fired the Court Minister. Then he sent for the farmer.

"From now on," said the King, "you will have the job of Chief Weatherman and Court Minister. Now tell me, how did you know it would rain?"

"I didn't," said the farmer. "It's my donkey who knows when it is going to rain. He puts his ears forward when wet weather is coming; he puts them back when it's going to be dry. So you see, Your Majesty, I cannot take the job."

The King sent the farmer away and sent for the donkey. And the King gave the donkey the job of Chief Weatherman and Court Minister.

"And that," said Lincoln, "is when the King made a great mistake."

"Why do you say that?" asked one of the job-hunters.

"Why, ever since that time," said Lincoln, "every donkey wants a job with the government."

The men couldn't help laughing. And then Lincoln told them, "Gentlemen, leave your letters and papers with me, and when the war is over, you will hear from me."

Abraham Lincoln, MATTHEW BRADY. National Portrait Gallery, Smithsonian Institution, Washington, D.C.

Developing Comprehension Skills

1. Why did President Lincoln tell this fable?
2. Why did the King come to the conclusion that he should fire his Chief Weatherman and hire the farmer?
3. Do you think that President Lincoln achieved his purpose for telling this story? Give a reason for your answer.

Reading Literature: Nonfiction

Finding the Organization. This anecdote contains two stories. How are they connected? In other words, how is the anecdote organized?

A Pass to Richmond

BEATRICE SCHENK de REGNIERS

During the Civil War, the North needed to take Richmond, Virginia. General McClellan was in charge of this mission but was not doing anything. How did Lincoln's humor help him deal with this problem?

President Lincoln had been trying for a long time to get General McClellan to march south with his army and take the city of Richmond, Virginia.

One day, while Lincoln was worrying about this problem, a businessman came to see him. The man asked for a pass so that he could go to—of all places—Richmond, Virginia.

"A pass to Richmond?" said Lincoln with a sigh. "My dear sir, it would do you no good. I have given McClellan passes for two hundred and fifty thousand men . . . and not one of them has got there yet!"

President Lincoln meeting General George B. McClellan at Antietam, Maryland, 1862. Culver Pictures, New York.

Developing Comprehension Skills

1. In what sense had Lincoln given 250,000 men passes? Who were the men? Why hadn't they gotten to Richmond yet?

2. Nowadays, you would not need a pass from the President to travel to another city. In the anecdote, why did the businessman need a pass to travel to Richmond?

Reading Literature: Nonfiction

1. **Learning about History from Literature.** Literature often tells much about the times and places in which it was written. Tell three things about the Civil War that you can learn from this anecdote.

2. **Evaluating Background Information.** Is it possible that Lincoln felt more deeply about the situation than this anecdote shows? Was he using humor because this was a light matter or to relieve a serious, tense problem? What else would you need to know in order to answer these questions?

Borrow the Army

BEATRICE SCHENK de REGNIERS

President Lincoln makes another joke about General McClellan's slowness. If you were General McClellan, how would you react to this statement?

"If General McClellan is not using the army," said Lincoln, "I would like to borrow it for a while."

Developing Comprehension Skills

1. From reading the previous selection, tell what Lincoln meant by McClellan "not using the army."

2. Why is it funny for Lincoln to ask to borrow the army? Whose army was it? Could Lincoln borrow it?

Reading Literature: Nonfiction

1. **Understanding the Tone.** What tone of voice do you think Lincoln used when he said these lines?

2. **Understanding Irony.** The term **irony** can mean saying something opposite to what you really mean. In this meaning, *irony* and *sarcasm* are almost synonyms. Is this anecdote an example of irony? Explain your answer.

Lincoln Gives a Book Review

In contrast to the anecdotes about McClellan, here President Lincoln is trying to avoid hurting someone's feelings. See how he manages it.

BEATRICE SCHENK de REGNIERS

A well-known man read aloud to President Lincoln some chapters from a book he was writing.

"Tell me, Mr. Lincoln," said the man, "what do you think of my book?"

Lincoln didn't think much of it. But he didn't want to hurt the author's feelings, so he said:

"Well, for those who like that sort of thing, I think it is just about the sort of thing they would like."

Developing Comprehension Skills

1. Write the last sentence of the story in your own words.

2. Do you think the man suspected that Lincoln didn't like his book? Give a reason for your answer.

Reading Literature: Nonfiction

Identifying Humor. Find a sentence in the anecdote that is funny partly because of the way it is worded. How does the wording make it funny?

A Bad Example

Here is another story Mr. Lincoln told. As you read it, try to decide why he liked it.

BEATRICE SCHENK de REGNIERS

President Lincoln told the story of a governor who visited the state prison.

The governor talked to the prisoners and asked what types of crimes they had committed. Each prisoner said he had never done anything wrong. To hear them talk, you would have thought they were all innocent, good men.

At last the governor came to one prisoner who said, "I am a thief and I deserve to be in jail."

"Then I must pardon you," said the governor, "and get you out of this place. You seem to be the only criminal in this prison, and I don't want you here setting a bad example to all these good men I have been talking to."

Developing Comprehension Skills

1. What did most of the prisoners tell the governor?

2. Was the last prisoner really "the only criminal in this prison"? Explain your answer.

Reading Literature: Nonfiction

1. **Recognizing Sarcasm or Irony.** The governor told the last prisoner that he would pardon him. Was the reason he gave true, or was he speaking sarcastically (ironically)? What did he mean?

2. **Making Inferences.** From what you now know about Abraham Lincoln, why do you think he liked this story?

Lincoln's Favorite Joke

We know that Lincoln could make jokes about other people. He could also laugh at himself. Can you find several reasons why this joke would appeal to him?

BEATRICE SCHENK de REGNIERS

Here is the joke about himself that Lincoln liked best of all. He said it was the best story about himself he had ever read in the papers:

Two Quaker women were talking about who would win the war—President Lincoln for the United States, or Jefferson Davis, who was President of the Confederate States.

First Quaker Woman. I think Jefferson Davis will win.

Second Quaker Woman. Why does thee think so?

First Quaker Woman. Because he is a praying man.

Second Quaker Woman. Abraham Lincoln is a praying man, too.

First Quaker Woman. Yes, but the Lord will think Abraham is joking.

Abraham Lincoln, L.G. WRIGHT. Collection of Kirby Rodriguez.

Developing Comprehension Skills

1. Where did Lincoln read this joke?

2. Why would the Lord "think Abraham is joking"?

Reading Literature: Nonfiction

1. **Making Inferences.** What quality of Abraham Lincoln is brought out in this anecdote that you didn't know from the other anecdotes?

2. **Understanding the Author's Purpose.** What do you think was the author's purpose in writing this joke? Was he criticizing President Lincoln, or predicting victory for the South, or commenting on something else? Why do you think President Lincoln liked the joke?

Developing Vocabulary Skills

Locating Information in the Encyclopedia. You have learned to use the dictionary to find the meaning of unfamiliar words in the stories you have read. There are also dictionary entries for the names of famous people or groups of people, places and events. For example, you can find Helen Keller and the Osage Indians entered in most dictionaries. However, the dictionary will give only a brief explanation of these entries. The **encyclopedia** will provide much more information. Words like *meteorite* also need more space for an explanation than a dictionary can provide.

The following words and names appear in the nonfiction selections you have read. Locate each item in the dictionary or glossary. Write the definition. Then locate each item in the encyclopedia. Write two facts about each topic that were not given in the dictionary or glossary.

1. gangrene
2. North Pole
3. Civil War
4. Jamaica
5. Dr. Alexander Graham Bell
6. Robert E. Peary

Developing Writing Skills

1. **Examining Anecdotes.** Not every anecdote about President Lincoln was true. We cannot tell which ones were entirely accurate. However, every anecdote was based on some quality of Lincoln that the people of his time appreciated and talked about. From the anecdotes in this section, what do you think were some of the qualities the people of his

time saw in President Lincoln? Write a paragraph explaining your conclusions.

2. **Understanding the Use of Humor.** How did President Lincoln's sense of humor help him solve or cope with the problems of being President at a critical time? Write a paragraph or more describing Lincoln's use of humor. Refer to specific sayings or anecdotes to illustrate your statements.

3. **Writing a Riddle.** Choose one of Abraham Lincoln's riddles on pages 430 and 431. Using this riddle as a pattern, write a riddle of your own. You should use a modern example, but your riddle should have the same meaning as Lincoln's.

Developing Skills in Study and Research

Scanning, Skimming, and Study-Type Reading. A good reader does not always read at the same rate. That is because not all reading is done for the same purpose. Your reason for reading influences how carefully and thoroughly you read. When you are reading for fun, you may concentrate less than when you are reading for information. When you are reading for different kinds of information, you can use different types of reading.

In **scanning,** you look for specific information. For example, you may be searching the sports pages of a newspaper for the mention of your school's team. You may be looking through a chapter of your science book for an explanation of Vitamin C. In both of these cases, nothing else on those pages is of interest to you. You are looking for only one word or phrase. When you scan, you are not reading for understanding. You can go through the pages much more quickly than when you do other kinds of reading.

In **skimming,** you look over the information on the page quickly to see what sort of material is there. You do not read every word, but you find out what topics are discussed. You look at the boldface heads, or heads in dark type. You get a general idea of whether there is anything on the page of interest to you. If there are any difficult words or passages, you skip over them. You are not trying to learn everything that is on the page. Skimming is not as fast as scanning, but it is still fast.

In **study-type reading** you go more slowly than in skimming and scanning. Now you are reading for understanding. You first read over anything in boldface type to get an idea of what the important ideas on the page are. You also find out how the material is organized. Then you read the material carefully. You stop to look up words in the glossary or dictionary when you need to. You read slowly enough to understand the main ideas in each paragraph.

Look up General George Brinton McClellan in an encyclopedia. First scan the article to find the following information:

a. The date of his birth
b. The date he took command of the Union Army in the East, also called the Army of the Potomac
c. The date of his death

Next, skim the article. On your paper, note three facts about General McClellan that you think are interesting.

Last, do a study-type reading of the article. Determine how the article is organized. On your paper, copy any boldface heads. Also, write the main idea of each paragraph of the article. If several important ideas are in one paragraph, restate them in your own words.

Essays

Most of us like to read about famous and important people. However, we also like to read about people and things closer to our own lives. The selections in this section challenge us to take a closer look at the things around us every day.

Woman with Plants, 1929, GRANT WOOD. Collection of the Cedar Rapids Museum of Art, Iowa.

R*eading Literature:* Types of Nonfiction

Two Types of Nonfiction

You have learned that nonfiction includes all writing that is based on facts rather than imagination. In general, there are two types of nonfiction.

In the first type of nonfiction, the writer reports facts about people, places, and events. Autobiographies, biographies, short sayings and writings, and anecdotes are all examples of the first kind of nonfiction. The last selection in this chapter, a vignette, also reports facts. These forms of nonfiction report things that were done or said.

The next three groups of selections belong to the second kind of nonfiction. In this writing, the author discusses ideas and opinions. Essays, letters, and speeches are some of the forms this writing can take. We read them purposely to find out what the writer thinks and feels about the topic.

In both types of nonfiction, the writers use both fact and opinion. In the first type, the writer is most concerned with giving information about people and events. However, in order to make this information clear, he or she often includes opinions.

In the second type, the writers tell what they believe and why. They base their opinions on facts and may use facts to support their statements. Frequently, they try to persuade their readers to agree with them.

Essays

The **essay** is a type of nonfiction writing in which writers state personal opinions and explain their reasons for those opinions. In a good essay, the opinions and reasons are organized. The writer's line of thought is clear and reasonable.

Almost any topic can be the subject of an essay. Some writers speak of common happenings. They give their reactions to these events and their thoughts about everyday life. The selections in this chapter are of this kind. Other writers use the essay form to discuss more serious topics, such as justice, peace, and truth. The writer's attitude, or tone, can range from serious thought to light humor.

Letters

The **letter** is one of the oldest and most popular forms of nonfiction writing. You have probably written letters yourself. Letters are written for many reasons, such as to describe the events of a trip, to tell news of daily life, and to make business arrangements. A writer can also write a letter to explain what he or she has done or what he or she thinks, and to give reasons.

The letters you will read, by Abraham Lincoln, are of this second type. They explain Lincoln's opinions on certain topics and his reasons for his opinions.

Speeches

A **speech** is a form of nonfiction written to be read aloud. The speeches that people remember are the ones that were both written well and presented well by skilled speakers.

Speech writers must have a special talent. They must be able to predict how certain phrases or sentences will be understood by a crowd of people. They must write speeches more boldly than other nonfiction forms, such as essays and letters. A speech should capture the listener's—or reader's—interest quickly. It should hold the attention of the audience. It should sound both important and sincere. Above all, the ideas in a speech must be well organized. A listener or reader should be able to understand the thinking of the speaker immediately and remember the ideas later.

A speech does not need to be long in order to develop its ideas clearly. Some of the best speeches are very short. The speeches by Abraham Lincoln in this chapter will prove that.

April and Robins

HAL BORLAND

This essay is about just what the title states: the beginning of April and robins. As you read it, see if you can tell why the author wrote it.

April 2

People who can't tell a bald eagle from a vulture know what a robin looks like, and they know that, when robins strut the lawn, April must be here. April just isn't April, in this part of the world, without robins. Spring couldn't come without them.

The robin long ago became a kind of national bird without a shred of legal backing. It didn't need legal proclamations, for the robin is one of the best known and widely distributed birds in all these United States. Perhaps most important of all, it is a cosmopolitan bird, equally at home in a city park, on a suburban lawn and in the open country. Unlike most other thrushes, it prefers to nest near a house. Being a comparatively large bird, big as a blue jay, and a conspicuous bird with its black head and cinnamon-red breast, the robin simply can't be overlooked. Besides, robins love to strut. And to sing, preferably from a street-side tree.

The robin's song is often underrated, probably because the robin is so common and so vocal. But the robin, after all, is a thrush, and the thrushes are accomplished songsters. The robin sings long, loudly and rather deliberately. Its notes are clear and rich in tone. And no two robins sing exactly the same way; they vary their songs, put the phrases together differently. An individual robin may sing as many as ten different songs, varying with the time of day.

Robins are already singing in many places. Their chorus will increase day by day. After all, it is April, even to a robin.

Developing Comprehension Skills

1. What two things does the author say almost everyone knows about robins? Look at the first paragraph of the essay to find out.

2. Read each statement below and decide whether it is a fact or an opinion. Give a reason for your decision.

   a. April just isn't April . . . without robins.
   b. But the robin, after all, is a thrush.
   c. The robin simply can't be overlooked.
   d. An individual robin may sing as many as ten different songs.

Reading Literature: Nonfiction

1. **Analyzing Organization.** A good essay is well organized. Reread each paragraph in this essay. Then in your own words identify the main idea of each paragraph. What is the connection between each main idea and the next?

2. **Identifying Mood.** The mood of a piece of literature is the feeling it gives you when you read it. How would you describe the mood of "April and Robins"?

The Prelude

HAL BORLAND

A prelude comes before the main event. What is the main event that follows this prelude?

June 6

Early Spring or late, cool May or warm, by June the days are alive with sound. It comes so gradually, increasing day by day from the cold silence of March, that we are scarcely aware of it. We must force our ears to listen. But there it is, in suburb and countryside, even in a city park, the buzz of the bumblebee, the low chirping of the lesser cricket at the grassroot, the scratch and rattle of the brash-winged grasshopper, the harsh rustle of the beetle in flight on stiff, inadequate wings. The insect sounds.

This is the lesser chorus, and it goes with daisies in the meadows and wild roses along the pasture margins. Not one of the sounds is really insistent, even when one listens closely; but in sum they are the voice of early June, untold millions of little hummings and buzzings and rustlings that set the long daylight hours to vibrating.

There is no true silence now, for the world is alive and teeming. What we hear is the urgency of life, the insistence of the unimportant which by its very numbers becomes of ultimate importance. Only the pollen of the trees and the spores of ferns and fungi outnumber the insect eggs, and all those eggs are hatching. Hatched, they must announce and praise life, mate, lay more eggs, perpetuate life. Later will come the high-pitched shrill of the cicada, the clamor of the katydid. But they await hot noontimes and warm evenings. They are the Summer itself. Now we hear the tune-up and the prelude. This, when we listen closely, is the voice of Summer still approaching.

Developing Comprehension Skills

1. What kind of sounds is the author talking about in this essay?

2. A prelude is often a part of a piece of music. It is like an introduction. In this essay, the author calls certain sounds of nature a prelude. What are they a prelude to?

3. Do you think the author likes the coming of summer? Give a reason for your answer.

4. Which of these two essays, "April and Robins" and "The Prelude," did you enjoy more? Give a reason for your answer.

Reading Literature: Nonfiction

1. **Recognizing Metaphor.** This essay is organized around a metaphor. A **metaphor** is a type of comparison that is not openly stated. In "The Prelude," the author compares the sounds and seasons to something that he does not openly state. What is it? Use these words from the essay as clues to your answer: *chorus, voice, hummings, high-pitched, tune-up, prelude.*

2. **Finding Onomatopoeia and Alliteration.** The use of words that sound like what they mean is onomotopoeia. For example, "whoosh" is onomatopoetic. Alliteration is the repetition of a single sound usually at the beginning of words. For example, "Peter Piper picked a peck of pickled peppers" is alliterative. In "The Prelude," the author uses both of those techniques. Find at least two examples of each technique. How do these techniques make the meaning of the essay clearer?

3. **Identifying Connotations.** Below are phrases from the essay. For each phrase, state whether the connotation is positive, negative, or neutral.

   a. alive with sound
   b. the harsh rustle of the beetle
   c. the cold silence of March
   d. the voice of early June
   e. high-pitched shrill
   f. stiff, inadequate wings

Shortest Month

HAL BORLAND

So far, we have read Mr. Borland's comments on spring and summer. Now we can find out how he feels about a winter month.

December 4

December is the shortest month of the year. No argument will be accepted, if it is to the contrary; and those who point to February are merely making gestures. True, December does have thirty-one days, such as they are. But can you really call days those hurried little spans that come zipping past, once Thanksgiving is behind and Christmas lies just ahead? Certainly not. Why, if you even pause to check them off on the calendar, you have no time for anything else! The Thanksgiving turkey vanishes, and you turn around, and there is the Christmas tree waiting to be decorated. New Year's Day is here, and January. December is gone again.

There is no mistake about it, except for those who are innate sticklers. In round figures, December has only 288 hours of daylight; and that counts in even those dreary times when the sun sulks behind a mass of clouds all day. Even March, of evil reputation, can muster that many hours of daylight in twenty-four days. And June, magnificent June, does as well by us in only nineteen days.

What is a December day, anyway? Nine hours of daylight, with a few minutes left over at each end to turn the lights on and off. And fifteen hours of darkness. With a moon, to be sure, and a great many stars. But darkness, just the same. You eat breakfast by lamplight, hurry to work in half-light, and get home in darkness. You have four weekends in which to watch the sun scurry across the southern quadrant of the sky.

December? By sundown tonight we will have had just a little over thirty-seven hours of December daylight. Enough said?

Arctic Owl and Winter Moon,
1960, CHARLES BURCHFIELD.
Private collection. Courtesy of Kennedy
Galleries, New York

Developing Comprehension Skills

1. What does December have less of than do March and June?

2. The first sentence of this essay is the topic sentence. December isn't really the shortest month, though. Change the underlined word below to another word or words so that the sentence tells what the author really means.

   "December <u>is</u> the shortest month of the year."

3. What is the author's opinion of December? Do you agree with him? Why or why not?

Reading Literature: Nonfiction

1. **Identifying Organization.** The author presents two arguments to show that December is the shortest month. What are those arguments? Do they use facts or opinions or both?

2. **Understanding Tone.** What is the tone of this essay? Would you call it serious, light, humorous, sad, or some other term?

3. **Recognizing Personification.** A writer using **personification** gives human qualities to non-human things. An example is "the lines of pine trees marched to the cliff's edge." Find at least three examples of personification in "Shortest Month."

Developing Vocabulary Skills

1. **Reviewing Context Clues.** The underlined word in each sentence below is from one of the essays by Hal Borland. The meaning of each underlined word can be figured out by using one of these context clues. On your paper, write each underlined word, its meaning, and the clue you used to figure out the meaning.

   (1) Main idea
   (2) Comparisons which relate ideas
   (3) Examples that explain an idea or word

   a. The robin is a cosmopolitan bird. For instance, it is at home in a city park, on a suburban lawn, and in the open country.
   b. Like other thrushes that are accomplished songsters, the robin sings long, loudly, and rather deliberately.
   c. Being a large bird, and a conspicuous bird with its black head and cinnamon-red breast, the robin simply can't be overlooked.

2. **Reviewing Word Parts.** In chapter two, you learned the meaning of several Greek and Latin prefixes. Another Latin prefix used in many English words is *quadra,* or *quadri,* meaning "four." For example, in one of the essays this phrase appears: "across the southern quadrant of the sky." A *quadrant* is one-fourth or one quarter of a circle.
   Read the following sentences. Choose the correct prefix to fill in the blank before each root word. Choose from among *quadri* and the other Latin and Greek prefixes listed on page 67. If you are unsure, check your answers in a dictionary.

a. A __lingual person speaks three languages, and a __lingual speaks four.

b. A __cycle has one wheel and a __cycle has four wheels.

c. A celebration marking the end of two hundred years is a __centennial, and one marking the end of four hundred years is a __centennial.

d. A __syllable word has many syllables, and a __syllable word has four.

e. A __gon is a figure with many sides, and a __agon has ten sides.

Developing Writing Skills

1. **Comparing Literary Works.** All three of these essays are related to seasons. Compare "Shortest Month" with either of the other essays. Discuss the author's opinions about the different seasons. Also discuss the author's use of figures of speech, such as personification, and the sounds of language, such as alliteration. Refer to examples from the essays to explain or to support your statements.

2. **Writing an Essay.** Write a two- or three-paragraph essay that expresses your feelings about a certain time of year. Start by organizing your essay on scratch paper. First, choose one time of year. Then think of two or three reasons for liking or disliking it. Put your reasons in order of importance, beginning either with the most important or with the least important. Think about how to connect your ideas. When you have your ideas well organized, write your essay.

Developing Skills in Speaking and Listening

Reading an Essay Orally. Prepare to read one of these essays by Hal Borland aloud. First make sure you understand the difficult words in the essay. Practice reading the phrases using onomotopoeia and alliteration. Try to read with expression, so that the mood of the essay is clear.

When you are ready to read the essay aloud, join four or five classmates. Members of the group should take turns reading their choices. After everyone has had a turn, discuss the differences between reading these essays silently and hearing them read aloud. Consider such questions as these: In what way is reading silently better? In what way is hearing the essay better? Which way did you understand the meaning better? Why do you think that is so?

Letters

Abraham Lincoln is most famous for his actions as President. However, he was not only a leader of his country. He had a family and felt deeply for his friends and acquaintances.

You will read two letters by Abraham Lincoln. One is a personal letter to his brother. The other is a letter he wrote as President. Although this letter is official, Lincoln's human sympathy and kindness shine through his formal words.

Army Boots, 1865, WINSLOW HOMER. Hirshhorn Museum and Sculpture Garden, Smithsonian Institution, Washington, D.C.

Abraham Lincoln:
A Letter to His Step-Brother

Here is a personal letter from Lincoln to his step-brother. Read it carefully to understand Lincoln's reasoning. Do you think it was easy for him to write what he did?

Dec. 24, 1848

Dear Johnston:

Your request for eighty dollars, I do not think it best to comply with now. At the various times when I have helped you a little, you have said to me, "We can get along very well now," but in a very short time I find you in the same difficulty again. Now this can only happen by some defect in your conduct. What that defect is, I think I know. You are not *lazy,* and still you are an *idler.* I doubt whether since I saw you, you have done a good whole day's work, in any one day. You do not very much dislike to work, and still you do not work much, merely because it does not seem to you that you could get much for it.

This habit of uselessly wasting time, is the whole difficulty; it is vastly important to you, and still more so to your children, that you should break this habit. It is more important to them, because they have longer to live, and can keep out of an idle habit before they are in it, easier than they can get out after they are in.

You are now in need of some ready money; and what I propose is, that you shall go to work, "tooth and nail," for somebody who will give you money for it.

Let father and your boys take charge of your things at home—prepare for a crop, and make the crop, and you go to work for the best money wages, or in discharge of any debt you owe, that you can get. And to secure you a fair reward for your labor, I now promise you that for every dollar you will, between this and the first of May, get for your own labor either in money or in your own indebtedness, I will then give you one other dollar.

By this, if you hire yourself at ten dollars a month, from me you will get ten more, making twenty dollars a month for your work. In this, I do not mean you shall go off to St. Louis, or the lead mines, or the gold mines, in California, but I mean for you to go at it for the best wages you can get close to home—in Coles County.

Now if you will do this, you will soon be out of debt, and what is better, you will have a habit that will keep you from getting in debt again. But if I should now clear you out, next year you will be just as deep in as ever. You say you would almost give your place in Heaven for $70 or $80. Then you value your place in Heaven very cheaply, for I am sure you can with the offer I make you get the seventy or eighty dollars for four or five months' work. You say if I furnish you the money you will deed me the land, and if you don't pay the money back, you will deliver possession—

Nonsense! If you can't now live *with* the land, how will you then live without it? You have always been kind to me, and I do not now mean to be unkind to you. On the contrary, if you will but follow my advice, you will find it worth more than eight times eighty dollars to you.

Affectionately,
Your brother,
A. Lincoln

Developing Comprehension Skills

1. Write the first sentence of the letter in your own words. It might help you to know that "comply" means to agree with or go along with.

2. Why did Lincoln refuse to lend his brother the money?

3. Do you think Abraham Lincoln had a fairly close relationship with his step-brother? Give reasons for your answer.

4. Do you believe Lincoln was right to answer as he did? Why or why not?

Reading Literature: Nonfiction

1. **Learning about History through Literature.** This letter reflects the society of the times. For instance, we learn that $80 was worth a lot and took a long time to earn. What else did you learn from this letter about what life was like a century ago?

2. **Recognizing Tone.** What is Lincoln's attitude toward his step-brother's request? What is his attitude toward his own proposal?

Abraham Lincoln:
A Letter to Mrs. Bixby

This letter was written sixteen years after the last one, after Lincoln had become President. It is an official letter, so its style is formal. How did Lincoln feel about Mrs. Bixby's sons?

Executive Mansion
Washington, Nov. 21, 1864

To Mrs. Bixby, Boston, Mass.

Dear Madam,

 I have been shown in the files of the War Department a statement of the Adjutant General of Massachusetts that you are the mother of five sons who have died gloriously on the field of battle. I feel how weak and fruitless must be any word of mine which should attempt to beguile you from the grief of a loss so overwhelming. But I cannot refrain from tendering you the consolation that may be found in the thanks of the republic they died to save. I pray that our Heavenly Father may assuage the anguish of your bereavement, and leave you only the cherished memory of the loved and lost, and the solemn pride that must be yours to have laid so costly a sacrifice upon the altar of freedom.

Yours very sincerely and respectfully,
A. Lincoln

Union supply base at Cumberland, used during McClellan's Peninsular Campaign in 1862. Library of Congress.

Developing Comprehension Skills

1. Because this letter was written over a century ago, the language is a little hard to understand. Take some time to "translate" it into modern English. Write the third sentence in your own words. The phrase "beguile you from" means "lead you away from."

2. What was Mr. Lincoln's feeling about these deaths?

3. Do you think this letter served its purpose? If you were Mrs. Bixby, how might you react to it? Give reasons for your answers.

Reading Literature: Nonfiction

1. **Comparing the Tone.** What is the tone of this letter? How is it different from Lincoln's letter to his step-brother?

2. **Analyzing Connotation.** Identify in this letter two examples of words with positive connotation. How does this connotation help President Lincoln make his point?

3. **Learning about History through Literature.** What does this letter tell you about the Civil War?

4. **Recognizing Alliteration.** One way that Lincoln made this difficult message easier to accept was by using a stately rhythm in the sentences. Another way was by using alliteration to connect phrases. In the last sentence, identify at least one instance of alliteration.

Developing Vocabulary Skills

Identifying the Correct Respelling and Part of Speech. Read the following sentences drawn from the nonfiction selections you have read. Each of the underlined words can be pronounced two different ways. Each word also has more than one part of speech. Decide how each word is used in the sentence. Then look up the word in the dictionary. On your paper, write the following for each word:

   a. The correct respelling
   b. The part of speech
   c. The correct meaning

1. If you abuse the horse, she will be ruined for ever.
2. My father's way of discipline was more appropriate.
3. I am filled with wonder when I consider the contrasts between the two lives which that day connects.
4. I returned again and again to the subject, eager for more information.
5. I did nothing but explore with my hands and learn the name of every object that I touched.
6. Lincoln was asked what would be the best attribute for a politician.
7. He said the attribute "would be the ability to raise a cause which would produce an effect and then fight the effect."

8. Lincoln refused his step-brother eighty dollars because of a defect in the step-brother's <u>conduct</u>.

9. The <u>defect</u> was that his step-brother didn't do a day's work in a day.

10. I blubbered a short <u>excuse</u>: "They were only girls."

Developing Writing Skills

1. **Comparing the Two Letters.** Both of these letters must have been difficult for Abraham Lincoln to write, although for different reasons. Write a paragraph telling which you think was harder to write. First, you will have to tell what was hard about writing each one. Then, give reasons to support your opinion.

2. **Writing a Personal Letter.** Write a letter to an imaginary person. In your letter, deal with a serious topic and serious feelings. It should be a personal letter, not a formal one. The letter should be at least three paragraphs long. There should be a clear development of your ideas.

Developing Skills in Critical Thinking

Analyzing Organization. Lincoln's letter to his step-brother starts out by saying that he doesn't think it is a good idea to send the $80. Lincoln then goes on to say why. He has an organized argument. Outline Lincoln's argument step by step. Here is the beginning of your outline. Use as many numbers as you need.

1. I have helped you before, but you soon had money problems again.

2. You are not lazy, but you are an idler.

3. You have a habit of wasting time.

Speeches

During his lifetime, Abraham Lincoln was not considered one of the great speakers of the country. Many audiences preferred long speeches filled with difficult words and complicated ideas. However, those complicated speeches have long been forgotten while Lincoln's short speeches are still remembered.

The Right To Know (detail), 1968, NORMAN ROCKWELL.
Printed by permission of the Estate of Norman Rockwell; Copyright © 1968 Estate of Norman Rockwell.

Farewell Address:
Delivered at Springfield, Illinois, February 11, 1861

ABRAHAM LINCOLN

When Lincoln was elected President, he had to move from Illinois to Washington, D.C. This is how he said goodbye to his friends and neighbors in his hometown.

My Friends:

No one, not in my situation, can appreciate my feeling of sadness at this parting. To this place, and the kindness of these people, I owe everything. Here I have lived a quarter of a century, and have passed from a young to an old man. Here my children have been born, and one is buried. I now leave, not knowing when or whether ever I may return, with a task before me greater than that which rested upon Washington. Without the assistance of that Divine Being who ever attended him, I cannot succeed. With that assistance, I cannot fail. Trusting in Him who can go with me, and remain with you, and be everywhere for good, let us confidently hope that all will yet be well. To His care commending you, as I hope in your prayers you will commend me, I bid you an affectionate farewell.

Developing Comprehension Skills

1. To what or whom did Lincoln feel he owed everything?

2. Write the last sentence of the speech in your own words. Here is some information to help you: "His" refers to God; "commending" is like "entrusting," or putting in the care of someone trustworthy.

3. Did Lincoln think that he was becoming President at an important time in history? Give a reason for your answer.

4. Remember that this speech was written just before the start of the Civil War. What did Lincoln mean by hoping "that all will yet be well"?

5. Very often a person elected to public office makes a speech just to get publicity. Do you feel that this was Lincoln's goal? If not, what was the purpose of this speech?

Reading Literature: Nonfiction

1. **Identifying Tone.** Basing your opinion on this speech, how do you think Lincoln felt when he gave it? Do you think he is being honest about his feelings? Give reasons for your answer.

2. **Identifying Important Details.** A good speech should give you ideas to think about after the speaker is finished. What ideas did Lincoln leave for his listeners to think about? Name at least two.

3. **Recognizing Literary Style.** Abraham Lincoln wrote very effective speeches. He used words, phrases, and sentence patterns carefully to achieve the effect he desired. This care in writing produced a "Farewell Address," which has an almost musical and prayerful quality. Lincoln achieved this quality by using several methods, or **techniques**, in writing.

   One method was the repetition of a certain pattern of words within a sentence. The third sentence, where he uses two related verb phrases, "have lived" and "have passed," is an example of this. Another technique was that of balancing related words or phrases, either within one sentence or in sentences close together. Examples are "born" and "buried," and "when or whether."

   Find in the "Farewell Address" an additional example of repetition of sentence patterns and another example of balance.

Developing Vocabulary Skills

Completing Analogies. In a word analogy, there are two pairs of related words. Each pair is related in the same way, for example, as synonyms or as antonyms. Complete the following analogies involving words used in this chapter.

1. intermittent is to constant as meager is to _____.

    abundant   gaudy   isolated   small

2. langor is to listlessness as grief is to _____.

    graciousness   sadness   height   laziness

3. hero is to inspire as sentinel is to _____.

    watch   confuse   immigrant   generation

4. solitary is to isolated as passionate is to _____.

    perplexed   emotional   rambling   sinister

5. stimulus is to response as incentive is to _____.

    action   incident   rebuke   gasp

6. rebuke is to sulky as _____ is to radiant.

    gesture   ramble   speculate   praise

7. stymie is to encourage as obstacle is to _____.

    intuitive   multitude   assist   oculist

8. President is to country as _____ is to state.

    general   cabinet member   governor   congressman

Developing Writing Skills

1. **Evaluating the Effectiveness of a Speech.** Lincoln's "Farewell Address" is very short. It probably took no more than a minute or two to deliver it. Did this shortness make the speech more effective or less effective? Would the speech have been better if it had been longer? Write a paragraph telling your opinion.

2. **Writing a Speech.** Think of a topic you feel strongly about. Write the first paragraph of a speech on this topic. The first paragraph should tell what the speech will be about and give some indication of your opinion. It should also set the tone of the speech.

The Gettysburg Address: Delivered at Gettysburg, Pennsylvania, November 19, 1863

ABRAHAM LINCOLN

In 1863, the Civil War was still raging. That fall, President Lincoln spoke at the dedication of a cemetery on the site of the Battle of Gettysburg. What did he want his listeners to learn from that awful battle?

Four score and seven years ago our fathers brought forth upon this continent a new nation, conceived in liberty, and dedicated to the proposition that all men are created equal.

Now we are engaged in a great civil war, testing whether that nation, or any nation so conceived and so dedicated, can long endure. We are met here on a great battlefield of that war. We have come to dedicate a portion of it as a final resting place for those who here gave their lives that that nation might live. It is altogether fitting and proper that we should do this.

But, in a larger sense, we cannot dedicate—we cannot consecrate—we cannot hallow this ground. The brave men, living and dead, who struggled here, have consecrated it far above our poor power to add or detract. The world will little note nor long remember what we say here, but can never forget what they did here. It is for us, the living, rather to be dedicated here to the unfinished work which they have, thus far, so nobly carried on. It is rather for us to be here dedicated to the great task remaining before us—that from these honored dead we take increased devotion to that cause for which they here gave the last full measure of devotion; that we here highly resolve that these dead shall not have died in vain; that this nation shall have a new birth of freedom; and that this Government of the people, by the people, for the people, shall not perish from the earth.

Civil War Drum, 9th Regiment
Infantry. Chicago Historical Society.

Developing Comprehension Skills

1. Some of the words in this speech may not be familiar to you. In the first sentence, for instance, a "score" is twenty; "conceived" means brought into existence; and a "proposition" is a proposal or a statement. Rewrite the first sentence of the speech in your own words.

2. Lincoln came to Gettysburg to dedicate a portion of the battlefield to the soldiers who died there. Then he said that could not be done. How did he arrive at this conclusion?

3. Lincoln was asking his listeners to do something. In your own words, say what he wanted them to do.

4. This speech contains many unusual words. Do you think Lincoln purposely chose words not used in everyday conversation? Why would he do such a thing?

5. Why do you suppose this speech is included in a literature book? Do you agree it still has meaning for us today? Why or why not?

Reading Literature: Nonfiction

1. **Describing the Mood.** How would you describe the mood of this speech? What feelings do you get when reading it?

2. **Recognizing Theme.** Lincoln thought that people would not remember what he said at Gettysburg. If the speech dealt only with the specific dedication of a battlefield, he probably would have been right. However, people are still reading his speech today. What themes did President Lincoln discuss in this speech that make it worth remembering?

3. **Identifying Author's Purpose.** What was the purpose for which President Lincoln was invited to speak? He had another, more general purpose in mind. What was it?

4. **Examining Style.** The third question under Reading Literature: Nonfiction for Lincoln's "Farewell Address" (page 464) pointed out two methods, or techniques, that Lincoln often used in his writing. These were repetition of sentence patterns and balance of related words or phrases. Lincoln used these techniques in his "Gettysburg Address," also. In addition, he varied the length of sentences to produce a stately, but not heavy, rhythm. Find examples of each of these three techniques in this speech.

Developing Vocabulary Skills

Using a Pronunciation Key. The following respellings are of words found in "The Gettysburg Address." Use the pronunciation key in the glossary of this text (page 569) to figure out the pronunciation of each word. Find the word in the speech to see how it is spelled. Write the word on your paper using the standard spelling. Then answer the questions below. Use context clues or a dictionary to find the answers.

a. kont'n ənt
b. prop'ə zish'ən
c. ded'ə kāt
d. en dùr'
e. kon'sə krāt'
f. di trakt'
g. di vō'shən
h. ri zolv'

1. Which two words in the third paragraph mean "to set apart for a particular reason"?

2. Which word means "a proposal or idea"?

3. Which word means "to last or keep on"?

4. Which word is a synonym for *dedication?*

5. Which word is the opposite of "add"?

Developing Writing Skills

1. **Comparing Two Works.** Compare "A Letter to Mrs. Bixby" and "The Gettysburg Address." Are the themes related? Is the difficulty of the vocabulary similar? Are there any similarities in sentence length or sentence patterns? How do the tones compare? Do you get the same feeling from each?

   If you noted differences, can you suggest any reasons for them? Does the author's purpose affect the answers to the questions above?

2. **Examining Style.** "The Gettysburg Address" ends in an emotional climax. Write a paragraph analyzing how the mood of the speech builds toward that climax. Consider the techniques discussed in Reading Literature: Nonfiction, 3, on page 464. Also consider Lincoln's use of words with strong connotations.

3. **Writing an Appeal.** If you could encourage a large group of people to do something important, what would you urge them to do? Choose a project you really believe is important. Then write a speech of three paragraphs (the length of Lincoln's "Gettysburg Address"). Use words with strong connotations to win the support and enthusiasm of your listeners or readers.

Developing Skills in Critical Thinking

Recognizing Slanted Writing. Slanted writing is not necessarily bad. All writers use it. It is the reader's job to be aware of how it is affecting his or her reactions to the writing.

In "The Gettysburg Address," Lincoln was encouraging his listeners to carry the war to victory. How did he do this? He used both a logical development of ideas and emotion-packed words.

To see more clearly how Lincoln constructed his speech, do the following exercise. Fold your paper in half. On the left half, write an outline of Lincoln's argument, using words with neutral connotations. Here is the first point:

1. Our ancestors started a country based on ideas of liberty and equality.

The last point on the outline should be this: "Therefore we should make sure that our government continues."

On the right half of the paper, across from each outline statement, list words from the speech with strong connotations. These should be words Lincoln used to express the idea in the outline statement.

After you have completed both halves of your paper, discuss how Lincoln blended both ideas and emotions in his speech.

Developing Skills in Speaking and Listening

Delivering a Speech. Choose one of the two speeches by Lincoln and prepare to say it to a group. For your speech to be effective, you must be sure that you understand exactly what Lincoln meant. Ask your teacher for help if you need it. If you understand what you are saying, your listeners will be able to understand you, too.

When you deliver your speech to the group, speak slowly. These are serious speeches and you should not rush through them. Say the words as if you mean them. Make sure you are standing straight and proud, speaking clearly and loudly, and looking at your audience.

Vignette

A **vignette** is a short piece of nonfiction writing that studies a person closely. A vignette is sometimes called a character sketch. Using a few words, the writer draws a picture of the person as you would draw a pencil sketch.

In the vignette you will read about Abraham Lincoln, the writer does not try to tell you everything about the man. She is interested only in introducing you to Lincoln as he was on that particular day in his life.

Abraham Lincoln, ALEXANDER GARDNER.
National Portrait Gallery, Smithsonian Institution, Washington, D.C.

Day of Light and Shadow

GENEVIEVE FOSTER

The following selection describes Abraham Lincoln's last day. As you read it, try to separate provable facts from the author's interpretation of the facts. Does the author's opinion of Lincoln show through?

April 14, 1865, was a great day for the United States and a happy one for Abraham Lincoln. Almost exactly four years after it had been fired upon, the Stars and Stripes were raised again above Fort Sumter! War was over! The Union had been saved. Slavery had been abolished. All that Lincoln had pledged himself to do had been accomplished.

The care that had weighed so heavily upon him for the last four years seemed to have slipped now from his shoulders. His lined face was almost radiant.

The last day he began, as usual, working at his desk, and then had breakfast at eight. Robert, his oldest son, now twenty-one, was with him. He had a picture of Robert E. Lee to show his father. Lincoln looked at it earnestly. "It is a good face," he said.

After breakfast he had several interviews and letters to write before the Cabinet meeting that was called for eleven o'clock.

"Today," said the President, "General Grant will be with us."

One by one, the cabinet members came in, entering into casual conversation over the day's news and speculating as to where the leaders of the rebel government had now gone.

"I suppose, Mr. President," said the Postmaster General, "you would not be sorry if they escaped from the country."

"Well, I should be for following them up pretty close to make sure of their going," answered Lincoln in a comical tone.

Then a half cloud passed over Lincoln's face, and he told of a strange dream that he had had the previous night. The dream itself was not so strange, he said, as the fact that he had had it several times before—and each time it had preceded some great victory or disaster.

It was a vague feeling of being on a strange phantom ship, sailing, or floating towards some vast, indefinite, unknown shore.

Someone ventured the suggestion that the anxiety in his mind may have led to the dream.

"Perhaps," said Lincoln thoughtfully, "that may be the explanation."

Stanton burst in—carrying a large roll of papers, and the group around the table was complete. General Ulysses S. Grant was then cordially introduced. Grant nodded and told in the fewest possible words the incidents of the surrender at Appomattox.

"And what terms did you give the common soldier?" asked Lincoln.

"I told them to go back to their homes and families, and that they would not be molested if they did nothing more," said Grant.

The President's face lighted with approval. That was right. There must be no hate shown or vindictiveness. Now that the war was over, everything must be done to help the bankrupt people of the South back to prosperity. So the talk turned to post-war plans. Stanton spread out his big roll of paper, showing charts for reconstruction. These were discussed until the meeting broke up at two o'clock.

As they were leaving, Lincoln spoke of going to the theater that evening to see "The American Cousin." Turning to General Grant, he said that he hoped that he and Mrs. Grant would accompany them. But there seemed to be some misunderstanding, because, though it had been advertised in the papers, General Grant said that they were to leave town that evening. Lincoln, himself, was not too eager about it, but since it had been announced, he thought he'd better go.

He made an appointment for the following day, and then went to lunch, from which his next callers saw him return munching an apple.

Then followed a talk with Vice-President Andrew Johnson. The time was growing short. It was past three o'clock. Lincoln could not stay much longer. There were only a few last things for him to do.

Towards late afternoon, he put on his high black hat and went for a drive with Mrs. Lincoln, alone. No, "just ourselves," he had told her when she had suggested guests. It was a fresh spring day, the lilacs were in blossom, the willows along the river were green, the dogwood was opening. Lincoln's face glowed.

"I never felt so happy in my life," he said, drawing a deep breath.

Returning, he walked across the gravel path to the War Department and "was more cheerful and happy," Stanton thought, "than he had ever seen him." Nevertheless, to the guard who walked back to the White House with him in the gathering dusk, he spoke of men who, he believed, would take his life. When they reached the steps it was "Good-bye, Crooks," that he said, for the first time, not "Good night."

The strands of happiness and tragedy that made Abraham Lincoln's life were twisting closely now for, in the next moment, seeing two friends from Illinois, the governor and a congressman, he called to them in the cheeriest tone. Laughing and chatting, he led them to his office, and read them one ridiculous story after another. His son Tad came to call him to supper, and he said he'd be right there. But first he wanted them to hear just one more story, the one perhaps in which the author poked fun at the "Goriller Linkin, whuz rane he had hoped wood be a short wun."

Then the author said, "The Confederacy is ded. It's gathered up its feet, sed its last words, and deceest . . . Linkin will serve his term out—our leaders will die off uv chagrin and inability to live long out uv offis. And so, Farewell, vane world!" And Lincoln left them laughing.

After dinner the Speaker of the House came for a few minutes, to say that, if there was to be no special session of Congress during the summer, he would take a trip to the West Coast where the transcontinental railroad was now being built.

The clock ticked on; it was just time to go to the theater when the congressman from Massachusetts was announced. Lincoln arranged to see him in the morning. Taking a small card he wrote a few words on it, and then he signed his name for the last time.

They were now at the door. Outside, the carriage was waiting. A breath of fresh cool air came in as the door was opened, and they walked out onto the portico in the moist spring night. Abraham Lincoln stood for a moment, then stepped into the carriage, its door closed behind him, the horses started, the carriage rolled down the driveway, the sound of the wheels on the gravel grew fainter and then died away and he was gone. Abraham Lincoln was gone.

Only then could the people of Abraham Lincoln's world realize how great he was. He was too tall when he walked beside them.

Developing Comprehension Skills

1. President Lincoln liked what General Grant told the common soldiers from the South. What did General Grant tell them? Why did Lincoln like that?

2. List at least five of Abraham Lincoln's activities on his last day. How do we know what he did?

3. The author says that only after Lincoln died did people realize how great he was. How does she phrase this statement?

4. Why do you think Lincoln told the Cabinet about his dream?

5. Why is this sketch called "Day of Light and Shadow"? Is it a good title?

Reading Literature: Nonfiction

1. **Recognizing Images.** In art, a **vignette** usually refers to a picture of someone's face. Find at least two words or phrases used to describe Lincoln's face in this written vignette. What do the words you found have in common with each other?

2. **Separating Fact and Opinion.** Tell which of the following statements are facts and which are opinions:
   a. War was over!
   b. "It is a good face."
   c. There must be no hate shown.
   d. Returning, he walked across the gravel path to the War Department.

3. **Recognizing Foreshadowing.** The vignette you read was written in a very lively and creative style. Even though it reports historical facts, the author develops suspense by dropping hints about what is to happen in the future. Such use of hints is called **foreshadowing**. Find the first hint that this day was Lincoln's last. Then locate at least three other instances of foreshadowing in this selection.

4. **Comparing Types of Writing.** Compare this vignette with the biographies you read earlier in the chapter. Can you identify some similarities? What are some differences?

Developing Vocabulary Skills

Reviewing Context Clues and Word Parts. Read these sentences (or groups of sentences) from the selection. Try to figure out the meaning of each underlined word by using context clues or word parts. Look especially for words that are similar or opposite in meaning. On your paper, write your own meaning of the word. Then write whether you used context clues or word parts to figure out the meaning.

1. The Union had been saved. Slavery had been abolished.

2. Lincoln's lined face that had grown so drawn and haggard was almost radiant.

3. The dream was like a vague feeling of being on a strange phantom ship, sailing towards some unknown shore.

4. Everything must be done to help the bankrupt people of the South back to prosperity.

5. Stanton spread out his big roll of paper, showing charts for reconstruction.

6. There seemed to be some misunderstanding with the Grants about the evening.

Developing Writing Skills

1. **Explaining Metaphor.** Read this sentence from the story: "The strands of happiness and tragedy that made Abraham Lincoln's life were twisting closely now." Write a paragraph telling what this means. Use examples of happiness and tragedy from the sketch.

2. **Writing a Well Organized Paragraph.** Some people think that fiction is read for enjoyment, but that nonfiction is read only for information, not enjoyment. What do you think? Write a paragraph explaining your opinion. Your first sentence should state your opinion. Then you should give arguments to support your opinion.

3. **Writing a Vignette.** Write a vignette about a day in your own life. First think over what happened on the day you choose. Write notes about the events you want to record. You will have to choose what you think is worth including. When you have made your choices, write at least six paragraphs describing your day. Try to show how

one event leads to the next. Include enough details to make your vignette interesting.

Developing Skills in Study and Research

Comparing Encyclopedias. Different encyclopedias often provide slightly different information or organize their entries differently. Using at least two different encyclopedias, look up the entries on Abraham Lincoln. Compare the two entries. Are they organized in the same way? Describe their pattern, or patterns, of organization. Does one encyclopedia provide more information than the other? Are they equally easy to understand? Do they both describe Lincoln's death in the same way? Based on this comparison, would you choose one of these encyclopedias over the other the next time you need to look up something?

Developing Skills in Critical Thinking

Identifying Words with Strong Connotations. Even though the vignette, "Day of Light and Shadow," reports the facts, it also includes many opinions. Frequently the reader does not notice the opinions. They are part of the picture the author draws for us. Examine each of the following sentences from the selection. Then find it in the selection in order to understand its context. What is the effect of the underlined word on the meaning of the passage?

1. Lincoln looked at it earnestly.   (page 472, paragraph 3)
2. "Perhaps," said Lincoln thoughtfully, "that may be the explanation." (page 473, paragraph 2)
3. Stanton burst in.   (page 473, paragraph 3)
4. The President's face lighted with approval.   (page 473, paragraph 6)
5. "I never felt so happy in my life," he said, drawing a deep breath. (page 473, column 2, paragraph 5)

Using Your Skills in Reading Nonfiction

The following is from *A Portrait of Myself*, by Margaret Bourke-White, a famous photographer for *Life* magazine. Read it. Then answer these questions: From what point of view is it written? How would you describe the tone that the writer is using?

A few months later, in the spring of 1929, I received a telegram from a man I had never met: HAVE JUST SEEN YOUR STEEL PHOTOGRAPH. CAN YOU COME TO NEW YORK AT OUR EXPENSE? signed: HENRY R. LUCE, TIME, THE WEEKLY NEWS MAGAZINE.

When I arrived, Mr. Luce and his associates explained that they were planning to launch a new magazine, which they hoped to illustrate with the most dramatic photographs of industry that had ever been taken. Did I think this was a good idea, he asked?

A good idea? I went back to Cleveland to pick up my belongings. Before I left again for New York, I wrote my mother: "I feel as if the world has been opened up and I hold all the keys."

Using Your Comprehension Skills

The following dialog is from a play you will read in Chapter 7. In it, Professor Pierson states both facts and opinions. Identify which statements are facts and which are opinions. Explain how each fact can be proved to be true.

Phillips. Professor, would you please tell our radio audience what you see as you observe the planet Mars through your telescope?

Pierson. Nothing unusual at the moment, Mr. Phillips. A red disk swimming in a blue sea. Stripes across the disk. The stripes are merely the result of atmospheric conditions peculiar to the planet.

Phillips. Then you're quite convinced that living intelligence does not exist on Mars?

Pierson. I should say the chances against it are a thousand to one.

Using Your Vocabulary Skills

The following are sentences from the plays you will read in Chapter 7. Locate the definition of the underlined words in the glossary of this text. On your paper, write the part of speech and the definition that fits the context below. Be prepared to pronounce the word correctly.

1. Merlin hath wrought a spell.
2. Stop the proceedings.
3. Her mistress is a captive in a vast and gloomy castle.
4. I wish I could convey the atmosphere of this fantastic scene.

Using Your Writing Skills

Choose one of the writing assignments below.

1. Choose from the selections in this chapter the person you found most admirable or appealing. Explain, in one to three paragraphs, why that person and his or her experiences interested you. Be sure to include specific examples of personal qualities.

2. Choose a famous modern-day person who interests you. Write two introductions about the person. Write the first as if you were the biographer of the person. Write the second as if you were the person. Remember to use the appropriate viewpoint for each introduction.

Using Your Skills in Critical Thinking

You have learned that one category of nonfiction records the lives, achievements, and personalities of people. List all the people about whom you have read in this chapter. What qualities, or personality traits, do some of the people share? What type of person does it take to overcome obstacles and achieve great things? What generalization can you make about this type of person? Be sure to support your generalization with at least five facts from the selections.

CHAPTER 7

Deep Bait, 1980, RICHARD HULL.
Photograph by William H. Bengtson,
Courtesy of Phyllis Kind Gallery,
New York and Chicago.

Reading Literature: Drama

What is Drama?

Drama is a form of literature in which a story is told through the words and actions of characters. Another word for a drama is a **play**. Plays are meant to be performed by actors and actresses in front of an audience.

The History of Drama

Drama, like other forms of literature, reflects what writers feel is important about life. Drama, therefore, has changed repeatedly in the thousands of years since the first play was acted out. That was long before the first play was written.

The first written plays we have today came from Greece. Around 600 B.C., a Greek poet named Thespis wrote a new kind of song. One person would pretend to be a character. A chorus of singers would have a conversation with him to tell a story.

Hundreds of years later, in countries such as Germany, France, and England, the Christian church made a different kind of play popular. Plays based on stories from the Bible were acted out. Much later, around 1500, people enjoyed **morality plays**. In these, characters had to choose between good and evil.

If you had lived in England in the late 1500's, you would have sensed the great excitement many people felt about drama. The best known playwright of that time was William Shakespeare. His plays told fascinating stories about kings and soldiers, witches and common people. Shakespeare wrote serious plays that ended in disaster called **tragedies** and light-hearted plays called **comedies**.

In recent times, plays have been written specially to be performed on radio and on television. This chapter has examples of plays written for radio.

The Elements of Drama

The Form of Written Drama. The written form of a play reminds you that the story is told through the words of the characters. The written play first gives the name of the character who is speaking. Then it prints the words, or lines, the character says.

Arthur: Good health to you both!
Clarence: Congratulations, Sir Boss.

Plays are divided into short sections called **scenes**. When the time or place changes, there is a new scene. Long plays are divided into **acts**, which are made up of a number of scenes.

Dramatic Conventions. A **convention** is an agreed-upon way of doing something. **Dramatic conventions** are the customary ways of writing and performing drama. Here are examples:

1. **Dialog**: Dialog refers to the conversations between characters in a play. The dialog tells the story.
2. **Aside**: In an aside, a character talks to the audience and acts as if the other characters cannot hear.
3. **Stage directions**: These are instructions to the director, actors, and actresses. They tell how to enter, move, and behave on the stage. They also help readers picture the play in their minds. They are usually printed in parentheses ( ).
4. **Sound effects**: These are sounds to be made as part of the play. In radio plays, they help listeners picture the action.
5. **Fade in**: In a radio play, this direction tells actors to speak softly and then louder, as if someone is coming closer.

How To Read a Play

1. Picture the play being performed by actors and actresses. Pay special attention to the stage directions and sound effects.
2. Cooperate with the writer. Enter the world he or she has made.

Comprehension Skills: Author's Purpose

Understanding the Author's Purpose

When preparing to write, writers decide what they want the piece of writing to do. Their purpose, or reason for writing, could be one or more of the following: 1) to entertain, 2) to express feelings, 3) to experiment with a new way of writing, 4) to teach, 5) to inform, 6) to persuade, 7) to make people laugh, 8) to inspire, 9) to shock, 10) to make people think seriously about a certain social problem.

Usually, a writer knows the purpose before he or she begins a piece of writing. Purpose affects many choices the writer makes, including the choices of topic, form, characters, setting, and plot.

To understand the author's purpose, study your own reaction to the piece. Were you entertained? Were you taught something? Did you gain a better understanding of other people's problems?

Not every writer achieves his or her purpose. Sometimes writers intend their work to be funny, but readers don't laugh. Sometimes a piece is meant to teach, but all it does is bore readers. Only the reader can tell if the writer has succeeded.

Evaluating the Author's Choice of Words

Suppose a story or play is set in the Middle Ages. The way the characters speak should suggest the time in which they live. As a reader, you would expect the characters to sound different from yourself. The writer might have the characters use old-fashioned words such as *thee, prithee,* and *verily.*

Suppose a second story is set in modern times. An army officer is reporting to the nation. Would you expect the officer to say, "Don't worry. No problem"? That would not sound like a real officer. This is how the general in *Invasion from Mars* speaks: "Situation arising from reported presence of certain individuals of un-identified nature is now under complete control." That sentence sounds believably stiff, formal, and official.

A writer chooses a character's words carefully. The words must fit the character and make him or her sound like a real person. You, as a reader, can judge when a writer has chosen the character's words well.

Exercises: Understanding the Author's Purpose and Choice of Words

A. Identify the purpose of each of these selections.

1. Mel works with scientists called marine archaeologists. They study the wrecks of old ships and all of the things that are brought up from the deep water.

   a. to inform you
   b. to persuade you
   c. to shock you

2. Small bird, forgive me.
   I'll hear the end of your song
   in some other world.

   a. to make you laugh
   b. to express feelings
   c. to teach

B. For each character below, choose the fitting line of dialog.

1. King Arthur:

   a. Thanks, Wiz. It's great to have you here at Camelot.
   b. Blessings upon thee, oh Great Wizard. I welcome thee to Camelot as my right-hand man.

2. Radio Announcer:

   a. Ladies and gentlemen, due to circumstances beyond our control, we are unable to continue the broadcast.
   b. We've been cut off! Oh, no! What'll I do?

Vocabulary Skills: Context Clues

Using Context Clues

What do you do when you are reading and you come to a word you can't understand? Do you skip it and go on with your reading, hoping that the word was not important? Sometimes, that's not a bad idea. Usually, however, a better idea is to figure out what the word means by using context clues.

Often you have to guess at the meaning of a new word. Then you test out your meaning in the sentence where you found the word. Here is an example. In these lines from *A Connecticut Yankee in King Arthur's Court,* the new word is underlined:

> **Connecticut Yankee:** The next time I saw Camelot, I knew at once that something was <u>amiss</u>. As I approached the gates of the castle, Clarence ran out to meet me and, by the worried look on his face, I knew that there was trouble.

What could *amiss* mean? To figure it out, first ask yourself what part of speech the new word could be. *Amiss* is probably an adjective because it describes the word *something*. Next, look at other clues. Clarence looked worried. The Yankee knew there was trouble. From all these clues, you can guess that something was wrong. *Amiss* probably means *wrong*.

Test your meaning in the given sentence. Replace *amiss* with *wrong*: "I knew at once that something was wrong." As you read on, you will know more surely whether your guess is correct.

This way of finding the meaning of a new word from context is called *inferring the meaning.* **Inference** is using what the writer has told you to figure out what the writer has not told you.

Here is another example of inferring meaning. This selection is from *Invasion from Mars*. Martians have killed forty people. The radio announcer is trying to keep the audience informed.

Announcer: Ladies and gentlemen, I have just been informed that we have finally established communication with an eyewitness of the tragedy. Professor Pierson . . . will give you his explanation of the calamity.

What does calamity mean? First, decide what part of speech it is. If you reread the sentence, you will see that calamity must be a noun, because the phrase "of the" needs a noun to complete it.

Now look for other clues. Professor Pierson saw a tragedy. You can guess that the thing he will explain will be that tragedy, or disaster. Calamity must mean disaster.

Exercise: Using Context Clues

Use context clues to find the meaning of each underlined word. Choose from the meanings following each selection.

1. **Connecticut Yankee:** Well, sir, there never was a man more dumbfounded than I was. I just couldn't get used to the idea. That's why when I woke again I thought the whole thing a dream, and, when I saw that page boy standing before me, I was more amazed than ever.

   a. Dumbfounded means "stupid."
   b. Dumbfounded means "found by accident."
   c. Dumbfounded means "surprised."

2. **Sound:** Clamor of crowd in the background

   a. Clamor means "silence."
   b. Clamor means "noise."
   c. Clamor means "sight."

3. **Announcer two:** Ladies and gentlemen, I have a grave announcement to make. Incredible as it may seem, those strange beings who landed in the Jersey farmlands tonight are the vanguard of an invading army from the planet Mars.

   a. Vanguard means "part of the army ahead of the main army."
   b. Vanguard means "a kind of vehicle."
   c. Vanguard means "a kind of guard."

A Connecticut Yankee in King Arthur's Court

In this play, the Connecticut Yankee goes back in time and lands in King Arthur's Camelot. As you read, decide whether he is a good time-traveler. Can he make himself comfortable in his new surroundings?

MARK TWAIN
Adapted from the novel

CHARACTERS

Connecticut Yankee
Worker
Clarence
King Arthur
Merlin

Alisande de la Carteloise
  (al'ə sänd də lä kär tel lwaz)
Women, *two*
Men, *two*

Music. *Pastoral theme, in and under.*[1]

Connecticut Yankee (*Elderly, as for all narrations*). I am an American, born and reared in Hartford, Connecticut. So, I am a Yankee of the Yankees—and practical. When I was little more than a lad, I went over to the great arms factory and learned my real trade; learned all there was to it. Why, I could make anything a body'd want—anything in the world. It didn't make any difference what; and if there wasn't any new-fangled way to make a thing quickly, I could invent one—and do it as easy as rolling off a log. I became a head superintendent—had a couple of thousand men under me. Now with all those men, you can see how easy it would be to fall into an argument. Well, one day. . . .

Music. *Reminiscent theme, in and under.*

Sound. *Factory noises softly in background.*

Conn. Yankee (*Younger than before, as for all dialog sequences*). Is that so, now? Well, sir, it just so happens that there *was* a total eclipse of the sun in the sixth century—matter of fact, it was on

---

1. **In and under**: a musical direction that directs the music to swell and then fade into the background.

the 21st of June, in the year 528 A.D., and began at three minutes after twelve noon.

Worker. Now look here, just because you're the foreman of this plant doesn't mean that you know everything. Ah, the trouble with you thick-headed types is that you're sure you do know everything.

Conn. Yankee. And just who are you calling thick-headed, sir?

Worker. Just you, sir.

Conn. Yankee. Is that right, now? Well, let me tell you something. . . .

Sound. *Angry voices fade off mike.*

Conn. Yankee (*Older voice*). Well, we argued and argued, and pretty soon we were taking off our shirts for a real fight. Everything was going along pretty smoothly, until he hit me a left under the chin that I didn't expect. The next think I knew, I was floating through space. . . .

Music. *Eerie, hypnotic dream theme, in and under.*

Sound. *Birds twittering gayly.*

Clarence (*A young boy*). Faith, sir, be ye awake?

Conn. Yankee (*Yawning*). Wha . . . Hmm? (*Alarmed*) Great green Jehoso-phat! Who are you?

Clarence. Clarence is my name. I be a page, sir.

Conn. Yankee. A page? A little thing like you a page? Go 'long, you aren't more than a paragraph. Hey, what is this place anyway? Where am I? Bridge-port?

Clarence. Camelot. You're in prison, sir.

Conn. Yankee. Prison! Then what are you doing all dressed up like you were going to a fancy ball?

Clarence. Marry,[2] sir, this is the latest thing for a page.

Conn. Yankee (*Suspiciously*). What's the date? This isn't April first, is it?

Clarence. No, sir. It's the twentieth of June, 528.

Conn. Yankee. Five twenty . . . look here. Is this a circus, maybe, or a lunatic asylum?

Clarence. No, sir, in faith it isn't.

Conn. Yankee. Well, then, either I am out of my mind, or something awful just happened. Now tell me, honest and true, where am I?

Clarence (*Simply*). Marry, sir, 'tis easy. You are in King Arthur's Court!

Music. *Delightful theme, in and under.*

---

2. **Marry**: exclamation of surprise used in Middle Ages.

Conn. Yankee (*Older voice*). Well, sir, there never was a man more dumb-founded than I was. I just couldn't get used to the idea. That's why, when I awoke again, I thought the whole thing a dream and, when I saw that page boy standing before me, I was more amazed than ever.

Clarence. Sir! Sir! Wake up!

Conn. Yankee. What? You here yet? Go along with the rest of the dream. Scat!

Clarence. Prithee, what dream?

Conn. Yankee. What dream? Why the dream that I am in Arthur's Court, and that I talk to you, who are nothing but a work of the imagination.

Clarence. Indeed! And is it a dream that you're to be burned at the stake tomorrow? Answer me that!

Conn. Yankee (*Astounded*). What?

Clarence. Aye, by the command of the King. Merlin suggested it!

Conn. Yankee (*Nervously*). Now, Clarence, my boy, you're the only friend I've got. You must help me devise some way to escape from this place.

Clarence. Verily, sir, it is impossible. The corridors are filled with guards, and worse than that, Merlin has woven a spell about this dungeon, and there bides not a man in this kingdom who would dare attempt to escape!

Conn. Yankee. Merlin hath wrought a spell. Merlin, forsooth! That cheap old humbug, that maundering old fake. (*Laughs*)

Clarence (*Frightened*). Oh beware! Any moment these walls may crumble upon us if you say such things!

Conn. Yankee. Do you know why I laughed? Because I'm a magician my-self. Why, I knew Merlin seven hundred years ago, and he doesn't amount to shucks as a magician, not next to me! Oh, he's all right for parlor magic and such, but he never learned the rudiments of the big stuff. Now listen to me. I want you to do me a favor; you said today is June 20, didn't you? Well, get word to the King that I am a magi-cian myself, and, if he dares to try burn-ing me tomorrow, I will blot out the sun at noon, and it shall never shine again. The fruits of the earth shall rot for lack of light, and the peoples of the earth shall die. Do you understand?

Music. *Mischievous theme, in and under.*

Conn. Yankee (*Older voice*). Well, the King believed that I was a magician, right enough. But that old fake, Merlin, persuaded him that I was a humbug. And so, at twelve the next day, I found myself tied to a stake in the middle of the courtyard. That didn't bother me, though; I knew that in about a minute and a half, I could expect a total eclipse of the sun.

Sound. *Clamor of crowd in background.*

Conn. Yankee *(Older voice).* Sure enough, just as they were about to light the pile of wood at my feet, I saw the skies darken slightly. Majestically, I raised my arm, pointing at the sun. Then everyone noticed the darkness. Poor fools, they thought I was really going through with my threat. Suddenly, the King rose, and shouted. . . .

Arthur *(Slightly off mike).* Stop the proceedings. Do not light the stake!

Merlin *(An old, crackling voice).* But Your Majesty. . . .

Arthur. Be quiet, Merlin. I, Arthur, King of England, command silence. But look you, the skies grow darker. *(Pleading)* Stranger, I am sorry! I beg of you: do not extinguish the sun!

Conn. Yankee. Stay where you are, all. If any man moves—even the King—before I give him leave, I will blast him with thunder and lightning.

Arthur. Be merciful, fair sir, and essay this peril no further, lest disaster follow. Name any terms, reverend sir, even to the halving of my Kingdom; but banish this calamity! Spare the sun!

Conn. Yankee *(Casually).* Give me time to consider.

Arthur. How long, oh, how long? Be merciful; look, it groweth darker, moment by moment. Prithee, how long?

Conn. Yankee. Oh, not long, Maybe an hour. For a lesson, I will let this darkness proceed, and spread night in the world; but, whether or not I will blot out the sun for good shall rest with you. These are the terms: you shall remain King over all your dominions, but you shall appoint me your perpetual minister and executive, so that I'll be The Boss, and give me as payment, one percent of all revenue I raise for the state. Is it satisfactory?

Arthur. Away with his bonds, and set him free! And show him homage, high and low, rich and poor, for he is a great wizard and magician. Now, sir, banish, if you will, this awful night.

Conn. Yankee *(To himself).* Ah, at last the eclipse is total. Now is the time. *(Aloud majestically)* Let the enchantment dissolve and pass harmless away!

Sound. *Tumultuous cheers in backgound.*

Arthur *(Proclaiming).* Blessings upon thee, oh Great Wizard. I, Arthur, welcome thee to Camelot as my right-hand man. And from this day henceforward, shall thy name be called . . . The Boss!

Sound. *Crowd cheers.*

Arthur *(Shouting).* Make way! Make way! Make way for The Boss!

Music. *Fanfare into royal theme, in and under.*

A Connecticut Yankee **491**

Conn. Yankee (*Older voice*). Well, that—miracle, shall we call it?—fixed things up as right as right could be. Soon news of it traveled throughout the Kingdom, and everybody knew what a wonderful person I was. Of course, I couldn't rest on my laurels. The Kingdom would get suspicious; besides, I was getting restless. I wanted some new glories. And so, I began—inventing things.

Music. *Out.*[3]

---

3. **Out**: a musical direction to indicate that the music should stop.

Conn. Yankee. Look, Your Majesty. My newest invention.

Arthur. It is a wondrous looking thing, but—but what is it?

Conn. Yankee. It's an artificial candle. It's cheaper to manufacture—I've already started a factory—and it'll give a hundred times the light that oil lamps give.

Arthur (*With awe*). Indeed! And what do you call your new miracle?

Conn. Yankee. I've given it the name . . . electric light bulb!

Music. *Low-pitched chord.*

Arthur. Another invention, Sir Boss?

Conn. Yankee. Yes. A collapsible sunshade—it'll protect you from rain, too. And when not in use, it can double as a walking-stick. I've got a factory producing twenty thousand of them a day. Do you like it?

Arthur (*In wonder*). Verily, I do. And what do you plan to call this wonderful device?

Conn. Yankee. How about—umbrella?

Music. *Higher chord.*

Conn. Yankee. Yes, Your Majesty, a new invention. It's a box that is capable of transfixing images of real things in miniature on paper. I call it a camera.

Music. *Higher chord.*

Conn. Yankee. It's a solution with which to get your skin much cleaner than with ordinary water. I plan to name it . . . soap.

Music. *Higher chord.*

Conn. Yankee. Yes, Your Majesty, I've just invented shoe polish. (*Pause*) That's right, Sire, it's my newest discovery: whipped cream. (*Pause*) Right again, King Arthur. Another invention: this one's the printing press.

Music. *A succession of chords mounting to a climax, then, fanfare.*

Arthur. I have sent for you, Sir Boss, to ask if you would like an adventure.

Conn. Yankee. An . . . an adventure?

Arthur. Yes. You must be tired of staying here in Camelot year after year, just working your humdrum miracles, so I thought—or, rather, Merlin thought—that you might like to go off on an adventure.

Conn. Yankee. Merlin did, did he?

Merlin. Yes, I did, did I.

Conn. Yankee. I'm awfully sorry, Sire, but much as I'd like to—well, I just couldn't. The factories have been going only a few months, and the Sunday schools have been in operation barely a week.

Merlin. You aren't afraid that I might get the upper hand while you're away, are you?

Conn. Yankee (*Not quite convincing*). Of course not. It's just that—well, what adventure could I go on?

Arthur. Ah, that's all settled. This lady that you see on my right has just come to Camelot with a marvelous tale. It seems that her mistress is a captive in a vast and gloomy castle, along with forty-three other young and beautiful girls.

Alisande (*A sweet, innocent voice*). Forty-four, an it please you, Sire.

Arthur. Ah yes; forty-four young ladies. The master of this castle is a giant, with four arms and one eye—in the center of his forehead. Your adventure is simply this: find the Princess and her ladies! Doesn't it sound exciting? I wish that I could go with you, but Guinevere would never hear of it. Oh, you must be thrilled!

Conn. Yankee (*Downheartedly*). Yes, yes, Sire. Thrilled. I can hardly control myself. (*Weakly, limply*) Three cheers for adventure.

Music. *Pastoral theme, in and under.*

Sound. *Horses trotting on a dirt road.*

Conn. Yankee. I still don't understand why you insist upon accompanying me on this fool's errand, young lady.

Alisande. How else then should you find the castle, Sir Boss?

Conn. Yankee. Oh come, come; you don't mean to say that there really *is* such a place. Your name, please?

Alisande. I'm called the Demoiselle Alisande de la Carteloise, an it please you.

Conn. Yankee. Now, Sandy—it's easier to call you that—have you brought any letters, any documents, any proofs that you are trustworthy and truthful?

Alisande. Of a surety, no; and wherefore should I? Have I not a tongue, and cannot I say all that by myself?

Conn. Yankee. But your saying it and someone else's saying it are different.

Alisande. Different? How might that be? I fear me I do not understand.

Conn. Yankee. Not understand? Can't you see the difference between you—why in Heaven's name do you look so innocent and idiotic?

Alisande (*Innocently*). I? In truth I know not, but it were the will of God.

Conn. Yankee. Oh, for the love of Heaven! (*Regaining his calm*) Now as to this castle—where is it?

Alisande. Oh, as to that, it lieth in a far country, many leagues away.

Conn. Yankee. Never mind the distance; whereabout does the castle lie, in what direction?

Alisande. Ah, please you sir, it hath no direction from here, by reason that the road lieth not straight but turneth evermore.

Conn. Yankee. But have you not a map—a good map?

Alisande (*Puzzled*). Is that peradventure[4] the manner of thing which of late the unbelievers have brought from over the great seas, which being boiled in oil, (*Fading*) and an onion and salt added thereto, doth . . .

---

4. **Peradventure**: Middle Age word for *perhaps*.

Music. *Pleasant theme, in and under.*

Conn. Yankee *(Older voice)*. Ah, I knew right then that the poor girl was a liar from the word "Go," and was only stalling for time. And here was I, a respectable Wizard of the Court of King Arthur, off gallivanting around the countryside with a beautiful young demoiselle named Sandy. Why, it was improper! It was indecent! It was scandalous! Especially since I was engaged to a telephone operator from East Hartford, Connecticut, named Kitty Flanagan. *(Sighs)* Ah, it was doubtful that I'd ever see her again, or ever call her on the telephone, with a "Hello, Operator." At first, I did think that there might be some chance of my returning to the nineteenth century—but as time went on, I realized that such would never be the case. And so, after much wandering around the countryside, I finally decided that it was time that Sandy and I were married. Therefore, we returned briefly to Camelot.

Music. *Wedding March, in and under.*

Note. *The next six speeches overlap each other in sequence, in a montage effect.*

Arthur. Good health to you both! Good health and long life!

Clarence. Congratulations, Sir Boss.

1st Woman. Long live Sir Boss and Lady Alisande!

1st Man. The best of luck in the world to you both.

2nd Woman. My heartiest congratulations and best wishes!

2nd Man. Long live the happy bride and groom!

Music. *Wedding March, in and under.*

Conn. Yankee *(Older voice)*. Although the first few months of our marriage were happy ones, in my dreams I still wandered thirteen centuries away. I could not get the face of that telephone operator—the one that I had been engaged to in Hartford—out of my mind. Night after night, I would toss upon my pillow, and whisper fitfully in my sleep: *(Whispering)* Hello, Operator! Hello, Operator! Hello, Operator! *(Pause)* In a little more than a year, Sandy presented me with a child, and, with great magnanimity, she saddled that cry of mine, uttered in my sleep, upon our little daughter, believing it to be the name of some lost darling of mine. It touched me to tears, and it nearly knocked me off my feet, too, when she smiled up at my face and said:

Alisande. The name of one who was dear to thee is here preserved, here made holy, and the music of it will abide always in our ears. Now thou'lt kiss me, as knowing the name I have given the child.

Conn. Yankee. Yes, I know, sweetheart—how dear and good it is of you, too! But I want to hear these lips of yours, which are also mine, utter it first. Then its music will be complete.

Alisande (*With deep feeling*). I have called our baby . . . Hello-Operator!

Music. *Lively theme, in and under.*

Conn. Yankee (*Older voice*). After a year and a half of traipsing arond the countryside in search of Sandy's mythical Princess, we returned once more to the Court of King Arthur. At first, I was worried about what I could tell His Majesty, but Sandy fixed that up just fine. She had lied me into the mess. Now, she lied me out again.

Music. *Lighthearted theme, in and under.*

Alisande. Yes, Your Majesty, we *did* find the forty-four maidens—*and* the Princess. But what do you think? They had been turned to swine! So we drove them back to the Kingdom from which they originally came, and the Sorcerer Glacklick turned them back into fair damsels.

Arthur. But why couldn't you turn them back into humans yourself, Sir Boss?

Conn. Yankee. Why, er . . . uh. . . .

Alisande (*Aghast*). Surely you wouldn't have someone as mighty as The Boss associate with swine, Your Majesty?

Music. *Delightful theme, in and under.*

Conn. Yankee (*Older voice*). Time marched on, and, I am pleased to say, England was altered. I had eradicated slavery, knight-errantry, serfdom, and ignorance. I had established schools everywhere, and even colleges. Baseball was the national pastime—King Arthur was my prize shortstop! A number of pretty good newspapers were in operation, and I even had established a weekly magazine. Only one thing troubled me; that was Merlin. He seemed jealous and was always slinking around in corners, whispering to his friends in low tones, and sneering whenever I passed. No matter, though, I thought; I had more important business on my mind. Then one day . . . .

Music. *Out.*

Alisande (*Breathless*). Sir! Sir Boss! Come quickly!

Conn. Yankee (*Kindly*). Easy, darling, easy. What is it?

Alisande. Hello-Operator. She's sick—the doctor says it's mem . . . membraneous croup. I don't know what that is—it's a word he learned in one of your colleges. But I'm frightened!

Conn. Yankee (*Calling out*). Clarence! Fetch my staff of physicians! And hurry!

Music. *Urgent theme, in and under.*

Conn. Yankee (*Older voice*). The doctors said we must take the child away if we would coax her back to health and strength again. And she must have sea air. Quickly, I had a yacht outfitted, and Sandy, the baby, and I took off for a cruise on the Mediterranean. I left Clarence in charge of things while I was away, and for three months I did not set foot on English soil.

Music. *Calm theme, in and under.*

Conn. Yankee (*Older voice; seriously, urgently*). The next time I saw Camelot, I knew at once that something was amiss. As I approached the gates of the castle, Clarence ran out to greet me and, by the worried expression on his face, I knew that there was trouble.

Clarence (*Breathless*). Sir Boss, at last you have come!

Conn. Yankee. What is it, Clarence? Speak!

Clarence. It was a plot—all of it—all Merlin's idea. As soon as your sails were out of the harbor, he started a revolution.

Conn. Yankee (*Numb with shock*). A— revo . . . lution?

Clarence. He brought back slavery, nobility—everything that you worked for years to remove. The people were only too ready for things to go back to their old state. It was no good for you to try to change them.

Conn. Yankee (*Heartbroken*). My dreams . . . my dreams of a republic . . . all gone, all smashed. What of the King?

Clarence. Dead. It is no use, I say. No use at all!

Conn. Yankee (*Determined*). Come, Clarence. There is work to do.

Clarence. Work? Where?

Conn. Yankee. We must destroy the schools, the factories, the colleges, lest they fall into Merlin's hands. We must destroy them; else, they destroy all of England.

Music. *Dramatic theme, in and under.*

Sound. *Explosions in the background.*

Conn. Yankee (*Bitterly*). Look at them, Clarence. Factories, schools, everything—blown to smithereens. And by my own hand; that's the irony of it.

Clarence. The work of a lifetime gone, in one fell swoop. What took you three-and-thirty years to build, destroyed in three-and-thirty minutes.

Conn. Yankee. It was the only way. I knew it would come to this, I think; yes, I knew it all along. That's why I had the dynamite charges set under all the buildings as soon as they were completed—in preparation for an event such as this. England simply wasn't ready for me, that's all.

Clarence. But it's not right, it's not fair.

Conn. Yankee. There can be no talk of right and fair. Go; see to the destruction of the newspaper office.

Clarence. The newspaper office? That too?

Conn. Yankee. That too. Go. I'll follow you in a moment.

Music. *Tense theme, in and under.*

Conn. Yankee (*To himself*). Just these last power lines to cut, and then it's finished. There . . . and . . . (*Exerting pressure*) . . . ugh! There! Now everything's done that must be done.

Merlin. Not everything, Sir Boss.

Conn. Yankee (*Surprised*). Wha . . . ? Who spoke? Merlin!

Merlin (*Maliciously*). Aye, Merlin. You see, Sir Boss, I win after all. I still have the upper hand here; I shall always have the upper hand here.

Conn. Yankee. Not as long as I am alive.

Merlin. Just so; and that is the one task that remains in the destruction of your Empire. I will not try magic with you; we understand each other too well for that. I shall only use—this dagger!

Conn. Yankee. Wha . . . ? Aggh!

Sound. *Body falling.*

Merlin. There now, Sir Boss! I, Merlin, am once again triumphant.

Alisande (*Fading on*). Husband, Clarence told me I might find you here . . . What's this? Merlin! Where is Sir Boss? (*Pause*) Stabbed!

Merlin. He's unconscious; aye, in my power at last!

Alisande (*Sobbing*). Husband!

Merlin. It is now my turn to work an enchantment—an enchantment to send Sir Boss back to wherever he came from. (*Calling aloud*) Thaglitch! Eerandabar! Sophoclus! Sophoclee!

Conn. Yankee (*A weird, echoing quality in his voice*). Goodbye, Alisande! Goodbye, Alisande! Goodbyyyyyye, Aaaalliiiiisaaaaaande!

Music. *Rapid succession of ascending chords.*

Sound. *Murmur of bewildered factory workers.*

Conn. Yankee (*Coming out of a coma*). Alisande! Alisande!

Worker (*Bewildered*). Alisande? Hey, who's Alisande? Come on, Boss, wake up. I didn't mean to hit you so hard, honest!

Conn. Yankee. Clarence . . . Merlin . . . eclipse.

Worker. Yeah, the eclipse, Boss. You were right about that. Now wake up, Boss. *(Pleading)* Please!

Conn. Yankee. Where . . . where am I?

Worker. You're in the factory, Boss. I was afraid you were never going to come around.

Conn. Yankee. Huh? What? You're sure this isn't Camelot?

Worker. It's the factory, the factory. Where did you think you were?

Conn. Yankee. Why in . . . oh, never mind. You'd probably never believe me, even if I told you. Besides, it was all just a dream.

Merlin *(Eerie and distant, speaking through miles and centuries).* It was the only way, Sir Boss. The only way.

Conn. Yankee *(Bewildered).* That voice. How can it be? It was only a dream. *(Pause)* Or . . . was it?

Music. *Full to finish.*

Developing Comprehension Skills

1. What caused the Connecticut Yankee to go back to 528 A.D.?

2. After the Yankee marries Lady Alisande, whom he calls Sandy, he tosses and turns in bed at night, whispering, "Hello, Operator! Hello, Operator!" Why does he do this? What is disturbing him?

3. In the factory where he worked in Hartford, Connecticut, the Yankee was head superintendent, with many men working under him. He is knowledgeable about his work. When he reaches Camelot, he uses this knowledge to "invent" things. Is he really inventing anything?

4. When the Yankee sets off dynamite charges to destroy all he has built in Camelot, he says, "England simply wasn't ready for me." Why was it wrong for the Yankee to bring about so much change?

5. To the Connecticut Yankee, the eclipse of the sun was an event that could be explained by natural causes. To the natives of Camelot, it was magic. Knowing this, can you suggest a definition of magic?

Reading Literature: Drama

1. **Appreciating Differences in Dialog.** This play uses two different speaking styles to show differences in characters and in their time periods. Remember that the Yankee moves back in time to Camelot. How does his style of speech differ from that of the characters he encounters there? Give examples from the early part of the play.

   Find two times that the Connecticut Yankee talks like the natives of Camelot. Does he change his speaking style on purpose? Why?

   Find a scene in which Alisande begins to talk like the Connecticut Yankee. Why does her language change?

2. **Understanding Dramatic Technique.** Look back at the stage directions for times when music is used. Notice that different musical themes, such as "delightful" and "mischievous," are used. These themes reflect the words and actions taking place in the play. Below are three types of musical themes used. Explain how they emphasize what has just taken place, or is taking place, in the play. Be sure to explain what is happening in the play.

   a. mischievous theme   (See page 490.)
   b. royal theme   (See page 491.)
   c. urgent theme   (See page 496.)

3. **Understanding Conflict.** The Yankee experiences both internal and external conflict in this play. How does he resolve his internal conflict over marrying Sandy instead of the telephone operator? In what way does Sandy try to help him with this problem? How is the Yankee's external conflict with Merlin resolved?

4. **Identifying Theme.** Although this play is more humorous than serious, the author still makes some statements about life. He points out that people tend to develop inventions even when there is no particular need for those inventions. He also points out that some of these inventions are so powerful that they are hard to control. What do you think is the author's opinion of our love of inventions? How does the play express his ideas?

5. **Understanding a Character.** In many ways, the Connecticut Yankee is a stereotype of an American. A **stereotype** person is a character whose ideas, actions, and words fit with a widely held idea of what that type of person is like. A stereotype has no individuality. He or she does only what is expected of that certain type of person. A stereotype does not change or grow.

   One stereotype of Americans pictures us as know-it-alls who are often rude and bossy. According to this stereotype, Americans depend on machines instead of people to solve their problems. This stereotype American believes that whatever is new is good, and whatever is old should be ignored or thrown away.

   The Connecticut Yankee often fits that stereotype in what he says or does. Find at least five details about the Yankee that prove this statement.

   Why would the author of this play want the hero to be a stereotype? With the theme of this play in mind, can you think of a reason? What might that reason be?

Developing Vocabulary Skills

Reviewing Context Clues. As you have learned in other lessons throughout this text, you can determine the meaning of an unfamiliar word from context in many ways. Sometimes there are key words that alert you to the meaning. For example, *is* is a clue to a definition, and *in other words* is a clue to a restatement. A comparison can be signaled by *in the same way,* while a contrast may be introduced with *unlike.*

Other context clues are not marked by key words. To discover meanings from cause and effect statements, for example, or from the main idea of a paragraph, requires careful reading. Sometimes you can infer the meaning of a word from the single statement in which it appears. Other times you must examine the entire paragraph or several paragraphs around the word.

Find the words listed below in the context of *A Connecticut Yankee.* For each word, read as many sentences or paragraphs as you need to determine the meaning. On your paper, write the word and the meaning you determined from the context. Then look up the word in a dictionary. After your meaning, write the dictionary definition that best fits the context.

1. newfangled (See page 488, The Connecticut Yankee's first speech.)
2. eclipse (See page 488, the Yankee's 2nd speech, and pages 490 and 491, the Yankee's speeches.)
3. devise (See page 490, the Yankee's 5th speech.)
4. humbug (See page 490 column 2, the Yankee's first and last speeches.)
5. homage (See page 491 column 2, Arthur's first speech.)
6. banish (See page 491 column 1, Arthur's 3rd speech and column 2, Arthur's first speech.)
7. humdrum (See page 493 column 2, Arthur's 2nd speech.)
8. gallivanting (See page 495, the Yankee's first speech.)
9. mythical (See page 496, the Yankee's 2nd speech.)
10. smithereens (See page 497 column 2, the Yankee's 4th speech.)

Developing Writing Skills

1. **Comparing Characters.** How were the Connecticut Yankee and Merlin similar? How were they different? Why were they in conflict with each other? Think about these questions and then write one or more paragraphs comparing the two characters. End by telling which character you found more interesting and why.

2. **Predicting Outcomes.** Go beyond the ending of this play. Write about the way the Yankee attempts to explain his experiences in

Camelot to his fiancée and the factory employees. Describe how the others will react to his story. Will anyone believe him? Write from two to four paragraphs explaining what you think might happen.

If you prefer, express your ideas in play form. Write an additional scene for the play, in which the Yankee talks with his fellow workers and his fiancée.

Developing Skills in Critical Thinking

Recognizing an Author's Purpose. Think back to Chapter 2 in this book, The Legend of King Arthur. What, if any, are the likenesses between Mark Twain's Camelot, set in 528 A.D., and Thomas Malory's, set in the Middle Ages? Twain was most likely familiar with Malory's legend when he wrote this play. Why do you think he made the changes he made? What was he trying to say in his play that was different from what Malory said in his book?

What tone does Mark Twain take toward Arthur and Merlin? Compare that to the tone Malory expressed. How does this difference in tone help Twain express his theme?

Developing Skills in Speaking and Listening

Giving a Dramatic Reading. Work with a group to present a portion of *A Connecticut Yankee in King Arthur's Court.* Each group member should select a role, study that character, and practice reading that character's lines aloud. Remember that two readers may be needed for the Connecticut Yankee—an older voice for the narrator and a younger voice for the dialog. Several group members should prepare music and produce background noises. Perhaps your music teacher can suggest melodies for the various musical themes asked for in the play.

The group should practice reading the selection together at least once. Make sure that every speaker talks loudly enough to be heard. Try to make your dialog sound as much like natural conversation as possible. Also, rehearse at least once, with sound effects if you plan to use them. Finally, present your reading to the other groups in your class.

Invasion from Mars

H. G. WELLS
From **The War of the Worlds**
Adapted by Howard Koch

This science fiction radio play uses radio news techniques to tell its story. As you read, think about why these techniques make such an impact upon those who are listening.

October 30, 1938: Shortly after 8 P.M., more than a million Americans, just tuning in their radios, heard a "news commentator" report that Martian invaders had landed in New Jersey. The monsters were reported armed with flames and poison gas and were marching toward New York. In a wave of mass hysteria, thousands of citizens fled to the highways. Churches overflowed. Soldiers and nurses volunteered for duty. A few of the terrified listeners tried to commit suicide; many had to be treated for shock.

The following selection is condensed and adapted from that famous radio broadcast. Announcements before, during, and after the show told listeners that the program was a regular Mercury Theatre presentation, starring Orson Welles. Perhaps, as you read, you'll understand the reactions of those who tuned in late—and didn't wait for the commercial.

ACT ONE

Sound. *Theme.*

Announcer. Ladies and gentlemen: the director of the Mercury Theatre on the Air, Orson Welles. . . .

Orson Welles. We know now that in the early years of the twentieth century this world was being watched closely by beings more intelligent than man and yet as mortal. We know now that, as human beings busied themselves about their various concerns, they were scrutinized and studied, perhaps almost as narrowly as a man with a microscope might scrutinize the tiny creatures that swarm and multiply in a drop of water.

Computerized image of Mars with exaggerated colors. NASA

Across an immense ethereal gulf, intellects vast, cool, and unsympathetic regarded this earth with envious eyes and slowly drew their plans against us. . . .

In the thirty-ninth year of the twentieth century, in the year 1938, came the great awakening.

It was near the end of October. Business was better. The war scare was over. On this particular evening thirty-two million people were listening in on radios. . . .

Fade in . . .

Announcer two. We now take you to the Meridian Room in the Hotel Park Plaza in downtown New York, where you will be entertained by the music of Ramon Raquello[1] and his orchestra.

Sound. *Spanish theme song . . . fades.*

Announcer two. Ladies and gentlemen, we interrupt our program of dance music to bring you a special bulletin from the Intercontinental Radio News. At twenty minutes before eight, Central Time, Professor Farrell of the Mount Jennings Observatory, Chicago, Illinois, reported observing several explosions of incandescent gas, occurring at regular intervals on the planet Mars. The gas seems to be moving toward the

---

1. **Ramon Raquello:** rä mōn' rä käl'yō.

earth with enormous velocity. Professor Pierson of the observatory at Princeton confirms Farrell's observation, and describes the phenomenon as (quote) like a jet of blue flame shot from a gun (unquote). We now return you to Ramon Raquello, playing the ever-popular "Stardust."

Sound. *Music.*

Announcer two. Ladies and gentlemen, following on the news given in our bulletin a moment ago, the Government Meteorological Bureau has requested the large observatories of the country to keep an astronomical watch on any further disturbances occurring on the planet Mars. Due to the unusual nature of this occurrence, we have arranged an interview with the noted astronomer Professor Richard Pierson, who will give us his views on this event. We now take you to the observatory at Princeton, New Jersey, where Carl Phillips, our commentator, will interview Professor Pierson.

Sound. *Entire interview in echo chamber; faint ticking sound.*

Phillips. Good evening, ladies and gentlemen. This is Carl Phillips, speaking to you from the observatory at Princeton. I am standing in a large semicircular room, pitch black except for an oblong split in the ceiling. Through this opening I can see a sprinkling of stars that cast a kind of frosty glow over the intricate mechanism of the huge telescope. The ticking sound you hear is the vibration of the clockwork. Professor Pierson stands directly above me on a small platform, peering through the giant lens. Professor, may I begin asking you questions?

Pierson. At any time, Mr. Phillips.

Phillips. Professor, would you please tell our radio audience exactly what you see as you observe the planet Mars through your telescope?

Pierson. Nothing unusual at the moment, Mr. Phillips. A red disk swimming in a blue sea. Transverse stripes across the disk. Quite distinct now because Mars happens to be at the point nearest the earth.

Phillips. In your opinion, what do these transverse stripes signify, Professor Pierson?

Pierson. Not canals, I can assure you, Mr. Phillips, although that's the popular conjecture of those who imagine Mars to be inhabited. From a scientific viewpoint the stripes are merely the result of atmospheric conditions peculiar to the planet.

Phillips. Then you're quite convinced that living intelligence as we know it does not exist on Mars? That there is no life on Mars?

Pierson. I should say the chances against it are a thousand to one.

Phillips. And yet how do you account for these gas eruptions occurring on the surface of the planet at such regular intervals?

Pierson. Mr. Phillips, I cannot account for them.

Phillips. By the way, Professor, for the benefit of our listeners, how far is Mars from the earth?

Pierson. Approximately forty million miles.

Phillips. Well, that seems a safe enough distance——Just a moment, ladies and gentlemen. Someone has just handed Professor Pierson a message. While he reads it, let me remind you that we are speaking to you from the observatory in Princeton, New Jersey, where we are interviewing the world-famous astronomer Professor Richard Pierson. . . . One moment, please. I shall read you the wire that Professor Pierson has just received from Dr. Gray of the Natural History Museum, New York. . . . "Seismograph registered shock of almost earthquake intensity occurring within a radius of twenty miles of Princeton. Please investigate. Signed. Lloyd Gray." . . . Professor Pierson, could this occurrence possibly have something to do with the disturbances observed on the planet Mars?

Pierson. Hardly, Mr. Phillips. This is probably a meteorite of unusual size, and its arrival at this particular time is merely a coincidence. However, we shall conduct a search as soon as daylight permits.

Phillips. Thank you, Professor. Ladies and gentlemen, we've just brought you a special interview with Professor Pierson, at Princeton Observatory. This is Carl Phillips speaking. We now return you to our New York studio.

Sound. *Fade in piano playing.*

Announcer two. Ladies and gentlemen, here is a special announcement from Trenton, New Jersey: "It is reported that at 8:50 P.M. a huge, flaming object, believed to be a meteorite, fell on a farm in the neighborhood of Grovers Mill, New Jersey, twenty-two miles from Trenton. The flash in the sky was visible within a radius of several hundred miles, and the noise of the impact was heard as far north as Elizabeth, New Jersey."

We have dispatched a special mobile unit to the scene, and we will have our commentator, Mr. Phillips, give you a word description as soon as he reaches the farm. In the meantime, we give you Bobby Millette and his orchestra, from the Hotel Martinet in Brooklyn.

Sound. *Swing band for twenty seconds . . . then cut.*

Announcer two. We take you now to Grovers Mill, New Jersey.

Sound. *Crowd noises . . . police sirens.*

Phillips. Ladies and gentlemen, this is Carl Phillips again, at the Wilmuth farm, Grovers Mill, New Jersey. Professor Pierson and I made the eleven miles from Princeton in ten minutes. Well, I . . . I hardly know where to begin, to paint for you a word picture of the strange scene before my eyes, like something out of a modern Arabian Nights.[2] I guess that's the—the *thing* directly in front of me, half-buried in a vast pit. Must have hit with terrific force. The ground is covered with splinters of a tree it struck on its way down. What I can see of the object itself doesn't look very much like a meteor, at least not the meteors I've seen. It looks more like a huge cylinder. It has a diameter of about thirty yards, and the metal on the sheath is—well, I've never seen anything like it. The color is sort of yellowish-white. Curious spectators are pressing close to the object, in spite of police efforts to keep them back.

Here's Mr. Wilmuth, owner of the farm. He may have some interesting facts to add . . . Mr. Wilmuth, would you please tell the radio audience as much as you remember of this rather unusual visitor that dropped in your backyard? Step closer, please. Ladies and gentlemen, this is Mr. Wilmuth.

Wilmuth. I was listenin' to the radio.

Phillips. Closer and louder, please.

Wilmuth. Yes, sir—while I was listenin' to the radio and kinda drowsin', that Professor fellow was talkin' about Mars, so I was half dozin' and half dreamin'——

Phillips. Yes, Mr. Wilmuth, and then you saw something?

Wilmuth. Not first off. First off I heard something.

Phillips. And what did you hear?

Wilmuth. A hissin' sound. Like this: sssssssss . . . kinda like a fourt' o'July rocket.

Phillips. Then what?

Wilmuth. I seen a kinda greenish streak and then zingo! Somethin' smacked the ground. Knocked me clear out of my chair!

Phillips. Thank you, Mr. Wilmuth. Thank you.

Wilmuth. Want me to tell you some more?

Phillips. No. That's quite all right, that's plenty. . . . Ladies and gentlemen,

---

2. **Arabian Nights**. A collection of fanciful Oriental folk tales

you've just heard Mr. Wilmuth, owner of the farm where this thing has fallen. I wish I could convey the atmosphere of this fantastic scene. Hundreds of cars are parked in a field in back of us. Police are trying to rope off the road leading to the farm, but cars are breaking right through. Their headlights throw an enormous spot on the pit where the object's half-buried. Some of the more daring souls are venturing near the edge. Their silhouettes stand out against the brightness of the metal.

Sound. *Faint humming.*

Phillips. One man wants to touch the thing . . . he's having an argument with a policeman. The policeman wins. . . . Now, ladies and gentlemen, there's something I haven't mentioned in all this excitement, but it's becoming more distinct. Perhaps you've caught it already on your radio. Listen: *(long pause)* . . . Do you hear it? It's a curious humming sound that seems to come from inside the object. I'll move the microphone nearer. Here. *(pause)* Now we're not more than twenty-five feet away. Can you hear it now? Oh, Professor Pierson!

Pierson. Yes, Mr. Phillips?

Phillips. Can you tell us the meaning of that noise inside the thing?

Pierson. Perhaps the unequal cooling of its surface.

Phillips. Do you still think it's a meteor, Professor?

Pierson. I don't know what to think. The metal casing is definitely not found on this earth. Friction with the earth's atmosphere usually tears holes in a meteorite. This thing is smooth and, as you can see, of cylindrical shape.

Phillips. Just a minute! Something's happening! Ladies and gentlemen, this is *terrific!* This end of the thing is beginning to flake off! The top is beginning to rotate like a screw! The thing must be hollow!

Voices. She's a-movin'!
  Look, the darn thing's opening up!
  Keep back there! Keep back, I tell you.
  Maybe there's men in it trying to escape!
  It's red hot—they'll burn to a cinder!
  Keep back there! Keep those idiots back!

Sound. *The clanking of a huge piece of falling metal.*

Voices. She's off! The top's loose!
  Look out there! Stand back!

Phillips. Ladies and gentlemen, this is the most terrifying thing I have ever witnessed. . . . Wait a minute! Someone's *crawling out of the top!* Someone or . . . *something!* I can see peering out of that black hole two luminous disks . . . are they eyes? It might be a face. It might be——

Sound. *Shout of awe from the crowd.*

Phillips. Good heavens, something's wriggling out of the shadow like a gray snake. Now it's another one, and another. They look like tentacles to me. There, I can see the thing's body. It's as large as a bear, and it glistens like wet leather. But that face. It—it's indescribable. I can hardly force myself to keep looking at it. The eyes are black and gleam like a serpent's. The mouth is V-shaped, with saliva dripping from rimless lips that seem to quiver and pul-sate. The monster's rising up! The crowd falls back. They've seen enough. This is the most extraordinary experience. I . . . I'm taking a new position as I talk. Hold on, will you please? I'll be back in a minute.

Announcer two. We are bringing you an eyewitness account of what's happening on the Wilmuth farm, Grovers Mill, New Jersey. We now return you to Carl Phillips at Grovers Mill.

Phillips. Ladies and gentlemen. (Am I on?) Ladies and gentlemen, here I am, back of a stone wall that adjoins Mr. Wilmuth's garden. From here I get a sweep of the whole scene. More state police have arrived. They're drawing up a cordon in front of the pit, about thirty of them. No need to push the crowd back now. They're willing to keep their distance. The captain is conferring with someone. We can't quite see who. Oh, yes, its Professor Pierson. Now the professor moves around one side, studying the object, while the captain and two policemen advance with something in their hands. I can see it now. It's a white handkerchief tied to a pole—a flag of truce. If those creatures know what that means—what anything means! *Wait!* Something's happening! I don't believe it——

Sound. *Hissing, followed by a humming that increases in intensity.*

Phillips. A humped shape is rising out of the pit. I can make out a small beam of light against a mirror. What's that? There's a jet of flame springing from that mirror, and it leaps right at the advancing men. It strikes them head on! Good Lord, they're turning into flame!

Sound. *Screams and unearthly shrieks.*

Phillips. Now the whole field's caught fire——

Sound. *Explosion.*

Phillips. The woods . . . the barns . . . the gas tanks of automobiles . . . it's spreading everywhere. It's coming this way. About twenty yards to my right——

Sound. *Crash of microphone . . . then dead silence. . . .*

Announcer two. Ladies and gentlemen, due to circumstances beyond our control, we are unable to continue the broadcast from Grovers Mill. Evidently there's some difficulty with our field transmission. However, we will return to that point at the earliest opportunity. In the meantime, we have a late bulletin from San Diego, California: "Professor Indelkoffer, speaking at a dinner of the California Astronomical Society, expressed the opinion that the explosions on Mars are undoubtedly nothing more than severe volcanic disturbances on the surface of the planet." We continue now with our piano interlude.

Sound. *Piano . . . then cut.*

Announcer two. Ladies and gentlemen, I have just been handed a message that came in from Grovers Mill by telephone. "At least forty people, including six State Troopers, lie dead in a field east of the village of Grovers Mill, their bodies burned and distorted beyond all possible recognition." The next voice you hear will be that of Brigadier General Montgomery Smith, commander of the State Militia at Trenton, New Jersey.

Smith. I have been requested by the governor of New Jersey to place the counties of Mercer and Middlesex under martial law. No one will be permitted to enter this area except by special pass. Four companies of State Militia will aid in the evacuation of homes within the range of military operations. Thank you.

Announcer. You have just been listening to General Montgomery Smith, commanding the State Militia at Trenton. In the meantime, further details of the catastrophe at Grovers Mill are coming in. The strange creatures, after unleashing their deadly assault, crawled back into their pit and made no attempt to prevent the efforts of firemen to recover the bodies and extinguish the fire.

We have been unable to establish any contact with our mobile unit at Grovers Mill, but we hope to be able to return you there at the earliest possible moment. In the meantime we take you—uh, just one moment please.

Sound. *Whisper, Long Pause.*

Announcer. Ladies and gentlemen, I have just been informed that we have finally established communication with an eyewitness of the tragedy. Professor Pierson has been located at a farmhouse near Grovers Mill where he has established an emergency observation post. As a scientist, he will give you his explanation of the calamity. Professor Pierson.

Pierson. Of the creatures in the rocket cylinder at Grovers Mill, I can give you no authoritative information—either as to their nature, their origin, or their purposes here on earth. Of their destructive instrument I might venture some explanation. For want of a better term, I shall refer to the mysterious weapon as a heat-ray. It's all too evident that these creatures have scientific knowledge far in advance of our own. It is my guess that they are able to generate an intense heat and project it against any object they choose by means of a polished parabolic mirror of unknown composition—much as the mirror of a lighthouse projects a beam of light.

Announcer. Thank you, Professor Pierson. Ladies and gentlemen, here is a bulletin from Trenton. It is a brief statement informing us that the charred body of Carl Phillips has been identified in a Trenton hospital.

Now here's another bulletin from Washington, D.C.: "Ten units of Red Cross emergency workers have been assigned to the headquarters of the State Militia stationed outside Grovers Mill, New Jersey." Here's a bulletin from State Police, Princeton Junction: "The fires at Grovers Mill and vicinity are now under control. Scouts report all quiet in the pit and no sign of life appearing from the mouth of the cylinder." . . . And now, ladies and gentlemen, in view of the gravity of the situation, we are turning over our entire broadcasting facilities to the State Militia at Trenton, at their request. . . . We take you now to the field headquarters of the State Militia near Grovers Mill, New Jersey.

Captain. This is Captain Lansing of the Signal Corps at Grovers Mill. Situation arising from the reported presence of certain individuals of unidentified nature is now under complete control.

The cylindrical object, which lies in a pit directly below our position, is surrounded on all sides by eight battalions of infantry, adequately armed with rifles and machine guns. All cause for alarm, if such cause ever existed, is now entirely unjustified. The things, whatever they are, do not even venture to poke their heads above the pit. I can see their hiding place plainly in the glare of the searchlights here. With all their reported resources, these creatures can scarcely stand up against heavy machine-gun fire. Anyway, it's an interesting outing for the troops. Now wait a minute! I see something on top of the cylinder. No, it's nothing but a shadow. Now the troops are on the edge of the Wilmuth farm. Seven thousand armed men closing in on an old metal tube. Wait, that wasn't a shadow! It's something moving . . . solid metal . . . kind of a shieldlike affair rising up out of the cylinder. . . . It's going higher and higher. Why, it's standing on legs— actually rearing up on a sort of metal framework. Now it's reaching above the trees and the searchlights are on it! Hold on! (*Long pause.*)

Announcer two. Ladies and gentlemen, I have a grave announcement to make. Incredible as it may seem, those strange beings who landed in the Jersey farmlands tonight are the vanguard of an invading army from the planet Mars. The battle, which took place tonight at Grovers Mill, has ended in one of the most startling defeats ever suffered by an army in modern times—seven thousand men armed with rifles and machine guns pitted against a single fighting machine of the invaders from Mars. One hundred and twenty known survivors. The rest strewn over the battle area from Grovers Mill to Plainsboro, crushed and trampled to death under the metal feet of the monster, or burned to cinders by its heat-ray. The monster is now in control of the middle section of New Jersey and has effectively cut the state through its center. Communication lines are down from Pennsylvania to the Atlantic Ocean. Railroad tracks are torn. Highways to the north, south, and west are clogged with frantic human traffic. By morning the fugitives will have swelled Philadelphia, Camden, and Trenton, it is estimated, to twice their normal population.

At this time, martial law prevails throughout New Jersey and eastern Pennsylvania. Bulletins too numerous to read are piling up in the studio here. Cables received from English, French, and German scientific bodies offer assistance. Astronomers report continued gas outbursts at regular intervals on planet Mars. Majority voice opinion that enemy will be reinforced by additional rocket machines. . . . Attempts made to locate Professor Pierson at Princeton, who has observed Martians at close range. It is feared he was lost in recent battle.

Langham Field, Virginia: "Scouting planes report three Martian machines visible above tree tops, moving north toward Somerville with population fleeing ahead of them. Heat-ray not in use. Although advancing at express-train speed, invaders pick their way carefully. They seem to be making conscious effort to avoid destruction of cities and countryside. However, they stop to uproot power lines, bridges, and railroad tracks. Their apparent objective is to crush resistance, paralyze communication, and disorganize human society." Here is a bulletin from Basking Ridge, New Jersey: "Coon hunters have stumbled on a second cylinder, similar to the first, embedded in the great swamp twenty miles south of Morristown. U.S. Army fieldpieces are proceeding from Newark to blow up second invading unit before cylinder can be opened and the fighting machines rigged. They are taking up positions in the foothills of Watchung[3] Mountains." Another bulletin from Langham Field, Virginia: "Scouting planes report enemy machines, now three in number, increasing speed northward, kicking over houses and trees in their evident haste to form a conjunction with their allies south of Morristown. Machines also sighted by telephone operator east of Middlesex within ten miles of Plainfield." Here's a bulletin from Winston Field, Long Island: "Fleet of army bombers carrying heavy explosive flying north in pursuit of enemy. . . ." Just a moment, please. Ladies and gentlemen, we've run special wires to the artillery line in nearby villages to give you direct reports in the zone of the advancing enemy. First we take you to the battery of the twenty-second field artillery, located in the Watchung Mountains. . . .

Officer. Projection thirty-nine degrees.

Gunner. Thirty-nine degrees.

Officer. Fire!

Sound. *Boom of Heavy Gun . . . Pause.*

Observer. A hit, sir! We got the tripod of one of them. They've stopped. The others are trying to repair it.

---

3. **Watchung** wä chung'

Sound. *Boom of heavy gun . . . pause.*

Observer. Can't see the shell land, sir. They're letting off a smoke.

Officer. What is it?

Observer. A black smoke, sir. Moving this way. Lying close to the ground. It's moving fast.

Officer. Put on gas masks. *(Pause.)* Get ready to fire. Shift to twenty-four meters.

Gunner. Twenty-four meters. *(Coughs.)*

Officer. Projection, twenty-four degrees. *(Coughs.)*

Gunner. Twenty-four degrees. *(Coughs.)*

Officer. Fire!

Sound. *Boom.*

Observer. Still can't see, sir. The smoke's coming nearer.

Officer. Get the range. *(Coughs.)*

Sound *Fade in coughing. Fade in sound of airplane motor.*

Commander. Army bombing plane, V-8-43, off Bayonne,[4] New Jersey. Lieutenant Voght, reporting to Commander Fairfax, Langham Field. . . . Enemy tripod machines now in sight. Reinforced by three machines from the Morristown cylinder. Six altogether. One par-

---

4. **Bayonne** bā yōn′

tially crippled machine believed hit by shell from army gun in Watchung Mountains. Guns now appear silent. A heavy black fog hanging close to the earth . . . of extreme density, nature unknown. No sign of heat-ray. Enemy now turns east, crossing Passaic[5] River into Jersey marshes. Another straddles the Pulaski Skyway. Evident objective is New York City. The machines are close together now, and we're ready to attack. Planes circling, ready to strike. A thousand yards and we'll be over the first—800 yards . . . 600 . . . 400 . . . 200 . . . There they go! The giant arm raised. . . . Green flash! They're spraying us with flame! Two thousand feet. Engines are giving out. No chance to release bombs. Only one thing left— drop on them, plane and all. Now we're diving on the first one. Now the engine's gone! . . .

Operator one. This is Bayonne, New Jersey, calling Langham Field. . . .

Operator two. This is Langham Field . . . go ahead. . . .

Operator one. Eight army bombers in engagement with enemy tripod machines over Jersey flats. Engines incapacitated by heat-ray. All crashed. One enemy machine destroyed. Enemy now discharging heavy black smoke in direction of——

---

5. **Passaic** pə sā′ik.

Operator three. This is Newark, New Jersey. . . . Warning! Poisonous black smoke pouring in from Jersey marshes. Reaches South Street. Gas masks useless. Urge population to move into open spaces . . . automobiles use routes 7, 23, 24 . . . avoid congested areas. Smoke now spreading over Raymond Boulevard. . . .

Sound. *Bells ringing over city gradually diminishing.*

Announcer. I'm speaking from the roof of Broadcasting Building, New York City. The bells you hear are ringing to warn the people to evacuate the city as the Martians approach. In last two hours, estimated three million people have moved out along the roads to the north. All communication with Jersey shore closed ten minutes ago. No more defenses. Our army wiped out. . . . This may be the last broadcast. We'll stay here to the end. . . . People are holding service below us . . . in the cathedral.

Sound. *Voices singing hymn.*

Announcer. Now I look down the harbor. All manner of boats, overloaded with fleeing population, pulling out from docks.

Sound. *Boat whistles.*

Announcer. Streets are all jammed. Noise in crowds like New Year's Eve in city. Wait a minute. . . . Enemy now in sight above the Palisades. Five great machines. First one is crossing river. I can see it from here, wading the Hudson like a man wading through a brook. . . . A bulletin's handed me. . . . Martian cylinders are falling all over the country. One outside Buffalo, one in Chicago, St. Louis . . . seem to be timed and spaced. . . . Now the first machine reaches the shore. He stands watching, looking over the city. His steel, cowlish head is even with the skyscrapers. He waits for the others. They rise like a line of new towers on the city's west side.

. . . Now they're lifting their metal hands. This is the end now. Smoke comes out . . . black smoke, drifting over the city. People in the streets see it now. They're running toward the East River . . . thousands of them, dropping in like rats. Now the smoke's spreading faster. It's reached Times Square. People trying to run away from it, but it's no use.

They're falling like flies. Now the smoke's crossing Sixth Avenue . . . Fifth Avenue . . . a hundred yards away . . . it's fifty feet . . . it . . . .

Developing Comprehension Skills

1. Professor Pierson says that it is "all too evident that these creatures have scientific knowledge far in advance of our own." Find at least three examples that support this statement.

2. Why does Captain Lansing of the Signal Corps say, on page 513, that the situation is under complete control? What is ironic about his statement? Identify two other instances of irony, when an expert says one thing and the exact opposite is true.

3. How do Professor Pierson and the other scientists quoted on the broadcast first explain the peculiar events that are happening all around? Why do they take so long to realize this is something new?

Reading Literature: Drama

1. **Following Time Order.** Events happen very quickly in this act. Sometimes two things happen simultaneously. This makes it difficult to keep track of what happens when. List the events and number them in the order in which they happen, not when they are described by the radio announcers. Events that happen simultaneously can be given the same number.

2. **Understanding Dialog.** To show differences in the personalities of his characters, the playwright has the characters use different types of language. For example, the radio announcers speak very formally.

Reread the dialog of the character named Wilmuth. What is his profession? How does Wilmuth's language contrast with the radio announcers' language? What level of language does Wilmuth use? Why does Phillips cut him off?

3. **Understanding Setting.** Because the play was written for radio, it is easy for the action to jump quickly from one place to another. What are some of the locations mentioned in the play? Why do you think the playwright chose to include so many areas of action, rather than concentrate on just one? What do you think he is trying to show?

4. **Using Description.** A radio play does not use sets, lighting, and costumes as a stage play does. Therefore, it must rely on other techniques to make the setting and actions clear for the listener. One technique is a strong use of description. Find two examples in which a long description explains a setting or an incident. Were you able to picture the place or event in your mind? Try to illustrate one setting or incident, for example, a Martian machine walking toward New York or the cylinder at Grovers Mill surrounded by infantry.

5. **Appreciating the Possibilities of Radio.** This play is more effective for radio than it would have been on stage. Why would you suppose that is true? Think about the many scene changes and the types of characters used to move the action along.

This play follows the format of a radio news show. How does this fact add to the believability of the invasion from Mars?

Developing Vocabulary Skills

Reviewing Word Parts, Dictionary Skills, and Context Clues. Read the following sentences drawn from the plays. Figure out the meaning of each underlined word by one of these methods:

  a. Knowing word parts
  b. Using the dictionary
  c. Using context clues indicated by clue words
  d. Using inference context clues

Write the meaning of the word and the method you used to find it.

1. I am standing in a large <u>semicircular</u> room, pitch black except for an oblong split in the ceiling.

2. That face is <u>indescribable</u>. I can hardly force myself to look at it.

3. Evidently, there's some trouble with our field <u>transmission</u>.

4. Those strange beings who landed in the Jersey farmlands tonight are the <u>vanguard</u> of an invading army from the planet Mars.

5. Enemy <u>tripod</u> machines are now in sight.

6. Oh, he's all right for parlor magic and such, but he never learned the <u>rudiments</u> of the big stuff.

7. You shall give me as payment one percent of all <u>revenue</u> I raise.

8. Have you brought any letters, any <u>documents</u>, any proofs that you are trustworthy and truthful?

9. Why, it was improper—<u>indecent</u>! Especially since I was engaged to a telephone operator from East Hartford, Connecticut.

10. I had <u>eradicated</u> slavery, knight-errantry, serfdom, and ignorance.

Developing Writing Skills

1. **Examining Illusions.** This first act of *Invasion from Mars* would take well under an hour to produce. The events it reports would take at least five or six times that long to take place. However, as you read or listen to the play, you get the feeling that you are finding out about the events as they happen. How does the play achieve this effect? How does it carry the audience forward in time without letting the audience notice the shift? Review the play to find some of the techniques the playwright uses to squeeze time. Then write one or more paragraphs explaining his methods. Give examples from the play.

2. **Creating an Alien.** Many science fiction plays, books, and movies are based on the idea of aliens visiting Earth. There have been evil aliens, as in this play and the movie *The Thing*. There have been friendly aliens, as in the movies *Close Encounters of the Third Kind* and *E.T.*

   Invent an evil or a friendly alien visiting Earth. In one or more paragraphs, describe your alien. Tell about its size, shape, color, and type of skin or fur. Does it have only one head? Are its organs for seeing, smelling, hearing, and eating all located on the head, like ours? Does it walk, ooze, or fly? How does it communicate with others?

Invasion from Mars

It's the end of the Earth as we know it. Or is it? What on Earth can possibly defeat the Martian machines?

H.G. WELLS
From **The War of the Worlds**
Adapted by Howard Koch

ACT TWO

Fade in . . .

Pierson. As I set down these notes on paper, I'm obsessed by the thought that I may be the last living man on earth. I have been hiding in this empty house near Grovers Mill—a small island of daylight cut off by black smoke from the rest of the world. All that happened before the arrival of these monstrous creatures now seems part of another life. I look down at my blackened hands, my torn shoes, my tattered clothes, and I try to connect them with a professor who lived at Princeton, and who, on the night of October 20, glimpsed through his telescope an orange splash of light on a distant planet. My wife, my colleagues, my students, my books, my observatory, my—my world . . . where are they? Did they ever exist? Am I Richard Pierson? What day is it? Do days exist without calendars? Does time pass when there are no human hands left to wind the clocks? . . . In writing down my daily life, I tell myself I shall preserve human history between the dark covers of this little book that was meant to record the movements of the stars. . . . But to write I must live, and to live I must eat. I find moldy bread in the kitchen and an orange not too spoiled to swallow. I keep watch at the window. From time to time I catch sight of a Martian above the black smoke.

The smoke still holds the house in its black coil. . . . Suddenly I see a Martian mounted on his machine, spraying the air with a jet of steam, as if to dissipate the smoke. I watch in a corner as his huge metal legs nearly brush against the house. Exhausted by terror, I fall asleep. . . . It's morning. Sun streams in the window . . . the black cloud of gas has lifted. I venture from the house. I make my way to a road. No traffic.

Here and there a wrecked car, baggage overturned, a blackened skeleton. I push on north. For some reason I feel safer trailing these monsters than running away from them. And I keep a careful watch. I must keep alive. I come to a chestnut tree and fill my pockets. Two days I wander in a vague northerly direction through a desolate world. Finally I notice a living creature—a small red squirrel in a beech tree. I stare at him and wonder. He stares back at me. I believe at that moment the animal and I shared the same emotion—the joy of finding another living being. . . . I push on north. I find dead cows and, beyond, the charred ruins of a dairy. The silo remains standing guard over the wasteland like a lighthouse deserted by the sea. Astride the silo perches a weathercock. The arrow points north. . . . *Fade out.*

Fade in . . .

Next day I came to a city vaguely familiar in its contours, yet its buildings are strangely dwarfed and leveled off, as if a giant had sliced off its highest towers. I reached the outskirts. Newark was undemolished but humbled by some whim of the advancing Martians. Presently, with an odd feeling of being watched, I caught sight of something crouching in a doorway. I made a step toward it, and it rose up and became a man—a man, armed with a large knife.

Stranger. Stop! Where did you come from?

Pierson. I come from . . . many places. A long time ago from Princeton.

Stranger. Princeton, huh? That's near Grovers Mill!

Pierson. Yes.

Stranger. Grovers Mill . . . *(laughs as at great joke)*. . . . There's no food here. This is my country—all this end of town down to the river. There's only food for one. . . . Which way are you going?

Pierson. I don't know. I guess I'm looking for—for people.

Stranger. Say, we're in the open here. Let's crawl into this doorway and talk.

Pierson. Have you seen any Martians?

Stranger. They've gone over to New York. At night the sky is alive with their lights. Just as if people were still living there. By daylight you can't see them. Five days ago a couple of them carried something big across the flats from the airport. I believe they're learning how to fly our airplanes.

Pierson. Then it's all over with humanity. Stranger, there's still you and I. Two of us left.

Stranger. They got themselves in solid; they wrecked the greatest country in the world. Those green stars, they're probably falling somewhere every night. They've only lost one machine. There isn't anything to do. We're licked.

Pierson. What will they do to us?

Stranger. I've thought it all out. Right now we're caught as we're wanted. The Martian only has to go a few miles to get a crowd on the run. But they won't keep doing that. They'll begin catching us, systematic like—keeping the best and storing us in cages and things. They haven't begun on us yet!

Pierson. Not begun!

Stranger. Not begun. All that's happened so far is because we don't have sense enough to keep quiet . . . bothering them with guns and such stuff and los-ing our heads and rushing off in crowds. Now instead of our rushing around blind, we've got to fix ourselves up according to the way things are now.

Pierson. But what is there to live for?

Stranger. There won't be any more con-certs for a million years or so, and no nice little dinners at restaurants. If it's amusement you're after, I guess the game's up.

Pierson. And what is there left?

Stranger. *Life* . . . that's what! I want to live. And so do you! We're not going to be exterminated. And I don't mean to be caught, either, and tamed and fat-tened and bred like an ox.

Pierson. What are you going to do?

Stranger. I'm going on . . . right under their feet. I gotta plan. We men as men are finished. We don't know enough. We gotta learn plenty before we get a chance. And we've got to live and keep free while we learn. I've thought it all out, see.

Pierson. Tell me the rest.

Stranger. Well, it isn't all of us that are made for wild beasts. That's why I watched you. All these little office workers that used to live in these houses—they'd be no good. They haven't any stuff to 'em. I've seen hundreds of 'em running wild to catch their commuters' train in the morning, for fear that they'd get fired if they didn't; running back at night, afraid they wouldn't be in time for dinner. Lives insured and a little invested in case of accidents. The Martians will be a godsend for those guys. Nice roomy cages, good food, careful breeding, no worries. After a week or so of chasing about the fields on empty stomachs, they'll come and be glad to be caught.

Pierson. You've thought it all out?

Stranger. You bet I have! And that isn't all. These Martians will make pets of some of them, train 'em to do tricks. Who knows? Get sentimental over the pet boy who grew up and had to be killed. And some, maybe, they'll train to hunt us.

Pierson. No, that's impossible. No human being——

Stranger. Yes, they will. There's people who'll do it gladly.

Pierson. In the meantime, you and I and others like us . . . where are we to live when the Martians own the earth?

Stranger. I've got it all figured out. We'll live underground. I've been thinking about the sewers. Then there's cellars, vaults, underground storerooms, railway tunnels, subways. And we'll get a bunch of strong men together. Get all the books we can—science books. That's where men like you come in, see? We'll raid the museums, we'll even spy on the Martians. We may not have to learn much before—just imagine this: four or five of their own fighting machines suddenly start off—and not a Martian in 'em. But *men*—men who have learned the way how. It may even be in our time. Imagine having one of them lovely things with its heat-ray wide and free! We'd turn it on Martians, we'd turn it on men. We'd bring everybody down to their knees.

Pierson. That's your plan?

Stranger. You and me and a few more of us, we'd own the world.

Pierson. I see.

Stranger. Say, what's the matter? Where are you going?

Pierson. Not to *your* world. Goodbye, Stranger. . . .

I came at last to the Holland Tunnel. I entered that silent tube, anxious to know the fate of the great city on the other side of the Hudson. Cautiously I came out of the tunnel and made my way up Canal Street.

I wandered up through the thirties and forties;[1] I stood alone on Times Square. I caught sight of a lean dog running down Seventh Avenue with a piece of dark brown meat in his jaws and a pack of starving mongrels at his heels. He made a wide circle around me, as though he feared I might prove a fresh competitor. I walked up Broadway past silent shop windows displaying their wares to empty sidewalks—past the Capitol Theater, silent, dark—past a shooting gallery, where a row of empty guns faced an arrested line of wooden ducks. I hurried on. Suddenly I caught sight of the hood of a Martian machine, standing somewhere in Central Park, gleaming in the late afternoon sun. An insane idea! I climbed a small hill above the pond at Sixtieth Street. From there I could see, standing in a silent row along the Mall, nineteen of those great metal Titans, their cowls empty, their steel arms hanging listlessly by their sides. I looked in vain for the monsters that inhabited those machines.

Suddenly, my eyes were attracted to the immense flock of black birds that hovered below me. They circled to the ground, and there before my eyes, stark and silent, lay the Martians, with the hungry birds pecking and tearing shreds of flesh from their dead bodies. When their bodies were examined in laboratories, it was found that they were killed by the disease bacteria against which their systems were unprepared . . . slain after all man's defenses had failed.

Strange it now seems to sit in my peaceful study at Princeton writing down this last chapter of the record begun at a deserted farm in Grovers Mill. Strange to see from my window the university spires dim and blue through an April haze. Strange to watch children playing in the streets. Strange to see young people strolling on the green, where the new spring grass heals the last black scars of a bruised earth. Strange to watch the sightseers enter the museum where the disassembled parts of a Martian machine are kept on public view. Strange when I recall the time I first saw it, bright and clean-cut, hard and silent, under the dawn of that last unforgettable day.

Sound. *Music*

---

1. **Thirties and Forties.** These numbers refer to street numbers in New York City.

Developing Comprehension Skills

1. This act shifts from focusing on many characters, as in Act I, to concentrating almost totally on one character. Who is that person? How does he "speak" to the audience?

2. How has the story changed to make possible the shift of focus described in question 1? How does this change affect tone and mood?

3. At the beginning of Act II, Pierson is alone. He is thinking and writing of how his life and surroundings have changed. What does he see around him? How would you feel if you were in Pierson's place?

4. Pierson informs us that the Martians were destroyed by disease bacteria, which their bodies could not fight. Reread the last paragraph, in which he describes life at present. What does Pierson find strange about it? What does the paragraph suggest about how people have recovered from the Martian invasion?

Reading Literature: Drama

1. **Recognizing Plot Development.** Make a plot diagram for this play. Which events belong in each of the five parts: introduction, rising action, climax, falling action, and resolution?

2. **Understanding Conflict.** Was the conflict in *Invasion from Mars* internal or external? Who or what was the source of that conflict? How was it resolved?

3. **Understanding the Central Character.** Professor Pierson is the central character in this play. As the play progresses, he changes. How is Professor Pierson different at the end of the play than he was in the beginning? Think about how he reacted on page 507 to the question about the seismograph reading. Also, think about your answer for question 3 in Developing Comprehension Skills, Act I (page 517).

4. **Examining Form.** Act II of *Invasion from Mars* has a slower, more thoughtful quality that Act I had. Think about this change of pace and the changes in the numbers of characters. Why did the playwright develop this act differently from the other act?

5. **Identifying Theme.** What general statement is this play making about life? What do Pierson's encounters with the squirrel and the Stranger have to do with the theme? Explain your answer.

Developing Vocabulary Skills

Reviewing Context Clues. The following words are located in the given paragraphs of the play. Read the paragraph in which each word is found. On your paper, write which context clue helped you figure out the meaning of the word. Also, write the meaning of the word.

1. hysteria   (page 504, paragraph 1)
   a. antonym   b. main idea   c. restatement

2. scrutinize   (page 504, Orson Welles' first speech.)
   a. words in a series   b. synonym   c. cause and effect

3. distinct   (page 506, column 2, Mr. Pierson's second speech)
   a. main idea   b. antonym   c. words in a series

4. gravity   (page 513, line 1)
   a. words in a series   b. example   c. main idea

5. incapacitated   (page 516, Operator One, second speech)
   a. restatement   b. antonym   c. cause and effect

6. dissipate   (page 520, column 2, paragraph 2)
   a. definition   b. comparison   c. cause and effect

Developing Writing Skills

1. **Developing Techniques for Radio Scripts.** The audience of a radio play cannot see the setting or the action of the play. There are, however, ways in which the playwright can make up for this difficulty. In some ways, in fact, the playwright can take advantage of the situation. List three or more ways in which the playwright can overcome the problem of the audience not seeing the action. Prove your point with examples from either of the two plays in this chapter.

2. **Comparing Plays.** In *A Connecticut Yankee in King Arthur's Court*, the central character thinks he can conquer Merlin and change King Arthur's world through his inventions. At first he seems successful. In *Invasion from Mars*, the Martians try to overcome Earth. At first, their superior weapons and machines suggest they will be successful. Are the authors of these two plays concerned with similar themes? If so, in what ways are the themes alike? How are they different? Can you find

other ways in which these plays correspond to each other? Write one or more paragraphs explaining what you have discovered.

3. **Presenting Your Opinion.** When this radio play was first presented, people believed that Martians really had invaded Earth. Some reacted out of fright and tried to run away. Think about what would happen if this play were presented over the radio now. Do you think that people would react the way they did in 1938? Why or why not? Be sure to include strong, solid reasons to support your argument.

4. **Writing a Radio Script.** For the six o'clock radio news, write a three- or four-minute broadcast describing the landing on Earth of life from another planet. If you created an alien for Developing Writing Skills, 2, for Act I (on page 519), you may use that creature in this script. If you like, include an interview with an eye-witness or an authority.

Developing Skills in Critical Thinking

Evaluating a Radio Play. You have read two complete radio plays in this chapter. If you were going to select a third one to include, what qualities would you look for in a radio play? List your requirements. Think about characters, sound effects, and any other characteristics you consider necessary for a good radio play.

Developing Skills in Speaking and Listening

Presenting A Monolog. Sometimes in a play there is only one character in a scene. The character talks to himself—and the audience. Such a speech is called a **monolog**. At the beginning of Act II of *Invasion from Mars*, Professor Pierson has a long monolog. At the end of the act he has another monolog.

A monolog can be tricky to present, especially in a radio play. Because there is only one person talking, there is less variety in voices and action. An audience can become bored quickly. To avoid boring the audience, the speaker must put strong feeling into his or her voice. The speaker's voice must show changes in mood, even if they are slight.

Work in small groups to practice reading either of Pierson's monologs. Discuss qualities of your speech that you can change, such as the speed with which you talk, the pitch of your voice, and its loudness. Then take turns reading the monolog and applying what you discussed.

Using Your Skills in Reading Plays

Read the following part of a play. List the characters in the scene, and briefly explain the goal of each character. What conflict do you see in the goals? Also, identify the stage directions.

ARTHUR AND GUINEVERE

(As the curtain opens, Arthur and Merlin are seated at Arthur's Round Table.)

Arthur. Merlin, my kingdom is in order, and all my subjects are happy. This castle's getting a little empty, though. I guess it's about time I got married.

Merlin. Who's the lucky lady?

Arthur (smiling). The most beautiful woman I've ever seen— Lady Guinevere!

Merlin (alarmed). Guinevere! Oh, no! She's not right for you! Let me fix you up with someone you'd be happier with.

Arthur. Arthur. No, I've made my choice. Guinevere is the only woman I'd ever want to marry. Go see if it's okay with her father, and let's get this show on the road! (He waves Merlin out.)

Using Your Comprehension Skills

The scene above contains dialog that is modern and informal. What effect does the level of language have on the mood of the play? What do you suppose might have been the author's purpose in using this language? Can you suggest a reason for writing a play about King Arthur in modern speech?

Which words in the scene above are not in keeping with a formal court scene? How might you change Arthur's words to create a greater air of royalty and authority?

Using Your Vocabulary Skills

Each of these sentences is from a selection in this book. In each, there is an underlined word. If you do not know the meaning of the word, which would be the best way to discover it? For each word, write one of the following: word parts, context clues, the dictionary.

1. You shall appoint me your <u>perpetual</u> minister and executive.
2. The farmer said he thought that was <u>unsound</u> reasoning.
3. The bishop looked upon the man with a <u>tranquil</u> eye.
4. The prisoner began <u>zealously</u> to study languages, philosophy, and history. He fell on these subjects with hunger.
5. Keesh strode into the village. There was importance in his step and <u>arrogance</u> in his speech.

Using Your Writing Skills

Choose one of the assignments below.

1. You have learned that, when reading drama, you should cooperate with the playwright and enter his or her created world. Write from one to three paragraphs describing the world created in *A Connecticiut Yankee in King Arthur's Court* or *Invasion From Mars*. Tell how the created world is different from your own.
2. Write one scene of an original play version of the King Arthur legend. If you like, you may use informal English. However, before you write, decide on the tone you will use. It might be, for example, admiring or mocking. Decide, also, on the mood you want your readers to get from your scene. Then, as you write, choose your words carefully to match your tone and mood.

Using Your Skills in Critical Thinking

Compare these three types of literature: short stories, nonfiction, and plays. How are the three alike? How are they different? Think of several categories you could use for discussing these three types of literature. On your paper, set up as many columns as you have chosen categories. Then fill in the columns with information about each of the three.

Handbook for Reading and Writing

Literary Terms

Alliteration. The repetition of consonant sounds is alliteration. The repeated sounds usually come at the beginnings of several words in a series of words. Alliteration can be used in prose and poetry.

> He clasps the crag with crooked hands;
> Close to the sun in lonely lands.
> ("The Eagle," page 286)

For more about alliteration, see pages 112 and 113.

Assonance. The repetition of vowel sounds within words is called assonance. Assonance can stress a certain mood and give a musical quality to the work. Notice how the repetition of *o*'s in this example stresses the feeling of smallness.

> The immense, the unknown, enfolded me.
> ("The Story of My Life," page 377)

For more about assonance, see pages 114 and 115.

Autobiography. A story that a person writes about his or her own life is an autobiography. It is written from the first-person point of view. An example of an autobiography is "The Story of My Life" by Helen Keller (pages 370 to 380).

For more about autobiography, see page 358.

Biography. A true account of a real person's life is a biography. It includes important events in a person's life and lets the reader know what the person was like. "Matthew A. Henson" (pages 392 to 400) is an example of a biography.

For more on biography, see page 384.

Character. Each person or animal who takes part in the action of a story, poem, or play is a character. Usually a story has one or two most important characters, called *major characters. Minor characters* would include everyone else in the selection. In "The Rocking Donkey" (pages 222 to 227), Esmeralda is a major character. Mr. Snye is a minor character.

For more about characters, see pages 3, 63, and 186.

See also *Character Trait.*

Character Trait. A quality that a character shows by his or her actions, statements, or thoughts is a character trait. For example, in "The Bet" (pages 165 to 169), the banker exhibits the character trait of greed.

Chronological Order. See *Time Order*.

Climax. The turning point of a story is called the climax. It often involves an important event, decision, or discovery. In "The Old Soldier," for example, the climax comes when the doctor discovers that the old soldier was a Hessian (page 192).

For more about climax, see page 135. See also *Plot*.

Comparison. A writer uses a comparison to show how two different things have something in common. In this example, children are compared to chicks.

> As he played, there came a sound of little hands clapping and feet pattering, of small voices chattering, like chicks in a barnyard when corn and grain are scattering. ("The Pied Piper of Hamelin," page 24)

See also *Contrast, Metaphor, Simile*.

Concrete Poem. See *Poetry*.

Conflict. The struggle that a character faces creates the conflict in a story. That struggle may be within one character, between two characters, or between a character and other forces. Conflict is necessary in any story or play.

For more about conflict, see pages 186 and 187.

See also *External Conflict, Internal Conflict*, and *Plot*.

Contrast. Writers often use contrast to show how different two things are. In "Hearts and Hands," contrast is used to tell about two passengers on the train.

> Among the newcomers were two young men, one of handsome presence with a bold, frank countenance and manner; the other a ruffled, glum–faced person, heavily built and roughly dressed. The two were handcuffed together. (page 158)

See also *Comparison*.

Description. In a description, a writer gives details that help the reader imagine a character, setting, or action. Often the details suggest a visual image, as in this example:

> Before him was our uncle Khosrove, an enormous man with a powerful head of black hair and the largest mustache in the San Joaquin Valley.
> ("The Summer of the Beautiful White Horse," page 213)

A description may also provide details of sound, smell, touch, or other senses. Sometimes a description lists actions or attitudes of a character.

See also *Direct Description* and *Indirect Description*.

Dialog. Conversation between characters in a story or play is called dialog. In writing, the exact words are set off by quotation marks.

"Will you keep it a secret?" asked the first man. "If so, I will tell you in a few words how we will bring it about."

"I promise, by my honor," said the other, "that I will not betray you." ("How the Three Young Men Found Death," page 143.)

For more about dialog, see page 483.

Direct Description. When a writer states how a character looks or acts, he or she is using direct description.

She was a cream-colored mare with a black forelock, mane, and tail and a black stripe along the middle of her back. Tall, slender, high-spirited, I thought then—I think now that she was the most beautiful of horses. ("I Get a Colt To Break In," page 359)

For more about direct description, see page 208.

See also *Description* and *Indirect Description*.

Drama. A story that is meant to be performed before an audience is a drama, or play. A drama is told through the words and actions of its characters. The word *drama* also refers in general to this type of writing. Like other forms of fiction, drama uses characters, setting, plot, dialog, and sometimes a narrator. In addition, a written drama makes use of stage directions and a cast of characters.

A long play is divided into parts called acts. Each act is divided into smaller scenes. In Chapter 7, there are two examples of drama. "A Connecticut Yankee in King Arthur's Court" is a one-act play. "The Invasion of Mars" is a two-act play.

For more about drama, see pages 482 and 483.

See also *Stage Directions*.

Essay. A type of nonfiction in which the writer expresses his or her own opinion is called an essay. An example of an essay is "April and Robins" by Hal Borland (page 446).

For more about the essay, see pages 444 and 445.

See also *Nonfiction*.

External Conflict. A struggle between two characters, or between a character and a force such as nature, is called external conflict. There are three external conflicts in "Spotted Eagle and Black Crow" (pages 35 to 39): the jealousy between the two warriors, Spotted Eagle's struggle to escape from the narrow ledge, and the battle between the Fox and Pahani tribes.

For more about external conflict, see page 186.

See also *Conflict*, *Internal Conflict*, and *Plot*.

Falling Action. Falling action is that part of the plot in which the story draws to a conclusion. It follows the climax. For example, in "The Six Horsemen" the climax occurs when Fadebi rescues Nassa from the fortress. The falling action occurs when Fadebi's five companions use their magic to get them across the river and away from Ballo (pages 46 to 47).

For more on falling action, see page 135. See also *Plot* and *Climax*.

Fiction. A work of fiction is the one that comes from the writer's imagination. Some types of fiction are short stories, legends, and drama. An example of fiction is "The Legend of King Arthur" (pages 68 to 94).

Figurative Language. A way of speaking or writing that looks at familiar things in a fresh, new way is called figurative language. Some particular kinds of figurative language are called figures of speech. Metaphor, simile, personification, and hyperbole are four figures of speech. They are all examples of figurative language.

Metaphor	The trees were soldiers, standing straight and tall.
Simile	The trees stood as tall as skyscrapers.
Personification	The trees pushed the clouds out of their way.
Hyperbole	A year went by as we stood there, waiting for the cat to climb down.

For more about Figurative Language, see pages 121 to 129.

See also *Hyperbole, Metaphor, Personification,* and *Simile.*

Humor. Writing that is funny has the quality of humor. A particular action in a story can suggest humor. For example, in "Lazy Peter" (pages 51 to 55), Peter's tricks make fun of the greedy farmer. A certain setting, character, or use of words can also suggest humor. "Casey at the Bat" (pages 306 to 308) has examples of all of these kinds of humor.

See also *Hyperbole* and *Irony.*

Hyperbole. An obvious exaggeration is called hyperbole. It gives the reader a humorous image of what the writer is describing.

And the much-despised Blakey "tore the cover off the ball."
("Casey at the Bat," page 306)

For more about hyperbole, see pages 128 and 129.

Imagery. Imagery is any kind of description that makes an object or experience so real that we can imagine it with our senses. Writers use sensory details to help us see, feel, smell, hear, or taste the things they describe.

In April, the party made another attempt in the face of icy winds that bore down from the North under the cold but continuous glare of a twenty-four-hour sun on blindingly white snow.
("Matthew A. Henson," page 395)

For more about imagery, see page 280. See also *Figurative Language.*

Indirect Description. A writer who states directly how a character looks or acts is using direct description. Any other way in which the writer leads you to understand the character is indirect description. A character's comments may also tell about himself or herself. For example, this speaker's treatment of his colt shows his patience and love for the animal.

> He went off downtown with my father, and I started away with my colt. I fed, I led, I cleaned her, gently, as if she were made of glass; she was playful and willing, a delight. ("I Get a Colt to Break In," page 361)

A reader can also learn about a character through seeing how other characters react to him or her.

> And curiosity was so strong on the men that the whole council, Klosh-Kwan to the fore, rose up and went to the igloo of Keesh. He was eating, but he received them with respect and seated them according to their rank.
> ("The Story of Keesh," page 179)

For more about indirect description, see page 369.
See also *Description*, *Direct Description*.

Internal Conflict. The struggle within a character's own self is called internal conflict. This struggle usually involves a decision the character must make. In "The Big Wave" (pages 199 to 207), Jiya must decide where he will live.

For more about internal conflict, see page 187.
See also *Conflict*, *External Conflict*, *Plot*.

Introduction. The first part of the plot is the introduction. It introduces the reader to the characters and the setting.

> It was a dark autumn night. The old banker was pacing from corner to corner in his room, recalling to his mind the party he had given in the autumn fifteen years before. ("The Bet," page 165)

For more about the introduction, see page 135.
See also *Plot*.

Irony. The contrast between what is expected, or what seems to be true, and what actually happens is called irony. For example, in "How the Three Young Men Found Death," the young men boast that they will kill death. Instead, they kill each other. The story ends with the ironic statement:

> And soon, like their friend, the two found Death. (page 144)

For more on irony, see pages 12 and 162.

Legend. A legend is a story about notable men and women of the past. Legends are often a mixture of fact and fiction. They reflect the values of the people who told the stories. An example of a legend is "Spotted Eagle and Black Crow" (pages 35 to 40).

For more on legends, see pages 2 and 3.

Lyric Poem. See *Poetry*.

Metaphor. A metaphor is a figure of speech that compares two unlike things having something in common. The comparison is made without the use of *like* or *as*, as in a simile. In the following example, Lincoln is compared to a pine tree.

> Lincoln was the green pine.
> Lincoln kept on growing.
> ("Abraham Lincoln," page 340)

For more about metaphor, see pages 124 and 125.
See also *Simile*.

Mood. The feeling you get as you are reading a selection is called the mood of that selection. *Sad* and *cheerful* are two possible moods. The mood of "I Was Born Today" (pages 264 to 265), for example, is hopeful.

For more about mood, see pages 187 and 271.

Narrative Poem. See *Poetry*.

Narrator. A narrator is the person who tells the story. There are different types of narrators. The first-person narrator is usually a character in the story, such as the boy in "The Disappearing Man" (pages 231 to 234). The third-person narrator tells the story from outside the story, as in "King John and the Abbot" (pages 15 to 18).

There are two types of third-person narrator. A narrator who knows how all the characters think and feel is *omniscient*, as in "The Big Wave" (pages 199 to 207). The third-person narrator may also be *limited*, telling only what one character thinks and feels, as in "The Rocking Donkey" (pages 222 to 227).

For more about narrator, see pages 3 and 135.
See also *Point of View*.

Nonfiction. Writing that tells about real people, actual places, and true events is called nonfiction. It is based on fact. An example of nonfiction is "Maria Tallchief" (pages 404 to 409).

For more about nonfiction, see pages 352 and 353.
See also *Autobiography*, *Biography*, and *Essay*.

Onomatopoeia. The use of words that sound like what they describe is called onomatopoeia.

> Back up he swims
>   Past sting-ray and shark,
>   Out with a zoom,
>   A whoop, a bark;
> ("Seal," page 278)

For more about onomatopoeia, see page 120.

Personification. A figure of speech that gives human qualities to animals, objects, or ideas is personification.

The Mountain and the squirrel
Had a quarrel,
And the former called the latter "Little
   prig;"
("The Mountain and the Squirrel," page
288)

For more about personification, see pages 126 and 127.

Play. See *Drama*.

Plot. The sequence of events in a story is the plot. In most stories, one event follows the next. Usually, each thing that happens is caused by what comes before it. The parts of the plot include the introduction, the rising action, the climax, the falling action, and the resolution.

For more about plot, see pages 63 and 135.

See also *Introduction*, *Rising Action*, *Climax*, *Falling Action*, and *Resolution*.

Poetry. Poetry is a form of writing in which words are arranged in lines rather than sentences. The sounds of the words and the way they are arranged are important. The lines are arranged in groups called stanzas. "The Dream Keeper" (page 249) has one stanza of eight lines. "Paul Revere's Ride" (pages 330 to 334), in contrast, has fourteen stanzas of varying lengths.

Sometimes a poet writes a poem in a special shape. This is called a *concrete poem*. "Seal" (page 278) is an example.

For more about poetry, see pages 242 and 243.

See also *Rhyme*, *Rhyme Scheme*, *Rhythm*, and *Stanza*.

Point of View. A story may be told from several points of view. This term refers to how the narrator tells the story. It may be a first-person point of view or a third-person point of view. "The Summer of the Beautiful White Horse" (pages 211 to 217) is told from a first-person point of view. "Richard the Lion-Hearted" (pages 8 to 11) is told from a third-person point of view.

For more about point of view, see pages 135 and 353.

See also *Narrator*.

Repetition. When a word or a group of words is repeated in a selection, the writer is using repetition. Poets often repeat a word or phrase to give special emphasis to a thought or action. Here, for example, repetition stresses the suspense of a foul shot.

The ball . . .
Plays it coy . . .
And then
      And then
            And then,
Right before ROAR-UP,
Dives down and through.
("Foul Shot," page 310)

For more on repetition, see page 219.

Resolution. The loose ends in a story are tied up in the resolution. It is the last part of the plot.

> Jiya smiled. Happiness began to live in him again. The good food warmed him, and his body welcomed it. Around him the love of the people who received him glowed like a warm and welcoming fire upon the hearth. ("The Big Wave," page 207)

For more about resolution, see page 135.
See also *Plot*.

Rhyme. The repetition of sounds at the ends of words is called rhyme. In poetry, rhyming words usually come at the ends of lines. The rhyming words in this example are *wore* and *more*, and *wear* and *spare*.

> The golden brooch my mother wore
> She left behind for me to wear;
> I have no thing I treasure more:
> Yet, it is something I could spare.
> ("The Courage That My Mother Had," page 253)

For more about rhyme, see pages 116, 117, and 243.
See also *Rhyme Scheme*.

Rhyme Scheme. Rhyme schemes are the different patterns in which rhyme can be used. When a rhyme scheme is written, different letters of the alphabet are used to stand for different rhyming endings. Here is an example of a rhyme scheme:

> Behold the hippopotamus! *a*
> We laugh at how he looks to us, *a*
> And yet in moments dank and grim *b*
> I wonder how we look to him. *b*
> Peace, peace, thou hippopotamus! *a*
> We really look all right to us, *a*
> As you no doubt delight the eye *c*
> Of other hippopotami. *c*
> ("The Hippopotomus," page 295)

For more about rhyme scheme, see pages 117, 270, and 271.
See also *Rhyme*.

Rhythm. The pattern of accented syllables in poetry is called rhythm. The accented or stressed syllables may be marked with /, while the unaccented or light syllables may be marked with ⌣.

> Some primal termite knocked on wood
> And tasted it, and found it good
> And that is why your cousin May
> Fell through the parlor door today.
> ("The Termite," page 294)

For more about rhythm, see pages 118, 119 and 242.

Rising Action. The second part of the plot is the rising action. In this part it becomes clear that the characters face a problem, or conflict. One event follows the other. In "The Disappearing Man" the rising action occurs when Larry witnesses a man dashing into an alley, followed by two police officers (page 231).

For more about rising action, see page 135.

See also *Plot*.

Sequence. A series of events or ideas may be put in an order, called sequence. Often the writer tells a story in chronological sequence, or time order. Sometimes a selection, such as an essay, has ideas arranged in a logical sequence. The writer might begin with an opinion and follow it with reasons to back it up.

For more on sequence, see page 136.

See also *Time Order*.

Setting. The time and place in which the events of the story occur are referred to as the setting. All stories have a setting, but some are described in more detail than others.

Kino lived on a farm that lay on the side of a mountain in Japan. The mountain rose so steeply out of the ocean that there was only a strip of sandy shore at its foot. Upon this strip was a small fishing village where Kino's father sold his vegetables and rice. ("The Big Wave," page 199)

For more about setting, see pages 3 and 63.

Short Story. A short story is a work of fiction short enough to be read at one sitting. It usually tells about one major character and one set of events. "Hearts and Hands" (pages 158 to 160) is an example of a short story.

For more about the short story, see page 134.

See also *Fiction*.

Simile. A simile is a figure of speech that compares two things that are not alike, but have something in common. The comparison uses the word *like* or *as*.

Cats sleep fat.
They spread out comfort underneath them
Like a good mat.
("Catalog," page 274)

For more about simile, see pages 122 and 123.

See also *Metaphor*.

Stage Directions. In drama, stage directions guide the actors in performing the play. These directions may tell the actors how to speak the words or what background sounds or actions are needed. In "A Connecticut Yankee in King Arthur's Court," the following stage directions may be found: *angry voices fade off mike, birds twittering gayly, yawning, alarmed, suspiciously*. (page 489)

For more about stage directions, see page 483.

Stanza. A group of lines in poetry is called a stanza. There is usually a space between two stanzas of a poem. An example of a poem with several stanzas is "Western Wagons" (page 338).

For more about stanza, see page 254.

Theme. The main idea that the writer wants the reader to understand from a selection is the theme of the selection. In "Lazy Peter and His Three-Cornered Hat" (pages 51 to 55), the theme is that one should not be greedy.

For more about theme, see page 187.

Time Order. Events in a story follow a certain order. It is important to understand which event comes first and how it causes the next event. The progression of events is called time order. For example,

look at "The Pied Piper of Hamelin" (pages 22 to 25). From the time the Pied Piper entered the town to the time he left with the children, the events follow one another in time order.

For more about time order, see pages 136 and 353.

Tone. The author's attitude toward what is being said is the tone. For example, in "Borrow the Army" (page 436), Lincoln's tone is sarcastic.

For more about tone, see page 353.

Summary of Comprehension Skills

Cause and Effect. Events are often related by cause and effect. The first event causes the second event. The second event, then, is the effect of the first event.

Some clue words tell the reader to look for cause and effect relationships. Among these clue words are: *because, since, so that, in order that,* and *if—then.*

Here is an example of a cause and an effect. The clue phrase is *so that.*

Mark reread all of his class notes so that he would do well on the test.

For more about understanding cause and effect, see pages 136 and 137.

Chronological Order. See *Sequence.*

Conclusions. See *Inferences.*

Connotation and Denotation. See *Slanted Writing.*

Details. See *Main Idea.*

Fact and Opinion. Writers often combine fact and opinion. Facts are statements that can be proved. Opinions, on the other hand, are statements that cannot be proved. They only express the writer's beliefs.

Sometimes writers list facts that lead you to believe their opinions, as in the example below. The opinion is underlined. Following the opinion are four sentences that state facts.

<u>Some of the most unusual scenery in the world is in our national parks.</u> The borders of Grand Canyon Park include most of the mile-deep canyon. In Yellowstone Park, visitors can see numerous geysers. Petrified Forest Park holds both ancient trees that have changed to rock and a brightly colored desert. Hawaii Volcanoes Park has two active volcanoes.

For more about separating fact and opinion, see page 354.

Figurative Language. Figurative language is a way of speaking or writing that forces the listener or reader to look at familiar things in a new way. While the words say one thing, their meaning can be very different.

For example, when people tell you to take a statement with a grain of salt, they don't want you to sprinkle salt on words. The expression "with a grain of salt" means you should not take something seriously. To understand this example of figurative language, you had to think about the words and look for a logical meaning.

For more about understanding figurative language, see pages 121 to 129.

Inferences and Conclusions. An inference is a logical guess based on evidence. You are often expected to make inferences as you read. You must infer what the writer hasn't said from what he or she has said. For example, a writer could describe this situation: A girl walks down a school hall past a boy who says "Hello." The girl doesn't answer. From this information, the reader might infer either that the girl did not hear the boy or that she didn't want to speak to him.

A conclusion is based on several inferences. Suppose that the writer added this information to the situation described above: A door slams loudly as the girl walks past, but she doesn't react. Then she stops to talk with another girl and watches the girl's lips closely during the conversation. From all these clues, the reader could draw the conclusion that the first girl was deaf.

For more about making inferences and drawing conclusions, see pages 64, 65, and 244.

Logical Sequence. See *Sequence*.

Main Idea. A paragraph is a group of sentences that work together to tell about one idea. This idea is the main idea. The main idea is often stated in one sentence called the topic sentence. The topic sentence may be at the beginning, middle, or end of a paragraph. Some paragraphs have no topic sentence at all. However, these paragraphs still have main ideas. All the sentences in a paragraph should be related to the main idea.

Read the following paragraph. The topic sentence has been underlined.

<u>Software for word processing can speed up your writing.</u> If you misspell a word, you can make the correction cleanly. If you are on your fifth sentence and want to add words to the first sentence, you can move everything else to fit in the new words. If you decide to change the order of sentences, you can rearrange your words without retyping them.

The main idea was stated in the topic sentence. The rest of the sentences gave details about the main idea.

For more about identifying the main idea of a paragraph, see pages 4 and 5.

Opinions. See *Fact and Opinion*.

Outcomes. When you make a reasonable guess about what will happen next in a story, you are predicting an outcome.

Some outcomes are easy to predict. For example, when you hear the band at the ball game play "The Star-Spangled Banner," you can predict that the game will start soon. Predicting other outcomes is not so simple. For example, you would not know at the beginning of the ball game, which team will win.

When you predict outcomes, base your guess on clues the writer gives you. To make a logical prediction, you should use what you know about the character, the plot, the setting, and your personal knowledge of what people usually do in certain situations.

For more about predicting outcomes, see page 245.

Paragraphs. See *Main Idea*.

Purpose. Before beginning any writing, an author decides what he or she wants the writing to do. Some purposes, or reasons for writing, are to entertain, to express feelings, to inform, to persuade, and to make people laugh. The topic of the writing and its organization are affected by the purpose of the writing. So are the choice of such elements as character, plot, and setting. A reader should be aware of the writer's purpose in order to understand the writing completely.

For example, the purpose of "The Disappearing Man" is to challenge the reader to solve the mystery with the same clues as the hero has. For that reason, the author tells the reader all the important clues and very few other details. He saves the explanation of the hero's thinking until the very end of the story.

For more about author's purpose, see pages 484 and 485.

Sequence. To understand a selection, it is important to recognize the sequence, or order, in which the information is presented. Three kinds of sequence are natural order, time order, and logical order.

Natural order is often used in descriptions. In natural order, a writer talks about things in the order in which you would notice them. In the play "Invasion from Mars," for example, Phillips describes "the thing" as he sees it.

> The eyes are black and gleam like a serpent's. The mouth is V-shaped, with saliva dripping from rimless lips that seem to quiver and pulsate.   (page 510)

Time order, or **chronological order**, is the order in which events happen. This order is usually used in stories to relate events.

Sometimes events are connected only by time order. Usually, however, the first event must take place before the second event may occur. Here is an example:

> The farmer held the chicken's head with one hand and then reached for the eggs with his other hand.

For more about recognizing time order, see pages 136 and 353, and Drawing a Time Line on pages 18 and 19.

Logical order is usually used to relate ideas or reasons. It may be used in stories to explain why a character does something. For example, read the sixth paragraph on page 38 to find Spotted Eagle's reasons for forgiving Black Crow.

Logical order is also used frequently in essays and similar nonfiction writing. It helps the reader understand why the writer believes or feels as he or she does. For example, read the third paragraph of "April and Robins" on page 446 to find out how the author feels about the robin's song.

Slanted Writing. Some writing appears to be telling nothing but facts, but it is actually presenting the writer's opinions. This kind of writing is called slanted writing. A reader must watch for such clues as those described below.

A writer can mix opinions with fact, as in this example:

> The custom of summer vacation from school started at a time when students were needed for farm work. Since students are no longer needed on farms, we no longer need summer vacation.

A writer can select only those facts that support his or her opinions. For example, support his or her opinions. Suppose you were trying to convince someone that your favorite actor or actress was the best. You might mention only the successful movies in which he or she appeared, and ignore those that got bad reviews.

A writer can report facts with words that lead the reader to feel a particular way about the facts. The writer will carefully choose words with the connotations he or she wants. That is, the writer chooses words that suggest certain ideas or feelings. For example, both sentences below report the same fact. One does it in a favorable way; the other strongly suggests disapproval.

> The school has invested in a new, more efficient copying machine.

> The school has thrown away more money on a newfangled copying machine that's supposed to be faster than the one we already have.

To avoid being influenced unwisely, a reader must watch for slanted writing.

For more about slanted writing, see pages 354 and 355.

Time Order. See *Sequence*.

Word Choice. A writer's choice of words depends on many influences. These include the following: the mood of the piece of writing; the author's tone; the author's personal style; and the setting, if the writing is a story. Characters must sound as if they fit in the time and place described. For example, if the story takes place in modern times, a character might use terms based on space travel, such as *liftoff* and *touchdown*.

For more about word choice for characters, see pages 181, 484, and 500. For more about other influences on word choice, see pages 219, 293, 309, 325, and 421.

Summary of Vocabulary Skills

1. Word Parts

To unlock some unfamiliar words, you can separate each word into two or more parts. If you know the meaning of each word part, you can figure out the meaning of the unfamiliar word. The two kinds of word parts are base words and affixes. There are two kinds of affixes: prefixes and suffixes. Many of the word parts found in English words are based on Greek and Latin words.

Base Word. A word to which other word parts are added is called a base word. For example, the base word in *careless* is *care*. The base word in *reappear* is *appear*. Sometimes the spelling of a base word is changed when other word parts are added to it. For example, the *n* in *win* is doubled when the word is changed to *winner*. For further information about spelling changes caused by combining suffixes and base words, see *Spelling Changes* below.

Prefix. A word part added at the beginning of a base word is called a prefix. Each prefix has a certain meaning. Adding a prefix to the beginning of a word changes the meaning of the word.

Prefix	+	Base Word	=	New Word
in-	+	correct	=	incorrect

For a list of frequently used prefixes, see page 66.

Suffix. A word part added at the end of a base word is called a suffix. Adding a suffix to a word changes the meaning of the word.

Base Word	+	Suffix	=	New Word
hope	+	-ful	=	hopeful

For a list of frequently used suffixes, see page 66.

Spelling Changes. Before endings can be added to some words, one of the following spelling changes may be necessary.

1. When a suffix beginning with a vowel is added to a word ending in silent *e*, the *e* is usually dropped.

   write + -er = writer

The *e* is not dropped when a suffix beginning with a consonant is added.

    late + -ly = lately

2. When a suffix is added to a word ending in *y* preceded by a consonant, the *y* is usually changed to an *i*.

    happy + -ness = happiness

Note that when the *y* is preceded by a vowel, it is not changed.

    joy + -ous = joyous

3. Words of one syllable, ending in one consonant preceded by one vowel, double the final consonant before adding *-ing*, *-ed*, or *-er*.

    swim + -ing = swimming

Note that when two vowels appear in a one-syllable word, the final consonant is not doubled.

    clean + -er = cleaner

Word Parts from Greek and Latin. Many Greek and Latin words are shortened and used as prefixes and suffixes in English words. Knowing the meaning of these Greek and Latin word parts will help you understand the meaning of English words they are a part of. For example, the Greek prefix *tele-* means "far off," and the word part *-gram* means "something written." For these two word parts, we have the word *telegram*.

For more about Greek and Latin word parts, see page 67.

2. Context Clues

Context refers to the sentence or paragraph in which you find a word. Clues about the meaning of a new word are often given in context. Look for the following kinds of context clues.

Antonyms. An antonym, or opposite, may be given in the same sentence as the new word. It may also be given in a nearby sentence. Often the antonym appears in the same position in its sentence as the new word. Like a contrast clue (page 548), an antonym leads you to understand the meaning of a new word by explaining what it is not.

> The group's decision on the date of the picnic was equivocal. However, their decision on the menu was clear and firm.

The antonyms both appear after the verb *was*. *Equivocal* means "the opposite of clear and firm."

For more about antonyms, see pages 32 and 33.

Comparison and Contrast Clues. Writers often compare one idea with another. They sometimes use an unfamiliar word in one part of the comparison. In that case, the other part of the comparison may give you a clue to the meaning of the word. Key words to look for in comparison clues are *like*, *as*, *similar to*, and *than*.

Here is an example of a comparison clue:

> Among people in our city, the <u>diversity</u> in languages is even more noticeable than the differences in foods.

The comparison tells you that *diversity* means "difference."

Writers also use contrast clues to give you hints about the meaning of a new word. Writers show that certain things or ideas are opposites. A contrast clue tells you what the new word is not. Look for these key words in contrast clues: *although*, *but*, *however*, *yet*, *on the other hand*, *different from*, and *in contrast*.

> Many of Karen's ideas are <u>irrational</u>, but her idea for a new city park certainly is sensible.

The contrast clue tells you that *irrational* is the opposite of *sensible*.

For more about comparison and contrast clues, see pages 246 and 247.

Definitions. In a definition clue, the writer tells the meaning of the new word. Certain words signal that a definition will follow. Look for these key words: *is*, *who is*, *which is*, *that is*, and *in other words*.

> The plans for the trip were <u>nebulous</u>. That is, they were not clear.

For more about definitions in context, see page 60.

Example Clues. In an example clue, a new word is related to a group of familiar words. The new word may be an example of a familiar term. Other times, the familiar terms are examples of the new word.

Key words and phrases tell you to look for examples in a sentence. Some key words are *an example*, *for example*, *one kind*, *for instance*, *some types*, *such as*.

> Ancient musical instruments, such as the <u>psaltery</u>, were displayed at the museum.

For more about example clues, see page 246.

Inference: Using Clues from Different Parts of the Sentence. Clues to the meaning of an unfamiliar word can be found in different parts of the same sentence. For example, clues to a new word in the subject can sometimes be found in the predicate.

> The <u>serape</u> that the Indian wore was made of a bright red and yellow wool.

From this sentence, you can guess that a *serape* is a brightly colored garment of some type.

Inference: Using Clues from Different Parts of the Paragraph. Sometimes the sentence in which a new word appears has no clues to its meaning. However, it is often possible to find clues to the meaning somewhere else in the same paragraph.

> This was Jan's first game of <u>lacrosse</u>. The other nine players on her team had all played before. She had a difficult time hitting the small rubber ball with the long-handled racket. To everyone's surprise, she was the first player to make a goal.

You can figure out the meaning of *lacrosse* from this information in the paragraph: lacrosse is a game played by two teams of ten players each; it is played with a long-handled racket; the players try to send the ball into a goal.

For more about inferring meanings from context, see pages 40 and 41.

Main Idea Clues. Sometimes you can figure out the meaning of a new word by understanding the main idea of the paragraph or selection in which it appears. In this example, several clues make the meaning of the underlined word clear.

> Mr. Bailey's decisions were <u>irrevocable</u>. No one ever persuaded him to change his scoring on an event. He was also firm about each contestant's behavior.

The main idea of the paragraph shows that *irrevocable* means "unchangeable."

For more about main idea clues to meanings, see page 502.

Prefixes and Suffixes. Your knowledge of affixes, that is, prefixes and suffixes, can lead you to context clues.

> Don't drink that unsafe water. You must boil it first to make it <u>potable</u>.

In this example, you know that the suffix *-able* means "can be." You can guess that *potable* water is water that can be drunk.

Restatement. To help you understand an unfamiliar word, a writer will often restate it. In other words, he or she says the idea again in a different way. Key words and punctuation tell you to look for the meaning. Some keys are the word *or*, dashes, commas, and parentheses.

> Next on the <u>itinerary</u>, or route, was a visit to the aquarium.

For more about restatements in context, see pages 6 and 7.

Words in a Series. A sentence may have a series of words that are similar in meaning or belong to the same group. If one of the words is unfamiliar to you, you can often guess its meaning by relating it to the familiar words. From the following example, you can guess that *tatting* is closely related to sewing and embroidery.

> Monica was very eager to learn sewing, embroidery, and tatting.

For more about words in a series, see page 247.

3. Denotation, Connotation, and Multiple Meanings

Denotation refers to the dictionary meaning of a word. **Connotation** refers to the feelings, ideas, and thoughts the word brings to the reader's mind. In order to understand most directions, explanations, and statements of fact, you need only recognize the denotation of a word. However, in order to understand most literature, and especially poetry, you need to be aware of the connotations of words.

For example, the denotations of the word *clever* are "bright, intelligent or skillful in doing some particular thing." However, its connotations may include trickery, deceitfulness or foul play in getting what one wants or needs. These are the meanings suggested in the following sentence.

Josh always has a <u>clever</u> way of getting out of his chores.

For more about the difference between connotation and denotation, see pages 354 and 355.

Multiple Meanings. Many words have more than one meaning. To choose the denotation that the writer intended, read the words in context. Read the words and sentences before and after the word. Try out possible meanings in the context of the sentence.

Use the context of this sentence to figure out which meaning of *knot* the writer intended.

The ship's speed was twenty knots.

There are at least three dictionary meanings for *knot*:

1. a tying or twining together
2. a unit of speed used on ships
3. a joint on the stem of a plant

Try each of the meanings in the sentence. It is clear that the second meaning must be the one the writer meant.

For more about choosing among multiple meanings, see page 138.

4. Levels of Language

Standard English is English that is acceptable anywhere, either in speaking or writing. It follows traditional rules of grammar and uses words that can be found in the dictionary. Most writing is done in standard English.

Standard English may be formal, as in classroom assignments, in speeches, and in most written literature. It may also be informal, as in conversations and in written literature that is trying to sound like natural speech.

Nonstandard English is English used by particular groups of people in particular circumstances. It may not follow the traditional rules of grammar. It may use **slang**. These are words not usually found as main entries in the dictionary or with meanings not listed in the dictionary.

Writers use nonstandard English only for special effects. For example, characters who are close friends might speak to each other in nonstandard English.

For more about recognizing the levels of language, see pages 235 and 236.

5. Reference Books: The Dictionary, Glossary, Encyclopedia, and Thesaurus

A **dictionary** is an alphabetical listing of words and their meanings. Sometimes context clues and word parts do not give enough information to allow you to understand unfamiliar words in your reading. Then you should use a dictionary to find the meaning.

If a word has multiple definitions, or meanings, they will all be listed. These denotations will probably be grouped by part of speech. To choose the right meaning for your selection, test each definition in the sentence in which you found the word.

A **glossary** is often found in the back of a nonfiction book. It contains an alphabetical listing of new or unfamiliar words that are used in the book. The definition given for a glossary word is often limited to the way it is used in a particular selection.

An **encyclopedia** is a book or set of books that gives information on a wide variety of topics. The articles about the topics are arranged alphabetically. You will find more detailed information about a word in an encyclopedia than in a dictionary.

Some dictionaries give information about connotations of a word. Another reference book that gives information about connotations is the **thesaurus**. In a thesaurus, a word is listed with other words of similar meanings, usually with some explanation of the differences.

For more about the dictionary, see page 356; the glossary, page 357; the encyclopedia, page 440; and the thesaurus, pages 325 and 326.

See also *The Dictionary*, *The Encyclopedia*, and *The Thesaurus* under Guidelines for Study and Research.

Guidelines for the Process of Writing

Every time you write, there are certain steps you should follow. Each step is essential for good writing. Together, the steps are called the process of writing.

The process has three stages: **pre-writing**, **writing** the first draft, and **revising**.

Stage 1: Pre-Writing

Pre-writing includes all the preparations you make before you begin to write. During the pre-writing stage, writers think, plan, do research, and organize. Below are the five steps of pre-writing.

1. Choose and limit a topic. Make a list of ideas that interest you. Go over the list carefully. Choose the topic that interests you most. Then list the things you could say about the topic. Limit this list to the ideas you can handle well.

For example, one student was asked to write a paragraph comparing any two legends. She skimmed the legends and chose "Richard the Lion Hearted" and "The Pied Piper of Hamelin." Then she listed all her ideas and circled the one she thought was most interesting.

mood	events	characters
setting	details	(use of music)

2. Decide on your purpose. Decide why you are writing. What do you want to say about your topic? Do you want to explain it, describe it, or criticize it? Are you trying to teach your readers or persuade them to do something?

The student writing about legends decided that the most interesting idea was the use of music. She decided to write her paragraph about music in the legends.

3. Decide on your audience. Decide who will read your writing. Then you will be better able to choose your level of language and the details to include. For example, your language in class will be more formal than at a friend's home.

4. Gather supporting information. List everything you know about the topic. It is possible that you will need more information. You may need to use reference sources, such as encyclopedias.

The student writing about legends re-read both her selections. She wrote notes on every part that had to do with music.

"RICHARD"

Richard—Shut up in dungeon, hidden
Blondel—Minstrel and singer
Made up tunes and songs together
Outside prison, Blondel sang song they
    had made up, and Richard sang back.

"PIED PIPER"

"A power—call it music or call it magic"
Piper played on pipe, led rats to river
Led children to hills
Piper's music told of a magic land.

5. Organize your ideas. Reread your list of details and information. Some details will be useful. Others will not. Cross out the ones that don't belong.

Choose a logical order for the details. For example, you may choose time order if you are writing a story. For a description, you may list details in the order you would notice them. Make a plan, or outline, showing the order in which you will present your ideas. Your outline should make sense to you.

Here is the student's outline for her paragraph. She has written out and underlined her main idea. This will help her keep her sentences on the subject.

COMPARISON OF LEGENDS

Main idea—<u>Music was in both "Richard" and "The Pied Piper."</u>
Important details—
    Blondel used music to find Richard.
    Pied Piper used music to lead rats away.
    Also, to lead the children away.

Stage 2: Writing a First Draft

Now you are ready to get your ideas down on paper. At this point, don't concentrate on getting your words perfect. That careful work will come later. For now, keep your purpose and audience in mind. Follow your outline as much as possible. Remember that you can change your outline if you get better ideas as you write. Leave space between the lines for later corrections and changes.

This is how the student in the example wrote the first draft of her comparison.

First Draft

When I read "Richard the Lion Hearted I enjoyed reading about how music saved king Richard's life, He was shut up in a dungeon so no one could find him, but Blondels song saved him. In "the Pied Piper Of Hamelin," music got rid of the rats. Also it led the children into a hill, from which They never returned. Music was used in both legends although they were very diffrent.

Stage 3: Revising

Revising means making changes in your writing to improve it. Read over your writing. Ask yourself these questions.

1. Is the writing interesting? Will others want to read it?
2. Did I stick to my topic? Are there any unnecessary details? Should any other details be added?
3. Is the organization easy to follow? Do ideas flow together smoothly?
4. Is every group of words a sentence? Is every word the best word?

Mark any corrections and notes on your first draft. Don't be surprised if you make corrections to your corrections. You may need to write several drafts before you are satisfied with your work.

Proofreading. Your writing should be correct as well as clear and interesting. Read it over again. This time, check for any errors in capitalization, punctuation, grammar, and spelling. Correct your errors. Use the symbols in the box at the top of page 555.

Here is a draft that is being revised. Notice how the writer has improved the piece by crossing out unnecessary words, by adding precise words, and by moving ideas around. The writer has also corrected errors in capitalization, punctuation, grammar, and spelling. The writer has used proofreading symbols shown in the box on page 555. First study this draft, then compare it with the final draft on page 555. See how changes that were marked here have been carried out in the final copy.

Revised Draft

¶ Music was important in both "Richard the Lion-Hearted" and "The Pied Piper of Hamelin."

In When I read "Richard the Lion-Hearted," I enjoyed reading about how music saved king Richard's life. He was shut up had been hidden in a dungeon, so no one could find him, but Blondel's song However, found him. When Blondel sang a song, the king answered him. saved him. In "the Pied Piper Of Hamelin," music got rid of the rats, Also it led the children into a hill, from but magic which They never returned. Music was used in both legends although they were very diffrent. legends

Proofreading Symbols

Symbol	Meaning	Example
∧	insert	diff∧rent
≡	capitalize	k≡ing
/	make lower case	Øf
∿	transpose (trade positions)	Also it
⌁	omit letters, words	they
¶	make new paragraph	¶ Music
⊙	insert a period	both⊙

Writing the Final Copy. As soon as you feel your writing is both clear and correct, write your final copy. Use your best handwriting or type carefully. Indent paragraphs correctly. Then proofread your work again. Read it aloud. Look for any errors you might have missed.

Notice that in making this final copy, the student found and corrected an error in punctuation. She also improved the wording of one phrase that had not been marked before.

Final Copy

Music was important in both "Richard the Lion-Hearted" and "The Pied Piper of Hamelin." In "Richard the Lion-Hearted," music saved King Richard's life. He had been hidden in a dungeon. However, the minstrel Blondel found him. When Blondel sang a song, the king answered him. In "The Pied Piper of Hamelin," music got rid of the rats, but it also led the children into a magic hill. They never returned. Although the legends were very different, music was used in both.

Checklist for the Process of Writing

Pre-Writing

1. Choose and limit a topic.
2. Decide on your purpose.
3. Decide on your audience.
4. Gather supporting information.
5. Organize your ideas.

Writing Your First Draft

1. Begin writing. Keep your topic, purpose, and audience in mind at all times.
2. As you write, you may add new details.
3. Concentrate on ideas. Do not be concerned with grammar and mechanics at this time.

Revising

1. Read your first draft. Ask yourself these questions:
   a. Do you like what you have written? Is it interesting? Will others want to read it?
   b. Does your writing make sense?
   c. Is your writing organized well? Do the ideas flow smoothly from one paragraph to the next? Are the ideas arranged in a logical order?
   d. Does each paragraph have a topic sentence? Does every sentence stick to the topic? Should any sentence be moved?
   e. Should any details be left out? Should any be added?
   f. Does every sentence express a complete thought? Are your sentences easy to understand?
   g. Is every word the best possible word?
2. Mark any changes on your paper.

Proofreading

Consider these questions as you check your writing for errors in grammar and usage, capitalization, punctuation, and spelling.

Grammar and Usage
a. Is every word group a complete sentence?
b. Does every verb agree with its subject?
c. Have you used the correct form of each pronoun?
d. Is the form of each adjective correct?
e. Is the form of each adverb correct?

Capitalization
a. Is the first word in every sentence capitalized?
b. Are all proper nouns and adjectives capitalized?
c. Are titles capitalized correctly?

Punctuation
a. Does each sentence have the correct end mark?
b. Have you used punctuation marks such as commas, apostrophes, hyphens, colons, semicolons, question marks, quotation marks, and underlining correctly?

Spelling
a. Did you check unfamiliar words in a dictionary?
b. Did you spell plural and possessive forms correctly?

Preparing the Final Copy

1. Make a clean copy of your writing. Make all changes and correct all errors. Then ask yourself these questions:

   a. Is your handwriting neat and easy to read?
   b. Are your margins wide enough?
   c. Is every paragraph indented?

2. Proofread your writing again. Read it aloud. Correct any mistakes neatly.

Guidelines for Study and Research

1. Using Reference Materials

The Dictionary

A **dictionary** is an alphabetical listing of words, called entry words, and their meanings. The **glossary** of a nonfiction book is a dictionary limited to entry words from that book.

How To Find a Word. In order to find a word in the dictionary, look first at the **guide words** on the pages. Two guide words are usually printed at the top of every page. They show the first and last words on the page. Keep looking until you find the guide words between which your word falls.

For example, here are the guide words for two pages of a dictionary. On which page will *radiant* appear?

radial—radium   radius—railway

You needed to compare the guide words to the fifth letter in order to find the answer. *Radiant* will appear on the first page, between *radial* and *radium*.

What the Entry Word Tells You. Use the **entry word** itself, printed in boldface (dark) type, to see how the word is spelled. Use the entry word, also, to find out where to break the word into syllables at the end of a line of writing.

How To Find the Pronunciation. Use the **respelling** that follows the entry word to determine the pronunciation of the word. The respelling usually appears within parentheses. It uses letters and symbols to stand for the sounds of the spoken word. To find out what each letter and symbol stands for, you must refer to the **pronunciation key** on that page or the page across from it. (For the meaning of the symbols in the sample respelling, see the pronunciation key in the Glossary.)

   entry word   respelling   part of speech

ra·di·ant (rā′dē ənt) *adj.* **1.** shining brightly. **2.** showing pleasure. **3.** coming from the sun or other source in rays.

       meanings

Accent marks in the respelling indicate which syllable to stress when you say the word. If the word has more than two syllables, it may have more than one accent. The heavy accent is called the **primary accent**. The lighter one is called the **secondary accent**.

How To Find the Part of Speech and the Meaning. Immediately following the respelling is an abbreviation that tells the **part of speech** of the word. Then you will find the **definition**, or meaning, of the word. If the word may be used as more than one part of speech, all the definitions for one part of speech are grouped together. After that you will find a second abbreviation and the definitions that fit that second part of speech, and so on.

After some entries, you will find subentries listed in dark, or bold, type. **Subentries** are familiar phrases in which the entry word appears. The special meaning of the phrase is then listed.

For more on the use of the dictionary, see pages 356, 367, and 368.

The Thesaurus

A **thesaurus** is a list of words followed by related words. You use a thesaurus when you need to find a word to express your exact meaning. The related words may be synonyms for the listed word. Some of the related words may be different parts of speech from the entry word. Other related words are antonyms, words with meanings opposite the entry word.

Imagine, for example, that you needed another word for the term *worried*. You would first find the listing for *worried* in the thesaurus. There you would read words such as *anxious* and *troubled*. You could choose one of those words.

Each thesaurus is organized in a different way. Look in the front of the thesaurus for directions. The index at the back of the book may also help you.

For more about using a thesaurus, see page 325.

The Encyclopedia

The **encyclopedia** is a collection of articles on a wide variety of topics. The articles are arranged in alphabetical order, according to their titles. Usually, if an encyclopedia is several volumes long, an index appears in the last volume.

When you are looking for information in an encyclopedia, begin with the index. The index tells which articles have information on each topic. It tells the volume and page where each article appears.

For more information about using the encyclopedia, see pages 77 and 440.

The Nonfiction Book

When you are looking for detailed information on a topic, your best source may be a nonfiction book concerning the topic. To decide whether the book will be useful to you, examine these parts:

The title page. Does the title mention your topic? Is the author or editor someone with knowledge about the topic?

The copyright page. If you need up-to-date information, is the copyright date a recent one?

The table of contents. Is the organization of the book clear? Do the part titles or chapter titles suggest what you can find in each section of the book, so that you can find your topic easily?

The index. Is there an adequate index? Does it list terms or names that you need information about? Does it use italic or boldface type to indicate the pages with maps, graphs, or illustrations?

---

2. Finding the Right Book

The Library

Books in a library are divided into two groups: fiction and nonfiction.

Fiction books are stories about imaginary happenings. They are arranged alphabetically according to the last name of the author. The author's last name is usually shown on the spine of the book.

Nonfiction books contain factual information. Most libraries arrange these books according to the **Dewey Decimal System**. Every book is assigned a number in one of ten categories. The number is called a **call number**. It is printed on the spine of the book. The books are then arranged on library shelves in numerical order.

THE DEWEY DECIMAL SYSTEM

000–099	General Works	encyclopedias, almanacs, handbooks
100–199	Philosophy	conduct, ethics, psychology
200–299	Religion	the Bible, mythology, theology
300–399	Social Science	law, education, government, folklore, legend
400–499	Language	languages, grammar, dictionaries
500–599	Science	mathematics, chemistry, physics
600–699	Useful Arts	farming, cooking, sewing, radio, nursing, engineering, television, business, gardening, cars
700–799	Fine Arts	music, painting, drawing, acting, games, sports
800–899	Literature	poetry, plays, essays
900–999	History	biography, travel, geography

The Card Catalog

The best way to locate a book in the library is to use the **card catalog**. The cards are arranged alphabetically according to the words in the top line of each card. On the top left corner of the card, you will find the call number. Using the call number, you can then locate the book on the shelves.

There are usually three cards for every book in the library: an author card, a title card, and a subject card. Each of the three cards contains the same information, but in a different order. The **author card** lists the author's name on the top line. The **title card** lists the title on the top line. The **subject card** lists the subject or topic of the book on the top line.

Author Card
973.7
K19   **Katz, William Loren**

An album of the Civil War.
Illustrated with original prints and
photos. N.Y.: F. Watts. © 1974.

Title Card
973.7
K19   **An album of the Civil War**

Katz, William Loren

An album of the Civil War.
Illustrated with original prints and

Subject Card
973.7
K19   **U.S. History—Civil War**

Katz, William Loren

An album of the Civil War.
Illustrated with original prints and
photos. N.Y.: F. Watts. © 1974.

3. Preparing To Study

Preparations in Class

Before you can begin an assignment, you must know what it is you are being asked for. The first step to studying is listening carefully to **directions**.

1. Focus your attention on only the directions about to be given.
2. Note how many steps there are.
3. Relate a key word to each step, such as *Read, Answer,* or *Write.*
4. Ask questions about any step you do not understand.

5. Repeat the completed directions to yourself and then write them down.

Keep an **assignment notebook** for making a record of what you must do. For each assignment, write the following:

1. The subject
2. The assignment and any details
3. The date the assignment is given
4. The date the assignment is due

Subject	Assignment	Date given	Date due

Your Study Area

The area where you read and study should meet these requirements:

1. It should be quiet.
2. It should be well lit.
3. It should be clean and neat.
4. It should be equipped with pencils, paper, and a dictionary.

Your Schedule for Study Time

It is important to set aside time to study and complete assignments.

Some reading and writing assignments require a small amount of time. These are called **short-term goals**. To be sure you will do these assignments, set aside a block of time each day to work on your studies.

Assignments that cannot be completed overnight are called **long-term goals**. If you break these assignments into smaller tasks, the job becomes manageable. Decide how long each small task will take. Then develop a plan for completing the tasks, one by one.

To make a **study plan**, write down what you will accomplish each day. On your plan, show the times each day when you will work on the project.

4. Studying

Three Types of Reading

There are three types of reading you can use when you are studying. Each is best for a particular purpose.

Scanning is a type of fast reading. It allows you to locate a specific piece of information quickly. To scan, move your eyes rapidly over the page. Look for key words that will lead you to the facts and ideas you need to answer your question.

Skimming is another type of fast reading. It helps you get an overview of the material you are about to read. To skim, move your eyes quickly over the material. Look for titles, subtitles, and illustrations that will give you clues about the content of the material.

The third type of reading is **study-type reading**. This is slower than scanning and skimming. When you do study-type reading, you are trying to get as much meaning as you can from the words. You are trying to find the order in which the information is arranged, and to make connections between statements. The SQ3R study method is a good description of effective study-type reading.

The SQ3R Study Method

The **SQ3R study method** is a sure way to improve reading and study skills. SQ3R stands for five steps: Survey, Question, Read, Recite, and Review.

Survey. Look over the material to get a general idea of what it is about. Read the titles and subtitles. Look at the illustrations, such as pictures, maps, graphs, or tables. Read the introduction or first few paragraphs. Read the summary.

Question. Read any study questions provided in the book or by your teacher. If there are no study questions, make up some for yourself by turning titles and headings into questions.

Read. Read the material. Identify main ideas. Keep the study questions in mind.

Recite. After reading, recite the answers to the study questions. Write down brief notes to help you remember any other important ideas.

Review. Look back at the study questions and try to answer them without using your notes. You may need to review the material to find the answers. Last, study your notes so that you will be able to remember the information later.

Note-Taking

As you read, you will probably recognize some main ideas and important facts. Write them down in a notebook.

Notes do not have to be written in sentences. They should be in your own words. Write them clearly so that, when you read these notes at a later date, they will still make sense to you.

Taking notes forces you to concentrate on the material. It also helps you understand the material since you are always looking for the most important facts. Besides, notes are useful as a study guide for later review.

Name of encyclopedia   Volume number

World Book Encyclopedia, Volume 15

Title of article   Page numbers

"George Brinton McClellan" pages 266-267

Fact

McClellan became general in chief of all Union armies in 1861. Lincoln removed him in 1862 because of his delay in pursuing the Confederates.

Summary of Skills in Critical Thinking

Analysis. The skill of analysis, or analyzing, is the ability to study something carefully, piece by piece. Many elements go together to make up a story or a poem. When you analyze, you focus on each part individually.

For example, when you analyze a poem, you may want to look at its rhyme scheme, its rhythm, its mood, or another element.

As you study each part separately, you begin to understand the whole selection better. Analyzing also helps you identify the ways in which a particular selection is similar to or different from other writing.

Throughout this text, study questions in Developing Comprehension Skills, Reading Literature, and Developing Writing Skills focus the reader's attention on individual elements in the selections. In addition, questions under Developing Skills in Critical Thinking develop specific skills of analysis on pages 27 and 46.

Evaluation. When you evaluate a piece of writing, you study it carefully and decide on its value. You use certain standards to judge the worth of a selection. Does the writing meet the standards or does it fall short?

Writing can be evaluated in two ways. First, the skill of the writers can be judged. For this type of evaluation you might ask yourself questions such as these: How well has the writer achieved his or her purpose? Has the writer chosen effective ways of presenting ideas? Is the organization logical? Does it help explain the ideas? Are the figures of speech clear?

You can also evaluate what the writers are saying. Is their writing truthful and accurate? How do you know the writers are qualified to write about this subject? Are the writers telling the whole truth or is their view incomplete? Are they biased in any way? What are the qualities of this piece that make it worth reading?

As you evaluate what writers write, stay alert for examples of faulty thinking such as the following:

1. unsupported generalizations
2. hidden confusion of fact and opinion
3. slanted writing

When you write, try to be as skillful and accurate as possible. When you read, demand that other writers do the same.

Some of the many study questions involving evaluation can be found on pages 220, 337, 465, and 530.

Fact and Opinion. Facts can be proved to be true. Opinions are only one person's beliefs. They may or may not be based on facts.

Fact: Water boils at 100 degrees Celsius. Opinion: This soup is too hot.

As you read, watch out for statements that sound like facts but cannot be proved. The writer's opinions will also influence his or her choice of details, and may result in slanted writing.

Some of the many study questions on identifying fact and opinion in the selections are on pages 402, 413, 475, and 478.

See also *Personal Opinions* and *Slanted Writing*.

Generalizations. Writers sometimes notice that some things occur in a pattern, that is, over and over again. They may make a general statement about what they notice happening. For example, a generalization about spring could be "Many trees grow new leaves in the spring."

Writers can make mistakes in generalizations. Sometimes they don't look at the facts in enough cases. They apply the generalization to more instances than the facts will support. Then the generalizations are too broad. They are not completely true.

For example, this generalization is too broad: *All trees lose their leaves in the fall.* In reality, some trees do not lose their leaves in the fall. In fact, if you can think of one tree that doesn't lose its leaves in fall, the generalization is faulty.

Study questions about generalizations can be found under Developing Skills in Critical Thinking on pages 237 and 327.

Personal Opinions. You are often asked to give your opinion about an issue or question. Your opinion should be based on evidence. You should be able to point out and explain the reasons why you think as you do.

Say, for example, you believe a certain story is realistic. If you want your opinion to be considered valid, you must be ready to back it up with evidence from the story. To explain your opinion, you might find examples of true-to-life situations and conversations in the story. You might point out the ways in which the story is like your own life or the lives of people you know.

Throughout this text, study questions in Developing Comprehension Skills, Reading Literature, and Developing Writing Skills ask the reader to form and present opinions, with supporting reasons. Some of these are on pages 27, 96, 257, and 412.

Slanted Writing. Writers are careful to choose words with the meanings they want. Denotations, or dictionary meanings, are important, of course. However, connotations, or the feelings or ideas the words give you, are equally important. In slanted writing, a writer uses many words with strong connotations. The connotations may lead readers to feel strongly in favor of a point of view. Other words with strong connotations may make a reader feel strongly against a subject.

Be aware of the power of slanted writing as you read. Don't permit the writer to trick you into agreeing with him or her without a good reason.

Read the following three sentences. Although they all deal with the same happening, they are very different. The first sentence is not slanted. The next two sentences are slanted. They use words with strong connotations. Notice how these words affect your reactions.

1. Bill sold his red bike to Todd for fifty dollars.
2. Bill cheated Todd when he sold him his old bike for fifty dollars.
3. Bill practically gave his classic bike to Todd for only fifty dollars.

For more about slanted writing and connotations, see the study questions on pages 292, 383, 411, and 469.

Glossary

The **glossary** is an alphabetical listing of words from the selections, along with their meanings. The glossary gives the following information:

1. **The entry word broken into syllables.**

2. **The pronunciation of each word.** The **respelling** is shown in parentheses. The most common way to pronounce a word is listed first. The Pronunciation Key below shows the symbols for the sounds of letters, and key words that contain those sounds. A key is repeated on every second page.

    A **primary accent** ′ is placed after the syllable that is stressed the most when the word is spoken. A **secondary accent** ′ is placed after a syllable that has a lighter stress.

3. **The part of speech of the word.** The following abbreviations are used:

    n. noun   *v.* verb   *adj.* adjective   *adv.* adverb

4. **The meaning of the word.** The definitions listed in the glossary apply to selected ways a word is used in these selections.

5. **Related forms.** Words with suffixes such as *-ing, -ed, -ness,* and *-ly* are listed under the base word.

ab·stract (ab strakt′ *or* ab′ strakt) *adj.* thought of apart from any particular act or object.

Pronunciation Key

a	fat	i	hit	͝o͝o	look	ə { a *in* ago	ch	chin
ā	ape	ir	here	o͞o	tool	e *in* agent	sh	she
ä	car, lot	ī	bite, fire	ou	out	i *in* unity	th	thin
						o *in* collect	*th*	then
e	ten	ō	go	u	up	u *in* focus	zh	leisure
er	care	ô	law, horn	ur	fur		ng	ring
ē	even	oi	oil			′l	able

This pronunciation key used with permission, from *Webster's New World Dictionary, Basic School Edition*; Copyright © 1979 by Simon & Schuster, Inc.

A

a·bate (ə bāt') *v.* to become less; weaken.

ab·bey (ab'ē) *n.* a place where a group of monks or nuns live.

ab·bot (ab'ət) *n.* a man who is the head of a group of monks.

a·bol·ish (ə bäl'ish) *v.* to do away with completely.

ab·stract   (ab strakt' *or* ab'strakt)   *adj.* thought of apart from any particular act or object.

a·buse (ə byoōz') *v.* to use improperly or wrongly.

a·byss (ə bis') *n.* a great, deep crack or opening in the earth.

ac·ro·bat (ak'rə bat) *n.* a performer who does tumbling tricks.

a·cute (ə kyoōt') *adj.* very severe.

ad·a·mant (ad'ə mənt) *adj.* not giving in; unyielding.

a·dapt (ə dapt') *v.* to change so as to be made usable for a specific purpose.

af·flic·tion (a flik'shən) *n.* pain; suffering.

a·ghast (ə gast') *adj.* feeling great shock or horror.

al·a·bas·ter (al'ə bas'tər) *adj.* smooth and white like alabaster, a stone that is carved into statues or vases.

al·cove (al'kōv) *n.* a small part of a room, set off from the main part.

al·der (ôl'dər) *n.* a small tree.

al·lies (al'īz) *n.* countries joined together by agreement or united for a special purpose.

al·lure·ment (ə loōr'mənt) *n.* something that attracts or tempts.

a·loft (ə lôft') *adv.* high above the ground.

am·ber (am'bər) *adj.* having a brownish-yellow color.

am·bi·tion (am bish'ən) *n.* **1.** strong desire to be successful or to gain fame. **2.** the thing that one strongly desires.

a·men·i·ties (ə men'ə tēz) *n. plural* the polite ways people are supposed to behave.

am·pu·tate (am'pyə tāt) *v.* to cut off, surgically.

an·nals (an''lz) *n. plural* a history or record of events.

an·vil (an'vəl) *n.* a steel or iron block on which heated metal objects are shaped.

anx·i·e·ty (ang zī'ə tē) *n.* the condition of being worried about what may happen.

a·poth·e·cary (ə päth'ə ker'ē) *n.* a person who makes and sells medicines.

ap·plaud (ə plôd') *v.* to show enjoyment or approval, usually by clapping one's hands or cheering. — **applause** *n.*

ap·por·tion (ə pôr'shən) *v.* to separate and give out in shares.

ap·pro·pri·ate (ə prō'prē it) *adj.* just right, or suitable for the purpose.

as·cend (ə send') *v.* to go up; rise.

as·sail (ə sāl') *v.* to attack with questions or arguments.

as·sault (ə sôlt') *n.* a sudden attack.

as·ton·ish·ment (ə stän'ish ment) *n.* the state of being filled with wonder; great surprise.

as·tound (ə stound') *v.* to amaze or greatly surprise.

a·stride (ə strīd') *adv.* having one leg on each side.

as·tro·nom·i·cal (as'trə nöm'i k'l) *adj.* having to do with the science of the stars, planets, and comets.

at·trib·ute (a'trə byoōt' *or* ə trib'yoōt) *n.* a quality or characteristic of a person or thing.

aug·ment (ôg ment') *v.* to become greater.

au·to·crat·ic (ôt'ə krat'ik) *adj.* having complete power over others; forcing others.

awe (ô) *n.* deep respect mixed with wonder and fear.

az·ure (azh'ər) *adj.* sky blue.

B

ban·ish (ban'ish) *v.* **1.** to force a person to leave his or her country as a punishment. **2.** get rid of. —**banishment** *n.*

bank·rupt (bangk' rupt) *adj.* not able to pay all of one's debts.

bap·tism (bap'tiz'm) *n.* the religious ceremony of dipping people in water or sprinkling water on them.

barge (barj) *n.* a large boat.

bar·rack (bar'ək) *n.* a building where soldiers live.

bar·ri·er (bar'ē ər) *n.* thing that blocks the way or keeps one from going on.

bat·tal·ion (bə tal'yən) *n.* a large group of soldiers.

ba·zaar (bə zär') *n.* a sale of many kinds of articles, usually to raise money for charity.

bed·cham·ber (bed'chām'bər) *n.* bedroom.

bel·fry (bel'frē) *n.* the part of a tower in which a bell is hung.

bel·low (bel'ō) *v.* to roar loudly.

be·nef·i·cence (bə nef'ə səns) *n.* a gift or kind act.

be·tray (bi trā') *v.* to fail to keep a promise or secret.

be·wil·der (bi wil'dər) *v.* to make confused.

bi·ol·o·gy (bī äl'ə jē) *n.* the science of living things.

blub·ber (blub'ər) *n.* the fat of whales.

blun·der (blun'dər) *v.* to move clumsily.

bolt (bōlt) *n.* a large amount of cloth on a roll.

boul·der (bōl'dər) *n.* a large rock.

bow·er (bou'ər) *n.* a place shaded by trees or vines.

brooch (brōch *or* brōōch) *n.* an ornamental pin often worn on a woman's dress.

buck·skin (buk'skin) *n.* a soft leather made from the skins of deer or sheep.

buf·fa·lo (buf'ə lō) *n.* a wild ox, sometimes tamed as a work animal.

bun·gle (bung'g'l) *v.* to spoil by clumsy work.

bus·tle (bus''l) *n.* a padding worn by women to puff out the back of a skirt.

C

ca·lam·i·ty (kə lam'ə tē) *n.* a terrible happening; deep trouble; misery.

can·ton (kan'tən *or* kan tän') *n.* a state or section of a country.

ca·pri·cious (kə prish'əs) *adj.* likely to change suddenly; flighty.

cap·tive (kap'tiv) *n.* a person caught and kept against his or her will.

car·cass (kär'kəs) *n.* the dead body of an animal.

ca·reen (kə rēn') *v.* to move from side to side while in motion.

ca·tas·tro·phe (kə tas'trə fē) *n.* a sudden happening that causes suffering or damage.

ca·the·dral (kə thē'dral) *n.* a church.

cen·taur (sen'tôr) *n.* a creature in myths that is part man and part horse.

cha·grin (shə grin') *n.* a feeling of being disappointed because one has failed.

chaise (shāz) *n.* a light carriage.

cham·ber (chām'bər) *n.* a room, usually a bedroom.

cha·os (kā'äs) *n.* confusion; disorder.

chap·el (chap''l) *n.* a place to worship in.

char (chär) *v.* to burn.

chime (chīm) *v.* to ring or sound.

chop·sticks (chäp'stiks) *n. plural* a pair of small sticks used to eat with.

chor·e·o·graph (kôr'ē ə graf') *v.* to plan dance steps and movements. —**choreographer** *n.*

---

at, āte, fär; pen, ēqual; sit, mīne; sō, côrn, join, took, fōōl, our; us, turn; chill, shop, thick, they, sing; **zh** *in* measure; **'l** *in* idle;

ə *in* alive, cover, family, robot, circus.

cin·der (sin′dər) *n.* a tiny bit of partly burned matter, such as coal or lava.

clar·i·fy (klar′ə fī) *n.* to make something easier to understand.

clas·sic (klas′ik) *n.* literature of high excellence.

cliff (klif) *n.* large, steep side of rock.

clois·ter (klɔis′tər) *n.* a place where nuns or monks live.

com·i·cal (käm′i k′l) *adj.* funny; amusing.

com·men·ta·tor (käm′ən tāt′ər) *n.* a person who works at reporting and commenting on the news, as on radio or TV.

com·mut·er (kə myo͞o′tər) *adj.* a type of vehicle used to take people to work or school.

com·pel (kəm pel′) *v.* to force to do something.

com·pet·i·tor (kəm pet′ə tər) *n.* a person who challenges another for something.

com·rade (käm′rad) *n.* a close friend or companion.

con·dense (kən dens′) *v.* to become more closely packed together; shortened.

con·de·scend (kän də send′) *v.* to mildly agree to do something beneath one's dignity.

Con·fed·er·a·cy (kən fed′ər ə sē) *n.* the eleven Southern States that seceded from the U.S. in 1860 and 1861.

con·firm (kən furm′) *v.* to make firm by approving or agreeing.

con·gest·ed (kən jest′əd) *adj.* overcrowded.

con·ges·tion (kən jes′chən) *n.* the condition of being filled with blood or other fluids.

con·jec·ture (kən jek′chər) *n.* guess; opinion formed without facts.

con·sci·en·tious (kän′shē en′shəs) *adj.* trying to be careful and correct.

con·se·crate (kän′sə krāt) *v.* to set apart as holy.

con·sent (kən sent′) *v.* to give approval.

con·stant (kän′stənt) *adj.* not changing; fixed.

con·tempt (kən tempt′) *n.* the feeling one has toward someone or something one considers low or evil.

con·ti·nent (känt′′n ənt) *n.* any of the large land areas of the earth.

con·tour (kän′to͞or) *n.* the outline of the shape of something.

con·trast (kän′trast) *n.* a comparison of things, noting the differences.

con·vent (kän′vent) *n.* the place where nuns live.

con·verse (kən vʉrs′) *v.* to talk; to have a conversation.

cor·don (kôr′ d′n) *n.* a line or circle placed around an area to guard or protect it, sometimes made up of police.

corpse (kôrps) *n.* the dead body of a person.

cor·ri·dor (kôr′ə dər) *n.* a long hall or passageway.

cos·mo·pol·i·tan (käz′mə päl′ət′n) *adj.* feeling at home anywhere.

coun·cil (koun′s′l) *n.* a group of people who gives advice to or makes laws for a village, town, or city.

coun·ci·lor (koun′sə lər) *n.* a person who advises, usually a member of a council.

coun·te·nance (koun′tə nəns) *n.* the look on a person's face.

cowl·ish (koul′ish) *adj.* shaped like a hood.

crin·o·line (krin′′l in) *n.* an old-fashioned hoop skirt.

crouch (krouch) *n.* the position of stooping with the legs bent close to the ground.

croup (kro͞op) *n.* a disease that causes hoarse coughing and hard breathing.

cyl·in·der (sil′ən dər) *n.* a rounded figure with two flat ends.

D

dank (dangk) *adj.* unpleasantly damp.

de·cath·lon (di kath′län) *n.* an athletic contest that includes ten different events.

de·cep·tion (di sep′shən) *n.* something that deceives, or fools.

ded·i·cate (ded′ə kāt) *v.* to set aside for a special purpose.

de·fect (dē′fekt *or* di fekt′) *n.* a fault or weakness.

de·fi·ance (di fī′əns) *n.* the act of opposing a person or thing.

dell (del) *n.* a valley or sheltered place.

de·scend·ant (di sen′dənt) *n.* one who is an offspring of, or has a trait of, certain family members or ancestors.

de·scent (di sent′) *n.* the act of moving down to a lower place.

des·per·ate (des′pər it) *adj.* having lost hope.

de·spair (di sper′) *n.* a giving up or loss of hope. *v.* to give up or lose hope.

de·spise (di spīz′) *v.* to dislike strongly.

des·tin·y (des′tə nē) *n.* one's fate.

de·tract (di trakt′) *v.* to remove something desirable.

de·vice (di vīs′) *n.* a thing made or invented for some special purpose or use.

de·vise (di vīz′) *v.* to think up or plan.

de·vo·tion (di vō′shən) *n.* loyalty or strong affection.

dice (dīs) *n. plural* small cubes marked on each side with a different number of dots, used in pairs for games of chance.

di·lem·ma (di lem′ə) *n.* a situation where one must choose between two equally difficult or unpleasant things.

dis·com·fit·ed (dis cum′fit id) *adv.* in a confused or embarrassed way.

dis·com·fort (dis kum′fərt) *n.* uneasiness or lack of comfort.

dis·may (dis mā′) *n.* fear; dread; uncertainty.

dis·pose (dis pōz′) *v.* to get rid of by giving or throwing away.

dis·po·si·tion (dis′pə zish′ən) *n.* one's general nature or mood.

dis·si·pate (dis′ə pāt) *v.* to break up or make disappear.

dis·tinct (dis tingkt′) *adj.* different; clearly seen, heard, or felt.

dis·trac·tion (dis trak′shən) *n.* a drawing away of attention.

doc·u·ment (däk′yə mənt) *n.* a printed or written record used to prove something.

doff (däf) *v.* to take off, as one's hat.

dole·ful (dōl′fəl) *adj.* very sad.

do·min·ion (də min′yən) *n.* land or country ruled over.

duch·y (duch′ē) *n.* land that is ruled by a duke or duchess.

du·el (dōō′əl *or* dyōō′əl) *n.* a pre-arranged fight with deadly weapons between two persons; the duel is governed by strict rules and must take place in front of witnesses.

doubt (dout) *n.* being unsure of something.

down·trod·den (doun′träd′′n) *n.* those forced to live in poverty and slavery.

draw·bridge (drô′brij) *n.* a bridge that can be raised or lowered to keep someone from crossing.

dumb·found (dum′found′) *v.* to astonish.

dun·geon (dun′jən) *n.* a dark underground room used as a prison.

dwel·ler (dwel′′r) *n.* one who lives in a particular place.

dy·na·mo (dī′nə mō) *n.* a machine for changing mechanical energy into electricity.

---

at, āte, fär; pen, ēqual; sit, mīne; sō, côrn, join, took, fōōl, our; us, turn; chill, shop, thick, *th*ey, sing; **zh** *in* measure; ′l *in* idle; ə *in* alive, cover, family, robot, circus.

E

e·clipse (i klips') *n.* a hiding of the sun by the moon as it passes between the sun and the earth.

ec·stat·ic (ek stat'ik) *adj.* full of joy.

em·bed (im bed') *v.* to set in earth.

e·ma·ci·ate (i mā'shē āt) *v.* to make very thin.

e·merge (i mʉrj') *v.* to come out so as to be seen.

em·i·nent (em'ə nənt) *adj.* very famous.

en·camp·ment (in kamp'mənt) *n.* a place set up for people to camp or rest.

en·dure (in dʊʊr' *or* in dyʊʊr') *v.* to put up with pain or weariness.

en·trails (en'trālz) *n. plural* the parts inside an animal's body.

e·rad·i·cate (i rad'ə kāt) *v.* to remove completely; get rid of.

e·rup·tion (i rup'shən) *n.* an explosion; a bursting or throwing forth.

es·cort (es kôrt') *v.* to accompany someone.

es·sence (es''ns) *n.* the most important or basic quality of something.

e·ter·nal (i tʉr'n'l) *adj.* seeming to have no end; continual.

e·the·re·al (i thir'ē əl) *adj.* like the upper regions of space.

e·vac·u·ate (i vak'yʊʊ wāt) *v.* to leave.

ex·as·per·ate (ig zas'pə rāt) *n.* to annoy very much.

ex·cuse (ik skyʊʊs') **1.** *n.* an explanation for an action. **2.** *v.* to forgive or pardon.

ex·e·cu·tion (ek'sə kyʊʊ'shən) *n.* the act of putting someone to death.

ex·pose (ik spōz') *v.* to let be seen; leave unprotected.

ex·ter·mi·nate (ik stʉr'mə nāt) *v.* to destroy completely.

ex·trav·a·gant (ik strav'ə gənt) *adj.* too ornate or showy. — **extravagantly** *adv.*

F

fa·ble (fā'b'l) *n.* a story that is not true.

fates (fāts) *n. plural* three goddesses who controlled human life in Greek mythology.

fath·om (fa*th*'əm) *n.* a length of six feet, used as a unit of measure for the depth of water.

fa·tigue (fə tēg') *n.* a tired feeling as from hard work or not enough rest.

feat (fēt) *n.* something done that shows great skill or strength.

fis·tu·la (fis'chʊʊ lə) *n.* an open sore or ulcer.

flex (fleks) *v.* to bend.

floss (flôs) *n.* soft and silky fiber.

fluc·tu·ate (fluk'chʊʊ wāt) *v.* to rise and fall; keep changing.—**fluctuation** *n.*

fol·ly (fäl'ē') *n.* a foolish action.

fore·man (fôr'mən) *n.* a person in charge of a group of workers.

for·feit (fôr'fit) *v.* to give up or lose something.

for·lorn (fər lôrn') *adj.* sad because of being lonely or uncared for.

for·tress (fôr'trəs) *n.* a building with strong walls for defending against an enemy.

fra·grance (frā'grəns) *n.* a pleasant smell.

fran·tic (fran'tik) *adj.* very upset with anger or worry.—**frantically** *adv.*

fraud (frôd) *n.* a cheating or tricking; dishonesty.

fric·tion (frik'shən) *n.* the contact of one thing against another.

frus·trate (frus'trāt) *v.* to keep a person from doing what that person wants, or to keep a thing from being done.—**frustration** *n.*

G

gal·a·vant (gal'ə vant') *v.* to go out in search of amusement or excitement.

gal·lant (gal'ənt) *adj.* brave and daring.

gan·grene (gang′grēn) *n.* decay of a part of the body from which the blood is blocked by injury or disease.

gar·ment (gär′mənt) *n.* a piece of clothing.

gasp (gasp) *v.* to breathe in suddenly, as in surprise.

gaud·y (gôd′ē) *adj.* bright and showy.

gav·el (gav′l) *n.* a small wooden hammer that a judge or chairperson taps on the table to call for attention.

gaunt (gônt) *adj.* looking worn and thin.

gen·darme (zhän′därm) *n.* a police officer in France.

gen·er·a·tion (jen′ə rā′shən) *n.* people born about the same time.

ges·tic·u·late (jes tik′yoo lāt) *v.* to make motions with the hands and arms.

gore (gôr) *v.* to stab with a horn or tusk.

gran·deur (gran′jər) *n.* great dignity or style.

gran·ite (gran′it) *n.* rock used for buildings and monuments.

grap·ple (grap′l) *v.* to fight or struggle.

grav·i·ty (grav′ə tē) *n.* the condition of being serious.

gren·a·dier (gren ə dir′) *n.* a soldier.

grieve (grēv) *v.* to feel deep sadness.

grim (grim) *adj.* frightful; cruel.

grope (grōp) *v.* to look for or find by feeling about.

grove (grōv) *n.* a group of trees.

guil·der (gil′dər) *n.* a unit of money in the Netherlands.

gul·ly (gul′ē) *v.* a narrow channel worn by water.

gust (gust) *n.* a strong, sudden rush of something carried by the air, such as rain.

H

hag·gard (hag′ərd) *adj.* having a wild-eyed, exhausted look.

halt (hôlt) *v.* to stop.

hap·haz·ard (hap haz′ərd) *adj.* not in any planned order.—**haphazardly** *adv.*

has·sle (has′l) *v.* to argue about the price of something.

haugh·ty (hôt′ē) *adj.* showing too much pride in oneself.

her·mit (hur′mit) *n.* one who lives alone.

her·mit·age (hur′mit ij) *n.* a place where a person can live apart from other people.

hid·e·ous (hid′ē əs) *adj.* very ugly.

hom·age (häm′ij *or* äm′ij) *n.* the act of showing honor or respect.

ho·ri·zon (hə rī′z′n) *n.* the line where the sky seems to meet the earth.

hos·pi·tal·i·ty (häs′pə tal′ə tē) *n.* a friendly and kind way of treating guests.

hov·er (huv′ər *or* häv′ər) *v.* to stay or wait near one place.

hulk (hulk) *n.* the body of a ship.

hum·bug (hum′bug) *n.* a fraud, or hoax.

hum·drum (hum′drum) *adj.* dull or boring, monotonous.

hu·mil·i·ate (hyoo mil′ē āt) *v.* to make one feel ashamed or embarrassed.

hys·te·ri·a (his ter′ē ə) *n.* an outbreak of emotional excitement or anxiety.

I

ig·loo (ig′loo) *n.* a small house built by using blocks of packed snow.

im·meas·ur·a·ble (i mezh′ər ə b'l) *adj.* too large or too much to be measured.

im·mi·grant (im′ə grənt) *adj.* relating to those who come into a different land to make a new home.

---

at, āte, fär; pen, ēqual; sit, mīne; sō, côrn, join, took, fool, our; us, turn; chill, shop, thick, they, sing; zh *in* measure; 'l *in* idle; ə *in* alive, cover, family, robot, circus.

im·pas·sioned (im pash′ ənd) *adj.* having or showing strong feelings or emotions.

im·pa·tient (im pā′shənt) *adj.* lack of patience.

im·pet·u·ous (im pech′ o͞o wəs) *adj.* rushing into action.

im·pulse (im′puls) *n.* a sudden feeling that makes one want to do something.

in·can·des·cent (in′kən des′′nt) *adj.* glowing with great heat.

in·ca·pac·i·tate (in′kə pas′ə tāt) *v.* to disable.

in·cen·tive (in sen′tiv) *n.* the thing that makes one want to work or try something.

in·ci·dent (in′si dənt) *n.* something that happened; event.

in·de·cent (in dē′s′nt) *adj.* not proper, moral, or modest.

in·de·scrib·a·ble (in′di skrī′bə b′l) *adj.* too beautiful or too horrible to describe.

in·dig·nant (in dig′nənt) *adj.* angry about something.

in·flux (in′fluks) *n.* a coming in or pouring in.

in·scrip·tion (in skrip′shən) *n.* something printed or written on a large stone, a coin, or in a book.

in·spi·ra·tion (in′spə rā′shən) *n.* an idea or action that gives one cause or influence to do something.

in·ter·mit·tent (in′tər mit′′nt) *adj.* stopping and starting again.

in·ter·vene (in tər vēn′) *v.* to come in so as to help or settle.

in·tri·cate (in′tri kit) *adj.* full of difficult or complicated parts.

in·tu·i·tive (in to͞o′ i tive *or* in tyo͞o′ i tive) *adj.* knowing about something without actually thinking it out. —**intuitively** *adv.*

in·vi·o·late (in vī′ə lit *or* in vī′ə lāt) *adj.* not broken or violated; kept sacred.

in·vis·i·ble (in viz′ə b'l) *adj.* cannot be seen.

ir·rel·e·vant (i rel′ə vənt) *adj.* having nothing to do with the subject. —**irrelevantly** *adv.*

ir·ri·gate (ir′ə gāt) *v.* to water by means of canals, ditches, or pipes. —**irrigation** *n.*

i·so·late (ī′sə lāt) *v.* to set apart from others; place alone. —**isolation** *n.*

J

joust (joust *or* just) *n.* a fight between two knights on horseback using a sword-like pole.

K

ki·mo·no (kə mō′nə) *n.* a loose robe with wide sleeves and a sash.

knap·sack (nap′sak) *n.* a leather or canvas bag worn on the back to carry supplies.

knight (nīt) *n.* a man who is given a military rank of honor for service or deeds.

knight·hood (nīt′ho͝od) *n.* the rank or position of being a knight.

L

la·bour (lā′bər) *n.* British spelling of *labor,* meaning work.

la·dle (lā′d'l) *n.* a cuplike spoon with a long handle.

land·scape (land′skāp) *n.* a stretch of land that can be seen in one view.

lan·guor (laŋ′gər) *n.* a feeling of being weak or tired.

lar·i·at (lar′ē it) *n.* a rope used for tying a horse or other animal.

le·gion (lē′jən) *n.* a large group of soldiers.

list·less (list′lis) *adj.* having little energy or interest because one is tired, sick, or sad. —**listlessly** *adv.*

lodg·ings (läj′iŋgz) *n. plural* a place to live, usually rented from somebody.

log·ger·heads (lôg′ər hedz) *n. plural* arguing; disagreeing.

lot (lät) *n.* **1.** a counter or slip of paper that people choose without looking, in deciding something by chance. **2.** one's condition; fate.

lu·na·tic (lo͞o′nə tik) *adj.* of or for insane or mentally ill persons.

M

mag·na·nim·i·ty (mag′nə nim′ə tē) *n.* the act of being generous.

mag·nif·i·cence (mag nif′ə s′ns) *n.* grand beauty; splendor.

mag·ni·fy (mag′nə fī) *v.* to make, look, or seem larger than is really so.

ma·jes·tic (mə jes′tik) *adj.* grand; stately; dignified. —**majestically** *adv.*

mare (mer) *n.* a female horse.

mast (mast) *n.* a tall pole set upright on a ship for supporting the sails.

mea·ger (mē′gər) *adj.* small amount.

mel·an·cho·ly (mel′ən käl′ē) *adj.* sad or depressed.

mem·bra·nous (mem′brə nəs) *adj.* of or like a thin layer of tissue that covers a part of an animal or plant.

mer·ci·ful (mur′si fəl) *adj.* kind; forgiving.

me·te·or (mēt′ē ər) *n.* a small solid body that moves with great speed from outer space into the air around the earth.

me·te·or·ite (mēt′ē ə rīt) *n.* a small chunk of metal or stone remaining from a meteor that has fallen upon the earth.

mill (mil) *v.* to move slowly.

min·i·a·ture (min′ē ə chər *or* min′i chər) *adj.* that is a small copy of something larger.

min·now (min′ō) *n.* a very small fish.

min·strel (min′strəl) *n.* an entertainer who travels about singing and reciting poems.

mi·ser (mī′zər) *n.* a greedy, stingy person who saves up money.

mod·er·a·tor (mäd′ə rāt′ər) *n.* a person in charge of a discussion or debate.

mole (mōl) *n.* a small, insect-eating, furry animal that burrows underground.

mon·arch (män′ərk) *n.* a ruler, as a king, queen, or emperor.

mon·grel (mun′grəl *or* mäng′grəl) *n.* an animal who has mixed breed or origin.

mo·not·o·ny (mə nät′′nē) *n.* lack of variety.

moor·ings (mo͞or′ingz) *n. plural* a place where a ship is anchored.

mor·sel (môr′s′l) *n.* a small bit of food.

mor·tal (môr′t′l) *adj.* of people as beings who must die.

moss (môs) *n.* tiny green plants.

moult (mōlt) *v.* British spelling of *molt,* meaning to shed skin, or feathers, before getting a new growth.

mount (mount) *n.* a horse for riding.

mul·ti·lat·er·al (mul′ti lat′ər əl) *adj.* having many sides.

mul·ti·tude (mul′tə to͞od *or* mul′tə tyo͞od) *n.* a large number of persons or things.

mul·ti·tu·di·nous (mul′tə′to͞od′′n əs *or* mul′tə tyo͞od′′n əs) *adj.* very many; numerous

mus·ter (mus′tər) *n.* the gathering.

mu·tu·al (myo͞o′cho͞o wəl) *adj.* shared.

myth·i·cal (mith′i k′l) *adj.* of, in, or like a myth; imaginary.

N

new·fan·gled (no͞o fang′g′ld *or* nyo͞o′fang g′ld) *adj.* new and strange.

North Pole (nôrth′ pōl′) *n.* that point on the earth that is farthest north.

nudge (nuj) *v.* to push or poke gently.

numb·ness (num′nis) *n.* the condition of not being able to feel, or feel very little.

---

at, āte, fär; pen, ēqual; sit, mīne; sō, côrn, join, took, fo͞ol, our; us, turn; chill, shop, thick, *th*ey, sing; zh *in* measure; ′l *in* idle;
ə *in* alive, cover, family, robot, circus.

O

o·be·di·ent (ō bē′dē ənt) *adj.* doing what one is told.

ob·serv·a·tory (əb zʉr′və tôr′ē) *n.* a building with telescopes and other equipment in it for studying things in space.

ob·sta·cle (äb′sti k′l) *n.* something that gets in the way or keeps one from going ahead.

oc·u·list (äk′yə list) *n.* a doctor who treats diseases of the eye.

om·in·ous (äm′ə nəs) *adj.* like a bad omen; threatening. —**ominously** *adv.*

om·nis·cient (äm nish′ənt) *adj.* knowing everything.

op·pres·sor (ə pres′ər) *n.* one who rules in a cruel way.

out·land·ish (ʊut lan′dish) *adj.* unusual or strange.

P

pact (pakt) *n.* an agreement between persons or groups.

pa·go·da (pə gō′də) *n.* a temple in the form of a tower, found in Japan or China.

pal·ate (pal′it) *n.* appreciation, or taste.

pal·lor (pal′ər) *n.* paleness of the face, that comes from being sick, worried, or tired.

pan·o·ra·ma (pan′ə ram′ə) *n.* a picture or model of a view or event.

par·a·bol·ic (par′ə bäl′ik) *adj.* curved, bowl-shaped.

par·a·sol (par′ə sôl) *n.* a light umbrella.

pas·sion (pash′ən) *n.* strong feeling or emotion. —**passionate** *adj.*

pass·port (pas′pôrt) *n.* an official paper given by a government to a citizen to prove that person's identity.

pas·tor·al (pas′tər əl) *adj.* peaceful, as life in the country.

pa·tience (pā′shəns) *n.* ability to bear discomfort while remaining calm.

pa·tri·ot (pā′trē ət) *n.* a person who shows great love for his or her country.

pa·tron (pā′trən) *n.* supporter or regular customer.

pea·cock (pē′käk) *n.* a large bird, having long tail feathers of bright colors.

peb·ble (peb′′l) *n.* a small stone.

pen·ance (pen′əns) *n.* suffering that one takes on to show apology for one's wrongdoing.

pen·e·trate (pen′ə trāt) *v.* to spread through.

per·cep·tion (pər sep′shən) *n.* the ability to understand.

per·di·tion (pər dish′ən) *n.* evil; ruin.

per·il (per′əl) *n.* a condition of possible danger and destruction.

per·ish (per′ish) *v.* to die; be destroyed.

per·pet·u·al (pər pech′ʊʊ wəl) *adj.* lasting for a long time or forever.

per·plex (pər pleks′) *v.* to make unsure of what to do; confuse or puzzle.

pe·so (pā′sō) *n.* a unit of money in Puerto Rico and other Hispanic countries.

phan·tom (fan′təm) *adj.* ghostly; shadowy.

phe·nom·e·non (fi näm′ə nän) *n.* something unusual or remarkable.

pi·ous (pī′əs) *adj.* dutiful; devoted.

pir·ou·ette (pir′ʊʊ wet′) *v.* to whirl on one's toes, as in dancing.

plague (plāg) *n.* a deadly disease.

plat·form (plat′fôrm) *n.* a stage higher than the ground or floor around it.

plum·met (plum′it) *n.* a metal weight hung at the end of a line, used to find how deep the water is.

plun·der (plun′dər) *v.* to rob or take something away.

poise (pɒiz) *v.* to balance or be held in balance.

pon·der (pän′dər) *v.* to think deeply; consider carefully.

pop·lar (päp′lər) *n.* a tall tree.

por·ti·co (pôr′tə kō) *n.* a porch or covered walk.

pounce (pouns) *v.* to spring on; attack.

pov·er·ty-strick·en (päv′ər tē strik′′n) *adj.* very poor.

prai·rie schoon·er (prar′ē skōo′nər) *n.* a large covered wagon used by pioneers.

pre·cede (pri sēd′) *v.* to go or come before.

prel·ude (prel′yōod *or* pre′lōod) *n.* the part that comes before or leads up to what follows.

prey (prā) *n.* a person or animal that is the victim of someone or something.

pri·mal (prī′m′l) *adj.* first in time; original.

prim·i·tive (prim′ə tiv) *adj.* like that of earliest times.

pro·ceeds (prō′sēdz) *n. plural* the money or profit from a business activity.

pro·ces·sion (prə sesh′ən) *n.* a group of persons or things moving forward in an orderly way.

pro·claim (prō klām′) *v.* to announce; make known publicly.

proc·la·ma·tion (prök′lə mā′shən) *n.* a public announcement.

pro·found (prə found′) *adj.* intense; very strong or deep.—**profoundly** *adv.*

pro·phet·ic (prə fet′ik) *adj.* telling what will happen in the future.

prop·o·si·tion (präp′ə zish′ən) *n.* a belief or idea, discussed and decided upon.

pros·per·i·ty (prä spar′ə tē) *n.* a condition of good fortune or success.

pros·trate (präs′trāt) *adj.* lying flat, as on one's back or one's face.

pul·sate (pul′sāt) *v.* to beat or throb in a regular rhythm.

pu·ri·fy (pyōor′ə fī) *v.* to make clean.

pur·sue (pər sōo′ *or* per syōo′) *v.* to follow in order to catch.—**pursuer** *n.*

Q

quad·rant (kwäd′rənt) *n.* section or part, usually a fourth of a circle.

quar·ry (kwôr′ē) *v.* take from a place where stone is cut or blasted out of the earth.

quest (kwest) *n.* a journey or search, often for adventure.

quick·sil·ver (kwik′sil′vər) *adj.* like the liquid metal mercury; often used to mean fast or flowing.

quill (kwil) *n.* a large tail feather of a bird. **quillwork**—a number of quills tied or sewed in a design.

R

ra·di·ant (rā′dē ənt) *adj.* **1.** shining brightly; **2.** showing pleasure.

ra·di·us (rā′dē əs) *n.* a distance measured from a line that goes from the center to the outside of a circular area.

ram·ble (ram′b′l) *v.* to walk along without any special goal.

ran·som (ran′səm) *n.* the price asked or paid for freeing a captured person.

rap·ture (rap′chər) *n.* a deep feeling of joy.

ras·cal (ras′k′l) *n.* a dishonest person, usually full of tricks.

raw·hide (rô′hīd) *n.* cattle hide; a kind of leather.

realm (relm) *n.* a region or area, sometimes of the imagination.

re·buke (ri byōok′) *v.* to scold sharply.

re·con·struc·tion (rē kən struk′shən) *n.* the process of rebuilding.

reed (rēd) *n.* the stem of tall grass, growing in wet land.

---

at, āte, fär; pen, ēqual; sit, mīne; sō, côrn, join, took, fōol, our; us, turn; chill, shop, thick, they, sing; **zh** *in* measure; ′l *in* idle; ə *in* alive, cover, family, robot, circus.

reign (rān) *n.* the rule of a king, queen, or emperor. *v.* to rule.

rein (rān) *v.* to pull or guide with reins, narrow straps used to control a horse.

re·pent (ri pent´) *v.* to feel sorry for having done something wrong.

rep·u·ta·tion (rep´yo͞o tā´shən) *n.* what people generally think about a person or thing.

res·er·va·tion (rez´ər vā´shən) *n.* land set aside for special use, as for Indians.

re·solve (ri zälv´) *n.* something decided upon; one's intention.

re·sound (ri zound´) *v.* to make a loud sound.

ret·i·nue (ret´'n o͞o *or* ret´'n yo͞o) *n.* the servants or followers of an important person.

rev·e·nue (rev´ə no͞o *or* rev´ə nyo͞o) *n.* money received, especially the money a government gets from taxes or duties.

re·vive (ri vīv´) *v.* to bring back, such as interest in something.

rheu·ma·tism (ro͞o´mə tiz'm) *n.* a disease in which the joints and muscles become stiff, sore, and swollen.

rogue (rōg) *n.* a tricky person, sometimes dishonest, who often likes to have fun.

ru·di·ment (ro͞o´də mənt) *n.* something to be learned first; something basic.

S

sa·cred (sā´krid) *adj.* having to do with a religious or holy purpose.

sac·ris·ty (sak´ris tē) *n.* a room in a church where the vestments, linens and altar articles are kept.

sash (sash) *n.* a band or scarf worn over the shoulder or around the waist.

sat·in (sat´'n) *n.* a cloth or like a cloth, having a smooth, glossy finish.

schol·ar (skäl´ər) *n.* a person who has learned much through study.

scorn·ful (skôrn´fəl) *adj.* showing dislike or hatred towards something mean or evil.

scoun·drel (skoun´drəl) *n.* a dishonest person; rascal.

scroll (skrōl) *n.* a roll of paper or parchment, usually with writing or a design on it.

scru·ti·nize (skro͞ot´'n īz) *v.* to look at very carefully; examine closely.

scur·vy (skʉr´vē) *n.* a disease that is caused by a lack of vitamin C; involves weakness and bleeding gums.

sedge (sej) *n.* a plant like coarse grass.

seed·ling (sēd´ling) *n.* a young plant grown from a seed.

seis·mo·graph (sīz´mə graf) *n.* an instrument used to measure the strength of earthquakes or explosions.

se·lect·man (sə lekt´mən) *n.* an officer elected to serve on a board, or committee, of a town or city.

sem·i·cir·cu·lar (sem´i sʉr´kyə lər) *adj.* having a half-circle shape.

sen·si·tive (sen´sə tiv) *adj.* quick to feel, notice, or appreciate.

sen·ti·nel (sen´ti n'l) *n.* a person who keeps watch to guard a group.

se·ren·i·ty (sə ren´ə tē) *n.* a state of calmness.

serf·dom (sʉrf´dum) *n.* the practice of keeping slaves, called serfs.

se·ver·i·ty (sə ver´ə tē) *n.* seriousness; harshness.

shaft (shaft) *n.* an arrow or spear.

sheath (shēth) *n.* a case for holding a sword.

sheer (shir) *adj.* straight up or down; very deep.

shep·herd (shep´ərd) *n.* a person who takes care of sheep.

shil·ling (shil´ing) *n.* a silver coin in Great Britain.

shorn (shôrn) *v.* cut.

shreds (shredz) *n.* pieces cut or torn off.

shrewd (shro͞od) *adj.* sharp; piercing, as in looks.

shroud (shroud) *n.* a sheet or gown which a dead person wears before burial.

shud·der (shud′ər) *v.* to tremble.

si·dle (sī′d′l) *v.* to move sideways.

sig·nif·i·cance (sig nif′ə kəns) *n.* importance.

si·lo (sī′lō) *n.* a storage tower, usually for grain.

sin·is·ter (sin′is tər) *adj.* that threatens something bad.

sledge (slej) *n.* a large sled for carrying loads over ice and snow.

smith·er·eens (smith ə rēnz′) *n. plural* small bits and pieces.

sol·emn (säl′əm) *adj.* serious.

sol·i·tar·y (säl′ə ter′ē) *adj.* living or being alone; single.

so·lo (sō′lō) *adj.* for or by one person, as a dancer or singer.

som·bre (säm′bər) *adj.* an old spelling of somber, meaning gloomy or serious.

spar (spär) *n.* a strong, heavy pole for holding up the sails on a ship.

spec·tral (spek′trəl) *adj.* ghostly; like a phantom.

spec·u·late (spek′yə lāt) *v.* to think about or make guesses; ponder. — **speculation** *n.*

sphere (sfir) *n.* the place or range of action or being.

sphe·roid (sfir′oid) *n.* a round object, shaped like a sphere, such as a planet.

sprat (sprat) *n.* a small fish.

stal·lion (stal′yən) *n.* a male horse.

stam·i·na (stam′ə nə) *n.* the strength to carry on or endure.

stealth·y (stel′thē) *adj.* quiet, so as not to be seen or heard.

steed (stēd) *n.* a horse, especially a lively riding horse.

stim·u·late (stim′yə lāt) *v.* to make more active; arouse.

stim·u·lus (stim′yə ləs) *n.* something that causes some action or activity.

sting·ray (stiŋ′rā) *n.* a large flat fish with a sharp spine on its tail, that can cause serious wounds.

stress (stres) *n.* pressure, mental or physical.

strew (strōō) *v.* to scatter or spread about. — **strewn.**

strid·u·late (strij′yə lāt′) *v.* a chirping or grating sound made by rubbing body parts, as certain insects do. — **stridulation** *n.*

strife (strīf) *n.* struggle; conflict.

stu·pe·fac·tion (stōō′pə fak′shən) *n.* amazement; astonishment.

sty·mie (stī′mē) *v.* to hold back a person from doing something.

sub·sti·tute (sub′stə tōōt *or* sub′stə tyōōt) *n.* a person or thing that takes the place of another.

sub·tle (sut′′l) *adj.* not strong; delicate.

suc·ces·sion (sək sesh′ən) *n.* a number of things coming one after another.

sulk (sulk) *v.* to turn away and be aloof.

sul·try (sul′trē) *adj.* hot and damp, without a breeze.

su·per·in·tend (sōō′pər in tend′) *v.* to direct or supervise.

su·per·in·tend·ent (sōō′per in ten′dənt) *n.* a person in charge of a large building or group of people.

sur·cin·gle (sur′siŋ′g′l) *n.* a strap put around a horse to hold a saddle or a pack.

sur·rey (sur′ē) *n.* a light covered carriage.

sur·vey (sər′vā) *n.* the act of measuring the size and shape of a piece of land by the use of special instruments.

swerve (swurv) *v.* to move or turn from a straight line or path.

---

at, āte, fär; pen, ēqual; sit, mīne; sō, côrn, join, took, fōōl, our; us, turn; chill, shop, thick, they, siŋ; zh *in* measure; ′l *in* idle; ə *in* alive, cover, family, robot, circus.

sym·met·ri·cal (si met′ri k'l) *adj.* balanced; alike in arrangement.

sym·pa·thize (sim′pə thīz) *v.* to share the feelings or ideas of another.

T

tan·gi·ble (tan′jə b'l) *adj.* that can be touched.

tan·ner (tan′ər) *n.* a person who makes leather from animal hides, by tanning (soaking in acid).—**tannery** *n.*

tat·tered (tat′ərd) *adj.* torn and ragged.

taunt (tônt *or* tänt) *v.* to make fun of; to tease with scorn.

taut (tôt) *adj.* tightly stretched, as a rope.

tax (taks) *v.* to accuse.

tech·nique (tek nēk′) *n.* style; a particular way of doing something.

tem·pest (tem′pist) *n.* a wild outburst of feeling or action.

ter·mite (tʉr′mīt) *n.* a small insect that eats wood and damages wooden buildings.

ter·race (ter′əs) *n.* a flat area of earth, as on a hillside.

ter·rain (tə rān′) *n.* ground or area of land.

thim·ble (thim′b'l) *n.* a cap of metal worn as a protection on the finger in sewing.

thong (thông) *n.* a narrow strip of leather, used as lace or strap.

thor·ough·fare (thʉr′ə fer) *n.* a main street or highway.

thresh·old (thresh′ōld *or* thresh′hōld) *n.* a piece of wood or stone beneath a door.

throb (thräb) *v.* to beat hard or fast, as the heart does when excited.

throne (thrōn) *n.* the position of power of a king or other monarch.

tour·na·ment (toor′nə mənt) *n.* a contest.

traipse (trāps) *v.* to walk or wander in an aimless way.

trai·tor (trāt′ər) *n.* a person who betrays his or her country, friends, or cause.

tran·quil (trang′kwəl) *adj.* calm; peaceful.

trans·con·ti·nen·tal (trans′kän tə nen′t'l) *adj.* that goes across a continent, or land area.

trans·fix (trans fiks′) *v.* to make unmovable; to hold fast.

trans·mis·sion (trans mish′ən) *n.* the moving of radio waves through space.

trans·verse (trans vʉrs′) *adj.* lying across; set crosswise.

trav·erse (tra vʉrs′ *or* trav′ərs) *v.* to pass over or through; cross.

treach·er·y (trech′ər ē) *n.* the act of disloyalty or betraying those who have trusted one.

tread (tred) *n.* a way or sound of walking.

trea·son (trē′z'n) *n.* the act of betraying one's country.

trem·u·lous (trem′yoo ləs) *adj.* trembling or quivering.

tri·col·ored (trī′kul ərd) *adj.* having three colors.

tri·pod (trī′päd) *n.* a stand or frame with three legs, often used to hold up cameras or telescopes.

troop (troop) *v.* to move in a crowd.

truce (troos) *n.* a stop in fighting or war, because both sides have agreed.

trun·dle (trun′d'l) *v.* to move or roll along.

tu·mult (too′mult *or* tyoo′mult) *n.* loud noise or uproar.

turn·key (tʉrn′kē) *n.* a person in charge of the keys of a prison.

tur·moil (tʉr′moil) *n.* an excited or confused condition.

tusk (tusk) *n.* a long, pointed tooth, usually one of a pair, that sticks out of the mouth, as in elephants.

tus·sle (tus′'l) *n.* a short struggle.

tyr·an·ny (tir′ə nē) *n.* a cruel and unjust use of power.

ty·rant (tī′rənt) *n.* a cruel person, often a ruler.

U

un·con·scious (un kän'shəs) *adj.* not able to feel and think.

u·nite (yoo nīt') *v.* to join together; combine.

un·prec·e·dent·ed (un pres'ə den'tid) *adj.* not done or known before.

ul·ti·mate (ul'tə mit) *adj.* greatest possible.

V

vag·a·bond (vag'ə bönd) *n.* a person who wanders from place to place.

vague (vāg) *adj.* not clear or definite as in form or meaning.

vain (vān) *adj.* **1.** having too high an opinion of oneself. **2.** with little or no result; not successful.—**vainly** *adv.*

val·iant (val'yənt) *adj.* brave; courageous.

van·guard (van'gärd) *n.* the front of an army.

van·i·ty (van'ə tē) *n.* the quality of being vain, having too high an opinion of oneself.

var·i·a·tion (ver'ē ā'shən) *n.* the act of changing, or differing.

venge·ance (ven'jəns) *n.* the act of getting even for a wrong or injury.

venge·ful (venj'fəl) *adj.* wanting to get even or punish someone for some wrongdoing.

ven·ture (ven'chər) *v.* to go in spite of danger or risk.

ver·ba·tim (vər bāt'əm) *adj.* in exactly the same words.

vex (veks) *v.* to trouble, disturb, or annoy.

vin·dic·tive (vin dik'tiv) *adj.* wanting to get revenge or do harm in return for harm.—**vindictiveness** *n.*

vis·age (viz'ij) *n.* the face, especially as showing one's feelings.

vi·sion (vizh'ən) *n.* something seen in the mind, in a dream, or in a supernatural way.

vo·cal (vō'k'l) *adj.* speaking or making sounds openly or strongly.

void (void) *n.* an empty space.

vol·ca·no (väl kā'nō) *n.* an opening in the earth's surface through which molten rock is thrown up.—**volcanic** *adj.*

vo·rac·i·ty (vô ras'ə tē) *n.* the act of eating food rapidly or greedily.

vow (vou) *n.* a solemn promise or pledge.

vul·ture (vul'chər) *n.* a large bird related to eagles and hawks that eats dead animals.

W

wasp (wäsp *or* wôsp) *n.* a flying insect.

wa·ver (wā'ver) *v.* to flutter; tremble.

wea·ry (wir'ē) *adj.* tired; worn out.

whin·ny (hwin'ē) *v.* to make a low neighing sound, as a horse.

whole·sale (hōl'sāl) *adj.* widespread; general.

wield (wēld) *v.* to use with skill.

wind·jam·mer (wind'jam'ər) *n.* a large sailing ship.

witch·craft (wich'kraft) *n.* the magic power of a witch.

wit·ty (wit'ē) *adj.* clever in an amusing way.

wrench (rench) *v.* to pull sharply.

writhe (rī*th*) *v.* to twist and turn; squirm.

Y

yawn (yôn) *v.* to open wide.

Z

zeal·ous (zel'əs) *adj.* very eager; enthusiastic.—**zealously** *adv.*

ze·nith (zē'nith) *n.* the highest point that one can see in the sky.

zone (zōn) *n.* an area set apart in some special way.

---

at, āte, fär; pen, ēqual; sit, mīne; sō, côrn, join, took, fool, our; us, turn; chill, shop, thick, they, sing; zh *in* measure; 'l *in* idle; ə *in* alive, cover, family, robot, circus.

Biographies of Authors

Joan Aiken

Joan Aiken *(born 1924)* has been writing stories and poems since the age of five. She grew up in England, the daughter of an American poet. Aiken's writing career included working for a magazine and a radio station. She has a rich imagination and makes use of fantasy, mystery, and humor. *The Whispering Mountain* and *The Wolves of Willoughby Chase* are two of her popular books.

Ricardo Alegría *(born 1921)* lives in San Juan, Puerto Rico, the place of his birth. He writes mostly about history, but is also well known for a collection of Puerto Rican folk tales, *The Three Wishes*. Alegria has taught history at the University of Puerto Rico and is now the director of the Center of Advanced Studies of Puerto Rico and the Caribbean.

Sally Andresen *(born 1947)* was raised on a farm in Iowa. After graduating from Iowa State University, she became a junior high school teacher. Andresen wrote the poem "Fall" when she was in the ninth grade, for an English assignment.

Isaac Asimov

Isaac Asimov *(born 1920)* came with his family to the United States from Russia at the age of three. As a boy, he loved reading science fiction magazines. This reading stimulated Asimov's interest in science. He studied at Columbia University and then became a professor at Boston University School of Medicine. Asimov has written hundreds of books and articles on scientific and other subjects, but is best known for his science fiction stories.

Herbert Asquith *(1881–1947)* was the son of a statesman who was a member of Parliament in England. He became a lawyer and served as a captain in the army. Asquith was known for his novels as well as his poetry.

Stephen Vincent Benét

Hal Borland

Pearl S. Buck

Katharine Lee Bates *(1859–1929)* was born in Massachusetts and graduated from Wellesley College, where she later taught. Bates won fame for writing the words for the patriotic song, "America the Beautiful." The melody for the song was written by Samuel A. Ward. Bates is also known for her short stories and travel books.

Stephen Vincent Benét *(1898–1943)* was born in Bethlehem, Pennsylvania, to a family of famous writers. He studied literature at Yale University and then traveled to Paris to study and write. There he met his future wife, Rosemary, who was working as a newspaper reporter. Benét's works include novels, short stories, and poetry, as well as radio and film scripts. He won fame for the short story "The Devil and Daniel Webster" and a short novel in ballad form, *John Brown's Body.*

Hal Borland *(born 1900)* grew up on the American frontier. He was greatly influenced by his childhood experiences. After completing high school, he worked his way through the University of Colorado by taking a job as a newspaper correspondent. Borland lived on a farm and had a deep interest in nature. His essays about outdoor life appeared in the *New York Times* for more than twenty years.

Pearl S. Buck *(born 1892)* left her birthplace of West Virginia as a child to live in China, where her parents were missionaries. She came back to the United States to attend college, but returned to China many times. Buck's stories and novels depict the lives of common Chinese people, many of them farmers or fishermen. *The Good Earth* won a Pulitzer Prize in 1932.

Dorothy Canfield *(1879–1958)* was born in Kansas, the daughter of a teacher and an artist. She attended college in Ohio, New York, and France, but felt most at home in rural Vermont. Canfield wrote short stories and novels, also under her married name of Dorothy Canfield Fisher. Two other popular books are *The Bent Twig* and *Understood Betsy.*

Frances Carpenter *(1890–1972)* was the daughter of a well-known geographer. Her father traveled all over the world on research trips and often took his family along. Frances Carpenter used information gained on those trips as background for much of her writing. Two of her popular books are *Tales of a Chinese Grandmother* and *African Wonder Tales.*

Geoffrey Chaucer

Geoffrey Chaucer *(perhaps 1340–1400)* is considered one of the greatest poets of all time. He was born in London, and served a while as a page to King Edward III's son. Chaucer was influenced by French literature and Italian culture. He used these sources, as well as his knowledge of English life, to create *The Canterbury Tales.* These tales are in poetry form, filled with humor and memorable characterization.

Anton Chekhov *(1860–1904)* was a noted Russian playwright and short story writer. He pursued a medical career while writing stories for magazines. Eventually Chekhov became a doctor, but still continued to write stories. After he married an actress, he turned to writing plays. Two of his well-known plays are *The Three Sisters* and *Uncle Vanya.* His plots are known for their humorous twists.

Anton Chekhov

Francisco A. de Icaza *(1863–1925)* was born in Mexico City, but lived in Spain for many years. He served as secretary to the Minister of Mexico in Spain, who was his friend. That career came to an end because of the Revolution of 1914. Icaza then turned to writing poetry and essays.

Walter de la Mare *(1873–1956)* was raised and educated in London, England. He began writing at the age of seventeen, when he founded a high school newspaper. While working as a bookkeeper; he devoted his spare time to writing. Eventually, he received a government grant, which allowed him to spend all his time writing. He is known for his poems, nursery rhymes, and stories. In 1953, he earned the Order of Merit from Queen Elizabeth II.

Walter de la Mare

Emily Dickinson

Ralph Waldo Emerson

Robert Francis

Beatrice Schenk de Regniers grew up in Crawfordsville, Indiana. She was active in a theater-dance group in Chicago, and then began writing books for young people. *The Snow Party, The Shadow Book,* and *May I Bring a Friend?* have won book awards. Regniers has served as editor of a book club.

Emily Dickinson *(1830–1886)* lived in Massachusetts. She led a normal life until the age of twenty-six, when she suddenly began to spend most of her time alone. Dickinson stayed indoors and had few visitors. Secretly, she wrote more than a thousand poems—most reflected deep feelings about life, love, and nature. Only seven of Emily Dickinson's poems were published while she was alive. The rest were discovered after her death, written on scraps of paper and hidden away in her bedroom.

Ralph Waldo Emerson *(1803–1882)* was born into a family of ministers. After working his way through Harvard University, he became the pastor of a Boston church. He gave up that vocation, however, because he felt better suited to the work of writing and lecturing. Two of Emerson's prose works are titled *The Conduct of Life* and *Essays. Poems* and *May-Day* are well known collections of his poetry.

Genevieve Foster *(1893–1979)* was inspired by her grandparents, who had a deep interest in history. Her favorite subjects to write about were historical figures, such as Columbus, the Pilgrims, and Abraham Lincoln. Born in New York City, Foster grew up and attended college in Wisconsin. She studied art and worked in advertising for a few years before writing became her career.

Robert Francis *(born 1901)* has devoted his life to writing and teaching. In his home on the outskirts of Amherst, Massachusetts, Francis lives a quiet life, gardening, reading, and writing. His award-winning works include fiction, essays, autobiography, and poetry. Robert Francis has published many collections of poems, including *Come Out into the Sun, The Orb Weaver,* and *The Sound I Listened For.*

O. Henry

Langston Hughes

Victor Hugo

O. Henry *(1862–1910)* was the pen name of William Sydney Porter. Before he achieved fame as a writer, O. Henry worked as a store clerk, journalist, and bank teller. He served a prison term for bookkeeping irregularities at the bank, but always claimed innocence. O. Henry's stories usually have surprise endings. Two popular collections of his stories are *Of Cabbages and Kings* and *The Four Million.*

Oliver Herford *(1863–1935)* was born in England, but moved to the United States with his family at an early age. He attended Antioch College in Ohio, and he also spent time studying in London and Paris. Herford was a popular literary figure of the early 1900's. His poems and humorous stories were published in many magazines, including *Life* and *Harper's Weekly.* Herford was also an artist. Animals were his favorite subjects, and his drawings often accompanied his writings.

Edwin A. Hoey *(born 1930)* attended Swarthmore College, served in the army, and then worked for a publishing company. His poems and articles have appeared in magazines, journals, and textbooks.

Langston Hughes *(1902–1967)* was a playwright, poet, song writer, and lecturer as well as an author of short stories and novels. He worked at many jobs before he achieved recognition for his writing talent. Hughes wrote about many facets of life, basing much of the writing upon his varied experiences, including travel to Africa. Many of Hughes's works reflect the speech patterns and jazz rhythms he heard on the streets of Harlem.

Victor Hugo *(1802–1885)* was a French author who had a deep interest in politics. Because his father was a general in Napoleon's army, Hugo was aware from childhood of his country's problems. He wrote twenty-three poems by the time he was fourteen, winning an early reputation as a genius. He eventually wrote plays, novels, and essays. One of his famous novels, *Les Miserables,* deals with a reformed criminal who tries to lead an honest life.

Helen Keller

Abraham Lincoln

Vachel Lindsay

Issa *(1763–1828)* was a Japanese poet, born in the Province of Shinano, Japan. He was a sad, lonely child who grew up to be rather unhappy. He had no fixed home until he reached the age of fifty, so Issa always considered himself an orphan. He loved living things and wrote many of his haiku about birds and insects. In his lifetime, Issa produced over fifteen thousand poems.

Helen Keller *(1880–1968)* overcame the loss of sight, hearing, and speech, caused by an illness at the age of two. For five years, she was cut off from contact with others until her teacher, Anne Sullivan, was hired. Sullivan taught her to communicate through touch, to write and read Braille, and eventually to speak. Keller graduated with honors from Radcliffe College. She mastered several languages and lectured throughout the world. Her speaking tours helped in raising money to improve conditions for blind people.

Richmond Lattimore *(born 1906)* is a graduate of Dartmouth College who became a Rhodes scholar. He has served on the faculty of Bryn Mawr College. Lattimore is known for his translations of Homer as well as his original poetry and critical writings.

Abraham Lincoln *(1809–1865)* was a self-educated man who grew up on the frontier of Kentucky and Indiana. He held jobs as postmaster and lawyer and served as a member of the Illinois legislature. Lincoln was elected to the Presidency of the United States in 1860. He remained in office until his assassination in 1865. As leader of the North during the Civil War, he was an inspiration to people all over the world. Lincoln's literary style, reflected in his speeches and letters, was straightforward and sincere. His sense of humor still delights readers today.

Vachel Lindsay *(1879–1931)* studied art when he was young and then later became a poet. He left his hometown of Springfield, Illinois, to travel around the country performing his poems. Lindsay tried to combine music, poetry, and stage directions into a form of poetry that sounds best when read aloud.

Jack London

Henry Wadsworth
Longfellow

Edna St. Vincent Millay

Jack London *(1876–1916)* was born in California. He had to work as soon as he was able, and ran away at fifteen to travel the country as a hobo. At nineteen, he returned to high school. The following year, after graduating, he went to Alaska in search of gold. His experiences there were all used in his highly imaginative stories. London is best known for *The Call of the Wild,* a novel.

Henry Wadsworth Longfellow *(1807–1882)* was one of the most popular and respected poets of his time. One of his narrative poems, "The Song of Hiawatha," sold more than one million copies in his lifetime. Longfellow was born in Portland, Maine, and graduated from Bowdoin College. He traveled and studied in Europe, and then returned to the United States to teach college. Much of his life was spent at Harvard University, inspiring students in their creative writing. Other well-known poems by Longfellow are "Paul Revere's Ride" and "The Village Blacksmith."

Edna St. Vincent Millay *(1892–1950)* won fame at the age of nineteen for her poem "Renascence." After graduating from Vassar College, she moved to New York City. There she lived in Greenwich Village among other noted writers of the 1920's and 1930's. Millay continued to write poetry, as well as stories and plays. She was awarded a Pulitzer Prize for *The Harp Weaver.*

Rosalie Moore *(born 1910)* has had a varied career. After graduating from the University of California, she worked at a radio station as a writer and announcer. She has lectured to college students at universities in the United States and in Mexico and has conducted poetry workshops. In 1977 she won an award for *Year of the Children,* a collection of her poems.

Lillian Morrison *(born 1917)* writes about subjects that interest her—jazz, dance, and sports. She was born in New Jersey and eventually moved to New York City. There she worked in the public library, interested mainly in improving services to young people. Morrison is known for *The Ghosts of Jersey City,* a collection of her own poems, and *Sprints and Distances,* an anthology of sports poems which she edited.

Ogden Nash

Carl Sandburg

William Saroyan

Ogden Nash *(1901–1971)* worked as a salesman, in an advertising firm, and for a book publisher before devoting himself to the job of full-time writer. He always was amused by the way misspelled words made a story or an article funny by chance. This led him to write poems with unusual rhymes, often using incorrect spelling. Nash became one of America's best known writers of humorous poetry.

Amado Nervo *(1870–1919)* studied for the priesthood in his native Mexico. He gave up that vocation to become a journalist, novelist, and poet. Nervo served as a diplomat in Madrid, Spain, for more than eighteen years. He enjoyed the friendships of many writers, who encouraged him to pursue a literary career.

Carl Sandburg *(1878–1967)* was the son of Swedish immigrants who settled in Illinois. Sandburg held a variety of jobs, served in the army, and traveled around the country. He sang and played his guitar, collected folk music, and listened to folk tales. Those experiences are reflected in his poetry, fiction, and nonfiction. Sandburg's language of writing—free verse, slang, dialect, and street talk—make his writing come alive with the sights and sounds of America of the past. Sandburg's biography of Abraham Lincoln, which won a Pulitzer Prize, is still popular reading.

William Saroyan *(1908–1981),* the son of Armenian immigrants, grew up in Fresno, California. He loved to read, and later claimed that he had read every book in the public library. He never finished his formal education because family financial problems caused him to leave school at the age of fifteen. Saroyan's wide reading led to his career in writing. *The Human Comedy* and *The Time of Your Life* are two of his well-known works.

William Jay Smith *(born 1918)* is known for his humorous poetry as well as plays, critical reviews, and English translations of other people's writings. Smith was born in Winnfield, Louisiana, and claims one-sixteenth Cherokee heritage from his mother. He has been a college professor and educational consultant, and has served as a member of the Vermont House of Representatives.

Lincoln Steffens

Alfred, Lord Tennyson

Mark Twain

Lincoln Steffens *(1866–1936)* wrote his autobiography in 1931, when he was sixty-five years old. By that time, Steffens had achieved fame as a writer, lecturer, and editor. He was born in San Francisco, attended the University of California, and further pursued his studies in Europe. His special interests were politics and the problems of business and labor.

Alfred, Lord Tennyson *(1809–1892)* was a shy, optimistic man who tried to deal positively with the unhappiness he encountered. His long poem *In Memorium* was written over a seventeen-year period and was about Tennyson's attempts to deal with the death of a close friend. Tennyson lived in England and was made its Poet Laureate by Queen Victoria. He became one of the best-known poets in the English-speaking world. His noted works include "The Lady of Shallot."

Ernest Lawrence Thayer *(1863–1940)* was born in Worcester, Massachusetts. He attended Harvard University, where he was the editor-in-chief of the student humor magazine, *Lampoon.* He joined his classmate William Randolph Hearst as a journalist on the *San Francisco Examiner.* Thayer wrote a number of poems for newspapers and is most noted for his famous poem, "Casey at the Bat."

Tobi Tobias *(born 1938)* has always been interested in people who have become famous in the arts. She enjoys researching and interviewing to get the information she needs for stories. Some people Tobias has written about include opera singer Marian Anderson; ballerina Maria Tallchief; and Isami Noguchi, a sculptor who grew up in Japan. Tobias also writes for television and magazines.

Mark Twain *(1835–1910)* was the pen name of Samuel Clemens. Twain grew up in Hannibal, Missouri, where he had many adventures as a boy on the Mississippi River. He loved the river and enjoyed fishing and rafting. Twain wrote about these experiences in *The Adventures of Tom Sawyer* and *The Adventures of Huckleberry Finn,* two of his most popular books. As a young man, he worked as a printer, a riverboat pilot, and a journalist. His humorous newspaper articles and lectures were well received by the public.

Louis Untermeyer *(1895–1977)* gave up a career as a professional pianist to become a writer. He has edited collections of written works and served as poetry editor of a magazine. Untermeyer translated traditional tales into modern English.

Alice Walker

Alice Walker *(born 1944)* was raised on a small farm in Georgia. She worked her way through college to become an award-winning writer. Walker, who has taught at several colleges, won an award in 1973 for *In Love and Trouble,* a collection of stories. *Revolutionary Petunias,* a book of poems, was nominated for an award in the same year. Walker has also written *The Third Life of Grange Copeland,* a novel.

H. G. Wells *(1866–1946)* was a noted British writer who believed strongly in scientific progress. He attended London University and received a science degree with honors. He published hundreds of books in various fields, but is best-known for his science fiction writing. His famous works include *The War of the Worlds* and *The Time Machine.* Wells wrote of airplanes, submarines, and moon voyages long before people believed such things could become reality.

H.G. Wells

William Carlos Williams *(1883–1963)* was born in Rutherford, New Jersey. He was a practicing physician who wrote forty-nine books. These included novels, short stories, plays, and poetry. Williams is praised for writing of everyday life in a style to which many can relate. Among his works are *Paterson,* a long poem set in Paterson, New Jersey, and *Pictures from Breughal,* for which he won the 1964 Pulitzer Prize.

Valerie Worth *(born 1933)* grew up in Philadelphia, Pennsylvania. She attended Swarthmore College, from which she earned a bachelor's degree. Worth has published *Small Poems,* a collection of poems about life, the earth, and the stars. In addition, Worth has written *Gypsy Gold,* a popular young adults' novel.

William Carlos Williams

Index of Titles and Authors

Index of Fine Art

Index of Skills

Skills in Comprehending Literature

Act 483

Alliteration 112–113, 130–131, 275, 277, 287, 449, 460, 532

Allusions 252

Assonance 114–115, 532

Author's Purpose 95, 368, 381, 440, 468, 484, 485, 503, 544

Autobiography 358, 367, 381, 532

Biography 384, 389, 401–402, 410–412, 415, 532

Cause and Effect 136–137, 161, 170, 196, 208, 238, 323, 410, 542

Character 3, 63, 64, 186, 289, 532
  Comparing Characters, 55, 163, 401
  Interpreting a Character's Actions, 32, 40, 75, 95, 155, 220, 228, 525
  Major and Minor Characters, 157, 186, 532
  Understanding Characters
    In Legends, 3, 19, 26, 32, 40, 84, 95
    In Nonfiction, 401, 417
    In Plays, 501, 525
    In Short Stories, 155, 157, 171, 197, 218, 228, 235

Character Traits 12, 48, 145, 426, 532

Chronological Order See *Time Order.*

Climax 26, 40, 49, 135, 146, 155, 181, 533

Comparison and Contrast 95, 183, 228, 297, 401, 422, 533
  Comparing Types of Literature, 389, 401, 426, 431, 475, 529

Conclusions 65, 244–245, 543

Concrete Poem See *Poetry.*

Conflict 19, 40, 49, 56, 186–187, 528, 533
  Internal and External Conflict, 155, 171, 186–187, 197, 208, 501, 525, 534, 536

Connotation 271, 354–355, 411, 449, 460

Denotation 271, 354–355

Description 26, 197, 208–209, 518, 533
  Indirect Description, 369, 536

Details 4–5, 26, 58, 305, 464

Dialog 210, 483, 500, 518, 528, 533–534

Drama 482–483, 500–501, 517–518, 525, 528–529, 534

Essay 443, 444–445, 447, 449, 452, 534

Exaggeration See *Hyperbole.*

External Conflict See *Conflict.*

Fact and Fiction 427

Fact and Opinion 354–355, 367, 381, 402, 452, 475, 478, 542

Falling Action 135, 146, 155, 534–535
  See also *Plot.*

Fantastic and Realistic 27, 98

Fiction See *Legends, Short Stories.*

Figurative Language 121–129, 243, 250, 263, 293, 305, 311, 318, 345, 535, 542
  See also *Hyperbole, Metaphor, Personification, Simile.*

First Person See *Narrator, First Person.*

Foreshadowing 475

Form 261, 282, 305, 335, 525

Free Verse 243, 302, 305

Haiku See *Poetry.*

Humor 299, 420, 437, 535

Hyperbole 128–129, 131, 309, 535

Vocabulary Skills

Part of Speech, 162–163, 182, 210, 239, 356, 460, 479, 559
Pronunciation, 209, 356, 479, 558
Pronunciation Key, 356, 367, 468, 558
Respelling, 356, 367–368, 424, 460, 558
Schwa Sound, 368
Syllabication, 210, 356
Word Origin, 356
Encyclopedia
Information about Word Meanings, 440
Formal and Informal English 138–139, 236, 550–551
See also *Levels of Language.*
Glossary 357, 402, 411, 479, 568–581
Homographs 197
Inference 486
Levels of Language 138–139, 235–236, 550–551
Multiple Meanings 138–139, 550
Inferring the Meaning, 41
Choosing the Correct Meaning, 146, 156, 318–319
Prefixes 66–67, 76, 85, 96, 546
Adding Prefixes to Base Words, 96, 453
Slang 163, 235
Standard and Nonstandard English 138–139, 163, 235, 550–551
See also *Levels of Language.*
Suffixes 66–67, 85, 96, 546–547
Adding Suffixes to Base Words, 96
Synonyms 6, 19–20, 26, 56, 559
Thesaurus 325, 551, 559
Word Parts 66–67, 85, 452
Finding the Meaning of a Word, 85, 98–99, 311, 346, 402–403, 476, 518, 529
Greek and Latin Word Parts, 67, 76, 98–99, 452, 547
See also *Base Words, Prefixes, Suffixes.*

Writing Skills

Anecdotes 440
Argument
Developing an Argument, 527
See also *Opinion.*
Author's Purpose 368
Autobiography
Writing about Yourself, 369
Biography
Writing a Biographical Sketch, 390, 479
Characters
Comparing Characters, 20, 41, 85, 163, 183, 502
Describing a Character, 77, 157, 198, 239, 347, 369, 403
Developing a Character, 183, 198
Comparing Selections
Comparing Autobiographies, 383
Comparing Biographies, 412
Comparing Nonfiction, 425, 453, 461, 469
Comparing Plays, 426
Comparing Poems, 267, 283, 326, 347
Conflict
Describing a Conflict, 220
Defining a Term 220–221
Description 59, 77, 312, 383, 479, 529
Dialog
Writing Dialog, 14
Drama
Creating an Alien, 519
Examining Illusions, 519
Writing a Scene, 503, 529
Endings
Suggesting Another Ending, 14, 85, 164, 229
Editing See *Revising.*

Study and Research Skills

Speaking and Listening Skills

Skills in Critical Thinking

Of Factual Content, 337, 389, 410, 435
Of Literary Technique, 56, 173, 421
Of the Organization of a Selection, 75–76, 345, 410, 419, 447, 461, 525
Of Reasoning Processes, 237, 410

Application
Of Literature to Life, 145, 181, 183, 265, 326, 390, 525

Classification
Determining Categories, 57, 320, 529
Identifying Common Characteristics, 57, 228, 346–347, 422, 479, 529

Comparison and Contrast
Of Characters, 20, 55, 85, 163, 401, 502
Of Ideas, 95, 181, 256, 366, 381
Of Selections, 48, 228, 237, 267, 283, 326, 346–347, 383, 401, 426, 469, 529

Conclusions
Drawing Conclusions, 32, 75, 84, 95, 145, 161, 228, 245, 316

Definition of Terms 181, 220, 250, 347

Evaluation 564
Of Accuracy of Content, 337, 427
Of Author's Credibility, 383, 415
Of Author's Slant, 34, 354, 369, 383, 460
Of Author's Style, 155, 235, 261, 464
Of Believability of Characters, Plot, and Setting, 12, 40, 48, 55, 84, 95, 218, 228
Of Elements of a Work, 32, 389, 411
Of Reasons, 12, 27, 40, 48, 57, 84, 97, 155, 196, 257, 461
Of Soundness of Opinions, 57, 94, 145, 220, 412   See also *Fact and Opinion.*

Fact and Fiction 27, 32, 49–50, 183, 427

Fact and Opinion 565
Separating Fact and Opinion, 354–355, 367, 381, 413, 475
Relating Facts and Opinions, 402, 452

Figurative Language 146, 196, 208, 250, 263, 265, 277, 287, 305, 311, 345

Generalizations 565
Identifying Generalizations, 96, 147, 252
Making Valid Generalizations, 19, 56, 84, 147, 228, 479
Qualifying Generalizations, 327, 389, 410
Using Generalizations, 75, 95, 237

Inferences
About Author's Purpose, 12, 95, 197, 237, 273, 440, 464, 503
About Characters, 12, 26, 55, 63, 75, 84, 95, 155, 198, 289, 339, 369, 426, 440
About Plot, 95, 164, 170, 235, 245, 266
About Setting, 50, 218, 389, 429, 518

Interpretation 40, 48, 84, 218, 280, 420, 436, 517

Main Idea
Distinguishing Between Main Idea and Details, 5, 13, 19, 26, 48, 58, 94
Of a Paragraph, 5, 13, 48, 58, 447

Outcomes
And Conclusions, 56, 85, 302, 341
Predicting Outcomes, 19, 97, 145, 502

Reasoning 14, 49, 94

Relationships
Chronological (Time Order) 18–19, 32, 75, 94, 136–137, 161, 517
Cause and Effect, 136–137, 161, 170, 196, 208, 286, 323
Detail to Main Idea, 26, 48, 94, 464

Slanted Writing 34, 271, 292, 354–355, 369, 383, 411, 449, 469, 477, 565

Summarizing
Of Character Description, 77, 95
Of Main Idea of Paragraph, 13, 19, 58
Of Plot, 389, 475
Of Theme, 68, 96, 229, 256, 261, 297

Art Credits

Cover

That, 1958–59, Kenneth Noland.
Collection, Mr. and Mrs. David Mirvish, Toronto, Canada.

Illustrations

Kinuko Y. Craft, 69, 72–73, 81, 83, 88, 92–93; William Cigliano, 30–31; Roberta Polfus, 51, 54, 474–475, 510, 515, 522; Jean Helmer, 107, 296, 447; Robert Masheris, 150, 154, 159; Sarah Woodward, 167, 168–169; Yoshi Miyake, 212, 217, 492, 499; Christa Kieffer, 225; John Sandford, 255; Glenn Wolff, 272–273; Judith Friedman, 360, 363; Dale Bēda, 376.

Photographs of Authors

The Bettmann Archive, Inc.: Stephen Vincent Benét, Pearl Buck, Geoffrey Chaucer, Anton Chekhov, Walter de la Mare, Emily Dickinson, Ralph Waldo Emerson, O. Henry, Langston Hughes, Victor Hugo, Helen Keller, Jack London, Carl Sandburg, William Saroyan, Alfred, Lord Tennyson, Mark Twain, H. G. Wells. Culver Pictures, Inc., Vachel Lindsay, Henry Wadsworth Longfellow, Ogden Nash, Lincoln Steffens, William Carlos Williams. Alex Gottfryd: Joan Aiken. Jill Krementz: Isaac Asimov. Library of Congress: Abraham Lincoln. Jerome Liebling: Robert Francis. New York Times: Hal Borland. Vassar College Library: Edna St. Vincent Millay. Newsweek; James Wilson: Alice Walker.

Acknowledgments

(continued from copyright page)

Lincoln," and "Benjamin Franklin" by Stephen Vincent Benét, from *A Book of Americans* by Rosemary & Stephen Vincent Benét, Holt, Rinehart and Winston, Inc.; copyright 1933 by Rosemary & Stephen Vincent Benét; copyright renewed © 1961 by Rosemary Carr Benét. For "The Rocking Donkey" by Joan Aiken, from *Smoke from Cromwell's Time and Other Stories;* copyright © 1959, 1966, 1969, 1970 by Joan Aiken. Delacorte Press/Seymour Lawrence: For "Seal," excerpted from *Laughing Time* by William Jay Smith; copyright © 1953, 1955, 1956, 1957, 1959, 1968, 1974, 1977, 1980 by William Jay Smith. Dodd, Mead & Company, Incorporated: For "Matthew A. Henson," from *Famous American Negroes* by Langston Hughes; copyright 1954 by Langston Hughes; copyright renewed 1982 by George Houston Bass. Doubleday & Company, Inc.: For an excerpt from *The Story of My Life* by Helen Keller; copyright 1902, 1903, 1905 by Helen Keller. For "The Six Horsemen," from *African Wonder Tales* by Frances Carpenter; copyright © 1963 by Frances Carpenter Huntington. For "Hearts and Hands," from *Waifs and Strays* by O. Henry; copyright 1917 by Doubleday & Company, Inc. Dover Publications, Inc.: For "The Dog (As Seen by the Cat)" by Oliver Herford, from *Rainbow in the Sky;* copyright 1935. E. P. Dutton, Inc.: For "The Flower-Fed Buffaloes" by Vachel Lindsay, from *Going to the Stars;* copyright 1926 by D. Appleton & Co., renewed by Elizabeth C. Lindsay. For "America the Beautiful" by Katharine Lee Bates, from *Poems.* Education Development Center, Inc.: For "Magic Words to Feel Better," from *Songs and Stories of the Netsilik Eskimos,* translated by Edward Field from text collected by Knud Rasmussen, courtesy Education Development Center, Inc., Newton, MA. M. Evans and Company, Inc.: Pages 41–43, 44–49, 56–57, 175–179, 191–194, 223–229, from *The World's Great Stories* by Louis Untermeyer; copyright © 1964 by Louis Untermeyer. Farrar, Straus & Giroux, Inc.: For "Sea Lions," from *More Small Poems* by Valerie Worth, with pictures by Natalie Babbitt; poems copyright © 1976 by Valerie Worth. Gail M. Griffin: For 'How the Three Young Men Found Death" by Gail M. Griffin, an adaptation of "The Pardoner's Tale" by Geoffrey Chaucer; copyright © 1969 by Gail M. Griffin. Harcourt Brace Jovanovich, Inc.: For "Summer of the Beautiful White Horse" by William Saroyan, from *My Name is Aram;* copyright 1938, 1966 by William Saroyan. For an abridged version of "I Get a Colt to Break In" by Lincoln Steffens, from *Boy on Horseback* by Lincoln Steffens; copyright 1931 by Harcourt Brace Jovanovich, Inc.; renewed 1959 by Peter Steffens. For "The Old Soldier," from *Four-Square* by Dorothy Canfield; copyright 1949 by Dorothy Canfield, renewed, 1977 by Sarah Fisher Scott. For excerpts from Chapter XVIII in *Abe Lincoln Grows Up* by Carl Sandburg; copyright 1926, 1928 by Harcourt Brace Jovanovich, Inc., renewed 1954, 1956 by Carl Sandburg. For "Women," from *Revolutionary Petunias & Other Poems* by Alice Walker; copyright © 1970 by Alice Walker. For "Chicago" from *Chicago Poems* by Carl Sandburg; copyright 1916 by Holt Rinehart and Winston, Inc.; renewed 1944 by Carl Sandburg. For an excerpt from "Fourth of July Night" in *Wind Song* by Carl Sandburg; copyright © 1956 by Carl Sandburg. Harper & Row, Publishers, Inc.: For "Snowy Benches," from *Out In the Dark and Daylight* by Aileen Fisher; text copyright © 1980 by Aileen Fisher. For an excerpt from page 24 (text only) of *Witcracks: Jokes and Jests* from American folklore collected by Alvin Schwartz (J. B. Lippincott Company). For "Cynthia in the Snow" (text only), from *Bronzeville Boys and Girls* by Gwendolyn Brooks; copyright © 1956 by Gwendolyn Brooks Blakely. For "Scene" (text only), from *River Winding: Poems* by Charlotte Zolotow (T. Y. Crowell Company); texty copyright © 1970 by Charlotte Zolotow. For "Strange Wind" (text only), from *A Light in the Attic* by Shel Silverstein; copyright © 1981 by Shel Silverstein. For an abridged and adapted version of *Maria Tallchief,* A Crowell Biography (Thomas Y. Crowell); copyright © 1970 by Tobi Tobias. Harvard University Press: For "The Duel" and "Bee! I'm Expecting You!" by Emily Dickinson, from *The Poems of Emily Dickinson,* ed. by Thomas H. Johnson, Cambridge, Mass.: The Belknap Press of Harvard University Press, copyright © 1951, © 1955, 1979, 1983 by the President and Fellows of Harvard College, reprinted by permission of the publishers and the Trustees of Amherst College. The Hoksueido Press: For a haiku poem "Woodpecker" by Issa, from *A History of Haiku* by R. H. Blyth: Vol. I, *From the Beginning up to Issa;* copyright © 1964. Holt, Rinehart and Winston, Publishers: For "Steam Shovel," from *Upper Pasture* by Charles Malam; copyright 1930, © 1958 by Charles Malam. International Creative Management, Inc.: For "Invasion from Mars" by Howard Koch, from *The Panic Broadcast;* copyright 1940 Princeton University Press, 1968 by Howard Koch. Richmond Lattimore: For "Sky Diving" by Richmond Lattimore, from *Poems from Three Decades.* Little, Brown and Company: For "The Hippopotamus," "The Canary," "The Panther," and "The Termite," from *Verses from 1929 On* by Ogden Nash; copyright 1935, 1940, 1942 by The Curtis Publishing Company, first appeared in *The Saturday Evening Post.* Liveright Publishing Corp., Inc.: For "Who knows if the moon's," from *Tulips & Chimneys;* copyright 1923, 1925 and renewed 1951, 1953 by E. E. Cummings, copyright © 1973, 1976 by the Trustees for the E. E. Cummings Trust, copyright © 1973, 1976 by George James Firmage. Macmillan Publishing Co.: For "Skating," from *Pillicock Hill* by Herbert Asquith, New York: Macmillan, 1926. Norma Millay Ellis: For "The Courage That My Mother Had" by Edna St. Vincent Millay, from *Collected Poems,* Harper & Row; copyright 1954 by Norma Millay Ellis. William Morrow & Company, Inc.: For "The Women's 400 Meters," from *The Sidewalk Racer and Other Poems of Sports and Motion* by Lillian Morrison; copyright © 1968, 1977 by Lillian Morrison, by permission of Lothrop, Lee & Shepard Books (A Division of William Morrow & Company). New Directions Publishing Corporation: For "Poem" by William Carlos Williams, from *Collected Earlier Poems of William Carlos Williams;* copyright 1938 by New Directions Publishing Corporation. The New Yorker Magazine:

Staff Credits

Editor-in-Chief: Joseph F. Littell
Project Director: Patricia Opaskar

Administrative Editor: Kathleen Laya
Managing Editor: Geraldine Macsai

Associate Editors: Elizabeth M. Garber, Bernice Rappoport
Rights and Permissions: Irma Rosenberg
Associate Designer: Linda Schifano FitzGibbon

Special Contributors

Nora Brooks Blakely; Katherine Fischer; Charlene Griffin-Jordan; Catherine Hobbins; Donna Levine; Sister Margaret Murphy, O.P.; Jeffrey Taggart; Gerry Tremaine.   Picture Research: Kitty Nolan.